RIVALS FOR POWER

RIVALS FOR POWER

PRESIDENTIAL-CONGRESSIONAL RELATIONS

Edited by
James A. Thurber
American University

A Division of Congressional Quarterly Inc.
Washington, D.C.

Printed in the United States of America

Cover design: Paula Anderson

Cover photo credits: *top row, left to right:* President Bill Clinton, by Reuters; Reps. Thomas J. Bliley Jr., R-Va., and John D. Dingell, D-Mich., by Richard Ellis, Congressional Quarterly; *middle row, left to right:* Vice President Al Gore and President Clinton, by Reuters; President Clinton, by Richard Ellis, Congressional Quarterly; President Clinton and Speaker of the House Newt Gingrich, by Reuters; *bottom row, left to right:* Speaker Gingrich, by Richard Ellis, Congressional Quarterly; Reps. Philip M. Crane, R-Ill., and Bill Archer, R-Texas, by Richard Ellis, Congressional Quarterly; Sens. Dianne Feinstein, D-Calif., and Orrin G. Hatch, R-Utah, by Richard Ellis, Congressional Quarterly.

Library of Congress Cataloging-in-Publication Data

Rivals for power : presidential-congressional relations / edited by
    James A. Thurber.
        p.   cm.
    Includes bibliographical references and index.
    ISBN 1-56802-152-6
    1. Presidents--United States.   2. United States.   Congress.
3. United States--Politics and government--20th century.
I. Thurber, James A., 1943–   .
JK585.R59   1996
320.973'09'049--dc20

95-48372
CIP

For Claudia, Mark,
Kathryn, and Greg

Contents

Tables and Figure

Preface

This book of twelve original essays is designed to explain the political dynamic between the president and the U.S. Congress. *Rivals for Power: Presidential-Congressional Relations* is an examination by scholars of the competition between the president and Congress using a variety of approaches and perspectives. After the Republican-controlled 104th Congress was swept into power as a result of the 1994 elections, a major transformation occurred in the relationship between Congress and the president. The tension between the two branches was prominently showcased again in the battle over the fiscal year 1996 budget. The system of separation of powers and checks and balances helps to check the power of both the president and Congress. However, for the political system to function, the president and Congress ultimately must cooperate. *Rivals for Power* examines the causes of cooperation and conflict between the two branches by presenting original research on a variety of topics, such as the battle over the budget; presidential leadership and coalition building; war powers; stability and change in the Congress and the White House; the politics of military base closures; and insights from empirical studies on presidential-congressional relations.

Rivals for Power grows out of the CQ Press volume that I edited entitled, *Divided Democracy: Cooperation and Conflict Between the President and Congress*. The title of that volume gave many the impression it was a study of divided party control of government, in the narrow sense of the term. In choosing the new title, I have sought to better describe and highlight the continued competition between the two branches, whether the White House and Congress are controlled by the same party or by different parties. This book focuses on the divisions in our democracy that create the rivalries between the president and Congress. It also explores the structural and behavioral factors that establish incentives for cooperation between the two branches.

Divided Democracy was translated into Russian and Spanish, revealing the international interest in the topic of legislative-executive relations. The relationship between the executive and the legislative assembly is, of course, a major concern in the former Soviet Union, where the Newly Independent States struggle to establish democracies. Since the publication of *Divided Democracy*, I have visited the Ukraine, Hungary, Cuba, and Kazakhstan to meet with academics and government officials to discuss executive-legislative relations, to help draft constitutions, and to explain our system of separated powers. Those meetings have been exceedingly helpful in my understanding of our system of governance and that of other nations. Those experiences helped to influence my selection of the authors and essays for *Rivals for Power*, since this book is intended not only for readers in the United States but also for those in other nations interested in the relationship between executives and legislative assemblies.

The only volume of original research that evaluates the relations between Congress and the presidency, it is useful to students of Congress, the presidency, and American government. The twelve essays address the most important questions about the rivalry between the president and Congress: What are the constitutional and political causes of presidential-congressional rivalry? How has change in Congress had an impact on the president? Has the rivalry between the president and Congress limited the political system's ability to produce timely and effective policy? Do a White House and Congress divided by partisanship produce only deadlock and delay? What are the causes of budgetary gridlock, and how do presidents and Congress overcome it? How do presidents build coalitions on Capitol Hill? Why are some presidents successful with Congress and others not, and how do we measure success? What are the war powers of the president and Congress, and are they infringing upon each other's prerogatives?

This book has no one viewpoint and no one dominant ideology for or against the Congress or the president. The authors at times disagree with each other in their observations about presidential-congressional rivalry. The authors generally do not advocate reform of our presidential-congressional system of governance. Although the debate over the power of the Congress and the president is at the heart of *Rivals for Power*, the book attempts to answer empirical questions about how the relationship works, rather than taking a reformist perspective calling for more or less executive or legislative power.

Acknowledgments

To write the essays in this book in the midst of the massive change in Congress and its relationship with the president is a difficult task. I am indebted to the authors of the essays in this volume for their careful analysis and willingness to make last-minute changes to reflect what has happened between President Clinton and the Congress.

I express special appreciation to the staff and advisers of CQ Press for producing *Rivals for Power* in a timely fashion. Acquisitions Editor Brenda Carter and Assistant Editor Gwenda Larsen carefully assisted me and all the authors through a year of many political changes and manuscript revisions. Their questions revealed insights into presidential-congressional relations that helped improve the content as well as the writing of this book. I would also like to thank Project Editor Chris Karlsten, Senior Editor Carolyn Goldinger, and freelance copy editor Barbara de Boinville for exceptional editorial work and for lessons on the fundamentals of good writing. Thank you also to the CQ marketing staff, who proved once again they are helpful and professional.

In addition to the many persons who have provided all of the authors with invaluable details about the relationship between Congress and the president, I thank my colleagues in the School of Public Affairs at American University. David Rosenbloom, Neil Kerwin, Candice Nelson, Jeff Fishel, Christine DeGregorio, Susan Hammond, Philip Brenner, Ron Shaiko, and Jeff Gill, my Ph.D. student and research assistant, are just a few who have been continuing sources of insight and support. I would also like to thank the many speakers in the Center for Congressional and Presidential Studies' Lobbying Institute who had observations about presidential lobbying on the Hill, especially Jack Bonner, Don Goff, William Sweeney, Charls Walker, and Anne Wexler. Charles O. Jones, Thomas Mann, Norman J. Ornstein, Robert S. Healy, and Roger Davidson were most helpful in this enterprise through their observations and writings on presidential-congressional relations. I also thank the students who have taken my "Congress and the Presidency" seminars for their fresh views and research.

Many interviews with persons in Congress and the White House were helpful to me in preparing this book, but nothing comes close to the hours I have spent with Pat Griffin, former assistant to the president for legislative affairs. I give special thanks to Pat for many insights on the relationship between the Clinton White House and the 103d and 104th Congresses. Also thanks to Dan Meyer, chief of staff to House Speaker Newt Gingrich, for his observations from the other end of Pennsylvania Avenue.

Thanks again to Neil Kerwin, dean of the School of Public Affairs at American University, for his continued support of my scholarship and the research agenda of the Center for Congressional and Presidential Studies.

This book is clearly a collective effort. I thank all of the contributors and those who have helped edit it. All of its flaws, however, are my own.

James A. Thurber

Contributors

Jon R. Bond is professor of political science at Texas A&M University. He has published articles on presidential-congressional relations, congressional elections, and public policy and is coauthor with Richard Fleisher of *The President in the Legislative Arena* (1990). He serves as coeditor of the *Journal of Politics.*

Cary R. Covington is associate professor of political science at the University of Iowa. He is coauthor with Lester G. Seligman of *The Coalitional Presidency* (1989) and author of numerous articles on presidential relations with Congress. His current research concerns the impact of newly elected presidents on the agendas of congressional committees.

Roger H. Davidson is professor of government and politics at the University of Maryland, College Park. He is author or coauthor of numerous books, monographs, and articles dealing with politics and policy making. His books include *Congress and Its Members*, 5th ed., coauthored with Walter J. Oleszek (CQ Press, 1996); *Remaking Congress: Change and Stability in the 1990s,* coedited with James A. Thurber (Congressional Quarterly Inc., 1995); and *The Postreform Congress* (1992).

Christopher J. Deering is associate professor of political science at George Washington University. He is coauthor with Steven S. Smith of *Committees in Congress* (CQ Press, 1990), editor of *Congressional Politics* (1989), and author of a number of articles and chapters on legislative politics and Congress's role in foreign and defense policy making.

Louis Fisher is senior specialist in separation of powers at the Congressional Research Service of the Library of Congress. His books include *Presidential War Power,* (1995); *American Constitutional Law,* 2d ed. (1994); *The Politics of Shared Power: Congress and the Executive,* 3d ed. (CQ Press, 1993); and *Constitutional Conflicts Between Congress and the President,* 3d ed. (1991).

Richard Fleisher is professor of political science at Fordham University. He has published articles on presidential-congressional relations, congressional elections, constituency influence in roll-call voting, and electoral realignments and is coauthor with Jon R. Bond of *The President in the Legislative Arena* (1990). He is currently writing a book on the presidency.

Scott R. Furlong is assistant professor of political science at the University of Wisconsin, Green Bay. His publications include a number of articles on regulatory politics and administration. His research interests are regulatory politics and presidential-congressional relations.

Glen S. Krutz is a Ph.D. student in the Department of Political Science at Texas A&M University. He served in the Washington office of Sen. Richard Bryan (D-Nev.) and was special policy assistant to the chancellor, University of Nevada System. His research interests are congressional policy making, specifically agenda setting and presidential-congressional relations.

Michael L. Mezey is professor of political science and dean of the College of Liberal Arts and Sciences at DePaul University. He is the author of numerous scholarly papers, articles, and book chapters in the areas of American politics, legislative politics, and comparative legislative behavior. He has published two books: *Congress, the President, and Public Policy* (1989) and *Comparative Legislatures* (1979).

Walter J. Oleszek is senior specialist in American national government at the Congressional Research Service and adjunct professor of political science at American University. With Roger H. Davidson, he wrote or edited *Congress and Its Members*, 5th ed. (CQ Press, 1996); *Governing: Readings and Cases in American Politics*, 2d ed. (CQ Press, 1992); and *Congress against Itself* (1977), as well as numerous other books and articles.

James P. Pfiffner is professor of government and public policy at George Mason University. His major areas of expertise are the presidency, American national government, and public management. His books include *Governance and American Politics* (1995); *The Modern Presidency* (1994); and *The Managerial Presidency* (1991).

Leroy N. Rieselbach, professor of political science at Indiana University, has written regularly on Congress. His publications include *Congressional Politics: The Evolving Congressional System* (1995); *Congressional Reform: The Changing Modern Congress* (CQ Press, 1994); and *Congressional Committee Politics*, coauthored with Joseph K. Unekis (1984).

Lester G. Seligman is professor emeritus of political science at the University of Illinois, Champaign-Illinois. He is coauthor with Cary R. Covington of *The Coalitional Presidency* (1989) and author of numerous books and articles on political leadership, the recruitment of political leadership, and the presidency.

James A. Thurber is professor of government and director of the Center for Congressional and Presidential Studies and the Campaign Management and Lobbying Institutes at American University. His books include *Remaking Congress: Change and Stability in the 1990s,* coedited with Roger H. Davidson (Congressional Quarterly Inc., 1995); *Campaigns and Elections: American Style,* coedited with Candice J. Nelson (1995); and *Divided Democracy: Cooperation and Conflict Between the President and Congress* (CQ Press, 1991).

RIVALS FOR POWER

1

An Introduction to
Presidential-Congressional Rivalry

James A. Thurber

The 1994 midterm congressional election reversed a generation of Democratic dominance in the House, brought divided party control of government again, and dramatically reshaped the rivalry between the president and Congress.[1] The 1994 election not only brought an overwhelming victory for the Republican party and major changes in the policy agenda and the structure of Congress, but it also dramatically changed the balance of power between the president and Congress. Having received an electoral mandate to implement their legislative program of cutbacks, devolution, and deregulation, Republicans in Congress boldly set about dictating the policy agenda. In contrast, President Clinton found that his negotiating power had been significantly diminished. The centralized decision-making system in the House of Representatives also limited the president's ability to influence Congress.

After the historic 1994 midterm election, President Clinton was impelled to reach out to the new Republican leadership in the House and the Senate. After Speaker Newt Gingrich, R-Ga., received a boost in power from a highly unified House Republican Conference and the structural reforms that it imposed upon the House, President Clinton's activist agenda during the 103d Congress was overshadowed by the Contract with America and the GOP-led drive to balance the budget and cut back the federal government.[2] However, ultimately, neither President Clinton nor the new Republican leadership could govern effectively without the cooperation of the other. Elections have an impact on presidential and congressional relations, as shown so clearly in the shift in political mood and policy from 1992 to 1994.

The 1992 presidential election brought a Democrat to the White House and unified party control of government for the first time in twelve years. At the heart of the 1992 presidential campaign was President Clinton's promise to fix the economy and to use the presidency to do so. He believed in an activist role for the federal government. The election produced the largest turnover of membership in the House of Representatives in more than forty years; 110 new members took office in January 1993. Although President Clinton had a majority of Democrats in the House and Senate, unified party control of government, and many new members of Congress who wanted change, he found out quickly that 43 percent support in the election (all but four House members ran ahead of him in absolute votes) did not translate into a mandate or easy coalition to push his activist agenda.[3] Clinton sent strong signals to the Hill that he wanted to cooperate with Congress as a "New Democrat" with a policy agenda along centrist lines. However, it was difficult for the president to find common ground for his centrist agenda with the Republicans and liberal Democrats.

Unified party control of government did not bring an end to the rivalry between the president and Congress. Within a few months, bitter struggles had broken out pitting the president not only against Republicans in Congress, but also against important congressional leaders within the Democratic party. Although President Clinton presented himself as a moderate, pragmatic president, he had to work with the majority of House Democrats, whose center of gravity had moved to the left on the political spectrum and who, as a result, frequently opposed the president's policies. For example, eleven Democratic House subcommittee chairs voted against President Clinton's economic package in May 1993, and the president's program barely survived. In a clear indication of the lack of discipline in the Democratic party, a subsequent demand by some House members, especially freshmen, that the eleven be stripped of their chairmanships was rejected by the House leadership.[4] Clinton also had to build cross-party coalitions with more conservative Republican leaders to pass several major bills on his agenda, such as the North American Free Trade Agreement (NAFTA) and the General Agreement on Tariffs and Trade (GATT). Many of President Clinton's initiatives were stopped or amended so thoroughly that they bore little resemblance to his original proposals. Unified government did not guarantee presidential dominance in Clinton's relationship with Congress.

President George Bush had similar "problems" with Congress. Immediately after his inauguration, President Bush, also in a gesture of good will, praised Congress: "To the Members of the Congress, to the institution of the House of Representatives and the Senate of the United States, may they flourish and may they prosper." [5] In response to President Bush's efforts to build better relations with Congress, Thomas S. Foley, D-Wash., then House majority leader, said, "That's another example of President Bush reaching out. We're going to respond very positively to that." [6] President Bush went on to have one of the lowest records of support for his policy initiatives in Congress in the last fifty years. Presidents Clinton and Bush had every good intention to work with broad bipartisan coalitions in Congress, but whether unified or divided party control of government, it did not work out that way.[7]

Good will does not generally characterize the institutional relationship between Congress and the president. President Clinton earned some of the highest presidential support scores (the percentage of presidential proposals that are approved by Congress, calculated annually by *Congressional Quarterly Weekly Report*) in his first two years of office, but never rose over 50 percent in the national public opinion polls. He is popularly known as a president that did not get his agenda through Congress—health care reform and welfare reform in particular.[8] However, he did continue to reduce the federal budget deficit, built bipartisan support for successful passage of NAFTA and GATT, and passed the family and medical leave law. In his first year in office, President Bush fared worse than any other president elected in the postwar era, winning only 63 percent of the roll-call votes on which he took an unambiguous position.[9] Despite Bush's popularity with the American people during Desert Storm (the highest in the polls of any postwar president at the end of his first year) and his sincere efforts to build bridges between the White House and Capitol Hill, executive-legislative relations during his presidency remained deeply rooted in political and institutional divisions. These divisions did not evaporate for President Clinton with unified government in 1993–1994, and they were clearly revealed in Clinton's relationship with Congress after the 1994 election. What are the roots of the rivalry between the president and Congress?

The Roots of Presidential-Congressional Rivalry

In this introduction I will examine seven root causes of the rivalry between the president and Congress: constitutional design, different constituencies, varying terms of office, weak political parties, divided party control of government, ongoing competition for power, and pluralism.

Constitutional Design

The Framers of the Constitution bequeathed to us one of the most enduring rivalries in government, that between the presidency and Congress.[10] The Constitution separates the three branches of government (legislative, executive, and judicial) but combines their functions, creating conflict and shared powers.[11] The president and the Congress are organized differently, and they are jealous of their constitutional prerogatives.

The Constitution invests Congress with "all legislative Powers," but it also authorizes the president to recommend and to veto legislation. If the president vetoes a bill, "it shall be repassed by two thirds of the Senate and the House of Representatives" (Article I, section 7). Because it is so difficult for Congress to gain a two-thirds' vote, presidential vetoes are usually sustained. Through 1994 presidents had used the veto 2,515 times; 1,065 of these were "pocket vetoes" not subject to congressional override. Congress overrode presidential vetoes slightly more than 7 percent of the time (104 times) when it had the opportunity to vote on them.[12] Thus, the threat of a veto in the legislative process gives the president an important bargaining tool; however, President Clinton did not use this tool until 1995, when he vetoed a $16 billion rescission bill. Clinton also used the veto in his confrontation with the Republican-led Congress over the cuts in Medicaid, Medicare, welfare, education, and federal environmental programs in the fiscal year 1996 federal budget. The greatest power of the president in divided government is often the power to say no. President Clinton embraced that notion in the budget battle when he said: "...this is one of those moments in history when I'm grateful for the wisdom of our Founding Fathers. The Congress gets to propose, but the president has to sign or veto, and that Constitution gave me that authority and one of the reasons for the veto is to prevent excess. They knew what they were doing and we're going to use the Constitution they gave us to stand up for what's right." [13]

Congress is given a broad list of powers in Article I, section 8, of the Constitution, but the greatest power of Congress is its authority to pass laws directly binding upon all citizens. Also of great importance is the power of the purse. Congress must authorize and appropriate funds for the president and the executive branch agencies. Presidents may propose budgets for the federal government, but Congress has the final say on spending, bringing automatic rivalry and conflict over spending priorities. Congress also has the power to levy and collect taxes, to borrow and coin money, and to regulate foreign and interstate commerce. A central element of the rivalry between the president and Congress has been battles over tax and trade policy. The powers to declare war, to provide for a militia, and to adopt laws concerning bankruptcy, naturalization, patents, and copyrights are also bestowed on Congress. The interpretation of presidential and congressional war power has changed over time and is another contemporary source of conflict. Congress has the authority to establish or eliminate executive branch agencies and departments and to oversee their operations. The Senate must approve cabinet nominees, ambassadors, and Supreme Court and federal judicial appointees before they can take office. A president cannot enter into a binding treaty with a foreign government without a two-thirds' vote of the Senate, nor can the president "declare war," a power the Constitution purposely gives to Congress. All of these constitutional congressional and presidential powers force both institutions to confront each other in governance, which more often than not creates rivalry and conflict.

A dramatic but rarely employed check on the president is impeachment. Executive branch officials can be impeached (formally accused) by a majority vote in the House and tried in the Senate. If two-thirds of the senators vote to convict, the official is removed from office. Only President Andrew Johnson has been tried on impeachment charges; the vote fell one short of the number required to convict him. The House Judiciary Committee recommended that Richard M. Nixon be impeached for transgressions in connection with the Watergate burglary of the offices of the Democratic National Committee and the ensuing cover-up. Nixon, however, resigned the presidency before a full session of the House could vote on the impeachment issue. The threat of impeachment establishes an important check on the president and executive branch.

The Framers of the Constitution deliberately fragmented power between the national government and the states and among the executive, legislative, and judicial branches.[14] They also divided legislative powers by creating two coequal houses, a bicameral Congress, which further magnifies rivalry and conflict. Although divided, Congress was designed to be independent and powerful, able to check the power of the executive and to be directly linked with the people through popular, periodic elections. The Framers wanted an effective and powerful federal government, but they wanted to limit its power in order to protect personal and property rights. Having experienced the abuses of English monarchs and their colonial governors, the men who wrote the Constitution were wary of excessive authority in an executive. They also feared "elective despotism," or excessive legislative power, something the Articles of Confederation had given their own state legislatures.

Therefore, the Framers created three branches of government with none having a monopoly. This separation of powers restricted the power of any one branch, and it required cooperation among the three in order for them to govern effectively. Today, as then, political action requires cooperation between the president and Congress. Yet the Constitution, in the way it divided power between the two branches, created an open invitation for conflict.[15] In sum, in creating a separated presidency and two equal legislative chambers, the Framers guaranteed on ongoing rivalry between the president and Congress.

Different Constituencies

The U.S. system of government, unlike parliamentary systems throughout the world, elects the executive and members of the legislature independently. The president is elected from vastly broader electoral coalitions than are representatives and senators, who have narrow constituencies in districts or states. Members of Congress, even those who belong to the president's party or hail from his home state, represent specific interests that can conflict with the interests of the president, who represents the nation as a whole. James Madison well understood this dichotomy of interests as an important source of conflict between the president and Congress: "The members of the federal legislature will be likely to attach themselves too much to local objects.... Measures will too often be decided according to their probable effect, not on the national prosperity and happiness, but on the prejudices, interests, and pursuits of the governments and the people of the individual States." [16]

Varying Terms of Office

The interaction of Congress and the president is shaped not only by their different constituencies but also by their different terms of office. The constitutional structure of U.S. government, which separates the Congress and the president, sets different terms of office for representatives, senators, and the president, and ensures they will be chosen from different constituency bases. House members are elected every two years; senators, every six. Presidents have only four years, possibly eight, in which to establish their programs. They are expected to set the national policy agenda and usually move rapidly in the first year before the traditional decline in their popularity.[17] Presidents are not concerned about reelection after the first four years of office; establishing good public policy and an honored place in history is their first priority. Other interests are certainly operative, but reelection concerns for members of Congress are most important, even for new members who support term limits.[18] Legislators, then, are often reluctant to allow their workload and policy agenda to be dictated by a president who has no electoral mandate to do so.

Congress moves more slowly than the president; it is deliberative and inefficient primarily because it represents a vast array of local interests. Congress passes new laws slowly and reviews old ones carefully. The House of Representatives of the 104th Congress had centralized power and was more efficient than the House of any other modern Congress, but this too caused conflict with President Clinton's agenda. The decision-making pace of Congress and of the president is not the same because of their different terms of office, electoral base, and perceived constituency mandates. The result of these differences is rivalry, conflict, and often deadlock.

Weak Political Parties

The federal system of state-based political parties contributes to the independence of members of Congress from the president. The president must work with weak, decentralized political parties that exercise little discipline and even less leverage over members. Senators and representatives usually run their own races with their own financing. The way they respond to local conditions has little to do with national party platforms or presidential politics. Members freely pursue their own interests without fear of discipline from the president.

Independence from political parties and the president allows legislators to seek benefits for their own constituents and to serve specialized interests. Thomas Mann argues further that:

> [t]he changes that swept through the political system during the 1960s and 1970s—the increase in split-ticket voting, the growing cost of campaigns and reliance on contributions from special interests, the rise of television, the expansion and growing political sophistication of interest groups in Washington, and the democratization and decentralization of Congress—may well have weakened the classic iron triangles, but they also heightened the sensitivity of politicians to all forms of outside pressure.[19]

For Republican members of the House, the 1994 election deviated from the normal individualistic election. The Contract with America, signed by three hundred Republican candidates for the House, "nationalized" the campaign for most of those candidates. No incumbent Republican House member lost in the 1994 election. Republicans earned a net gain of seventeen in the fifty-two open-seat House contests and lost only four Republican-controlled House open seats to the Democrats. Thirty-five House incumbent Democrats lost. With the Democrats losing fifty-two seats in the House and eight Senate seats, the mandate of the new Republicans was to be loyal to the contract, to the House Republican leadership, and to the reduction of individualism in the House. Party discipline came from the congressional party leaders, not from the grass-roots party organizations throughout the United States. This was unique in modern congressional elections and created the basis of conflict with President Clinton.

Divided Party Control of Government

Another electorally based impediment to legislative-executive cooperation is divided government, as shown by the dramatic election of 1994, which left a Democrat in the White House working with Republican majorities in the House and Senate.[20] There are two varieties of divided government (the condition that exists when the majority party in either or both houses of Congress differs from the party of the president): divided party control of Congress and split control of Congress and the White House. Opposing parties have controlled the presidency and one or both houses of Congress in twenty-two of the past twenty-eight years (79 percent of the time from 1969 through 1996), with the Republicans mainly controlling the White House and the Democrats controlling Congress. From 1887 to 1954, divided party control of government occurred only eight years (14 percent of the time), but from President Dwight D. Eisenhower's first year (1953) through President Clinton's fourth year in office (1996), it occurred twenty-eight years (56 percent of the time) (see Table 1-1). Therefore, divided party control of government at the federal level has been the norm in modern U.S. politics.

The trend toward ticket splitting between presidential and congressional candidates further exacerbates already strained relations. Election returns for Congress have increasingly diverged from national presidential returns; "the range in the ... variance, which measures the extent to which changes in local returns differ from the change in national returns, has more than doubled."[21] During the past thirty years, as the power of political parties has declined significantly, there has been a corresponding rise in individualistic candidacies for the presidency, the Senate, and the House. Fewer and fewer members of Congress ride into office on the electoral "coattails" of the president. This has led to the election of presidents who find it difficult to translate electoral support into governing support. The scarcity of presidential coattails by Bush in 1988 and Clinton in 1992 brings the conclusion that "the emperor has no coat."[22] Bush was the first candidate since John F. Kennedy

Table 1-1 Unified and Divided Party Control of Government, 1901–1996

Year	President	Senate	House
1901–1903	R	R	R
1903–1905	R	R	R
1905–1907	R	R	R
1907–1909	R	R	R
1909–1911	R	R	R
1911–1913	R	R	D
1913–1915	D	D	D
1915–1917	D	D	D
1917–1919	D	D	D
1919–1921	D	R	R
1921–1923	R	R	R
1923–1925	R	R	R
1925–1927	R	R	R
1927–1929	R	R	R
1929–1931	R	R	R
1931–1933	R	R	D
1933–1935	D	D	D
1935–1937	D	D	D
1937–1939	D	D	D
1939–1941	D	D	D
1941–1943	D	D	D
1943–1945	D	D	D
1945–1947	D	D	D
1947–1949	D	R	R
1949–1951	D	D	D
1951–1953	D	D	D

(Continued on next page)

to win the White House while his party lost seats in the House. Clinton ran behind all but four members of the House. With the decline of presidential coattails, strong-willed members of Congress are largely beyond the president's control. They are often more responsive to district and specialized interests than to the national agenda of the president.

Unified party control of government does not mean the two branches will work closely together. Divided government does not mean that the two

Table 1-1   *(Continued)*

Year	President	Senate	House
1953–1955	R	R	R
1955–1957	R	D	D
1957–1959	R	D	D
1959–1961	R	D	D
1961–1963	D	D	D
1963–1965	D	D	D
1965–1967	D	D	D
1967–1969	D	D	D
1969–1971	R	D	D
1971–1973	R	D	D
1973–1975	R	D	D
1975–1977	R	D	D
1977–1979	D	D	D
1979–1981	D	D	D
1981–1983	R	R	D
1983–1985	R	R	D
1985–1987	R	R	D
1987–1989	R	D	D
1989–1991	R	D	D
1991–1993	R	D	D
1993–1995	D	D	D
1995–1996	D	R	R

☐ Unified party control of government

■ Divided party control of government

Source: "Political Party Affiliations in Congress and the Presidency, 1789–1991," *Congressional Quarterly's Guide to Congress,* 4th ed. (Washington, D.C.: Congressional Quarterly Inc., 1991), 93-A and 94-A.

branches will fight. David Mayhew found that when it comes to passing major legislation or conducting investigations, it "does not seem to make all that much difference whether party control of the American government happens to be unified or divided." [23] However, we do know that it was generally easier for presidents to govern during periods of unified government—such as the early days of the New Deal (1933–1937), during World War II (1941–1945), and during the Great Society (1964–1965)—than in periods of divided government (especially since 1981, Reagan's first year in office).

Ongoing Competition for Power

The balance of power between and within the institutions of Congress and the presidency is dynamic and conflict is inevitable, another root cause of the rivalry between the president and Congress. The 1994 election brought the most centralized power structure in the House since Republican Speaker Joseph G. "Czar" Cannon, who served from 1903 to 1911.[24] Just one year before, the 103d Congress under Speaker Thomas Foley was decentralized and fragmented. What the public expects from each institution varies over time, as dramatically shown by the differences between the 103d and 104th Congresses.[25] For two hundred years Congress has continued to represent local interests and to respond (some think too much) to political preferences and public pressures.[26] Nevertheless, the institution has changed dramatically. The reforms of the past two decades have made Congress even more representative and accountable and, in the 104th Congress, more centralized. The reforms of the last twenty years have changed the way it makes laws, passes budgets, oversees the executive branch, and confronts the president.

As the congressional leadership is centralized and made more effective by one party, the power of the president is often diminished, as we have seen in the 104th Congress. This creates more tension between the two branches, with a clash between the president's national policy agenda and the agenda of Congress. President Clinton's legislative successes during the 103d Congress (1993–1995) were impressive, with a remarkable 86.4 percent win record on the votes on which he took a position. The 1994 election changed his success and the competitive environment with Congress; he was overshadowed by the Contract with America, the leadership of Speaker Newt Gingrich, and the Republican drive to balance the budget. Unified government and a decentralized Congress helped his legislative successes in 1993 and 1994; a massive loss in the midterm elections to the Republicans created conflict and deadlock between the two branches. If the president is popular with the American public, he has electoral coattails bringing many new members into Congress that are beholden to him, and if he has a well-organized and well-run White House and administration, he is more able to control the national policy agenda. An example of a president meeting these criteria is President Lyndon Baines Johnson during his first two years of office, before the war in Vietnam undermined his influence in Congress and popularity with the American voters. His central core of authority in dealing with the Congress reduced conflict between the two branches. Structural reforms within the presidency (for example, the establishment of the Bureau of the Budget and, later, the creation of the Office of Management and Budget and the expansion of the post–World War II

White House staff) and change in Congress (for example, the centralization of power by the Republican party congressional leadership and increased party unity in the 104th Congress) have direct impacts on the ability of the president to dominate the legislative agenda and for the Congress to act independently from the president. Thus, cooperation and conflict between the two branches are the norm.

Pressure to check the power of the president through the War Powers Resolution of 1973 and the Budget and Impoundment Control Act of 1974 brought changes that helped Congress reclaim some of the power it had lost to the president during the previous decades. Many institutional reforms of the 1970s, however, resulted in decentralization, which made Congress more democratic but also less efficient. With the new openness came greater accountability and responsiveness but at the price of efficiency and effectiveness as a lawmaking body. Modern presidents find Congress harder to influence than did their predecessors in the White House. Members of Congress are more independent. And with the weakening of strict seniority rules wielded by strong parties, coordinating the legislative process was more difficult for congressional party leaders until the House reforms of the 104th Congress that centralized power with the Republican leadership.

Although Congress created new ways of checking presidential power in the 1970s, ultimately legislative-executive relationships are not zero-sum games. If one branch gains power, the other does not necessarily lose it. The expansion of the federal government since World War II has given vast new power to both branches. Events and public policy issues contribute to the policy-making power of both the president and Congress. The war on drugs, environmental concerns, the savings and loan crisis, Desert Storm, and continuing budget deficits have led to new administrative (and legislative) powers expanding the scope of both branches. Even these crises, however, are not enough to reduce the rivalry between the two institutions.

The decentralization and fragmentation of power within Congress was dramatically altered as a result of the 1994 election. The Speaker, the only structural feature of the House dictated by the Constitution, had significant power before Speaker Gingrich expanded that power even more. Gingrich appointed the committee chairs and increased his influence over committee assignments, placing freshmen on the Ways and Means, Appropriations, Rules, and Commerce Committees. Of the eleven Republican openings on the Appropriations Committee, Speaker Gingrich appointed nine freshmen, thus assuring cohesion and loyalty from the new Republicans in the House. Gingrich's control over committee assignments for freshmen and over the selection of chairs was a dramatic break from the decentralized and more democratic House of the last twenty years. He abolished proxy voting in committees, thus limiting the power of committee chairs. He reduced committee staffing, abolished independent subcommittee staff, and placed six-year term limits on committee chairs, thus reducing the power of the chairs and increasing the power of the leadership. Gingrich, with the support of the Republican Conference, also limited committee assignments and restructured the committee system generally. All of these reforms helped to centralize power in the Speakership. Under the reformed House of Representatives, Speaker Gingrich gained substantial power to control the policy agenda using key provisions in the GOP Contract with America. He was able to overshadow President Clinton (and the Senate) and pass far-reaching legislation that projected a balanced budget in seven years, cut taxes, cut back spending on Medicare, Medicaid, and welfare, and decentralized federal government, sending more programs and money to the states. Not only the Republican party dominance of the House and Senate, but also the internal change in the House power structure changed fundamentally the relationship with the president in 1995.[27]

Pluralism

Pluralism, group-based politics, limits the power of the president and Congress to pursue their own agendas and thereby increases the competition between them. Policy-making gridlock often comes from competition among organized interests in society, not from divided party control of government. As more people are organized, as the political process is opened to more groups and classes than ever before, and as the demands and needs of those competing interests are weighed and mediated in the political process, the power of the president and Congress to control the policy agenda is reduced. The constitutional First Amendment rights, especially freedom of speech, freedom of assembly, freedom of the press, and freedom to petition government for grievances, are the foundation of pluralism in U.S. politics. The decay of political party organizations in the last thirty years in the United States has helped the growth of pluralism.[28] As political parties have lost power to recruit and elect candidates that are loyal to party leaders in government, interest groups have gained political power. The United States is experiencing "hyperpluralism," or extreme competition among groups that makes it almost impossible to define the public good in terms of anything other than the collection of special narrow interests. Hyperpluralism contributes fundamentally to the rivalry between the president and Congress and often leads to deadlock between the two branches of government (as with the fiscal year 1996 budget) by making it difficult to make the necessary compromises between the national interests of the president and the parochial interests of members of Congress.[29]

Conclusion

Organization theorists suggest that conflict produces incentives for organizations to centralize decision-making power.[30] When an organization is threatened, a premium is placed on efficiency, effectiveness, and cohesiveness in setting strategy. After forty years of Democratic control and two years of conflict from the Clinton White House, the House Republicans centralized their decision-making power structure in unprecedented ways. The House Republican centralization of decision making in the 104th Congress reduced individualism and brought about a more efficient and cohesive institution in its battle with President Clinton. Threatened by a unified Republican House, President Clinton reorganized and centralized his White House staff through Leon Panetta, his chief of staff. He simplified his policy agenda and built a more tightly knit and effective legislative affairs operation. Faced with a Democratic majority in the House in the 1980s, then-Minority Whip Newt Gingrich helped to build a cohesive, centralized, and efficient opposition that was eventually used as a majority party organization against President Clinton and the congressional Democrats in 1995.

Intense rivalry between the president and Congress is inevitable in an electoral system that can produce divided party control of the two branches. Cooperation may be more likely when both the president and Congress are of the same party. Even so, because of the wide range of views within a party, unified government is no safeguard against conflict, as was shown with President Clinton and the congressional Democratic party in 1993 and 1994. Partisanship may also serve to move legislation. For example, the 1986 tax reform law benefited from the battle between the Democrats and Republicans because both sides saw political advantage in moving the bill or disadvantage in being seen as obstructionist. The give-and-take between national and local representation, deliberation and efficiency, openness and accountability, specific interests and the "public good" ensures a certain amount of confrontation between Congress and the president. As we have seen, their relations are shaped by an amalgam of factors: constitutional design, different constituencies, different terms of office, weak political parties, divided party control of government, ongoing competition for power, and pluralism. Although the rivalry and conflict between Congress and the president are inherent in our system of government, presidents must find support in Congress and members must seek assistance from the White House. To succeed in office every president must surmount the constitutional and political obstacles to pass their legislative program and establish a working relationship with Congress.

Separation of powers and the division of political control between presidents and congresses do not present an insurmountable barrier to good public policy making. Presidents need to lead both public opinion and a consensus among the policy communities in Congress to solve the problems that are so readily visible. Overcoming divided government, changing public opinion, building consensus, and establishing the nation's policy priorities calls for leadership from the president or from inside Congress. Congress and the president must work together. Unified partisan control of both branches of government does not guarantee cooperation. Divided government does not guarantee conflict. Governing calls for bargaining, accommodation, and compromise by Congress and the president, the basis of our "separated" system of government.[31]

An Overview of the Book

The authors of each chapter in this book address the rivalry between the president and Congress in a variety of ways. They explain the relationship between the president and Congress and advance suggestions about how conflict and cooperation between the two institutions help and hinder democracy.

In chapter 2, "The Presidency and Congressional Time," Roger H. Davidson argues that the two branches run on different but related time frames, which has a major effect on the rivalry between the president and Congress. Presidents are limited to four or eight years and are forced to focus on the most important policy issues and get immediate results. Congress has more continuity with longer tenure and can take years to nurture policy. A number of indicators can be used to reveal legislative productivity—bills introduced, committee workloads, recorded votes, laws passed, and issues addressed. Using these measures Davidson suggests three recent lawmaking eras—a bipartisan conservative coalition from 1937 to 1964, liberal activism from 1965 to 1978, and financial restraint and political stalemate from 1979 to 1992. We may now be in a fourth era, driven by a conservative partisan majority. The overall history shows little relationship between legislative productivity and either unified party control or presidential leadership.

Walter J. Oleszek analyzes several important global and domestic changes that have had an impact on the policy-making process in Congress, in chapter 3, "The New Era of Congressional Policy Making." The end of the Cold War and concerns about the environment and the global economy, as well as recent demographics, have changed the legislative agenda. Members of Congress are overburdened, short of time, increasingly influenced by foreign lobbyists, and increasingly dependent on ad hoc solutions. Parties are in decline, with more independent voters and more candidate-centered campaigns. Despite all these new problems, successful policy making can happen if there is a popular consensus for purposeful action.

In chapter 4, "Presidential Leadership with Congress: Change, Coalitions, and Crisis," Lester G. Seligman and Cary R. Covington define presidential leadership in Congress as actions that consist of facilitating change and building coalitions from people who share similar goals—not merely following the latest poll. The decline in parties has made presidential leadership more difficult by reducing the sense of shared fate between the president and fellow partisans in Congress, as well as reducing party resources available. The modern media has also made presidential leadership more difficult by a greater inclination to cover scandals and a lesser tendency to trust the president. The debate over health care reform shows that the environment for building coalitions has worsened. Presidents have responded by expanding their staffs and, in order to rally support for an especially important policy or proposal, declaring national crises, neither of which promises success.

Although unified party control of government after the 1992 elections did not end gridlock, President Clinton succeeded in building presidential coalitions in Congress that helped to redirect public policy, according to Leroy N. Rieselbach in chapter 5, "One Vote at a Time: Building Presidential Coalitions in Congress." Rieselbach argues that the Constitution deliberately divided power between the branches of government. Presidential leadership must take account of the slow pace of Congress, as well as congressional constituencies and foreign and domestic events. It is possible that the 1994 election brought the start of a new "responsible party system," with a disciplined majority in Congress passing its own agenda: the Contract with America, budget cuts, devolution, and deregulation. This outcome would reduce the power of the president to affect legislation, but even if the old decentralized, individualistic system returned, the president would still have to struggle to build coalitions to support his agenda.

Chapter 6, "An Overview of the Empirical Findings on Presidential-Congressional Relations," by Jon R. Bond, Richard Fleisher, and Glen S. Krutz, is a thorough, critical review of the major empirical studies on presidential-congressional relations. Measures of legislative success should be reliable, valid, and generalizable. Such measures include presidential box scores, presidential support scores of individual members, and success on winning roll-call votes, when the president has publicly stated his position. Bond et al. argue that all three have their advantages and disadvantages, but roll-call votes seem to be the best overall approach for analysis. More research is needed in all areas of presidential-congressional relations, especially in the areas of agenda setting and committee decision making.

Building on the work of Bond, Fleisher, and Krutz, Scott R. Furlong, in chapter 7, "Congressional Support for Presidential Action," examines the impact of congressional factors that influence presidential success with Congress. Furlong explains presidential success with members of Congress for the years 1989, 1992, and 1993. He uses political party, ideology, an interactive variable based on party and ideology, leadership position in Congress, public support for the president in the member's district (based on presidential election returns), and the member's independence (based on the member's margin of victory in his last election) to explain the president's success in Congress.

Christopher J. Deering's chapter 8, "Congress, the President, and Automatic Government: The Case of Military Base Closures," evaluates congressional decisions regarding military base closures. Funding of military bases has been influenced by pork barrel politics and legislative-executive conflict since the beginning of the United States. The base closure commission created by Congress in 1988 is also a product of these factors. The base closure commission process illustrates both the difficulty of the necessary cooperation between the legislative and executive branches, and the efforts made by Congress to avoid blame when making difficult decisions.

President Clinton won a number of important legislative struggles, but ultimately lost the war over his primary policy agenda, according to James P. Pfiffner's findings in chapter 9, "President Clinton and the 103d Congress: Winning Battles and Losing Wars." President Clinton had a high success rate when he took a stand, but his successes were limited, and despite strong party unity, he did not get the level of support from the Democrats that he needed. Clinton's overall record with the 103d Congress was mixed, but he started with many factors against him, and did well to accomplish as much as he did.

Decisions about the federal budget are at the heart of American politics. Budgets quickly reveal the degree of cooperation and conflict between the president and Congress over public policy priorities. James A. Thurber analyzes the causes and characteristics of the intense presidential-congressional battles over the federal budget in chapter 10, "Congressional-Presidential Battles to Balance the Budget." In addition to evaluating the effect of congressional budget process reforms over the last twenty years on the rivalry between the president and Congress, the chapter analyzes the historic 1995–1996 budget confrontation and compromise between the president and Congress.

Louis Fisher's chapter 11, "President Clinton as Commander in Chief," describes Clinton as a president who has embraced a broad definition of his power as commander in chief. In June of 1993, Clinton ordered air strikes against Iraq, on questionable grounds and without congressional approval. In Somalia Clinton expanded original goals (begun under Bush) in an effort at "nation building" and stopping a so-called war lord, Mohammed Farad. And in Bosnia, Clinton claimed that he did not need congressional approval to order air strikes or commit troops. In reaction to the administration, Senator Dole introduced a bill in 1995 to clarify the war powers of Congress and the president, perhaps signaling a new effort by Congress to defend basic constitutional principles. The confrontation between the president and Congress over Bosnia continues the historic battle over basic constitutional rights and responsibilities in foreign policy.

Michael L. Mezey cautions us in chapter 12, "Congress Within the U.S. Presidential System," to be careful about exporting the U.S. presidential-congressional structure to other nations. The American political system is distinguished by remarkable political continuity, despite arguments that presidential systems are prone to political instability. The Founding Fathers were concerned about political instability and wanted a government with a strong legislature, but did not want a dominant legislature driven by popular pressures. The political stability of the United States results from the unique circumstances of its history and from American society and culture. For these reasons, nations imitating American political institutions are unlikely to succeed.

Notes

1. See James A. Thurber, "Thunder from the Right: Observations About the Elections," *The Public Manager* (Winter 1994–1995): 13–16.
2. On September 27, 1994, Republican congressional candidates signed the Contract with America, pledging that if elected they would support changes in congressional procedures and bring votes in the House on a series of proposals such as: a balanced budget amendment, a line-item veto, and term limits for members of Congress. For more on the Contract with America see Ed Gillespie and Bob Schellhas, eds., *Contract With America* (New York: Times Books, 1994).
3. For more on the 1992 elections see Michael Nelson, ed., *The Elections of 1992* (Washington, D.C.: CQ Press, 1993).
4. Beth Donovan, "Maverick Chairmen Forgiven as Clinton Reworks Bill," *Congressional Quarterly Weekly Report,* June 12, 1993, 1251–1252.
5. Erwin C. Hargrove, "The Presidency: George Bush and the Cycle of Politics and Policy," in *The Elections of 1988,* ed. Michael Nelson (Washington, D.C.: CQ Press, 1989), 175.
6. Quoted in James A. Barnes, "Political Focus," *National Journal,* February 11, 1989, 377.
7. For a description of presidential-congressional policy battles see Lance T. LeLoup and Steven A. Shull, *Congress and the President: The Policy Connection* (Belmont, Calif.: Wadsworth, Inc., 1993).
8. See chapter 6, "An Overview of the Empirical Findings on Presidential-Congressional Relations," for a full discussion of how "presidential support scores" are measured.
9. Janet Hook, "Bush Inspired Frail Support for First-Year President," *Congressional Quarterly Weekly Report,* December 30, 1989, 3540.
10. See James A. Thurber, "Congress and the Constitution: Two Hundred Years of Stability and Change," in *Reflections on the Constitution,* ed. Richard Maidment (Manchester, England: University of Manchester Press, 1989), 51–75.
11. For this constitutional basis of conflict see Louis Fisher, *Constitutional Conflicts Between Congress and the President* (Lawrence: University Press of Kansas, 1991); Fisher, *The Politics of Shared Power: Congress and the Executive* (Washington, D.C.: CQ Press, 1993); and Charles O. Jones, *The Presidency in a Separated System* (Washington, D.C.: Brookings Institution, 1994).
12. A pocket veto is the act of the president in withholding his approval of a bill after Congress has adjourned. See Harold W. Stanley and Richard G. Niemi, *Vital Statistics on American Politics,* 5th ed. (Washington, D.C.: CQ Press, 1995), 258. For vetoes and overrides from the 80th to the 103d Congresses (1947–1994), see Norman J. Ornstein, Thomas E. Mann, and Michael J. Malbin, *Vital Statistics on Congress, 1995–1996* (Washington, D.C.: Congressional Quarterly Inc., 1996), 167.
13. Todd S. Purdum, "President Warns Congress to Drop Some Budget Cuts," *New York Times,* October 29, 1995, 30.
14. See Jones, *The Presidency in a Separated System.*
15. See George C. Edwards III, *Presidential Influence in Congress* (San Francisco: Freeman, 1980); and Cecil V. Crabb, Jr., and Pat M. Holt, *Invitation to Struggle: Congress, the President, and Foreign Policy,* 4th ed. (Washington, D.C.: CQ Press, 1992).
16. James Madison, *Federalist* no. 46, in *The Federalist Papers,* ed. Clinton Rossiter (New York: New American Library, 1961), 296.
17. See Stephen Wayne, *The Legislative Presidency* (New York: Harper & Row, 1978).
18. David R. Mayhew, *Congress: The Electoral Connection* (New Haven: Yale University Press, 1974).
19. Thomas E. Mann, "Breaking the Political Impasse," in *Setting National Priorities: Policy for the Nineties,* ed. Henry J. Aaron (Washington, D.C.: Brookings Institution, 1990), 302.

20. On divided party control of government see David R. Mayhew, *Divided We Govern: Party Control, Lawmaking, and Investigations, 1946–1990* (New Haven: Yale University Press, 1991); James A. Thurber, ed., *Divided Democracy: Cooperation and Conflict Between the President and Congress* (Washington, D.C.: CQ Press, 1991); and Gary C. Jacobson, *The Electoral Origins of Divided Government* (Boulder, Colo.: Westview Press, 1990).

21. Ornstein, Mann, and Malbin, *Vital Statistics*, 49.

22. Nelson Polsby quoted in *Congress and the Nation, vol. VII, 1985–1988* (Washington, D.C.: Congressional Quarterly Inc., 1990), 21–22.

23. Mayhew, *Divided We Govern*, 198.

24. For more on Speaker Cannon see Ronald M. Peters, *The American Speakership: The Office in Historical Perspective* (Baltimore: Johns Hopkins University Press, 1990).

25. See Stephen J. Wayne, "Great Expectations: What People Want from Presidents," in *Rethinking the Presidency*, ed. Thomas E. Cronin (Boston: Little, Brown, 1982), 185–199; and Glen R. Parker, "Some Themes in Congressional Unpopularity," *American Journal of Political Science* 21 (February 1977): 93–119.

26. See Committee on the Constitutional System, *A Bicentennial Analysis of the American Political Structure* (Washington, D.C.: Committee on the Constitutional System, 1987).

27. James A. Thurber, "The 104th Congress Is Fast and Efficient, But at What Cost?" *Roll Call*, March 4, 1995, 16.

28. See Joel H. Silbey, "The Rise and Fall of American Political Parties," in *The Parties Respond: Changes in American Parties and Campaigns*, ed. L. Sandy Maisel (Boulder, Colo. : Westview Press, 1994), 3–18.

29. See Jonathan Rauch, *Demosclerosis* (New York: Times Books, 1994).

30. See James G. March and Herbert A. Simon, *Organizations* (New York: John Wiley and Sons, 1958).

31. See Jones, *The Presidency in a Separated System*.

2

The Presidency and Congressional Time

Roger H. Davidson

The legislative workload is a major component of the structure and substance of legislative-executive relations. Given the Constitution and the political history of the United States, it could not be otherwise. Articles I and II, after all, are largely devoted to the interleaved lawmaking responsibilities of the two branches—from initiation ("He [the president] shall from time to time ... recommend to their [Congress's] consideration such measures as he shall judge necessary and expedient....") to implementation ("He shall take care that the laws be faithfully executed...."). Beginning with George Washington, activist presidents have always inserted themselves into the legislative process. Franklin D. Roosevelt and his successors institutionalized "the legislative presidency": today's chief executives are expected to present their legislative agendas to Congress, and to provide their allies on Capitol Hill with guidance and leadership.

As for Congress, one attribute sets it apart from virtually all the world's other national assemblies: it is a working body that writes, processes, and refines its own products, relying to a large degree on "in-house" resources. Until quite recently scholars paid scant attention to legislative business as a research topic. Yet Congress's agenda and workload shape not only the behavior and operations of the Senate and House of Representatives, but also the two chambers' relationships with the executive branch. What is more, the legislative workload reminds us of "what Congress actually does and how it does it, with all its duties and all its occupations, with all its devices of management and resources of power." [1]

Legislative activity is, of course, only one aspect of the interactions between presidents and congresses. Executive communications to Congress, for example, have grown so rapidly over the past two generations that almost as many of them are referred to committees as are bills and resolutions. Making federal appointments is another joint enterprise that has become ever more burdensome at both ends of Pennsylvania Avenue. Implementation and oversight, not to mention administrative and judicial rule making, are other functions that repeatedly propel the president and Congress into joint action. Given the breadth and reach of modern government, these oversight duties remain burdensome even when few new statutes are produced. Yet oversight activities bear a close relationship to lawmaking: they flow from previously enacted statutes, they influence how these statutes are carried out or revised.

Thinking About Political Time

Thinking in terms of political time ought to come naturally to students of U.S. politics. After all, the Constitution separates the two policy-making branches, the presidency and Congress, chronologically as well as functionally. An interlocking system of terms of office—four years for the president, two years for representatives, and staggered six-year terms for senators—creates a perpetual timetable for electoral renewal or replacement of officials. If the constitutional system resembles an intricate machine of interlocked moving parts, that machine could very well be a timepiece.[2]

The two policy-making branches run on different but related time frames; rarely do they experience change at precisely the same moment or at exactly the same rate. Because presidents are limited to four or eight years, they are forced to focus on the most pressing policy issues and to seek quick results.[3] By contrast the houses of Congress display a durable continuity maintained by overlapping tenure and by the presence of experienced careerists. As a consequence policies are typically incubated and nurtured by Capitol Hill policy entrepreneurs, oftentimes years or even decades before someone in the White House decides to elevate the item to a short-list for urgent action.

These divergent time perspectives suggest why it is misleading to tell political time strictly according to electoral periodicity. Every new Congress is to some degree unique, but not every election makes substantial changes in the two chambers. As a continuing body the Senate is especially resistant to change; despite respectable turnover rates in the 1990s, the average senator had served 10.2 years, or nearly two terms.[4] The House of Representatives formally reconstitutes itself every two years, but only rarely is it as radically transformed as when it convened in January 1995. And even then, the continuities were tangible: the average representative in the 104th Congress had served 7.75 years, slightly less than four terms.

Categorizing presidencies might seem a simpler matter, and indeed most historians and political scientists use particular presidencies as their unit of analysis. But even here things are not always what they seem. First, an administration may undergo substantial midcourse corrections—caused by midterm elections, crises, or other events. Bill Clinton is only the most recent president whose second two years in office encountered conditions very different from those of his first two years. Such occurrences, as Charles O. Jones reminds us, can alter a president's governing strategy and effectiveness.[5] Second, essential presidential governing strategies or styles may conceivably extend beyond a single administration—as, for example, in the Nixon-Ford or Reagan-Bush successions.

Political scientists tend to measure political time in terms of underlying and enduring political party coalitions. These "party systems" are initiated by realigning elections or periods: most notably, the election of Andrew Jackson in 1828, the ascendancy of the Republican party in 1860, the "Sys-

tem of 1896," and Franklin D. Roosevelt's election in 1932. Such a categorization assumes the existence of mass-based parties that can effectively
mobilize the votes of loyal supporters in elections, unless and until these stable loyalties are disturbed by short-term forces or a more permanent
reordering of party divisions.[6] The theory conforms to political developments during the heyday of U.S. political parties, roughly from the 1830s
through the 1960s; it is less persuasive in explaining events either before the
rise of mass-based parties, or during the more recent period of "dealignment," or collapsing party loyalties. Nonetheless, party alignment theory
yields interesting insights into changes in presidential and congressional
policy making.[7]

A related classification is offered by Stephen Skowronek, who links
changing political apparatus to what he calls "emergent structures" of presidential policy making, depending on whether a given president challenges
or adheres to the prevailing political order.[8] Skowronek plants himself right
in the middle of the Oval Office; political time is "presidentially driven
sequences of change encompassing the generation and degeneration of
coalitional systems or partisan regimes."[9] He describes how presidents
"make politics" by tirelessly building constituencies for change and striving
to remove obstacles that stand in the way of their high-priority projects. It
is hard to square this presidentially centered vision with, for example, the
varied patterns of legislative-executive relations. Presidents are not always at
the center of policy making, nor are they invariably agents of change. In our
separated system, as the evidence shows, innovation and incubation of major
policy departures can occur in many places, not the least of which are on
Capitol Hill.

What we need is a way of counting political time in terms of policy-
making activity and outcome. Here we attempt such a measure, based on a
critical but often neglected variable: legislative productivity.

Overall Legislative Trends

Today both the president and Congress confront a number and variety
of demands unmatched in all but the most turbulent years of the past.
"What is equally true, as the history of [Congress] readily demonstrates, is
that the volume of output demands as well as the degree of their complexity, uniformity, and volatility, vary greatly over time."[10] Aggregate legislative
statistics from the post–World War II period show how variable these workload measures can be.[11]

One workload indicator is the number of bills and resolutions introduced by senators and representatives. In both chambers, bill introduction
showed long-term growth from the mid-1940s until the early 1970s, followed by gradual and then precipitous decline (see Figure 2-1). In the
House, a portion of that decline can be traced to changes in cosponsorship
rules in 1967 and again in 1978. Both chambers, however, have experienced

Figure 2-1 Measures Introduced, 80th-103d Congresses (1947-1995)

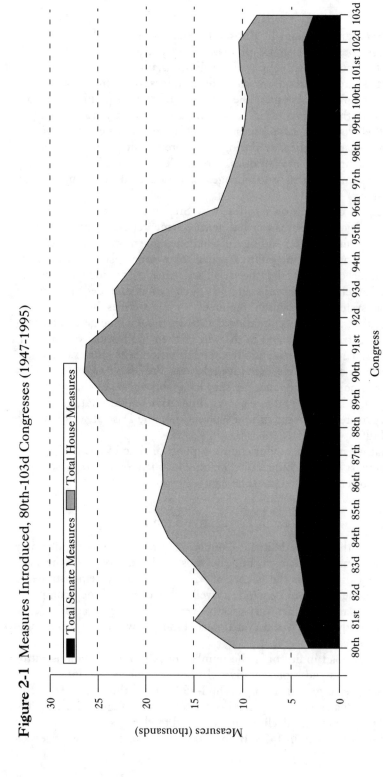

Note: Measures include all bills and joint resolutions and exclude simple and concurrent resolutions, which do not have the force of law when enacted.

Source: Rozanne M. Barry, "Bills Introduced and Laws Enacted: Selected Legislative Statistics, 1947-1994," *CRS Report* 95-233C (February 2, 1995), 2.

parallel cycles: gradual buildup, then a period of extraordinary legislative activity followed by a sudden and striking contraction.

Bill introduction and sponsorship vary widely among individual senators and representatives. Some lawmakers are inveterate sponsors of bills and resolutions; others shy away from sponsoring measures. In 1947–1949 (80th Congress), House members on average authored about eighteen bills or resolutions, compared to thirty-three for senators. In the late 1960s figures peaked at about fifty measures per representative and forty-nine measures per senator. Then in the late 1970s the figures plummeted, reaching a plateau in the mid-1980s that remains to this day. Today's lawmakers introduce fewer measures than those who served in Congress at the beginning of the post–World War II period—fewer than thirty per senator and fewer than half that number per representative.

Legislators today are doubly disadvantaged: not only do they introduce fewer bills and resolutions, but their proposals are less likely to be approved by the full chamber. A Senate bill or resolution introduced in the post–World War II years had better than an even chance of passage; the odds are now about one in four.[12] A House bill or resolution used to have nearly one chance in four of passage; today the odds are about half that.[13] This trend, as will be seen, stems in large part from the elimination or contraction of large numbers of administrative or noncontroversial measures.

Overall workload levels reverberate, to a greater or lesser degree, in the committee rooms of the two houses. To be sure, every committee is unique, as Richard F. Fenno, Jr., reminds us; one committee's business may soar while other panels are looking for work.[14] Yet most committees conform more or less to the overall boom-and-bust cycle, at least in terms of bills and resolutions referred to them.[15] In the boom years of the 1970s, activity levels reached modern-day peaks. After about 1978 committee workload indicators declined markedly, hitting a plateau in the mid-1980s and early 1990s. In 1993–1995 (103d Congress), for example, the number of measures referred to House committees was only one-third what it had been two decades earlier. In the Senate, referrals to committees were down by 40 percent.[16]

Five of the House committees studied by Fenno were reexamined in four selected congresses: the preform 90th (1967–1969), the reform 94th (1975–1977), and the postreform 98th (1983–1985) and 102d (1991–1993). The results can be seen in Table 2-1. Committee activity and workload soared in the 1970s, as an overflowing policy agenda found a newly decentralized power structure that offered multiple channels for initiative and action. In the mid-1970s the number of measures referred to the committees rose by more than 20 percent, despite the fact that House rules by this time permitted cosponsorship of measures. The five committees scheduled more than twice as many hearing days as they had a decade earlier. By the mid-1980s the trend had reversed itself: referrals were cut almost in half and days of hearings were down by about one-third. Committee activity levels rebounded somewhat in the early 1990s: although total referrals continued

Table 2-1 Referrals and Hearings in Five House Committees, Four Selected Congresses

Committee	Measures Referred (by Congress)				Days of Hearings (by Congress)			
	90th (1967–1969)	94th (1975–1977)	98th (1983–1985)	102d (1991–1993)	90th (1967–1969)	94th (1975–1977)	98th (1983–1985)	102d (1991–1993)
Education and Labor	831	1,084	487	647	228	377	260	290
Foreign Affairs	288	798	564	639	154	363	261	406
Interior/Natural Resources	735	1,036	463	568	40	279	281	345
Post Office and Civil Service	1,183	1,543	835	721	167	213	93	172
Ways and Means	3,714	3,740	1,908	1,994	74	267	135	295
Totals	6,751	8,201	4,257	4,569	663	1,499	1,030	1,508

Note: Committee names are those used in the Congresses in question. In 1995 the new Republican majority eliminated the Post Office and Civil Service Committee and transferred its jurisdiction to another panel. Names were also changed: Education and Labor became Economic and Educational Opportunities, and Foreign Affairs became International Relations.

Sources: Committee calendars and activity reports; Joint Committee on the Organization of Congress, *Background Materials*, S. Prnt. 103–55 (Washington, D.C.: U.S. Government Printing Office, 1993), 491–493.

to lag, committees held more days of hearings and printed more of them than in earlier peak years of productivity.[17]

One panel that compiled extensive records throughout this period was the House Committee on Commerce (named Interstate and Foreign Commerce until 1981, then Energy and Commerce until 1995). Though by no means an "average" committee (if such a thing exists), Commerce is nonetheless a good barometer of workload trends. The panel has historically been a major player in domestic policy making: its jurisdiction, expansive and jealously guarded by its chairmen and staff, has brought it more than one out of every ten measures referred to House committees in recent years. Even under Republican rule the committee remains a powerhouse, although in 1995 it ceded some jurisdiction and the "Energy" part of its name. The panel's incoming demands—for example, bills referred and issues covered—peaked in the 93d Congress (1973–1975); its activity—for example, days of hearings, hours of sitting, and pages of testimony—crested later in the decade. The committee is still regarded as one of the most aggressive and active on Capitol Hill. In the 103d Congress (1993–1995) it handled such issues as health care reform, telecommunications, food safety, and environmental protection, not to mention implementation of such trade pacts as the North American Free Trade Agreement (NAFTA) and the General Agreement on Tariffs and Trade (GATT). Yet in that two-year period it covered fewer than one-fifth the bills and spent fewer than one-fourth as many hours in hearings or markup sessions as it had done nearly two decades earlier in the 95th Congress (1977–1979).[18] Its activity record, in short, roughly parallels the overall cyclical pattern for the chamber as a whole.

Recorded votes on the House and Senate floors underscore these shifts in legislative activity. The numbers of recorded votes remained quite low in the 1940s and 1950s, accelerated in the 1960s, and then exploded in the 1970s.[19] The rise in floor activity was linked directly to changes in rules and procedures that made it easier for members to offer floor amendments and to gain recorded votes. This shifted power perceptibly from the committee rooms to the chambers themselves.[20] Party and committee leaders, especially in the House, soon fought back with procedural tactics aimed at limiting contentious floor votes. Accordingly, the number of recorded votes fell off markedly after 1978, more or less stabilizing in the 1980s and 1990s—(from 900 to 1,000 in the House and from 600 to 800 in the Senate)—far below the rate for the peak congresses of the 1970s.

Finally, consider the end product of lawmaking: bills and resolutions that survive the labyrinthine legislative process to become law. Working in tandem, Congress and the executive strictly regulate the flow of legislative outputs. Of the nearly ten thousand bills and resolutions introduced in the House and Senate in a given Congress, only about 6 percent find their way into the statute books. The size and shape of the legislative product are a function not only of political support or opposition but also of changing rules specifying which matters must be resolved by statute and which can be handled by other means.

Overall legislative output figures—measures passed by the two chambers, measures signed into law—look quite different from the input and activity figures described thus far. Only a modest upsurge in volume occurred during the activist era of the 1960s and 1970s; since then, there has been only a slight decline. The number of enacted public bills (those dealing with general legislative matters) began at a high level after World War II, peaking in the mid-1950s.[21] Levels have descended gradually since then. The number of enacted private bills (that is, granting benefits to named individuals, as in pension or land claims) has slowed to a trickle. In the early postwar period, private bills typically equaled or exceeded public laws; today they are rare.

Legislative output is shaped not only by the size and shape of the public policy agenda but even more by Congress's periodic decisions to include or exclude categories of items from legislative consideration. The burgeoning legislative agenda produced by the Great Depression and World War II, for example, led to demands for simplification and streamlining. As George B. Galloway, staff director of the 1945–1946 Committee on the Organization of Congress (the La Follette-Monroney Committee), described the legislative branch's predicament:

> Still functioning for the most part with the machinery and facilities inherited from the simpler days of the mauve decade, its calendars and committees became increasingly congested, its councils confused, and its members bewildered and harassed by multiplying technical problems and local pressures.[22]

Not surprisingly, one of the objectives of the 1946 Legislative Reorganization Act was to trim and systematize the legislative agenda. Minor or administrative questions were to be delegated to administrative agencies or tribunals.

The 1946 act's goal of shrinking the legislative workload, though initially frustrated, eventually came to pass. The most dramatic development was the long-term decline of private bills—mostly private immigration and claims cases. That trend has remained relatively steady over the past forty years.

Categories of administrative matters have also gradually been jettisoned. More than half of all public laws produced in the late 1940s and 1950s addressed administrative matters rather than general policy questions.[23] Examples include Native American tribal claims settlements, land conveyances, interstate compacts, legislative housekeeping matters, pay adjustments, and income disbursements. Less than 40 percent of the laws embodied major or generalized policy decisions—appropriations, authorizations, or even substantive amendments to prior authorizations. Fewer than one out of twenty laws were commemorative in nature—that is, established commemorative days, weeks, or months; authorized commemorative stamps, medals, or coins; or named federal buildings or other facilities. During the 1960s, however, the proportions shifted roughly as follows: substantive, 45 percent; administrative, 40 percent; commemorative, 5 to 8 percent. By 1977–1978, nearly three-quarters of all public laws were substantive, with administrative and commemorative measures accounting for 15 percent and 10 percent, respectively.

The most striking trend of the 1980s was the growth of commemoratives at the expense of substantive laws. Commemoratives came to comprise nearly half of all statutes produced in a given Congress, whereas substantive laws accounted for about 30 percent and administrative matters 20 percent. The shrinkage in the volume of substantive legislation is commonly attributed to the policy "gridlock" that resulted from split party control of the White House and Capitol Hill. But it was equally a byproduct of the increasingly common stratagem of packaging legislative proposals into massive measures—for example, continuing resolutions, reconciliation bills, tax reform packages, and broad-scale reauthorizations. This is attested by the steady growth in the length of public statutes, despite the upsurge in brief commemorative measures. Between 1947 and 1992, the average public law ballooned from 2.5 pages to nearly 13 pages. In the late 1960s, more than two-thirds of all public laws took up no more than a single page; in the 1980s, fewer than half of all laws were that brief.[24] And the proportion of truly long enactments—twenty-one pages or more—grew threefold in that same period. Legalistic verbosity is only partly to blame; legislative packaging is also at work.

These statistical trends, especially the activity and workload figures, lend strong support to the thesis that contemporary lawmaking has passed through three, or perhaps four, distinct stages or eras (see Table 2-2). Legislative-executive relations follow different paths during each of these periods. The first was a relatively static era dominated by a bipartisan conservative coalition (roughly 1937–1964); the second was an era of liberal activism and reform (1965–1978); and the third was an era of contraction, of fiscal restraint and political stalemate (1979–1992). A fourth congressional era, driven by a conservative partisan majority, may presently be under way.

Like any artifacts of historical categorization, these eras are bound to arouse debate over their precise definitions and boundaries, and perhaps even over their validity or utility in illuminating legislative-executive relations. Historical developments, after all, are continuous and multifaceted, rarely yielding unambiguous boundaries. Although my primary data sets begin in 1947, I have extended the first era back to the second Roosevelt administration (1937–1941) by relying on fragmentary statistical indicators and a wealth of qualitative data. The boundaries of the second, liberal era are also problematic: reformist skirmishes broke out over a period of years starting in the late 1950s; by the time the climax occurred in 1974–1975, the era's energy was already waning. The third, postreform era was one of instability in which elements of the prior era coexisted uneasily with sub-

Table 2-2 Four Eras in the Operation of the Modern Congress

Congressional Era	Approximate Dates	Environmental Forces	Leadership Mode	Member Goals	Activity and Workload
Bipartisan Conservative	1937–1964	Intraparty divisions	Chairmen of "corporate" committees	Public policy, internal influence sought by careerists; reelection stressed by marginal members	Stable (much of it routine in nature)
Liberal Activist	1965–1978	Liberal majorities	Democratic caucus	Public policy now competes with reelection for most members; internal influence is dispersed	Rising rapidly with legislative innovation, jurisdictional expansionism
Postreform	1979–1992	Divided government	Party leaders versus committee majorities	Public policy sought by many, internal influence by a few; reelection important for most members	Declining rapidly (jurisdictional protectionism, oversight stressed)
Partisan Conservative	1993–	Interparty conflict	Republican leadership	Public policy predominant; careerism deemphasized or shunned	Short-term rise; party leaders push committee productivity

sequent adjustments to economic and political trends. The years following the third era resist categorization, too, perhaps because of their very nearness.

Despite these caveats, it is intriguing how closely these three eras coincide with changing journalistic and scholarly understandings of the legislative process. The "textbook Congress" that emerged from the first era was well-researched and descriptively persuasive.[25] The same can be said for the liberal activist, or reform, era, which still dominates journalistic and textbook treatments of the subject. There has even emerged a measure of scholarly consensus on the nature and characteristics of the recent postreform era. Fashionable theoretical paradigms have also shifted roughly in tandem with changing legislative characteristics. Explaining these eras of lawmaking, then, can illuminate our understanding of policy formation and presidential-congressional relations.

The Bipartisan Conservative Era (1937–1964)

According to popular legend, Franklin D. Roosevelt overwhelmed Congress with his New Deal programs, dictating legislation that gained virtually automatic approval. The facts by no means support this legend. Putting aside the emergency measures approved quickly during the first months of his administration, Roosevelt's legislative record drew heavily on proposals already introduced and incubating on Capitol Hill. This interbranch cooperation increased in the late 1930s. For the years 1931–1940, Lawrence H. Chamberlain found joint presidential-congressional influence at work in 52 percent of the major pieces of legislation; the president prevailed in 37 percent of the cases and Congress in 11 percent.[26] His findings affirmed "the joint character of the American legislative process," even in years of powerful presidential leadership.

The New Deal soon gave way to a long period of bipartisan conservative dominance, which lasted roughly from the second Roosevelt administration through the mid-1960s. Both parties were split internally between a progressive, internationalist wing and a reactionary wing. Although the progressives tended to dominate presidential selections, the conservatives held sway on Capitol Hill. An oligarchy of senior leaders, oftentimes called "the barons" or "the old bulls," wielded the gavels and commanded the votes in the committees and on the floor. Whichever party was in power, congressional leaders overrepresented safe one-party regions (the Democratic rural South, the Republican rural Northeast and Midwest) and reflected the limited legislative agenda of the bipartisan conservative majority that controlled so much domestic policy making.

This Capitol Hill regime proved a hostile environment for activist presidents and their ambitious legislative agendas. "'For God's sake,' a congressional spokesman telephoned the White House in April 1938, 'don't send us any more controversial legislation!'" Recounting this anecdote from

Franklin Roosevelt's second term, James MacGregor Burns summed up legislative-executive relations as "deadlock on the Potomac." [27]

Harry Truman's clashes with Congress began early and continued throughout his administration. "Except for the modified Employment Act of 1946," relates Robert J. Donovan, "the [Democratic] Seventy-ninth Congress had squelched practically every piece of social and economic legislation Truman had requested." [28] Truman's other congresses were equally frustrating, though in different ways. The Republican 80th Congress "gave [Truman] his most enduring image. Facing an opposition-controlled legislative body almost certain to reject any domestic program he proposed, he adopted the role of an oppositionist." [29]

Truman campaigned successfully in 1948 by attacking the "awful, do-nothing 80th Congress." Yet the Democratic 81st Congress rejected virtually all his major Fair Deal initiatives, and the 82d, marked by depleted Democratic majorities and the Korean War stalemate, was even more hostile to new domestic legislation.

The 1950s were years of outward quiescence accompanied by underlying, accelerating demands for action and innovation. Dwight Eisenhower, with far more modest legislative goals than Truman's, was increasingly placed in the position of offering scaled-down alternatives to programs launched on Capitol Hill by coalitions of activist Democrats and moderate Republicans.

The legislative workload throughout this era was, accordingly, relatively stable and manageable from year to year. A large proportion of the bills and resolutions were routine and dealt with matters not yet delegated to the executive branch for resolution—for example, immigration cases, land claims, and private legislation. Demands were building, however, for bolder legislation to address civil rights and other concerns of urban and suburban voters.

On Capitol Hill, the powerhouse committees (the taxing and spending panels plus House Rules) were cohesive groups— "corporate," to use Fenno's term—with firm leadership and rigorous internal norms of behavior.[30] They kept a tight lid on new legislation, especially in fiscal affairs. The appropriations committees, in particular, stood as guardians of the U.S. Treasury, holding in check the more rapacious inclinations of the program-oriented authorizing panels.

In both houses of Congress power gravitated to a cadre of strong committee leaders. The best of them were able, vivid personalities whose safe constituencies enabled them to devote their time and skills to Congress and its work. If they often behaved autocratically, they usually enjoyed the tolerance if not support of a majority within their committees. Southern Democrats, who chaired most of the key committees during those days, reached across the aisle to build their working majorities, often cultivating a close bond with their ranking minority counterparts. Younger and more liberal members, recalling bitterly how they were initially treated by the old bulls, slowly succeeded in restraining or replacing the committee barons. As members' memories of this era fade, however, there survive many colorful anecdotes and stories, some of them no doubt apocryphal, about the exploits and foibles of the old bulls—among them Rules Chairman Howard W. Smith, D-Va.; Ways and Means Chairman Wilbur Mills, D-Ark.; Senate Minority Leader Everett M. Dirksen, R-Ill.; and, most of all, Senate Majority Leader Lyndon B. Johnson, D-Texas.

Journalists and political scientists closely studied post–World War II congresses, constructing a detailed and persuasive picture of their operations. Borrowing research concepts and techniques from sociology and anthropology, behaviorally trained political scientists, in particular, illuminated Congress's workings through close personal observation, interviews, and statistical analysis. The Senate of this era was lovingly described by journalist William S. White and systematically analyzed by political scientist Donald R. Matthews.[31] Richard F. Fenno, Jr., wrote powerful, detailed accounts of committee operations and the budgetary process.[32] To do justice to the many scholars who illuminated the workings of the postwar Congress would require a lengthy listing of names and citations.

The picture of the postwar Congress that emerged from the behaviorists' assault upon Capitol Hill was so persuasive that one scholar labeled it "the textbook Congress." [33] According to the leading intellectual framework from that period, the institution was viewed as an interlocking pattern of personal relationships in which structure and function worked in rough equilibrium. Ironically, by the time observers got around to completing this coherent picture of a tight, closed, internally coherent congressional world, that world was already being turned upside down. Pressures for change and "reform" mounted, heralding a prolonged period of liberal reformist politics.

The Liberal Activist Era (1965–1978)

The cozy domains of the barons were eventually pulled apart by what journalist Hedrick Smith called a "power earthquake." [34] The metaphor is attractive but inexact. Although many observers (Smith included) associate the changes with the post-Watergate "class of 1974" and the subsequent overthrow of three House committee chairmen, these events signaled the high-water mark rather than the outset of the era of legislative activism and procedural reformism.

The boundaries of the liberal era, like those of the other eras, are somewhat imprecise. The process of change began in earnest after the 1958 elections, when the Democrats enlarged their ranks by sixteen senators and fifty-one representatives, many of them urban and suburban liberals. The elections had an immediate effect in both chambers. Senate Majority Leader Johnson's heavy-handed leadership style softened perceptibly; in the House a small band of liberal activists formally organized the Democratic Study Group, which set about launching a drive for procedural reforms. Two years later, Johnson relinquished the Senate majority leadership to the mild-mannered, liberal Mike Mansfield, D-Mont., while Speaker Rayburn struggled to break the conservatives' control of the powerful Rules Committee. The reform era reached its high-water mark in the mid-1970s with successive waves of changes in committee and floor procedures and, in 1975, the ouster of three of the barons from their committee chairmanships.

One underlying cause of the upheaval was the policy demands of urban and suburban voting blocs as well as minority groups—demands heeded by activist presidents.[35] The spirit of the era was reflected in the popular "movements" that came to prominence: civil rights, feminism, environmentalism, consumerism, and opposition to the Vietnam War. These movements provided not only an extensive legislative agenda, but also grassroots activists who promoted that agenda—some of whom wound up serving in the House or Senate. Longer-range causes of the era's liberal activism included reapportionment and redistricting, demographic shifts, widened citizen participation, social upheaval, and technological advances in transportation and communications.

The resulting changes pointed Congress in the direction of a more open and participatory process that encouraged legislative innovation and productivity. Individual lawmakers had greater leverage; influence was dispersed among and within the committees. More leaders existed than ever before, and more influence could be exerted by nonleaders. More staff aides were on hand to extend the legislative reach of even the most junior members.

Individual senators and representatives, while enjoying their enhanced legislative involvement, were at the same time forced to devote increasing attention to their constituents back home. No longer was frantic constituency outreach confined to a few senators from large states and a few representatives from swing districts; it was practiced by all members (or their staffs) in order to purchase electoral security in an age of dwindling party support. In their officeholding activities, members tended to exchange the role of workhorse, or legislative specialist, for that of showhorse, becoming legislative generalists, advertisers, and credit seekers.

The reforms were propelled by, and in turn helped to facilitate, an ambitious and expansionary policy agenda, as such themes as John F. Kennedy's "New Frontier" and Lyndon B. Johnson's "Great Society" suggest. This era witnessed a flood of landmark enactments in civil rights, education, medical insurance, employment and training, science and space, consumer protection, and the environment, not to mention five new cabinet departments and four constitutional amendments. Legislative activity soared by whatever measure one chooses to apply—bills introduced, hearings, reports, hours in session, floor amendments, recorded floor votes, and measures passed.[36] The processing of freestanding bills and resolutions became the centerpiece of committee and subcommittee work.

This legislative outpouring formed a gigantic "bulge in the middle," which David R. Mayhew noticed in his study of lawmaking between 1946

and 1990.[37] Fifty-two percent of the 267 "major" enactments Mayhew identified over the forty-four-year period were enacted between John F.
Kennedy's inauguration in 1961 and the end of Gerald Ford's administration in 1976. Over this period 74 measures were produced under eight years
of divided party control (Nixon, Ford) and 66 under eight years of unified
control (Kennedy, Johnson). We will presently have more to say about this
aspect of our analysis, which bears out Mayhew's thesis that party control
makes little difference in the output of major enactments or investigations.

The decentralization of the 1960s and 1970s was accompanied by a
weakening of the appropriations committees' grip over spending and by a
strengthening of the power of the authorizing committees (for example,
Agriculture, Banking, Commerce). By ingenious use of "backdoor spending"
provisions—such as contract authority, budget authority, direct Treasury
borrowing, and especially entitlements—the ascendant authorizing committees stripped the appropriations panels of much of their former fiscal
guardianship role.[38] Three-quarters of the domestic spending growth
between 1970 and 1983 occurred in budget accounts lying outside annual
appropriations—that is, beyond the appropriations committees' reach.[39]

The procedural autonomy of another prereform power center, the
House Ways and Means Committee, was not breached until nearly the close
of the liberal activist period. "During the congressional revolution of the
1970s," wrote Abner J. Mikva and Patti B. Saris, "the Ways and Means
Committee became a 'bastille' that symbolized the inequities of the old
order." [40] The panel's independence was curtailed not only by chamberwide
reforms (caucus ratification of committee chairmanships, modified or open
rules for floor deliberation, open committee meetings), but also by provisions aimed explicitly at the committee (enlargement of the committee,
transfer of Democratic committee assignments to the Steering and Policy
Committee, jurisdictional encroachments, and, finally, mandated subcommittees). By this time Chairman Mills's remarkable House career was drawing to a close, and he was succeeded by far weaker leadership.[41]

Like the earlier period, this reform era was well documented by journalists and scholars.[42] The most popular scholarly paradigm of the era,
drawn from economics, focused on the decentralization and fragmentation
of the period.[43] Lawmakers were viewed not as role players enmeshed in a
complex system of interactions in equilibrium but as individual entrepreneurs competing in a vast, open marketplace that rewarded self-interested
competitiveness with little or no regard for the welfare of the whole.

The Postreform Era (1979–1992)

During the 1980s Congress again faced an environment that departed
in significant ways from what had gone before. Although the shift is popularly associated with the Reagan administration, it was under way by
1979–1981 (the 96th Congress).

The advent of what economist Lester Thurow called the "zero-sum society" no doubt lay at the root of the changed political atmosphere.[44] Between World War II and the early-1970s, the nation's productivity levels had soared, along with real incomes for average citizens. These engines had enabled the nation to raise its standard of living while underwriting an expanding array of public services. After 1973 both the nation's productivity and the individual worker's real income stagnated, in comparison with both our economic rivals and our previous record. Indeed, the 1970s and 1980s were the poorest productivity decades of this century.[45] The economy no longer seemed to support the federal government's vast array of services, many of them enacted or enlarged during the liberal activist period.

Lagging productivity affected not only government tax receipts but also citizens' attitudes toward their economic well-being. In the late 1970s the economy was buffeted by "stagflation," a coexistence of high inflation and high unemployment. Serious recessions occurred in the early 1980s and again in the early 1990s. Meanwhile, the government's costly and relatively impervious system of entitlements, coupled with President Reagan's 1981 tax cuts and program reallocations, turned the "fiscal dividends" of the postwar era into "structural deficits."

Intellectual fashions and political realities repudiated the notion that government could solve all manner of economic and social ills. Disenchantment with the results of government programs, many of which had been shamelessly oversold to glean support for their enactment, led to widespread demands for a statutory cease-fire: disinvestment, deregulation, and privatization. At the same time, "bracket creep" raised the marginal and real tax rates of millions of citizens and spurred a series of tax revolts that swept through the states to Washington.

In the 1980s the president and Congress were fixated on resolving fiscal and revenue issues, rather than on designing new programs or establishing new agencies in response to constituent preferences or national needs. In the domestic realm, the emphasis was on reviewing, adjusting, refining, or cutting back on existing programs. "There's not a whole lot of money for any kind of new programs," remarked Senator Thad Cochran, R-Miss., "so we're holding oversight hearings on old programs ... which may not be all that bad an idea." [46] Accordingly, fewer individual members were tempted to put forward their ideas as freestanding bills or resolutions. Such new ideas as were salable were more likely to be contained in amendments to large-scale legislative vehicles: reauthorizations, continuing appropriations, and debt limit or reconciliation bills.

The environment of constraint in the 1980s reversed the previous era's liberal activism. Government revenues were curtailed by lagging economic productivity, exaggerated after 1981 by tax cuts, program reallocations, and soaring deficits. Few new programs were launched, and few domestic programs were awarded additional funding. Although the public continued to expect Congress to take action to solve problems, there was equal sentiment for cutting back "big government" and reducing public sector deficits. Public faith in government's capacity to solve problems plummeted in the wake of criticisms of waste and ineffectiveness of government programs.

Elected officials at both ends of Pennsylvania Avenue sought profit from cutback politics. They engaged in creative bookkeeping to give the appearance of balancing revenues and outlays and trimming the deficit as required by the 1985 Gramm-Rudman-Hollings law. Conservatives seized upon revenue shortfalls as a way of snuffing demands for new programs and new spending. Liberals blamed the situation on the failures of the Reagan and Bush administrations and pledged to protect federal programs favored by middle-class voters. As for the voters, they naturally tried to have it both ways. As Gary C. Jacobson put it, "They can vote for Republican presidential candidates committed to the diffuse collective goods of low taxes, economic efficiency, and a strong national defense, and for congressional Democrats who promise to minimize the price they have to pay for these goods in forgone benefits." [47]

When all was said and done, however, the economic predicament severely curtailed legislative productivity. "Rarely in peacetime has a single issue dominated politics here the way the budget deficit is doing now," observed a *New York Times* correspondent. "The most important legislative measures of the year—tax cuts, expansion of child-care benefits, changes in Medicare and Medicaid and many others—are paralyzed." [48] In some cases zero-sum politics was practiced literally, as members bartered such programs as congressional mailing costs for pressing demands for spending on eastern Europe or a war on drugs. Senate Majority Leader George J. Mitchell, D-Maine, characterized the deficit dilemma as "the whale in the bathtub that leaves no room for anything else." [49]

The phenomenon of cutback politics influenced the postreform Congress in at least six ways. First, fewer bills were sponsored by individual senators and representatives. Second, key policy decisions were packaged into huge "megabills," enabling lawmakers to gain support for provisions that would be unlikely to pass as freestanding measures. Third, lawmakers employed techniques of "blame avoidance"—for example, in closing military bases—to protect themselves from the adverse effects of cutback politics. Fourth, more noncontroversial "commemorative" resolutions were passed—nearly half of all laws produced by congresses in the 1980s. Fifth, party-line voting on Capitol Hill, driven mainly by changes in the parties' demography, soared to modern-day highs. Finally, leadership in the House and Senate was markedly stronger than at any time since 1910. Congressional leaders benefited not only from powers conferred by reform-era innovations of the 1960s and 1970s; they also responded to widespread expectations that they were the only people who could, and should, untangle jurisdictional overlaps and orchestrate the legislative schedule. [50]

The House Ways and Means Committee mirrored the shifts of the postreform era in Congress as a whole. Randall Strahan described the changed agenda that the committee faced after 1978. Following the reform-era assaults on the committee and hiatus in leadership, Chairman Dan Rostenkowski, D-Ill., set about systematically to strengthen the panel's position.[51] According to Allen Schick, the chairman's efforts succeeded in the main: "Ways and Means has regained its status and effectiveness by resorting to a simple formula that worked for it in the past: the committee is successful when it controls the House and when the chairman controls the committee." [52]

As the committee's exhaustive bicentennial history explained, the chairman "centralized control over staff and substantially diminished the autonomy of subcommittee chairs." [53] Rostenkowski's personal leverage was enhanced by his influence over Democratic assignments to the panel as well as his selective use of sanctions. To promote cohesiveness, he scheduled more closed meetings and arranged for weekend retreats and seminars to discuss policy questions.[54] The panel's internal politics settled somewhere between the extremes of bipartisan consensus of the prereform Mills era and the reform period's divisive partisanship.[55]

Confronted by a lagging economy, a divided government, and the public's doubts about the efficacy of government programs, the president and Congress in the postreform era changed the way they approached the legislative workload. Presidents trimmed their agendas and hampered congressional initiatives through a combination of curtailed revenue and veto threats. Interbranch negotiations frequently took the form of high-level summitry. Divided control of the White House and Congress, along with rising party voting on the Hill, placed a premium on tough bargaining between the president, Senate leaders, and House leaders. Congress, for its part, moved away from the decentralized system established during the 1960s and 1970s to facilitate that era's frenetic legislative activity. A knowledgeable British scholar put it this way: "There can be little doubt that the Congress of the mid-1980s differed from that of the late 1970s in terms of its emphasis on parliamentary reform, legislative activity, constituency attentiveness and distribution of power." In sum, "the reform orientation of the New [or reform-era] Congress [was] left far behind." [56]

Consider the kinds of institutional innovations made by the postreform Congress. Beginning in the late 1970s, Congress confronted an altered set of demands for legislative action. The political agenda shrank, narrowing the prospects for new programs or spending priorities. While many of the structural innovations of the earlier reform era remained intact, procedures were adjusted to cope with the altered environment. Committee and floor agendas contracted. Important decisions were more apt to be folded into lengthy omnibus vehicles, often processed by more than one committee and typically superintended by party leaders. Members and committees explored new categories of policy making, or rather they exploited existing categories—for example, oversight, commemorative, indexing, and symbolic measures—that were well suited to the uncertain policy environment.

Now, the Partisan Conservative Era?

The 1990s brought a new mix of challenges to governmental institutions—some continuations of long-term trends, others startlingly new. Prolonged economic uncertainty—manifested in sluggish growth, heightened foreign competition, and widely reported job layoffs—weakened citizens' self-confidence and optimism. Widening racial, ethnic, religious, and even sexual fissures, along with a seemingly permanent disadvantaged underclass, fueled growing suspicions that the nation had become uncontrollable and perhaps ungovernable. The public services that most people came in contact with—public schools, police, courts, welfare—seemed especially flawed. The end of the Cold War brought only fleeting satisfaction: losing the menace of the Soviet "evil empire" in fact also meant losing a certain sense of national purpose.

By the 1990s public unrest had deepened into what can only be called a crisis of governance. One member of Congress called it a massive "civic temper tantrum." [57] Few institutions escaped public censure. Scarcely more than a year after celebrating the Persian Gulf War in a burst of civic pride, citizens turned President George Bush out of office. With a plurality of only 43 percent, successor Bill Clinton's public-opinion "honeymoon" hardly survived the wedding night; his job ratings remained precarious. Although surveys uncovered public disgust with partisanship and "gridlock," the Democrats' victories in 1992 ended divided government only in a formal sense, and the 1994 elections dissolved even that deceptive unity.

Of all public institutions, Congress bore the largest measure of public scorn. On top of the generalized public discontent, a series of scandals on Capitol Hill targeted the "Keating five" senators who had championed a failed savings and loan magnate, forced closure of the House "bank" (payroll office), and cast doubt on the personal ethics of numerous members. By the spring of 1992, only 17 percent of those questioned in a national survey approved of the way Congress was doing its job, whereas 54 percent approved of their own representative's performance. Both figures were all-time lows.[58] This exceeded the usual level of Congress bashing and recalled the public unrest that preceded the reforms adopted in the early 1970s.

The 1990s saw a dramatic changing of the guard on Capitol Hill. The 1992 elections brought 110 new House members (87 of whom returned two years later) and 14 new senators. The 1994 contests added 86 new representatives and 11 new senators. When the House convened in January 1995, nearly a majority of its members had arrived in the 1990s. Although the Senate naturally changes more slowly, 29 of its members were 1990s arrivals.

Do these events signal a new era of legislative policy making? This is a more complicated question than it may seem; it is far easier to find order in past events than in developments that are still unfolding. Commentators lost no time calling what had happened a "political earthquake." But it is well to remember that the Watergate reforms of 1974, when the earthquake analogy was last employed, were not so much a turning point as the zenith of a more extended political time period. Nor is high membership turnover itself an indicator of such a transition. Generational changing of the guard that took place on Capitol Hill in the immediate post–World War II years and again in the mid-1970s had short-term political effects but did not upset the sequence of legislative regimes we have outlined.

Despite the attention paid to the 1994 party changeover, we are unquestionably faced with something that spans more than a single election. In fact, Congress has been undergoing an extended period of upheaval in which the postreform equilibrium has become increasingly unstable, so much so that by the early 1990s a crisis had developed. Elements of this crisis included: uncertain leadership, dysfunctional committees, partisan bickering, interchamber tensions, increasingly redundant procedures, scandals both large and small, and a fraying of the unwritten rules of comity needed to manage and contain conflict in the legislative arena.

The 1994 elections had instant and visible effects. The party balance of nearly two generations was reversed. The public policy agenda was transformed. Issues that had long been simmering suddenly boiled over: downsizing the federal establishment, devolution of power to states and localities, welfare reform, budget stringency, and a regulatory cease-fire. Facing a struggling Democratic presidency, the resurgent congressional Republicans seized command of policy initiatives, media attention, and public expectations.

Inside Congress, party leaders flexed their muscles, activity levels soared, and innovative procedures were explored, tested, and adopted. House Republicans, led by the vigorous leadership of Speaker Newt Gingrich, R-Ga., and backed by an unusually cohesive party numerically dominated by newcomers, effected wide-ranging changes in structures and procedures. Cuts were made in the number of committees, committee assignments, and committee staffs; committee and floor procedures were altered; administrative arrangements were streamlined; and most of all, the Speaker and other party leaders gained greater leverage over committee assignments, committee staffing, floor scheduling, and administrative management. House leaders used all these tools, and the votes that backed them up, to win committee approval of and floor votes on all ten items of the Contract with America within the first hundred days of the 104th Congress.

The Senate was not unaffected by the party turnover of 1994. Although senators initially resisted major procedural reforms or staff cuts, they did move to trim committee spending and limit subcommittees. Younger Republican conservatives, moreover, pressed for tighter party discipline in selecting and ratifying committee leaders. And the chamber was under pressure to take action on House-passed elements of the contract.

Have the momentous events of the early 1990s ushered in a new legislative regime, one dominated by conservative Republicans and their policies? No one can say for sure. In all probability recent developments have yet to run their full course. Today's Republicans command impressive demographic, organizational, and financial resources; public opinion and political trends are apparently running in a conservative direction. But instability also marks contemporary politics: with voters restless and events volatile, no governing coalition can be confident of a long-term lease on power.

Conclusion

Shifting the viewpoint from the Oval Office to Capitol Hill radically changes one's perspective on congressional-presidential relations. Rather than measuring political time in terms of successive presidencies, we have sought to identify congressional equivalents. By tracking one cluster of variables—legislative workload and productivity figures—we have identified three, or perhaps four, distinctive congressional eras or regimes. Examining legislative attributes within each era, and between succeeding eras, casts new light on interbranch policy making since the New Deal and even helps resolve some puzzling historical anomalies (for example, Franklin Roosevelt's mixed legislative record and the unexpected productivity of the Nixon-Ford period).

Our foray into the thicket of legislative activity and productivity reveals two general truths about modern-day politics and policy making. First, legislative productivity does not necessarily coincide with the tenure of individual presidencies. Second, legislative productivity is less determined by party control than many scholars contend.

Presidencies and Legislative Regimes

The bipartisan conservative era outlasted several presidents of widely varying goals and skills. Roosevelt failed after 1936 to keep Capitol Hill safe for New Deal initiatives and, after 1940, was preoccupied with the war effort. Truman repeatedly broke his lance in efforts to push legislation through conservative congresses—most memorably in housing, labor-management relations, civil rights, and medical care. Eisenhower's modest, moderately right-of-center legislative instincts were a better fit with the objectives of the conservative coalition that ruled Capitol Hill. More aggressive than Eisenhower, Kennedy enjoyed considerable success in a transitional period when the old order in Congress was crumbling.

The liberal activist era, with its huge working majorities in both chambers of Congress, spanned the presidencies of Lyndon Johnson, Richard Nixon, Gerald Ford, and (in part) Jimmy Carter. Johnson's presidency was perhaps the most productive in history, legislatively speaking. Yet the most telling point is that the flow of legislation continued unabated during the presidencies of Nixon and Ford. A recitation of legislative high points from the Nixon years suggests that the mutual hostility between the Republican president and the Democratic Congress did not stand in the way of significant legislative enactments. These laws included: a comprehensive tax code revision, the National Environmental Policy Act of 1969, major air and water pollution control measures, endangered species protection, a comprehensive organized crime bill, postal reorganization, urban mass transit and rail reorganization plans, the Occupational Safety and Health Act of 1970 (OSHA), the Consumer Product Safety Act, the Comprehensive Employment and Training Act (CETA), the Federal Election Campaign Act, coastal zone management, the trans-Alaska pipeline, the War Powers Resolution, and the Congressional Budget and Impoundment Control Act of 1974—not to mention the Twenty-sixth Amendment giving eighteen-year-olds the right to vote and a proposed amendment (the Equal Rights Amendment) on equal rights for women.

The liberal juggernaut continued during these conservative presidencies for at least two reasons. First, the Nixon and Ford presidencies were under relentless siege from Capitol Hill's liberal majorities, composed of Democrats and a scattering of moderate or liberal Republicans. Between 1973 and 1976, write Ornstein and his colleagues, these forces "attempted a much higher number of veto overrides than any of the other Congresses in the previous thirty years, and a large number of their attempts were successful." [59] Second, Nixon saw his primary mission to be in foreign affairs and diplomacy, which left his aides in the domestic departments relatively free to negotiate as best they could with Capitol Hill majorities. Nixon may have been a conservative president, but the legislative record compiled during his administration was expansive and liberal. This historical irony deserves more careful and dispassionate reassessment by historians and political scientists than it has yet received.

The next legislative regime, the postreform era, spanned part or all of the presidencies of Jimmy Carter, Ronald Reagan, and George Bush. The advent of zero-sum, stalemate politics was popularly associated with the Reagan administration, which took office in 1980 pledging to cut taxes, domestic aid, and welfare programs. To be sure, his election was interpreted at the time as a sea change in American politics; some of Reagan's initiatives—especially the 1981 revenue cuts and repeated threats to veto new domestic spending or taxes—helped to curtail the legislative agenda. However, deteriorating economic conditions and shifting attitudes had already caused President Carter to begin to curtail his legislative agenda.[60] By the 96th Congress (1979–1981) the altered environment had led to a decline in legislative workload. Had Carter been reelected in 1981, it is likely that he, and Congress, would have traveled farther down the road toward zero-sum politics.

Party Control and Legislative Regimes

Party control influences policy outputs. No proposition is more widely accepted among scholars and other observers. Many would further contend that "things go better" when the same party controls both the executive and legislative branches and that divided government is a prescription for confusion, delay, and deadlock. Legislative productivity is, without a doubt, affected by party control. And certainly presidents are more apt to achieve their legislative goals if their partisans comfortably control both chambers.

Equally to the point, shifts in Capitol Hill partisan ratios can yield meaningful changes in policy outputs, quite apart from any questions of party control or alignment. The recession-driven influx of Democrats in 1959–1960, the Johnson landslide class of 1964, the Watergate class of 1974, and the GOP shift of 1981–1982 were dramatic changes in partisan strength on Capitol Hill that led in turn to policy redirections and procedural innovations. Probably these changes far exceeded any underlying shifts in attitudes or voting habits within the electorate as a whole, not to mention any long-term partisan realignment.

Yet party control is an incomplete guide to legislative activity and productivity. The administrations of Roosevelt, Truman, and Carter testify to the fact that party control of both branches is no guarantee of legislative productivity. By the same token, the Nixon-Ford period and the Reagan administration (in its first year and last two years) saw productivity far beyond what would be expected from divided government. The correlation between party control and legislative productivity seems even more tenuous when we consider Mayhew's most intriguing piece of evidence: during what we term the liberal activist era, annual productivity under split party control actually exceeded that under unified control.[61]

Legislative activity and workload, in short, fit imperfectly with conventional political thinking that stresses presidential leadership or the locus of party control of the two branches. The record of the past two generations, moreover, casts doubt on the assumption of many observers that unified party control raises legislative productivity and that divided government necessarily leads to stalemate.

Notes

1. Woodrow Wilson, *Congressional Government* (1885; reprint, Baltimore: Johns Hopkins University Press, 1981), 56. For a recent interpretation, see Charles O. Jones, "A Way of Life and Law," *American Political Science Review* '89 (March 1995): 1–9.
2. See Michael G. Kammen, *A Machine that Would Go of Itself: The Constitution in American Culture* (New York: Alfred A. Knopf, 1986).
3. Many scholars, including myself, have pointed to the varying time perspectives of the two branches. See, for example, Jean Reith Schroedel, *Congress, the President, and Policymaking: A Historical Analysis* (Armonk, N.Y.: M. E. Sharpe, 1994), 10–11.
4. Mildred L. Amer, "Membership of the 104th Congress: A Profile," *CRS Report* 95–205GOV (January 25, 1995): 4.
5. Charles O. Jones, *The Presidency in a Separated System* (Washington, D.C.: Brookings Institution, 1994), 48–50, 197–201, et passim.
6. The *locus classicus* of party alignment theory is V. O. Key, Jr., "A Theory of Critical Elections," *Journal of Politics* 17 (February 1955): 3–18. More detailed analyses are

found in: William N. Chambers and Walter Dean Burnham, eds., *The American Party Systems: Stages of Political Development* (New York: Oxford University Press, 1967); Walter Dean Burnham, *Critical Elections and the Mainsprings of American Politics* (New York: W. W. Norton, 1970); and James L. Sundquist, *Dynamics of the Party System*, rev. ed. (Washington, D.C.: Brookings Institution, 1983), esp. chaps. 1–3.

7. See, for example, David W. Brady, "Electoral Realignments in the U.S. House of Representatives," in *Congress and Policy Change*, ed. Gerald C. Wright, Jr., Leroy N. Rieselbach, and Lawrence C. Dodd (New York: Agathon Press, 1986), 46–69.

8. Stephen Skowronek, *The Politics Presidents Make* (Cambridge: Harvard University Press, 1993), 29–58.

9. Ibid., 50.

10. Joseph Cooper, "Organization and Innovation in the House of Representatives," in *The House at Work*, ed. Joseph Cooper and G. Calvin Mackenzie (Austin: University of Texas Press, 1980), 332.

11. Anyone using legislative statistics should be aware of their limits. Definitions of terms are neither simple nor self-evident. Data collection, moreover, requires making decisions, sometimes arbitrary, on methods to be followed—what sources to rely on, what dates to use as benchmarks, and so forth. If legislative statistics are interpreted as indicators of demands or workloads, extra caution must be exercised. A shift in numbers may indicate changing demands; alternatively, it may signify innovative management of those demands by legislative strategists. Finally, available data convey only a partial picture of the scope and volume of legislative activity. Despite all these caveats, a careful study of trends can reveal a great deal about contemporary relations between the branches of government.

This essay draws upon statistical data compiled by the author, his former colleagues at the Congressional Research Service, and other investigators. Interested readers are invited to consult original sources such as Roger H. Davidson, "Congressional Committees as Moving Targets," *Legislative Studies Quarterly* 11 (February 1986): 19–33; Davidson, "The Legislative Work of Congress" (Paper presented at the annual meeting of the American Political Science Association, Washington, D.C., August 28–31, 1986); Roger H. Davidson and Carol Hardy, "Indicators of House of Representatives Workload and Activity," *CRS Report* 87-492S (June 8, 1987); Davidson and Hardy, "Indicators of Senate Activity and Workload, *CRS Report* 87-497S (June 8, 1987); Robert Moon and Carol Hardy Vincent, "Workload and Activity Report: U.S. House of Representatives," *CRS Report* 93-707GOV (July 30, 1993); Moon and Hardy Vincent, "Workload and Activity Report: United States Senate, 1946–1992," *CRS Report* 93-789GOV (August 30, 1993); and Norman J. Ornstein, Thomas E. Mann, and Michael J. Malbin, *Vital Statistics on Congress 1993–1994* (Washington, D.C.: Congressional Quarterly Inc., 1994), esp. chap. 6.

12. Moon and Hardy Vincent, "Senate Workload and Activity," 12.

13. Moon and Hardy Vincent, "House Workload and Activity," 9.

14. Richard F. Fenno, Jr., *Congressmen in Committees* (Boston: Little, Brown, 1973), 280.

15. Davidson and Hardy, "Indicators of House Workload and Activity," 29; "Indicators of Senate Activity and Workload," 60–61. Recent figures are found in Moon and Hardy Vincent, "Senate Workload and Activity," 54–55; and "House Workload and Activity," 54–55.

16. Rozanne M. Barry, "Bills Introduced and Laws Enacted: Selected Legislative Statistics, 1947–1994," *CRS Report* 95-233C (February 2, 1995): 2.

17. Davidson, "Congressional Committees as Moving Targets," 19–33. Recent figures are from Moon and Hardy Vincent, "House Workload and Activity," 53–57.

18. House Committee on Energy and Commerce, *Activity Report*, 103d Cong., 2d sess., 1995, H. Rept. 103-882, 331. Earlier figures are contained in House Committee on Interstate and Foreign Commerce, *Activity Report*, 92d Cong., 2d sess., 1973, H. Rept. 92-1634, 44–45.

19. John S. Pontius, "Congressional Roll Call and Other Recorded Votes: Statistical Summary of 1st through 103d Congresses (1989–1994)," *CRS Report* 95-257GOV (February 6, 1995): 7–11.
20. Steven S. Smith, *Call to Order: Floor Politics in the House and Senate* (Washington, D.C.: Brookings Institution, 1989), 130–131.
21. Davidson, "Legislative Work of Congress," 26–27; Barry, "Selected Legislative Statistics, 1947–1994," 2.
22. George B. Galloway, *Congress at the Crossroads* (New York: Thomas Y. Crowell, 1946), 53.
23. Davidson, "Legislative Work of Congress," 30–33.
24. Ibid., 29; Moon and Hardy Vincent, "Senate Workload and Activity," 15.
25. Kenneth A. Shepsle, "The Changing Textbook Congress," in *Can the Government Govern?* ed. John E. Chubb and Paul E. Peterson (Washington, D.C.: Brookings Institution, 1989), 238–266.
26. Lawrence H. Chamberlain, *The President, Congress and Legislation* (New York: Columbia University Press, 1946), 450–453.
27. James MacGregor Burns, *Roosevelt: The Lion and the Fox* (New York: Harcourt, Brace, 1956), 337, 339
28. Robert J. Donovan, *Conflict and Crisis: The Presidency of Harry S Truman, 1945–1948* (New York: W. W. Norton, 1977), 260.
29. Alonzo L. Hamby, "The Mind and Character of Harry S Truman," in *The Truman Presidency*, ed. Michael J. Lacey (Cambridge: Woodrow Wilson International Center for Scholars and Cambridge University Press, 1989), 46.
30. Fenno, *Congressmen in Committees*, 279.
31. William S. White, *Citadel: The Story of the U.S. Senate* (New York: Harper and Brothers, 1956); and Donald R. Matthews, *U.S. Senators and Their World* (Chapel Hill: University of North Carolina Press, 1960).
32. Fenno, *Congressmen in Committees* ; and Richard F. Fenno, Jr., *The Power of the Purse: Appropriations Process in Congress* (Boston: Little, Brown, 1966).
33. Shepsle, "Changing Textbook Congress." By the 1970s and 1980s, however, this view had been supplanted by a revised reform-era "textbook" view that stressed the institution's decentralization and fragmentation. For an expression of this view, see Hedrick Smith, *The Power Game: How Washington Works* (New York: Random House, 1988).
34. Smith, *Power Game*, chap. 2.
35. James L. Sundquist, *Politics and Policy: The Eisenhower, Kennedy, and Johnson Years* (Washington, D.C.: Brookings Institution, 1968), chap. 10.
36. Davidson and Hardy, "Indicators of Senate Activity and Workload, 23–32"; and Davidson and Hardy, "Indicators of House Workload and Activity," 19–22, 26–27, 65–67.
37. David R. Mayhew, *Divided We Govern: Party Control, Lawmaking, and Investigations, 1946–1990* (New Haven: Yale University Press, 1991), 76.
38. Allen Schick, *Congress and Money: Budgeting, Spending and Taxing* (Washington, D.C.: The Urban Institute Press, 1980), 424–436.
39. John W. Ellwood, "The Great Exception: The Congressional Budget Process in an Age of Decentralization," in *Congress Reconsidered*, 3d ed., ed. Lawrence C. Dodd and Bruce I. Oppenheimer (Washington, D.C.: CQ Press, 1985), 315–342.
40. Abner J. Mikva and Patti B. Saris, *The American Congress: The First Branch* (New York: Franklin Watts, 1983), 292.
41. See Randall W. Strahan, *New Ways and Means: Reform and Change in a Congressional Committee* (Chapel Hill: University of North Carolina Press, 1990), 92–101.
42. For example, Roger H. Davidson and Walter J. Oleszek, *Congress Against Itself* (Bloomington: Indiana University Press, 1977); James L. Sundquist, *The Decline and Resurgence of Congress* (Washington, D.C.: Brookings Institution, 1981); and Leroy N.

Rieselbach, *Congressional Reform: The Changing Modern Congress* (Washington, D.C.: CQ Press, 1994), esp. chap. 3.

43. David R. Mayhew, *Congress: The Electoral Connection* (New Haven: Yale University Press, 1974).

44. Lester Thurow, *The Zero-Sum Society* (New York: Basic Books, 1980).

45. Paul Krugman, "We're No. 3—So What?" *Washington Post*, March 24, 1990, C1–2.

46. Quoted in Helen Dewar, "Congress Off to Slowest Start in Years," *Washington Post*, November 21, 1989, A18.

47. Gary C. Jacobson, *The Electoral Origins of Divided Government: Competition in U.S. House Elections, 1946–1988* (Boulder, Colo.: Westview Press, 1990), 112.

48. David E. Rosenbaum, "Why the Deficit Is Paralyzing Congress," *New York Times*, October 22, 1989, E1.

49. Quoted in Helen Dewar, "At Finish of Slow-Starting Session, Lawmakers End Up Eyeball to Eyeball," *Washington Post*, November 21, 1989, A18

50. Barbara Sinclair, *Legislators, Leaders, and Lawmaking: The U.S. House of Representatives in the Postreform Era* (Baltimore: Johns Hopkins University Press, 1995), 48–57.

51. Randall Strahan, "Agenda Change and Committee Politics in the Postreform House," *Legislative Studies Quarterly* 13 (May 1988): 185–194.

52. Allen Schick, "The Ways and Means of Leading Ways and Means," *Brookings Review* 7 (Fall 1989): 17.

53. U.S. House of Representatives, *The Committee on Ways and Means: A Bicentennial History, 1789–1989* (Washington, D.C.: U.S. Government Printing Office, 1989), 369.

54. Ibid., 370–372.

55. Schick, "Ways and Means," 21.

56. Christopher J. Bailey, "Beyond the New Congress: Aspects of Congressional Development in the 1980s," *Parliamentary Affairs* 41 (April 1988): 246.

57. Quoted in Lawrence N. Hansen, "Our Turn: Politicians Talk about Themselves, Politics, the Public, the Press, and Reform," Centel Public Accountability Project (March 1992), 5.

58. Richard Morin and Helen Dewar, "Approval of Congress Hits All-Time Low, Poll Finds," *Washington Post*, March 20, 1992, A16.

59. Ornstein, Mann, and Malbin, *Vital Statistics*, 151. See also Table 6-6, 160–161.

60. Charles O. Jones, *The Trusteeship Presidency: Jimmy Carter and the U.S. Congress* (Baton Rouge: Louisiana State University Press, 1988), chap. 7.

61. Mayhew, *Divided We Govern*, 7.

3

The New Era of Congressional Policy Making

Walter J. Oleszek

W"e have to maximize the opportunity for substantial change," said Speaker Newt Gingrich, R-Ga. "This [Washington, D.C.] is a city which is like a sponge. It absorbs waves of change, and it slows them down, and it softens them, and then one morning they cease to exist." [1] Or as former Senate majority leader George J. Mitchell (1989–1995), D-Maine, said: "The genius of the American system has been its ability to adapt to change." [2]

There is little question that change is the order of the day in national governance. Fundamental issues are being raised in the aftermath of the Republican party's dramatic election victory of November 1994. After forty straight years as the "permanent minority" in the House of Representatives, the GOP won control of that chamber and reclaimed control of the Senate as well. Hence, the public dialogue is focused on topics that Republicans campaigned on and that resonate with a good portion of the American populace. The important questions that orient much of today's public discussion are: What are the appropriate role and reach of the national government? What are the nation's obligations in the international arena in the post–Cold War world? If the national government's social programs are reduced or terminated, should those who are well-off assume a larger individual responsibility for the less fortunate?

The decade of the 1990s, in short, will be a tumultuous period for lawmakers, for both chambers of Congress, and for legislative-executive relations. Procedural innovations and unconventional lawmaking, such as the utilization of a variety of formal and informal legislative devices to craft public policies rather than the traditional committee system, are almost commonplace today and highlight the flexibility and adaptability of Congress's decision-making processes. New congresses, new lawmakers, new electoral circumstances, and new agendas are among the many interconnected forces that generate new forms of policy making.

To give the reader some understanding of how the larger political environment affects House, Senate, and executive branch politics and priorities, this chapter will discuss three contemporary developments that are likely to endure into the next century. They are national agenda changes, flux in the party system, and divided government. Each affects how Congress makes decisions.

Congress and Agenda Change

Politics is sometimes called the art of the possible. It might also be called the art of defining the possibilities. As the nations of the world become increasingly interdependent, the U.S. Congress is confronting a host of new issues that challenge its capacity for defining the possibilities. Far-reaching global changes in the environment, in economics, in diplomacy, and startling changes in U.S. demographics and in the national government's role are reshaping Congress's agenda and political discourse. To be sure, legislative implications flow from these changes.

The Environment

Once perceived as largely a local or regional concern, the environment is now viewed by many as an urgent planetary challenge. The contemporary press and media are filled with stories about oil spills, nuclear and toxic waste dumps, soil depletion, acid rain, water shortages, and deforestation—as well as related stories about population growth, energy consumption, and economic development. One scientist put it this way:

> When my grandfather was born, environmental concerns were almost all based on housekeeping and trash in the back yard. By the time I was born there was demonstrable regional impacts. The birth of my children coincided with entire river systems and estuaries being affected. Now ... major global systems, upon which society depends for its welfare, are being destroyed.[3]

Some commentators have even suggested that the global environment "may become the overarching issue for the next 40 years in the way the Cold War defined our worldview during the last 40 years."[4]

Economics

The United States is part of an increasingly competitive world economy. Discussions of budget and trade deficits occupy a lot of Congress's and the White House's time; however, another "deficit" also arouses intense concern: the lack of competitiveness in some of the nation's industries and in the society at large.

To be sure, there is growing recognition that the nation's economic prosperity hinges on its continuing ability to develop markets overseas. A source of frustration for our elective politicians is that our involvement in the global economy means that public officials have less influence over the domestic economy. Industries have the whole world to choose from when deciding where to locate their plants and facilities; moreover, the 1990s restructuring and downsizing of many domestic companies, undertaken in order to make them globally competitive, have cost American workers, especially the unskilled, thousands of jobs. It comes as no surprise, then, that here and in other developed nations there is popular dissatisfaction with representative government. Lawmakers bear the brunt of citizen frustration when there are insufficient productive and well-paying jobs to go around even when the national economy is growing.

Diplomacy

Diplomatically and militarily, international relations in the post–Cold War period is without a broad national consensus. Understandably, with the collapse of the Soviet empire, most Americans want to make domestic issues and problems their top priority. And the domestic problems that confront us are large: crime, drugs, joblessness, homelessness, medical costs, racial tensions, decrepit schools, and more. On the other hand, in a world that is interconnected culturally, economically, and technologically, and as the sole global military power, the nation cannot help becoming involved in international affairs. How it will achieve some balance between domestic and international activism is not clear. "Uncertain," in short, seems to best express the country's position on the issue of its role in the world.

Absent a coherent or unifying theme about our world role, every significant involvement of our military, money, and material is likely to require its own separate rationale and justification, unless an event plainly jeopardizes our national security or, as in the case of an opportunity to prevent mass starvation, energizes our sense of morality. Hence, the country seems to move from wanting to act alone to emphasizing a collective approach to international issues. Citizens who expected a new world order after winning the Cold War now watch violent disorder on the Cable News Network (CNN) and other media outlets; reports come from faraway places (Bosnia, Somalia, or Chechnya, for instance) where our national interest seems remote. Furthermore, the violence often occurs not between nations but within the borders of so-called nations. In sum, as the world grows more complex and confusing, the case for internationalism becomes harder to make. Thus, the imperatives of nationalism and transnationalism coexist today in uneasy tension.

Demographics

There are scores of significant demographic changes influencing public attitudes about Congress's agenda. Two crucial developments are the aging of the population and the changing structure of the American family. They have raised many new issues. Child care, parental leave, nursing and home health care for the elderly, child poverty, and the shrinking pool of young workers are among the concerns of the electorate.

Dramatic transformations in the American family—the prevalence of single-parent households, the frequency of divorce and unwed motherhood, and the influx of women into the workforce, among others—have triggered debate about whether scores of social problems, such as crime and poverty, are primarily economic or moral issues. Fatherless families, for example, "are five times more likely to be poor and almost 10 times more likely to be extremely poor" than dual-parent households.[5] Conservatives and some religious groups assert that diverse moral, cultural, and social forces are to blame for the decline of the family unit. The Christian Coalition, for instance, has submitted to Congress its own Contract with the American Family (no funding for gays or lesbians, sex education, or abortion, for example), a take-off on Speaker Newt Gingrich's Contract with America.[6]

Role of the National Government

Although the role of the national government is a traditional issue in American politics, the topic has taken on renewed importance. With Republicans in charge of the 104th Congress, the House and Senate proposed budget blueprints that eliminated or dramatically reduced federal programs and entities. One House plan, for example, suggested the elimination of 3 cabinet departments (Commerce, Education, and Energy), 284 programs, 69 commissions, and 13 agencies. In addition, "3 broad government-run commercial activities" were to be "terminated, converted into block grants or sold to private investors."[7] These budget objectives, including a tax reduction, were less about making spending or program cuts than about achieving the fundamental long-term goal of Republicans: shrinking the size and reach of the federal government. Today, the two parties, the two houses of Congress, and the legislative and executive branches are debating which functions are national responsibilities and which can be returned to the states and localities or handled by the private sector. The theme that undergirds the activities of the 104th Congress is "Toward a New Federalism." This theme, no doubt, will remain operative in legislative sessions to follow.

A dilemma in sorting out which responsibilities are national and which are either state or private obligations is that policy makers disagree on the criteria for distinguishing among them. Broadly, many people agree on the responsibilities of the federal government: national security, diplomacy, maintenance of a sound currency, and physical safety and security. Assuming consensus on these four roles, it becomes much harder thereafter to determine which level of government can best perform what types of functions. For example, schools, roads, transit issues, and fire and police protection are traditionally state and local concerns. "That does not mean," stated Rep. David R. Obey, D-Wis., "that they're exclusively state and local concerns." He continued:

> We have a national Constitution that guarantees individual rights to schoolchildren, and those rights were not, in fact, guaranteed historically by all our state and local jurisdictions. The national government has a moral, legal, and constitutional obligation in those cases to exercise its responsibilities.[8]

In short, it is too early to tell whether the contemporary emphasis on devolution and deregulation, with President Clinton striving to "reinvent" government and Republicans seeking to "deinvent" government, will clarify federal-state roles and responsibilities. Compounding the problem is a citizenry that usually lambastes "big government" but argues strongly for particular programs that benefit them. Citizens may pay lip service to Thomas Jefferson's admonition that the best government is one that governs least, but their actions frequently belie their words.

Legislative Implications

What are the legislative implications of these sorts of agenda changes? First, as already noted, new, complex, interdependent, and not easily resolvable issues—especially in an era of scarce resources—are being added to an already heavy congressional schedule. In addition to the regular items that appear on Congress's agenda (the annual money bills, measures requiring reauthorization, emergency legislation, and bills and amendments advanced by entrepreneurial members), House and Senate leaders and committee chairs are now obliged to find some way to accommodate even more legislative business.

Second, legislators' schedules are long, fragmented, and unpredictable. Representatives and senators work, on average, at least an eleven-hour day. With their time splintered into tiny bits and pieces, how will members find the time to think, read, and learn about so many new issues? Washington is so filled with movers and shakers, remarked the late Norman Cousins, that there is hardly any room for thinkers: "We have everything we need except the most important thing of all—time to think and the habit of thought. We lack time for the one indispensable for safety." [9] Perhaps as members reflect on the interconnectedness of many issues (sometimes dubbed "intermestic," after international and domestic), they will begin to broaden their representational focus to encompass a "home style" that includes transnational constituencies.

Third, lobbying by or for foreign governments, corporations, or interest groups has greatly increased. For instance, 152 Japanese companies and government agencies hired 113 American firms to represent them in Washington. The cost exceeded $100 million, "more than the combined budgets of the U.S. Chamber of Commerce, the National Association of Manufacturers, the Business Roundtable, the Committee for Economic Development and the American Business Conference—the five most influential business organizations in Washington." [10] Foreign presidents, prime ministers, foreign ministers, and parliamentarians are seen regularly on Capitol Hill lobbying lawmakers in behalf of their nations' interests. Senate Majority Leader Bob Dole, R-Kan., was so impressed by Pakistan Prime Minister Benazir Bhutto that "he offered her the use of his offices as he collared more than fifteen senators from the nearby Senate floor to meet her." [11]

The surge in foreign lobbying stems in part from Congress's more assertive role in international affairs and from the issues on the legislative agenda. Among them are trade imbalances, joint ventures in manufacturing, foreign investments in the United States, and conflicts between national security and the export of sophisticated technology. One study pointed to a related issue that needs legislative attention: "use of former federal officials by foreign governments to lobby the executive branch." [12] Part of the reason that this lobbying activity may require special attention is that there is a lack of sufficient information on the extensiveness of the practice.

Finally, Congress has increasingly relied on ad hoc devices to address new concerns. Party leaders now employ a wide variety of informal procedures and mechanisms—working groups, leadership amendments, task forces, outside commissions, or study groups—to consider complex substantive and fiscal issues. For example, in a joint appearance in New Hampshire, President Clinton and Speaker Gingrich agreed to establish a bipartisan commission to make recommendations on lobbying and campaign finance reform. Both Speaker Gingrich and Senate Majority Leader Dole commonly employ task forces to consider legislative proposals often handled by the standing committees. "We envision using task forces a lot," said a top Gingrich aide, "as a device for finessing some institutional obstacles to decision making." [13]

To address contemporary issues, rank-and-file members frequently form ad hoc caucuses. The majority Republicans changed the rules of the House at the start of the 104th Congress to restrict the use of taxpayer dollars to fund these informal entities. This change caused some caucuses to discontinue their operations, but around 125 are still active on Capitol Hill. These entities, which are often bicameral and bipartisan, provide members with the organization, ideas, and votes to influence legislation and to adapt to new agenda demands.

Internal power fluctuations in Congress and legislative assertiveness in nearly every policy arena have lessened Congress's reliance on the president's traditional agenda-setting role. To be sure, competition in agenda-setting will continue to characterize relations between the legislative and executive branches. In a remarkable development that occurred during the 104th Congress, Speaker Gingrich's Contract with America (comprising measures designed largely to reduce the federal government's role, such as regulatory reform and balanced budget proposals) set the national agenda. Functioning somewhat like a prime minister in a parliamentary setting, with Republican lawmakers voting in overwhelming numbers to back the contract, Speaker Gingrich eclipsed (or certainly rivaled) the White House in determining and shaping the national discourse.[14] The "bully pulpit" seemed to move from the White House to Capitol Hill. This type of competition need not be a formula for stalemate, however. As former senator J. William Fulbright, D-Ark., once counseled: "Our proper objective is neither a dominant presidency nor an aggressive Congress but, within the strict limits of what the Constitution mandates, a shifting of the emphasis according to the needs of the time and the requirements of public policy." [15]

Flux in the Party System

Whether one believes that political parties are undergoing decline, dealignment, realignment, or resurgence, it seems clear that the two-party system is in ferment.[16] With the decline of the machine politics, patronage, and voter loyalty of the past, both parties are adjusting to new circumstances. Citizens who call themselves independents now rival voters who identify with either of the two major parties.[17] Democrats, long the advocates of an activist national government, are struggling to redefine their message in an era when the public says it wants to downsize the federal establishment. "We're saying we don't like what [Republicans] are doing, but we don't say what we would do. It's a big blur," declared Sen. John B. Breaux, D-La.[18] Republicans, longtime proponents of smaller government, appreciate the government's role in assisting the truly needy, but they differ internally on how best to achieve this and related objectives.

The aging of the electorate and the addition of new immigrant groups (Asians and Latinos, for example) are forcing both parties to reshape their strategy, theme, message, and demographic base. Technology has also changed the parties. Candidates often rely more on computer software than on shoe leather to win elections. Professional campaign consultants provide an enormous range of services, including fund raising, polling, and media advertising, which enable candidates to reduce their reliance on party organizations. There are even "cyberPACs" to help congressional candidates employ e-mail and faxes to raise money for their campaigns. Candidate-centered elections are generally replacing party-centered elections.

These changes in the party system strongly influence the institutional environment in the House and Senate. At least three areas in this connection are worth exploring: the nature of the membership, the effect of the campaign "money chase" on legislative business, and members' heightened stress on constituency service.

Nature of the Membership

The membership of today's Congress differs from that of earlier Congresses in an especially important regard: the number of Democratic seats that come from the South. Regionally, the Democratic "lock" on the South has been ended by the apparent rise of a GOP "lock" on this region. In the aftermath of the November 1994 election, the Republican party has emerged as the dominant electoral force at all levels of public officeholding. More southern voters identify with that party, and Republicans have increased their share of southern seats in the House and Senate.

As one election analyst noted, "Democrats were outpolled by Republican House candidates [in November 1994] in every southern state except Mississippi, where most of the Democratic members are so conservative that they could just as readily be Republicans." [19] The result: for the first time since Reconstruction, Republicans hold a majority of House seats in the states of the Confederacy. In short, congressional strength in this region has been transformed. The South, once solidly Democratic, now belongs to the Republicans.

Changes in the South (economic, electoral, social, and demographic) and in other regions have had significant legislative and policy repercussions. For example, the seventy-three freshmen GOP members elected in November 1994 campaigned on the Contract with America. Compared to many other classes of newcomers, those elected in 1994 are younger, less politically experienced, and more outspoken, ideologically committed, and aggressive. They are also ardent backers of term limits for lawmakers, and they share a determination to transform the federal establishment. "This is an ideological class," said freshman Matt Salmon, R-Ariz., "that really believes we were sent here to make a difference." [20] As a group, the GOP freshmen voted for Speaker Gingrich's Contract with America nearly 97 percent of the time.

A look at what happened to the Georgia delegation illustrates a fundamental shift between the parties. In the 103d Congress, the delegation had 9 Democrats and 1 Republican (Gingrich). After the 1994 election and the defection of conservative Democratic representative Nathan Deal to the Republican party, the delegation contained eight Republicans and three Democrats, who represented "majority-minority" districts. (Created to promote minority representation in the House, majority-minority districts contain high concentrations of a single minority group.) This kind of development has produced a Democratic party that is largely liberal and a Republican party that is dominated by conservatives.

The ideological gulf between the parties means that it is difficult for them to reach compromises, especially on issues that involve the role of government in problem solving. It has also produced intraparty factional disputes. Conservative House Democrats, for example, often criticize their liberal leadership for being intolerant of their views. Similarly, young and ideologically aggressive Senate Republicans are not overly sympathetic to the views of moderates within their party.

The Money Chase

There is no question that it costs a lot to win and hold House and Senate seats. Election expenditures have escalated in the past few election cycles. Inflation, the expense of hiring professional consultants, and the cost of campaigning in the age of television account in large part for the increases. In 1976, for example, the winner of a Senate seat spent on average $610,000; in 1986 the cost was a little more than $3 million. Eight years later the average cost of winning a Senate seat was around $4 million. (It is worth noting that in November 1994 former representative Michael Huffington, R-Calif., spent $30 million of his own money to try, unsuccessfully, to defeat incumbent senator Dianne Feinstein, D-Calif.) The average cost of winning a House seat in 1994 was about $550,000. It is a political fact of life, wrote a commentator, "that those in the Congress, and those who aspire to be in it, need money." [21]

This financial reality affects the scheduling of House and Senate business. Members' fund-raising activities take more and more of their valuable time, leading to scheduling conflicts. Members cannot "chase money" and debate and vote on legislation at the same time. To minimize the conflicts between electoral and lawmaking activities, explained a former senator,

> the practice has grown up in the last several years of providing "windows" in the Senate schedule. A window is a period of time in which it is understood that there will be no roll-call votes. Senators are assured that they won't be embarrassed by being absent for a recorded vote. Windows usually occur between six and eight in the evening, which is the normal time for holding fund-raising cocktail parties. [22]

"They'll never admit it," noted one Washington political consultant, "but certainly some members [of the House] and some senators spend a majority of their time raising money." [23]

As long as large sums of money are required to get elected, public and congressional debate about money and policy making will continue. Legislators, lobbyists, and citizens sometimes question the propriety of fund-raising practices. Members are concerned about the implied obligation when they accept money from political action committees (PACs). Lobbyists resent pressure from members to buy tickets to their fund-raisers. And citizens are concerned that the tie between lobbyists and money raising pushes Congress to enact laws that benefit the few and not the many.

Finally, the money chase affects the somewhat mysterious process of selecting party leaders. Not only are party leaders selected by secret ballot in closed-door party sessions, but also the choice involves many intangible factors, such as a candidate's parliamentary shrewdness, media presence, and skill in coalition building. To these qualities can be added a host of others, including the leader's fund-raising capabilities. Party leaders are expected to raise and contribute campaign money for partisan colleagues. As one observer noted, "the job of fund-raiser is becoming more important to senators' expectations of what a majority leader should do. The candidates thus are not trying to buy votes so much as to demonstrate how well they can fulfill that role." [24]

Constituency Service

To maintain popularity back home is not always easy, especially in an era of resource scarcity and government cutbacks. Lobbyists and their PAC affiliates can raise large sums of money for candidates. They can employ sophisticated new techniques to generate grass-roots pressure campaigns. They can combine with other groups to form potent electoral alliances. Thus, legislators sometimes complain that they are competing to represent their state or district against the information distributed there by interest groups.

Furthermore, legislative actions are scrutinized more closely by the media than in the past. Consequently, members may be less able or willing to make compromises or modify their positions once they have been expressed in public. Constituents, too, are far better educated than ever before. "The effects of this educational transformation are profound," explained former Lyndon Johnson presidential aide Horace W. Busby. "[A] more self-reliant populace is less attracted to Government intervention and, at the same time, is more disposed to be independent of party dictates." [25] The party, as a result, no longer acts as the main bridge or mediator between the elected leader and the voter. Instead, voters learn about their members of Congress largely from media and other electronic accounts. Conversely, legislators base their assessments of constituency opinion not simply on what local political leaders tell them but also on what the legislators' own personal surveys and visits reveal.

It is small wonder that legislators create their own personal party organizations back home. Attentiveness to voter interests is crucial to political survival even in a "power of incumbency" era. The paradox is that incumbent members seem safer than ever (despite today's pro-term limit and anti-government mood), yet they are sometimes reluctant to take positions that may be controversial back home. "The problem with politicians is they're all risk minimizers," said House Majority Leader Dick Armey, R-Texas.[26] Part of the explanation for this is the speed with which "instant constituencies" can be manufactured by special interests to make life difficult for and electorally threatening to incumbents. For example, an outpouring of nationwide support for an issue can be quickly generated from Washington, D.C., by lobbying organizations that specialize in organizing "grass roots" campaigns (or "astroturf" campaigns, to use a term more descriptive of the high-tech methods employed by these organizations).[27]

The effect of these diverse developments (sophisticated grass-roots lobbying, better educated constituents, and more media coverage) is greater attention to constituency service, even in the Senate. Sen. Richard C. Shelby of Alabama, who was elected as a Democrat in 1986 but became a Republican eight years later, highlighted the expanded notion of constituency service:

> Many freshmen view their role differently than twenty-five years ago, when a Senator was only a legislator. Now a senator is also a grantsman, an ombudsman, and a caseworker.... When we are asked by our constituents to help, we can't say we don't have time because we are focusing on national and international issues.[28]

Travel to the states is another indicator of constituency attentiveness. "Two trips a year," recalled Sen. Strom Thurmond, R-S.C., was about how frequently senators went home in the 1950s.[29] Today senators, like House members, travel to their states to meet with constituents much more frequently. Senate Democratic Whip Wendell H. Ford said he averaged about forty-eight weekends a year in Kentucky, his home state.[30] One consequence of this constant travel is some loss of collegiality. The Senate "is no longer a group of guys who get together and socialize, who go to [each] other's offices after a vote, sit down, and have a few drinks.... Instead, we're on planes back to our home states," explained Sen. John McCain, R-Ariz.[31]

Other indicators of the emphasis today on constituency service include the greater number of staff aides working in members' districts or states, scheduling House and Senate business with an eye toward accommodating members' frequent need to return home, and the increase in franked mail. In short, the parochial nature of much congressional activity may help to account for the proclivity of voters to split their tickets and create the "split personality" government that has been common since the 1950s.

Divided Government

In recent years scholars and commentators have examined divided government with renewed attention. Heightened interest in divided government stems from at least three factors: its near permanent condition in recent decades; its probable meaning (a weakening of the parties' traditional role in promoting public accountability and fostering unity in the U.S. system of separated powers); and its encouragement, in the judgment of some analysts, of "trench warfare" between the legislative and executive branches and of political "gridlock" in addressing important national issues.

There are two overlapping, yet different, types of divided government. The first is split party control of Congress; the second is one party in charge of Congress and the other in charge of the White House. Each will be discussed in turn to illuminate some of its policy, political, and procedural implications. Either variant of divided government may be perceived as another informal "check" in the system of separated powers. More than three decades ago, Douglass Cater observed that a "sizeable body of public opinion appears to believe that a President of one party and a Congress of the other can do a better job of keeping tabs on each other. In an era of big and irrevocable decisions, why not add this new check to the numerous ones already written into the Constitution?"[32] Cater's question about the value of divided government is still debated by today's commentators.

Split Party Control of Congress

Until the 1981–1987 period, only twice during this century had there been divided party control of Congress: the 62d Congress (1911–1913) and the 72d Congress (1931–1933). One explanation for split party control of the House and Senate involves the staggered terms of senators. The entire House faces reelection every two years; only one-third of the Senate is thus exposed. This means that the Senate is apt to be more resistant than the House to short-term electoral tides that occasionally sweep the nation and slower to respond to longer term political trends. Particularly when one party has a large "cushion" over the other, a single senatorial election is unlikely to transform the majority senatorial party into one of minority status.

During the 1981–1987 period, split party control of Congress (the Senate in GOP hands and the House controlled by Democrats) affected bicameral and legislative-executive relations in at least four broad ways. First, President Reagan needed the support of some House Democrats to pass his proposals. Particularly in 1981, Reagan's successes in the House resulted from disunity in Democratic ranks and unity among House Republicans. Democrats held nominal control of the House, but real control on important issues rested with an ideological majority that consisted of conservative Democrats and Republicans.

Second, the Senate played a pivotal role during the 1981–1987 period by accelerating action on the Reagan agenda (pressuring House Democrats in the process), blocking unwanted Democratic proposals, or seizing the initiative on issues when the White House failed to do so. For instance, national efforts to curb the deficit often emanated from the GOP-controlled Senate, led by Majority Leader Bob Dole of Kansas. It often fell to the Senate, acting as gatekeeper, broker, facilitator, or referee, "to find and open the door to compromise when confrontation between Reagan and the House threat[ened] to disrupt the government's business." [33]

Third, conference committees assumed greater importance as each chamber sought to enact its own version of disputed legislation—often packaged in massive megabills—or to draft the law in conference (the case with the 1985 Gramm-Rudman-Hollings deficit reduction statute). The use of sizable bills, an unconventional form of lawmaking that continues to flourish in an era of cutback budgeting, contributed to huge conferences. Often hundreds of conferees were involved in resolving interchamber disagreements on crucial legislation.[34]

With omnibus bills frequently short-circuiting normal floor routine, conference committees became the penultimate policy maker for Congress. "Let the conference decide" was an often-heard refrain. (It is still heard today as the majority Republicans in the House and Senate strive to reconcile their intraparty policy differences.) And with the partisan division accentuating the natural rivalry between the House and Senate, conference committees did not just reconcile the "differences between the two houses of Congress," but they also resolved "the differences between two political parties." [35]

Finally, bicameral maneuverings became more complex as a result of Democratic control of the House and Republican control of the Senate. For example, when House Republicans became frustrated in advancing their policy goals, they turned on occasion for legislative aid to their partisan Senate colleagues. Yet bicameral discussion of Congress's agenda typically involved the two majority parties rather than members of the same party. As one account noted, "House Democratic and Senate Republican leaders have developed a closer relationship with each other than with their party colleagues in the other chamber, leaving some feeling of isolation among House Republicans and Senate Democrats." [36]

Split Party Control of Congress and the White House

This second type of divided government has characterized the political system for many years (see Table 1-1, pp. 8–9). Since 1956, the first time in this century that a newly elected president faced a Congress controlled by the opposition party, the GOP has won the White House in six of nine presidential elections. Also beginning in the mid-1950s, Democrats always controlled the House—and usually the Senate as well—until the electoral earthquake of November 1994. It is hardly surprising that Republicans during this period were viewed as the "executive party" and Democrats as the "legislative party." Interestingly, it was only after Republicans lost the White House, in November 1992, that they won control of the House and Senate two years later.

Explanations. Numerous theories purport to explain truncated partisan control of Congress and the White House. One suggests that Republicans enjoy a majority "lock" on the electoral college because their partisan strength is concentrated in growing geographic areas that are increasingly congenial to the GOP. People are moving from the central cities, which have been traditionally Democratic, to Republican communities surrounding the cities. In addition to these suburbs, states in the South, West, and Southwest are generally presumed to be more sympathetic to the GOP than to the Democratic party. Democratic president Clinton's election in 1992 (he won 43 percent of the popular vote, the smallest winning margin in eighty years), like Jimmy Carter's before him, is considered an aberration under this theory.

Another theory holds that the ticket-splitting electorate of the United States prefers divided government because it wants different things from Congress and the White House. When Republican presidents occupied the White House, they were often accorded high marks for their handling of national priorities concerning the economy and defense; Democratic Congresses acted to protect the social programs that citizens wanted. With Democrat Clinton in the White House, citizens may want the president to protect various social programs from termination or to head off overzealous spending reductions by the GOP-controlled Congress.

Another explanation is that the power of incumbency promotes divided government. Given the advantages of incumbency, such as name recognition, fund-raising ability, and staff resources, it is extraordinarily difficult for challengers to defeat Democratic or Republican incumbents. House Democrats long were the beneficiaries of the incumbency factor because, by political skill or luck, they were in the majority in Congress when this reelection factor took hold. In the November 1986 and 1988 elections, for instance, nearly 99 percent of the House members who sought reelection won. Even in November 1994, 90 percent of the incumbents who ran were returned to Congress. (Senate incumbents are more easily defeated than their House counterparts, in large part because there are fewer problems in recruiting credible and adequately financed Senate challengers.)

The November 1994 election broke the forty-year Democratic "lock" on the House. (The Senate also returned to GOP control in this election, but in the future the Senate may function more than the House as a "swing" branch of government.) One result of this changeover was that House Republicans raised more money "in the first four months of 1995 [than they] raised in all of 1993." [37] This development, along with others such as the GOP's control of national debate and the retirement of Democratic incumbents, suggested that it would be difficult for the minority Democrats to win back control of the House in November 1996.

Finally, it is worth noting that the Constitution permits divided government. Voters separately choose candidates for the House, the Senate, and the White House. Perhaps more surprising than the recent occurrence of divided government is its comparative absence during much of U.S. history. Today's voter, it seems, cares less about party label and more about the qualities of the candidates. This tendency has produced several political and policy consequences that merit some mention.

Consequences. However one views divided government, it seems plain to many that the "split level" arrangement contributes to heightened partisanship. "I never want to see divided government again in my lifetime," declared Sen. Robert C. Byrd of West Virginia, when he was Democratic leader and Republican Ronald Reagan was in the White House.[38] His sentiment reflects the partisan warfare and legislative-executive conflict that characterize much contemporary congressional policy making.

Many factors contributed to greater partisanship. One was the election of Reagan as president. He (like Speaker Gingrich) advanced an ideologically charged and controversial agenda that aroused strong congressional opposition. A skilled partisan leader, Reagan often battled Congress, especially its Democratic leaders, in numerous policy areas and publicly blamed Congress when it frustrated his initiatives. (A lasting legacy of the Reagan era, with its mushrooming fiscal deficits, was to curtail the activist governmental ambitions of the Clinton White House.) Split party control of Congress also fostered partisanship as Senate Republicans often functioned as an instrument of the GOP-controlled White House.

Another indicator of heightened partisanship was the parliamentary warfare that erupted periodically, even in the Senate where party conflict is often muted. Senators criticized each other personally; they campaigned against colleagues of the opposite party; party leaders clashed heatedly on the floor; and legislators traded charges of partisan excesses. No wonder many senators became concerned about the decline of comity in the Senate. As the glue of personal and political camaraderie began to dissolve, and as many new senators pushed their individual agendas to the detriment of institutional obligations, the atmosphere of the Senate shifted from one of cooperative politics to one of confrontation politics.

The trend toward confrontation politics was particularly evident in the House, where the rules emphasize majority rule. When Republicans were in the minority for four decades, they assumed an aggressive posture toward the Democratic-led House. Through a combination of parliamentary, public relations, and political guerrilla warfare strategies, Republicans confronted Democrats on a host of issues.

The issue of ethics also became a weapon of partisan warfare in the House. In June 1989 Speaker Jim Wright, D-Texas, became the first Speaker ever to be forced to leave the House because of charges of financial irregularities. The charges against Wright were brought by then House GOP whip Newt Gingrich of Georgia. A fundamental objective of these tactics was to dislodge the Democrats from their majority status.

> The idea is to accuse the Democrats of ruling the House through a system of entrenched corruption. If people see enough corruption, they will get the idea that the whole system has to be overthrown—and the Democratic majority will be swept away.[39]

Democrats were swept away, as already noted, in the November 1994 election. (Political campaigns, too, were replete with attack ads designed to vilify opponents.) In the 104th Congress, Democrats employed many of the same political and parliamentary tactics used by Republicans when they were in the minority. Democrats, for example, lodged a half-dozen ethical charges against Speaker Gingrich. Almost daily, in an orchestrated effort, Democrats discussed the charges on the House floor for the press and the C-SPAN (Cable Satellite Public Affairs Network) viewing public. Further, with a cohesive GOP majority, House Democrats were often marginal players in legislative decision making; hence, they devoted considerable effort to devising communications strategies that attacked Republican initiatives and promoted their counter messages.

Another manifestation of heightened partisanship was in legislative-executive relationships. The president's veto weapon is a good example. Difficult to overturn because doing so requires a two-thirds' vote of each house, the veto poses risks (if the president is overridden, he may be viewed as weak and ineffective) and rewards (Congress will heed the president's policy suggestions when it drafts legislation). President Clinton used his veto pen for the first time on June 7, 1995, when he rejected an appropriations bill (a rescission of fiscal year 1995 money) sent to him by Republicans. Chances are, however, during times of divided government, that each branch will employ the "politics of differentiation" as the November elections draw near. That is, the president may look for items to veto, and Congress may send him measures it fully expects him to veto, so each party can stake out its positions clearly to the electorate. Speaker Gingrich stated in June 1995 that if President Clinton vetoed GOP initiatives, they would be added to "must pass" legislation. The president, Gingrich said, "will have to sign on to spending cuts that will inflame his Democratic supporters or veto them and force the shutdown" (as happened) of the federal government.[40]

Divided government also provided an incentive for aggressive, partisan oversight. Opposition lawmakers monitored and supervised agency activities with an eye toward politically bashing the administration. In the 104th Congress, Republicans conducted investigations, such as the Whitewater hearings, to embarrass the Clinton White House. Speaker Gingrich, for instance, directed the House Banking Committee to schedule Whitewater hearings during the August recess period. He "wanted to do this during a slow news time," said a GOP committee aide.[41]

For its part, the Clinton administration complained about the oversight activities of House Republicans. "It seems a pattern has developed where [House Republicans] are requesting information not so they can evaluate the effectiveness of the government's performance," stated a White House spokesman, "but so that they can use [requests for information to] thwart those who might be carrying out the laws as they've been properly passed by Congress." In response, a House GOP spokesperson said: "For two years they've gotten nothing from Democratic oversight chairmen but postcards from Hawaii saying, 'Wish you were here.'" [42]

Yet for all its allegedly negative consequences, divided government has produced many policy successes. One example is the Tax Reform Act of 1986, the most sweeping overhaul of the Internal Revenue Code since World War II:

> Ironically, the fact that government was split in 1985 and 1986—with the GOP controlling the White House and the Senate, and the Democrats controlling the House—proved to be a boost to the passage of tax reform. Tax reform's progress reflected a continuous fear on the part of one party that the other party would steal the issue from them. It was that competition that helped keep tax reform alive.[43]

The Democratically controlled 100th Congress (1987–1989), with Reagan as president, was one of the most productive since the mid-1960s. It passed significant legislation on health, welfare, immigration reform, trade, deficit reduction, and defense. As one scholar noted, the 100th Congress gave "the lie to the notion that the system can't produce" during a president's lame-duck years.[44] President Clinton and the GOP-led 104th Congress also worked together to achieve some policy successes. The president, for example, signed into law legislation making it more difficult for Congress to impose unfunded federal mandates on state governments.

Other post–World War II presidents who faced Congresses controlled by the opposition party—Harry S. Truman, Dwight D. Eisenhower, and Richard Nixon, for example—also achieved major successes, such as the Marshall Plan, civil rights legislation, and the normalization of relations with China. And some presidents who had their party in control of both houses of Congress, such as Democrat Jimmy Carter, encountered significant difficulties in getting their proposals through the legislative branch. "So there is something more than just having your party in power in all three places," noted one analyst. "You've got to know [how] to build political coalitions that work, that pull together, that sustain policies that you as President effectively articulate." [45] In short, while same-party control of Congress and the White House might be better for policy making and accountability, divided government, despite its drawbacks, can be made to work.

Conclusion

Our constitutional system of shared powers, reinforced by today's heightened partisanship, presents challenges and opportunities. Still, the White House and Congress are capable of adjusting to contemporary political reality and to the societal circumstances and values that give their activities direction. Whether institutional leaders achieve a harmony of purpose often depends on whether there is consensus among the citizenry for purposeful action. As Rep. Lee H. Hamilton, D-Ind., said about Congress and policy making:

> When the nation clearly wants change, the Congress can respond decisively. But when public opinion is more mixed, the legislature responds with delay and inaction. The Congress can often work out compromises of conflicting interests and act on the basis of a national consensus, but it cannot impose a consensus where none exists. [46]

Put somewhat differently, Speaker Gingrich said: "You reach the American people, and they reach Congress." [47]

Notes

1. David S. Cloud, "Gingrich Clears the Path for Republican Advance," *Congressional Quarterly Weekly Report*, November 19, 1994, 3322.
2. *Congressional Record*, daily ed., 101st Cong., 1st sess., January 25, 1989, S88.
3. *Congressional Record*, daily ed., 101st Cong., 1st sess., March 21, 1989, E878.
4. William Schneider, "Welcome to the Greening of America," *National Journal*, May 27, 1989, 1334.
5. Marilyn Gardner, "Male Joblessness Fosters Rise of Fatherless Families," *Christian Science Monitor*, April 25, 1995, 3.
6. Cheryl Wetzstein, "Friends of Family Values Mail Wish Lists," *Washington Times*, April 27, 1995, A2.
7. *Wall Street Journal*, June 15, 1995, A14.
8. *U.S. News and World Report*, December 14, 1981, 65.

9. Norman Cousins, "Take Time to Think," *Christian Science Monitor,* September 26, 1989, 18.
10. Pat Choate, "How Foreign Firms Buy U.S. Clout," *Washington Post,* June 19, 1988, C1.
11. Elaine Sciolino, "New Protocol: Heads of State Now Court Congress," *New York Times,* April 8, 1995, 3.
12. *Congressional Record,* daily ed., 101st Cong., 1st sess., September 19, 1989, S11301.
13. Deborah Kalb, "Government by Task Force: The Gingrich Model," *The Hill,* February 22, 1995, 3.
14. David S. Cloud, "Speaker Wants His Platform To Rival the Presidency," *Congressional Quarterly Weekly Report,* February 4, 1995, 331–335.
15. J. William Fulbright, "The Legislator As Educator," *Foreign Affairs* 58 (Spring 1979): 726.
16. See David Broder, *The Party's Over* (New York: Harper & Row, 1972); and Xander Kayden and Eddie Mahe, Jr., *The Party Goes On* (New York: Basic Books, 1985).
17. Richard Berke, "The Specter of Perot Haunts Major Parties," *New York Times,* June 6, 1995, A20.
18. *Washington Times,* June 1, 1995, A4.
19. Rhodes Cook, "Rare Combination of Forces May Make History of '94," *Congressional Quarterly Weekly Report,* April 15, 1995, 1079.
20. *Wall Street Journal,* May 11, 1995, A18.
21. Andy Plattner, "The High Cost of Holding and Keeping Public Office," *U.S. News and World Report,* June 22, 1987, 30.
22. Charles Mathias quoted in Philip M. Stern, "The Tin Cup Congress," *Washington Monthly,* May 1988, 4.
23. Michael Oreskes, "Congress," *New York Times,* July 11, 1989, A17.
24. Stephen Gettinger, "Potential Senate Leaders Flex Money Muscles," *Congressional Quarterly Weekly Report,* October 8, 1988, 2276.
25. Horace W. Busby, "The New Politics of Who We Are," *New York Times,* September 9, 1984, E25.
26. Melissa Healy, "Richard Armey," *Los Angeles Times,* June 26, 1995, A12.
27. Jane Fritsch, "The Grass Roots, Just a Free Phone Call Away," *New York Times,* June 23, 1995, A1.
28. Richard Cohen, "Assertive Freshman," *National Journal,* May 2, 1987, 1061.
29. Peter Osterlund, "The Senate's Business As Usual Just Isn't What it Used to Be," *Christian Science Monitor,* April 22, 1988, 1.
30. *Congressional Record,* daily ed., 99th Cong., 1st sess., October 1, 1985, S12343.
31. Helen Dewar, "Defeat of Tower Reflects Dramatic Changes in Senate," *Washington Post,* March 13, 1989, A6.
32. Douglass Cater, "Split Personality of the Voter," *New York Times Magazine,* January 24, 1960, 71.
33. "GOP Senate Plays Gatekeeper Role in 1983," *Congressional Quarterly Weekly Report,* December 3, 1983, 2548.
34. The largest conference in history met on the Omnibus Reconciliation Act of 1981. More than 250 House and Senate conferees, meeting in more than fifty subconferences, settled over three hundred matters that were in disagreement.
35. This observation was made by a top aide to Thomas P. "Tip" O'Neill, Jr., former Speaker of the House. Steven V. Roberts, "The Nitty-Gritty of Conference," *New York Times,* July 17, 1985, A18.
36. Richard E. Cohen, "A Congress Divided," *National Journal,* January 18, 1986, 131.
37. Tim Curran, "House GOP Claims Fundraising History," *Roll Call,* May 29, 1995, 1.
38. Helen Dewar, "Full Plate of Leftovers Awaits Hill, Reagan in 1988," *Washington Post,* December 23, 1987, A6.
39. William Schneider, "Jim Wright's Capitol Punishment," *Los Angeles Times,* pt. 5, June 4, 1989, 1.

40. *Time,* June 5, 1995, 23.
41. *Congressional Quarterly's Congressional Monitor,* June 15, 1995, 4.
42. *Washington Times,* April 7, 1995, A1.
43. Alan S. Murray and Jeffrey H. Birnbaum, "Lawmakers, Lobbyists, and the Unlikely Triumph of Tax Reform," *Congress & the Presidency* (Autumn 1988): 190.
44. Charles O. Jones quoted in Janet Hook, "100th Congress Wraps Up Surprisingly Busy Year," *Congressional Quarterly Weekly Report,* October 29, 1988, 3117.
45. Hedrick Smith, "Considerations on the Power System," *Presidential Studies Quarterly* (Summer 1988): 497.
46. *Congressional Record,* daily ed., 101st Cong., 1st sess., March 15, 1989, E805.
47. Richard E. Cohen, "The Transformers," *National Journal,* March 4, 1995, 530.

4

Presidential Leadership with Congress: Change, Coalitions, and Crisis

Lester G. Seligman and Cary R. Covington

The concept of presidential leadership is elusive. It is difficult to state precisely what constitutes leadership, and just as difficult to distinguish good leadership from bad. Students of the presidency lack agreed-upon standards by which to evaluate individual presidents. Consequently, observers often come to divergent conclusions about whether a president provided leadership or whether a president's leadership was effective.

Similarly, a president judged at different times can produce contrasting evaluations of leadership. Thus, the image of corruption and ineptitude that hounded Truman from office gave way to more recent judgments that rank him with some of the best presidents in history. And Eisenhower's reputation has been burnished by scholars who resifted the record of his presidency. Who knows what the next generation of scholars may think of presidents like Carter or Reagan?

We begin by considering the boundaries of presidential leadership, identifying the range of behaviors that can reasonably be expected of presidents. Then we describe changes in the presidency's political environment over the past quarter-century, tracing their implications for how presidents lead. Next, we present an approach to presidential leadership based on the concept of coalition building. We construct an analytical framework to describe and explain how presidents build coalitions. We describe the structures of those coalitions, and identify different situations within which coalition building takes place. We use this framework to explain President Clinton's efforts to lead Congress to adopt his health care reforms. We conclude by offering observations about the task confronting the modern presidency and about the prospects for leadership by presidents.

The Boundaries of Presidential Leadership

One approach to defining a concept is to identify characteristics that are not a part of the concept, and so place boundaries on it. Given the ambiguity of the concept, presidential leadership is well-suited to this approach. We begin our inquiry into presidential leadership by discussing what it is not.

Two recent books on the presidency help identify end points on the range of behaviors that constitute presidential leadership. At one extreme, George Edwards, by distinguishing between "president as director" and "president as facilitator," helps establish the upper limit of presidential leadership. At the other end, Paul Brace and Barbara Hinckley, in their study of opinion polling by presidents, help define the lower limit of leadership.

Edwards creates one version of presidential leadership (president as director) that he supplants with a more realistic portrayal (president as facilitator). A director governs by "leading others where they otherwise would not go" and "creates a constituency" that did not exist.[1]

Presidents as directors are unlikely to exist for at least three reasons. First, it is difficult to imagine that, in a democratic society such as the United States, in which interests are well-defined and well-organized, presidents could get others to act against their own interests or to act on preferences that they did not realize they possessed. Presidents are elected because their views coincide in some fashion with those of the voters who selected them. The electorate is unlikely to choose a president who promises to disregard its wishes and strike out in a direction that it either opposes or does not think is important.

Second, as a practical matter, it is unlikely that presidents could create a policy option (much less an entire agenda) for which there was not a pre-existing constituency. Regardless of the direction in which a president leads, there will be groups that previously established their intent to move in that direction. As a consequence, no matter how innovative a president's policy proposal, the president is a facilitator.

Finally, a president concerned with reelection and retaining popular support would have no incentive to act like a director. A director could not be politically oriented, since a director would have to show disregard for existing patterns of public and interest group attitudes. It is not surprising, then, that Edwards offers no evidence of presidents who acted as directors.

Ironically, the absence of examples of the director model demonstrates its value: the director model exceeds the range of behaviors that can meaningfully be labeled presidential leadership. Leadership cannot be expected to consist of presidential actions that open the eyes of the public, or Congress, or interest groups, to a reality to which they had previously been blind. People, and especially organized groups and institutions, are bound to know enough about their own interests that the likelihood that presidents can spring unconsidered policy options on them is virtually nil.

Instead, presidential leadership consists, in Edwards's terms, of actions that facilitate change, enabling those with goals similar to the president's to achieve them. Presidential leadership "reflects and perhaps intensifies widely held views, using [its] resources to achieve [its] constituency's aspirations." [2]

At the opposite end of the leadership continuum is Brace and Hinckley's account of the "public-relations presidency." [3] In their study of the connections among presidents' rankings in the public opinion polls, their behavior in office, and the political consequences of their actions, Brace and Hinckley find evidence that, to at least some degree, recent presidents (with the exception of Harry Truman) make decisions on the basis of what makes them popular, rather than on the basis of the intrinsic merit of their goals.

"Leadership by polling" undermines the concept of leading by inverting the leader-follower connection between presidents and those they would lead. Presidential leadership would consist of putting one's finger to the wind, allowing decisions to be pushed along by prevailing sentiments. Thus, Brace and Hinckley provide us with the balancing end point to presidential leadership. Leadership ceases when presidents seek to remain in the public's good graces rather than to guide and shape its wishes into coherent and appropriate public policies.

Presidential leadership consists neither of imposing the presidents' wishes on "unwilling" others, nor of uncritically composing their own agendas from the wishes of others. Instead, it consists of presidents working, within the existing preferences and powers in the political system, to direct the participation of others in the governing process toward presidential goals.

Changes in the Presidency and Its Environment

To fully appreciate the manner in which presidents provide leadership today, we need to place the presidency in its historical setting, identifying the origin of expectations for presidential leadership and the changes that have occurred within the presidency's political context.

The Modern Presidency's Progressive Roots

The origin of modern expectations for presidential leadership can be traced to the doctrines of the Progressive Era, which were prominent around the turn of the century. These doctrines form the foundation of our expectations for the modern presidency.

Progressive values relevant to modern presidential behavior include beliefs that: (1) the national government should actively participate in defining and achieving national purposes through regulation of the economy; (2) the presidency is preeminent over Congress because the presidency's national constituency makes it more representative of the national interest; and (3) the political parties should be democratized, or opened up to greater public participation.

Activist government. Progressives' support for active government sprang from the belief that the public's interests and the interests of big business were diametrically opposed. Progressivism expressed "the conviction that government should actively pursue the public interest in a society whose private sector seemed increasingly indifferent or hostile to that interest." [4] The movement voiced urban middle-class resentment toward the economic power of large corporations and their political allies, the urban party machines, which Progressives believed had corrupted political life. [5]

Government's job was to intervene in conflicts between private and public interests, acting as an umpire to resolve disputes. According to Richard Hofstadter, government was to be a neutral party among society's special interests, subordinating those interests to the common good and dispensing justice in an even-handed way.[6]

Presidential leadership of government. According to Progressives, government should be led by the president. They wanted a role for the presidency in domestic policy comparable in prominence to its constitutionally defined role in foreign affairs. Progressives justified the presidency's preeminence by stressing the legitimacy conferred by its status as the only elective office with a national constituency. In contrast, Congress was tainted by localized politics and narrow self-interest, leaving the president as "the rightful champion of public opinion against the failed legislatures." [7]

Theodore Roosevelt and Woodrow Wilson shared certain Progressive values and a low regard for Congress. Both used the presidency to reform political processes and reshape government's relationship to the economy. Both helped shift the balance among the legislative, judicial, and executive branches to the presidency's advantage. And both set forth legislative agendas and cultivated the press, modeling what became aspects of modern presidential leadership.

Democratizing the parties. The final way in which Progressives helped shape our expectations for presidential leadership was by laying the groundwork for restructuring the role of parties in the electoral and governing arenas. Progressives were devoted to dismantling party "machine" politics. They sponsored reforms that weakened party organizations and leadership, including those that established the civil service system of public employment and created direct primaries for nominating candidates.

Progressives hoped that such reforms would reduce the control of machine bosses over party organizations, elections, and government. By broadening opportunities for public participation, Progressives hoped to recruit new leaders who would raise the level of competence and moral tone in public affairs and inspire greater public involvement in government.

When fully implemented, these reforms had their intended effects. The decline of patronage undermined the parties' ability to deliver large blocs of votes to preferred candidates. The adoption of direct primaries in the 1970s opened the door to self-starting candidates who could secure a party's nomination without the party organization's endorsement. As a result, parties have been pushed to the periphery of electoral and governmental politics, profoundly affecting the methods by which presidents lead.

The Presidency's Changing Political Context

Progressives also put into motion events that would dramatically alter the context in which presidents would try to provide leadership. We will consider the following changes in the features of the presidency's environment: (1) the declining role of political parties, (2) the expanding impact of the mass media, (3) the proliferation of political interest groups, (4) the centralization and decentralization of power in Congress, (5) the increasingly corporate character of the presidency, and (6) the growing demands placed on the presidency.

Declining role of political parties. Changes in the role of parties in the presidential selection process have dramatically altered the role of parties in presidential strategies for leading the government.[8] The decline of parties has been thoroughly explored by others.[9] We want to highlight a few key issues.

Throughout the 1960s, party organizations provided candidates with a sure and certain route to presidential nominations. Parties also provided candidates with the structure and strategy necessary for running in the general elections. The same was true for congressional candidates. Consequently, parties were integral to any president's plans for winning office and governing.

Since the 1970s, however, the parties have moved from caucus/convention systems of nomination to direct primaries.[10] In 1992, for example, over 75 percent of all delegates to both parties' national conventions were chosen through primaries. This changed the characteristics of the nomination process and, consequently, those of the general election process. The revised process of candidate selection gave candidates both the incentive and the means to discount their parties and to appeal directly to the electorate. Today, candidates in presidential and congressional elections are self-starters who mobilize the resources needed to win nominations without having to subordinate themselves to their parties. As a result, the central mediating structures in the candidate-selection process, the state and local party organizations and leaders, have lost their pivotal role. Instead, primary voters and the media determine who wins nominations.

The decline in the parties' organizational power has been mirrored by their weakening in the electorate. Generally speaking, partisan attachments are weaker today than in the past. This produces higher rates of split-ticket voting, which results in districts that elect congressional candidates of one party and presidents from the opposing party.

The diminished role of parties in the electoral arena has had important ramifications for the governing arena. In general, parties are less able to provide the basis for stable, broad-based governing coalitions. In Congress, for example, the sense of shared fate that once gave presidents a basis for appealing for support from their copartisans on Capitol Hill has been greatly diminished.[11] Similarly, parties are less able to serve as umbrellas for political interest groups, which are more inclined to seek their goals independently of parties.

The decline of parties has also affected the way presidents organize and use their staffs. Rather than depending on parties, presidents rely on White House office staffs. Political appointments, for example, were once handled by and for party officials, but are now directed by the White House.[12] Similarly, where presidents once turned to state party officials for help in persuading members of Congress, they now rely on the White House congressional liaison staff.

Expanding impact of the mass media. Changes in the mass media have made presidential leadership more difficult. The press has, since Watergate, been increasingly predisposed to cover stories that deal with scandals, internal dissension, and presidential gaffes.[13] Such stories have undermined the authority and legitimacy of the presidency.

Moreover, the media have become more skeptical of presidents as sources of information.[14] Presidential news management during the Vietnam War and the Watergate scandal elevated the press's cynicism toward the office.[15] Michael Grossman and Martha Kumar observe that whereas journalists of an earlier period were willing to ally themselves with and protect the White House, today's press corps covers the administration from an antagonistic point of view. Nonetheless, presidents and the press must cooperate to achieve their respective goals.[16]

The media have expanded the scope of their reporting to encompass presidents' personal lives. Reporters once looked the other way when it came to presidents' private behavior. Today, the coverage given to stories like Gary Hart's trysts, and the allegations of Gennifer Flowers and Paula Jones against President Clinton, helps undermine the stature presidents need to claim the nation's allegiance.

In addition, the sheer growth in the number of news agencies and reporters covering the presidency has intensified the scrutiny to which presidents are subjected. Rich in financial, technological, and human resources, the broadcasting industry has used its considerable wealth to examine aspects of the presidency not previously explored. In the process, it has uncovered and, in many cases, magnified the faults of the presidency.[17]

Each of these developments has contributed to a situation in which presidents confront a press that is less responsive as an instrument of leadership and more inclined to challenge presidents' claims to leadership.

Proliferation of political interest groups. Among the most noteworthy developments in the governing arena has been the growth in the number of political interest groups, especially single-issue interest groups. It is difficult to identify, and so to count, all of the political interest groups active in Washington. However, figures documenting the proliferation of political action committees (PACs) give us some indication of how large and how fast the interest group community has grown. Whereas in 1974 there were fewer than 1,000 PACs, by 1987 there were 4,100.[18]

The influence of these groups has grown over the past decades. The weakening of parties helps explain that growth. In the past, when parties were stronger, interest group demands were resisted by party leaders, who argued that giving in to them would alienate party adherents, or that party loyalty precluded yielding to a single interest. Today, these arguments arise less frequently, and parties avoid taking stands on some issues, leaving interest groups free to advocate without partisan constraints.

The growing importance of interest groups has affected the policy-making process, accelerating the switch by policy makers from decentralized "iron triangles" to more fluid "issue networks"—the "fairly open networks of people that increasingly impinge upon government." [19] As David Ricci observes: "When additional actors insisted on joining the older establishments, the fairly simple pattern of regular interactions among a finite number of long-standing players could not survive. New Washingtonians overwhelmed it.... Indeed, the clamorous practices that they employed led to interminable jostling with unpredictable outcomes." [20] The in-depth study of policy making conducted by John Heinz, Edward Laumann, Robert Nelson and Robert Salisbury reinforces the emerging perception of policy making as an open process involving many participants, rather than a closed system dominated by a cohesive elite.[21] "[R]ather than a wheel with a hub and spokes, the networks of communication among influentials resemble a soap bubble, with an empty center and thin surface—hence, the 'hollow core' ... [which] takes us beyond the obsolete notion of the iron triangle and lends precision to [the] notion of the porous but diffuse policy network." [22]

Today, groups polarize policy debates rather than seek compromises. This strategy helps keep the groups' members mobilized and encourages financial contributions. As R. Kent Weaver of the Brookings Institution notes, "few people are likely to send money to an organization because of its intense, flaming moderation." [23] As a result, "extremism in the defense of ideology is no vice. Moderation in the pursuit of donor dollars is no virtue." [24]

In addition, single-issue groups are often better at blocking changes than achieving their own goals.[25] When groups are satisfied to act as "veto groups," they have little incentive to join others. As President Clinton's experience with his 1994 health care reforms revealed, when groups settle for blocking others' initiatives rather than enacting their own, they have little incentive to exhibit the flexibility required to create constructive coalitions.

The proliferation of single-issue groups has made the task of presidential coalition building more complicated. The key to successful coalition building lies in finding common ground and making common cause with other groups. As political interest groups move away from the time-honored strategy of compromise and toward the "politics of bombast," potential coalition partners are less inclined to make the sacrifices needed to join, thereby making the task of presidential leadership more difficult.[26]

Centralization and decentralization of power in Congress. Congress has, over the past quarter-century, experienced twin developments. The first decentralized power from party leaders and committee chairs to subcommittee chairs and the rank-and-file, while the second recentralized some power in the hands of party leaders and a few key committee chairs. On balance, these trends have made presidential leadership of Congress more difficult.

On the one hand, power in Congress has been diluted among its members as a result of decisions in the 1970s to increase the number and autonomy of subcommittees, to weaken the seniority system, and to enlarge the staffs of committees and members. Each of these changes weakened the power of the congressional hierarchy and enhanced the opportunities for personal initiative by individual members.[27]

On the other hand, other reforms of the era strengthened the party leadership and party caucuses. At the same time, the "fiscalization" of congressional politics centralized power in the hands of the committees that handle taxes and spending.[28] The election of Newt Gingrich, R-Ga., as Speaker of the House further accelerated the growing centralization of power of the House party leadership.

Overall, these two trends have made presidential leadership more difficult. The proliferation of bargaining partners in Congress and the limited ability of congressional leaders to persuade the rank-and-file to accept guidance mean that coalition building in Congress becomes increasingly time-consuming and costly.[29]

Increasingly corporate character of the presidency. Another important development with implications for presidential leadership has been the growth, formalization, and internal differentiation of the presidency. What was once, prior to FDR, a small, informal, and highly personalized staff structure created on an ad hoc basis by each president has taken on the characteristics of a large-scale bureaucracy. Presidential actions today are the outcomes of interactions among many individuals and organizations within the presidency. Presidents once relied on state and local party officials to solicit support from their congressional copartisans. Since the Eisenhower presidency, the White House Office of Legislative Affairs has performed this role. White House staffs now lay the foundations for congressional coalitions.

Parties once formed the glue that held together political interest groups. Since the Ford presidency, however, the White House Office of Public Liaison has taken over that function, providing presidents with access to and the means of coordinating the actions of many diverse groups.

When we talk about "the president" acting, or about "presidential" leadership, we are often talking about a corporate product rather than an individual's behavior. Both the personal authority and the organizational structure of the presidency are involved. And while presidential staffs are committed to serving their presidents, they must at the same time exercise an important degree of discretion. Thus, we must consider where the impetus for policy direction and leadership comes from: Who is making the decisions? Who is providing leadership? To what extent is it a personal product of the president, or of the institution of the presidency?

Changes in the demands placed on the presidency. The president's job today is undoubtedly more difficult than in the past. As Hedley Donovan observed in 1982, "to be a 'good' President in the 1980s may be even harder than to be a 'great' President in the days of Antietam or Pearl Harbor." [30] There are three reasons why being president has become more difficult.

First, we expect more of presidents than we once did. According to Fred Greenstein, "There's been a lot of cranking up of expectations." [31] Recent presidents have been involved in more issues than their predecessors. Many of today's pressing issues either did not exist until a few years ago or have only recently fallen within the domain of the public sector. Consequently, there are more issues on the president's plate.

Second, the problems requiring presidential attention are less amenable to solution. For example, the intractability of today's problems of budget deficits and entitlement spending far exceeds that of the perceived difficulties of initiating the War on Poverty. Similarly, the clarity and seriousness of purpose that the Cold War gave to U.S. foreign policy has been supplanted by a fog of uncertainty about what constitutes our vital interests and how we should pursue them in a post–Cold War world.

Third, the standards to which we hold a president's efforts at leadership have become more stringent. As one observer notes, the nation's "political processes are nastier and less forgiving than they were. The nation has become a harder place to govern than it used to be. It isn't likely to get any easier." [32]

The implications of these developments for presidential leadership are clear. Presidents must act on a wider array of issues that are more difficult to address, through a governing process that is less supportive and responsive. To be sure, the political context has rendered presidential leadership a more forbidding and intimidating task.

A Framework for Describing
and Understanding Presidential Leadership

Conceptions of leadership have historically fallen into two categories, with occasional subcategories. The older approach viewed leadership as a function of the traits of the individual who was the leader. Leaders were a part of the natural order of society. Historically, leadership derived from prophetic religious figures or from groups of primary relationships. Leadership was personalized, vested in the person with the power to lead. In its more extreme forms (for example, Thomas Carlyle's 1841 book *On Heroes, Hero-Worship, and the Heroic in History*), we have the "great man theory of history." Leaders act upon their environment. Leadership flows from the leader to the followers.

More recent and nuanced treatments within this "traits" approach claim that certain personality characteristics or behaviors constitute leadership. However, empirical studies using traits to define leadership have been unable to identify a common set of characteristics or behaviors that set leaders apart.

The second way to categorize leadership has been labeled a "situational" approach. Examined in detail by Harold Lasswell and James MacGregor

Burns, it focuses on the interaction between leaders and followers. From this perspective, leadership requires acceptance by the followers. Following is a choice made by the follower, informed by the follower's sense of self-interest and the situation in which the relationship takes place. Since the leader's goal is to induce others to follow, the leader has an incentive to make following an attractive option. Consequently, influence in the leader-follower relationship becomes contingent, a two-way rather than a one-way flow, as followers also affect the actions of leaders.[33]

This approach emerged during the twentieth century in response to two developments. The first was the rise of democracy in the eighteenth and nineteenth centuries. Democratic regimes placed authority in laws and offices rather than in persons, thus depersonalizing leadership. Second, the positivist influence of the social sciences further modified the concept. The older "instinct-and-trait," psychology of leadership gave way to a conception of leadership as a role that satisfied the mutual expectations of both leaders and followers.[34]

We view presidential leadership as an interaction between a leader and followers. Presidents operate within a pluralistic society of organized and competing interests. As a result, they exercise leadership by building governing coalitions from discrete groups and interests.[35] Presidents develop proposals around which coalitions can form and then induce others to join. Potential coalition partners accept or reject the president's offers, thereby deciding whether to follow the president. That gives them influence over what the president proposes and what the president offers as inducements to join.

These coalitions can be ad hoc or strategic in character. Ad hoc coalitions are formed by presidents on an issue-by-issue basis. Presidents with substantial agendas have to create as many ad hoc coalitions as there are issues on their agendas. In contrast, a strategic coalition consists of a configuration of support that is broad-based and stable. Coalition partners follow the president on most if not all the issues on the president's agenda, not just on their salient issues. The changes in the presidency's political context discussed earlier have affected presidents by making it more likely that, beginning in the 1970s, presidents have been less able to create strategic coalitions, and so have had to rely more on ad hoc coalitions.

Regardless of the types of coalitions being formed, this conditional, interactive perspective on leadership directs us to three topics: (1) who is leading, (2) who is following, and (3) in what situation the leader-follower relationship is being pursued.

Who Is Leading

The growth in both the size and internal complexity of the presidency means that presidential behavior consists of much more than the actions of the single individual who is president. Presidential action is an organized, corporate product, with the president acting as the head of the team. Presidential coalition building is more than the personal efforts of the president to set a policy agenda and attract supporters. Many people and staff units help decide what the objectives of the presidency should be. Executive Office of the President (EOP) agencies such as the National Economic Council, the National Security Council, the Domestic Policy Council, and the Council of Economic Advisers all help formulate the president's policy agenda. Similarly, White House office units such as the Office of Legislative Affairs, the Office of Public Liaison, and the Office of the Press Secretary are all integral to the presidency's efforts to solicit and retain the support of the groups participating in a governing coalition.

Who Is Following

Governing coalitions do not exist as amorphous, homogeneous masses of support. They are constructed out of discrete sets of actors. To understand the dynamics of coalition building, we must distinguish among the various components from which a coalition may be constructed. Coalitions exist on three levels: the elite, the intermediary group, and the mass public levels.

The elite level. The elite level of coalitions exists within the presidency itself. Although we argue that presidential leadership incorporates the activities of both the institution of the presidency and the individual president, that does not mean the presidency is a single, monolithic actor. The process of presidential coalition building begins within the presidency, as presidential factions are influenced by and seek to influence the choices of the president. Recent administrations illustrate these internal divisions.

For example, White House "home state personal loyalists" (whose relationship with the president predates their involvement in national politics) frequently compete with "Washington insiders," who are added to the president's staffs to contribute expertise about Washington politics. Reagan's choice of Edwin Meese and Michael Deaver as loyalists, along with James Baker as an insider, reflects this division, as does Clinton's replacement of longtime friend Mack McLarty with Leon Panetta as White House chief of staff.

Presidencies also often include advocates of conflicting policy options. Carter's appointment of Zbigniew Brzezinski as national security adviser and Cyrus Vance as secretary of state laid the foundation for disputes between hard-line and more accommodating foreign policy options. Similarly, when Nixon chose Daniel Moynihan as chief domestic policy adviser and Arthur Burns as special counsellor, he created a situation in which each adviser competed for his own vision of good domestic policy. As part of building a governing coalition, presidents must pull together an elite coalition within their own administrations. When opposing groups within the presidency exist in uneasy balance, coalition building outside the White

House is hampered. Images of conflict and inconsistency attendant to these intramural disputes undermine the reputation for confidence and reliability that presidents need to enlist outside support.

The intermediary group level. This level of a president's governing coalition consists of the leaders of national institutions: Congress and its staffs, the career bureaucracy, political parties and interest groups, and the mass media. Some combination of these groups is essential for successful presidential coalitions. For example, before a bill becomes a law, Congress must pass it, and before Congress will pass a bill, it must possess substantial interest group support. Similarly, to get a law enacted into policy, presidents need the cooperation of career civil servants and of the clienteles of the relevant government agencies.

The changing context for presidential leadership significantly affects how presidents build coalitions among these actors. The fragmentation of authority in Congress and the proliferation of single-issue interest groups mean that presidents build many single-issue coalitions, rather than a few broadly focused coalitions. Empowered congressional party leaders help presidents in general, but can be damaging to presidents under conditions of divided government or when leaders defect.

The mass public level. Presidents once gave the mass public only secondary consideration. When all the important action was "inside the Beltway," the public was neither a participant nor even an especially interested observer, and so could be brought along later. Samuel Kernell describes this situation as "institutionalized pluralism." [36] Today, the ready availability of public opinion polls and the omnipresent media give public opinion greater weight.

The public contributes to a president's governing coalition in at least two ways. First, by electing and providing continued support for a president, the public lends legitimacy to the president's claim to leadership. Jeffrey Tulis traced this role for the public back to Woodrow Wilson.[37] According to Tulis, Wilson rejected the traditional understanding of presidential authority as residing solely in the Constitution. In its place, Wilson claimed that the president's authority stems from winning elections. This gives the president the right to lead a government that is prone to deadlock and stalemate. As the only elected official with a national constituency, the president earns deference from intermediary groups.

This deference does not extend to an obligation to follow the president's lead. The antiauthoritarian bias in our nation's political culture is too strong to permit such an imposition.[38] But the president's electoral success does induce others to look to the president for direction in setting and enacting a governing agenda.

With the emergence of public opinion polling, proof of the legitimacy of presidential leadership has shifted from the one-time test of the general election to repeated measurements of the president's current level of popularity. Recent presidents have been preoccupied with their popularity, going so far as to periodically review their popularity against that of their predecessors at comparable points in time.[39]

Second, the public contributes to a president's governing coalition through what Kernell refers to as the "going public" strategy. In this case, presidents pursue the public's endorsement of their policy objectives by giving speeches and making public appearances designed to mobilize the public to pressure Congress on behalf of those policies. The public has become an integral component and target of presidential coalition-building efforts.

Situations for Leading and Following

According to Richard Neustadt, as presidents enter office, they are expected to take the initiative in responding to important national problems.[40] Within the context of this general expectation, however, the specific situations in which presidents try to lead can vary substantially. In some situations, expectations are clearly focused on the president, while in others, the president is only one among many potential policy makers. Some situations are crises, others are more routine. The type of situation involved should be considered, because it can significantly affect the president's prospects for leading. We identify four types of situations: (1) initiating, (2) crisis, (3) maintaining, and (4) secondary. We then examine the implications of these situations for presidential leadership.

Initiating situations. In many respects, this is the classic presidential situation. Presidents are expected to take the initiative in identifying problems and proposing solutions. These expectations can originate from within the presidency, from the president's electoral campaign promises, or from actors in the presidency's environment.

The benchmark of a president's "first one hundred days" gives voice to this expectation: What has the president done to enact his agenda? Presidents often name their new policy agendas (for example, FDR's "New Deal," Kennedy's "New Frontier," or Nixon's "New Federalism").

Presidents who do not adequately respond to these expectations will be criticized for failing as leaders. Dwight Eisenhower, for example, was attacked by the media and his own party when he did not prepare an explicit agenda for Congress in 1953.[41] Similarly, many analysts lay a portion of the blame for George Bush's 1992 defeat on his failure to propose a substantive domestic package early in his term. Thus, the key feature of an initiating situation is that the president is expected to take the lead in proposing solutions to the nation's problems. However, in this situation those demanding leadership are not obligated to follow.

Crisis situations. Crises consist of situations that arise unexpectedly and require specific and concrete responses—they are not likely to be part of a planned agenda.[42] Some crises have major ramifications (for example, the Cuban missile crisis during Kennedy's administration, or Operation Desert

Storm during Bush's presidency), while others have more narrow and limited effects (for example, Reagan's Grenada invasion).

The characteristic that distinguishes crises is that the president can expect others to follow. In crises, there is a "rally 'round the president" phenomenon that strengthens the president's hand; presidential leadership is accepted, and blame or judgment of the president is deferred so long as the crisis prevails. That willingness to follow can be short-lived, but is present for some significant period of time. For instance, Sen. Edward M. Kennedy's challenge to Carter's renomination in 1980 was thwarted in large part when the public rallied to Carter after Iran took American diplomats hostage in Tehran. However, as the hostage crisis dragged on, public support sagged, and Carter's inability to solve the crisis contributed to his loss to Reagan.

While more common in the realm of foreign policy, crises also occur in the domestic policy arena. Consider, for example, the banking crisis in 1933. Franklin Roosevelt declared a "banking holiday" (which closed the banks to protect them from demands for withdrawals that might force them into bankruptcy) prior to the convening of Congress. Even though his action was based on a dubious interpretation of an outdated law, it went basically unchallenged.[43]

In situations that are not crises, followership is problematic. Indeed, securing followers is the heart of presidential efforts in noncrisis situations. In contrast, the key to presidential success during a crisis rests on creating a consensus that the crisis indeed exists.

The dynamics of coalition building in crises differ markedly from those in other situations. In a crisis, the president's efforts are directed toward creating a perception among the public that the president's declaration of a crisis is warranted. Debate focuses on whether or not the president is objectively correct. Therefore, the debate is over the facts of the situation. In contrast, in a noncrisis situation, the president's efforts center on persuading others that what the president wants them to do is in their own best interests. Thus, in a crisis, attention focuses on the public and its willingness to believe that a crisis exists. The public's role in a crisis is more prominent than in other situations because in many ways the intermediary groups will fall into line when the public is unambiguous in its support for the president's declaration of an emergency.

Many examples of presidential attempts at leadership through crises exist. Gerald Ford used his "Whip Inflation Now" (WIN) campaign to persuade the public that there was an inflationary crisis. Jimmy Carter went on television in a sweater to try to persuade the public that there was an energy crisis. Both presidents were ultimately unsuccessful in their attempts to paint a portrait of crisis, and their policy initiatives failed.

Maintaining situations. Presidents on occasion may be expected to protect or only marginally alter existing policies. The fact that some policy issues are not subject to strong pressures for change allows presidents to focus their energies on those policies for which, because of personal inclination or external pressures, they feel an obligation to provide initiative.

In a fundamental sense, George Bush found himself in a maintaining situation in 1989. Proposals for policy change could be seen as tacit criticisms of Reagan. While Bush was subject in general to the expectation that presidents should provide initiative, his particular situation strongly deterred him from doing so. He was constrained by his own conservative inclinations and by his predisposition to address issues of foreign policy. Those circumstances placed Bush in a difficult, almost "no-win," situation, subject to criticism and second-guessing regardless of the path he chose.

Secondary situations. Finally, presidents may find themselves facing a policy for which the presumption of initiative rests elsewhere. These policy areas generally do not warrant the president's personal attention. Most "iron triangle" policy issues exist in this type of situation. Responsibility for making policy rests with a decentralized policy process, and presidents constitute an unwelcome intrusion. Generally, presidents tread in these policies at their own risk. Only occasionally, as Reagan's program of broad-ranging budget cuts showed in 1981, can presidents take on iron triangles and build coalitions that thwart existing power structures. And as the Reagan experience demonstrates, even his successes were only temporary, as budget making returned to normal in most iron triangles after Reagan's first two years in office.[44]

Implications of situations. What can we learn from this framework for classifying leadership situations? Three points suggest themselves. First, most of the important action during a president's term will occur in the initiating and crisis situations. Presidents can put maintaining and secondary situations on the back burner and focus their attention on the other two. Second, policy issues are moving out of the maintaining and secondary situations and into the initiating situation. As a result presidents face increasingly demanding expectations. Finally, the coalition-building advantages of the crisis situation give presidents an incentive to try to interpret initiating situations as crisis situations.

President Clinton and the National Health Care Debate

President Clinton's efforts to pass comprehensive health care reforms through Congress provide a good case study for understanding presidential leadership as coalition building (also see James P. Pfiffner on national health care, chapter 9). The perspective of presidential leadership on health care reform through coalition building provides insights and facilitates our understanding of those events.[45]

Defining the Policy Situation

As both candidate and president, Bill Clinton pronounced the existence of a health care crisis. Through his first year in office, a majority of the public shared his views. This would have provided a context in which he, as the initiator, would be greatly advantaged.

However, opponents of comprehensive reform repeatedly challenged the president's characterization, and by mid-1994 Americans had rejected the crisis context by a two-to-one margin. This change clearly affected the dynamics of coalition building. Members of Congress felt little constituency pressure to act, and so had no incentive to sign on early to the president's proposals. The slow pace also gave Clinton's congressional and interest group opponents time to organize and critique his proposals. Thus, the context reverted from the crisis to the less-pressing initiating situation. Clinton was expected to lead, but the rest of the political system now felt little obligation to follow. As a result, his prospects for success were greatly diminished.

Building a Coalition for Health Care Reform

The elite component. Once in office, Clinton created a task force headed by First Lady Hillary Rodham Clinton. Early on, it focused on the substance of health care policy. At this stage, Clinton was creating the elite component of his coalition. A wide variety of alternatives had support within the administration, ranging from decentralized, private, market-driven reforms to a centralized, top-down, government-controlled system. In the end, Clinton's plan tried to achieve a middle ground—not by adopting a single, moderate approach, but by incorporating elements that appealed both to market-oriented conservatives and to liberals who preferred government controls. The corporate nature of the presidency in both the policy formulation and persuasion processes was strongly evident. Although Clinton would get the blame or credit for the fate of health care reform, it was clear that the success or failure of reform would hinge not just on the president, but on the entire presidency.

The intermediate groups. Clinton's reforms, promised for the spring of 1993, were not delivered until September. Moreover, the White House did remarkably little to attract coalition partners following the plan's introduction. The White House appeared to believe that "high public support for their goal of universal coverage would help ensure their success on Capitol Hill." [46] By July 1994, observers concluded that the White House had "pretty much blown it" in building support for the plan, though they still gave the president a chance to pull out a win in the final stages of the process. [47]

The difficulty of that task was reflected in the range of conflicting views found within the interest group community as well as in the depth of opposition the president's plan engendered. Interest groups did not align themselves into a few monolithic groups. Instead, they were "fragmented and idiosyncratic ... a kaleidoscope of narrowly focused coalitions." [48] The seriousness of the threat that some groups perceived in the president's plan raised further obstacles to its success. For example, the Health Insurance

Association of America, which represented small health insurance companies, spent $15 million to defeat the plan.

The president's task was also made more difficult by the range of alternatives (six to ten) being considered by Congress, and by the complicated and decentralized nature of the legislative process from which any reform would eventually emerge. Various parts of the president's plan, for example, were reviewed by ten different House committees. In such a decentralized setting, and in the absence of committed support and cooperation from the House and Senate party and committee leaders, there were more issues to address and coalition partners to satisfy than the White House could handle. The approaching midterm elections solidified Republican resolve to resist compromise, which further complicated the president's task.

The mass public. Despite the six-month delay in presenting a plan, the public was initially disposed to support Clinton's proposal. In the days following his speech introducing the plan, support for the president's reforms stood at 59 percent. However, support waned when opponents of the plan argued that it would create massive federal bureaucracies and impose limits on patients' ability to choose their own physicians. By May of 1994, a majority of Americans said they opposed Clinton's plan.

Last-Minute White House Adaptations

The refusal of potential coalition partners to join with Clinton signaled their desire that the president change his proposals. Clinton responded by watering down his commitment to universal health care and by endorsing two moderate initiatives that already had substantial support—the Mitchell plan in the Senate and the Gephardt plan in the House.

As the time for voting drew near, Clinton stepped up his coalition-building efforts. He enlisted support at the intermediary group coalition level among interest groups like the American Association for Retired Persons, the National Council of La Raza, the National Education Association, and the National Governors' Association. He also appealed to the mass public, participating, for example, in campaign-like health care bus caravans. He and his staff made extensive use of the mass media and contacted individual members of Congress, seeking their support for at least parts of the proposal.

Ultimately, however, the president failed. The growing risk of voter dissatisfaction with the costs and constraints of reform as well as clear interest group opposition deterred Democrats from rallying to the president. Republicans, who felt they could enhance their prospects for electoral success in November by handing the president a defeat on this high-priority agenda item, backed away from every presidential concession. The 103d Congress ended without passing any version of health care reform.

Presidential Leadership and the 1994 Elections

The 1994 midterm elections fundamentally shifted the balance of power between Democrats and Republicans, and between the presidency and Congress. Voters gave Republicans control of Congress for the first time in forty years. What can the coalition-building perspective tell us about why these changes occurred and what effects they are likely to have? A review of events at the elite, intermediate, and mass public coalition levels suggests the following.

In many respects, Clinton's problems originated in the elite level of his governing coalition. His administration was disorganized, lacked focus, and exhibited poor discipline.[49] These problems muddied his message and created an image of indecision. The administration proposed comprehensive reforms featuring federal controls over the health care system. It then allowed opponents to portray the plan as a new federal bureaucracy. This led the public to view Clinton as a politician who talked like a moderate but relied on traditional Democratic programs that expanded the size of government. The White House clearly failed Clinton in his efforts to fulfill his electoral pledge to govern as a "new style" Democrat.

Coalition building at the intermediate group level was complicated by the mass media. Both legitimate and tabloid media outlets rehashed allegations of Clinton's personal indiscretions and characterized his administration's attempts to balance competing demands as vacillation and a lack of principles. The press's portrayal of Clinton as indecisive and unprincipled undercut his efforts to rally group and mass support.

Finally, the elections revealed important changes in the mass public. Support for the Republican party grew dramatically in the South, and an anxious middle class found the Republican promises of social order and economic prosperity appealing. As a result, not a single incumbent Republican lost a congressional race, and the party achieved majority status in both houses. It is too early to tell whether this election signals a realignment, but Republicans took a substantial step in that direction.

Clinton's subsequent coalition-building strategy clearly reflected his reaction to these changes. At each level of coalitions, Clinton attempted to portray himself in more moderate terms. Within his administration, he signaled a move to the center by firing his controversial surgeon general, Joycelyn Elders. His appeals to Congress prominently featured calls for bipartisanship and a rejection of "politics as usual." He also shifted from talking about what he wanted Congress to do, to talking about what he promised to prevent Congress from doing (for example, repealing the ban on assault weapons or transforming funds earmarked for hiring additional local police into block grants). Finally, early attempts to create a new centerpiece for the Clinton presidency focused on a "Middle-Class Bill of Rights," in a clear attempt to appeal for moderate voters who had deserted him for Republicans in 1994. At every level Clinton's coalition-building efforts refocused toward creating a moderate base of support that would enable him to succeed with Congress and win reelection in 1996.

Conclusions

The demands placed upon presidents have clearly increased and accumulated over the past half-century. The number of policy issues that presidents are expected to address are increasing, the public's expectations are more demanding, and the problems are more intractable. More and more issues are moving into the presidents' initiating situations.

The environment in which presidents must construct their coalitions is changing, to the presidents' detriment. The large proto-coalitions that once filled the national scene have been replaced by a plethora of single-issue interest groups and egocentric members of Congress. Anthony King's admonitions about trying to "build coalitions in the sands" seem increasingly apt.[50]

To help cope with this trend, presidents have expanded the resources available to them, especially the size and complexity of the White House staff. In the face of weakened political parties, to provide the connective links that would hold a governing coalition together, presidents have developed their personal staffs as surrogates. These staffs function to develop agendas and to create and maintain coalitions on the president's behalf. However, this expansion in the size of the presidency is not the same thing as a growth in unilateral presidential powers. Presidents still exist in what Charles Jones refers to as "a separated system," depending on the cooperation of others to enact their own preferences.[51]

The other tool likely to tempt presidents in the future is the strategy of declaring the existence of a crisis. When the public is persuaded that a crisis exists, presidents can provide real leadership, as the government and interest groups become more willing to follow the president. As a result, presidents have an incentive to portray those areas in which they choose to seek important policy change as crises, because crises increase their ability to engender "followership" among others, and so successfully build coalitions. The risk, of course, is that presidents will cry wolf too often and lose their credibility. Presidents must be circumspect in their use of this strategy, or otherwise it will lose its effectiveness.

Notes

We wish to express our appreciation for the helpful comments and suggestions offered by several colleagues, especially Alexander George and Fred Greenstein.

1. George C. Edwards III, *At the Margins: Presidential Leadership of Congress* (New Haven: Yale University Press, 1989), 4, 5.

2. Ibid., 5. While we concur with Edwards in his depiction of presidents as facilitators, we take exception to his minimalist implication that presidents function only "at the margins."

3. Paul Brace and Barbara Hinckley, *Follow the Leader: Opinion Polls and the Modern Presidents* (New York: Basic Books, 1993), x.

4. David M. Kennedy, *Over Here: The First World War and American Society* (New York: Oxford University Press, 1980), 97.

5. Richard L. McCormick, "The Discovery That Business Corrupts Politics: A Reappraisal of the Origins of Progressivism," *American Historical Review* 86 (1981): 247–274.

6. Richard J. Hofstadter, *The Age of Reform* (New York: Alfred A. Knopf, 1977), 232.

7. Barry D. Karl, *Charles E. Merriam and the Study of Politics* (Chicago: University of Chicago Press, 1974), 17.

8. Lester G. Seligman and Cary R. Covington, *The Coalitional Presidency* (Pacific Grove, Calif.: Brooks/Cole, 1989).

9. See, for example, Sidney M. Milkis, *The President and the Parties: The Transformation of the American Party System Since the New Deal* (New York: Oxford University Press, 1993); and Nelson W. Polsby, *Consequences of Party Reform* (New York: Oxford University Press, 1983).

10. Of course, we do not intend to draw too dramatic a distinction between pre- and post-1970s presidential elections. Any imposed threshold is necessarily arbitrary and therefore somewhat misleading. The changes that manifested themselves in the 1970s and beyond had roots that extended back at least to Franklin Roosevelt's presidency. Nonetheless, given the confluence of party changes with other changes in the political environment, it is useful to consider the onset of the widespread use of primaries as a turning point in the manner in which presidential candidates get elected, and also in the manner in which presidents seek to lead once in office.

11. Morris P. Fiorina, "The Presidency and Congress: An Electoral Connection?" in *The Presidency and the Political System*, 3d ed., ed. Michael Nelson (Washington, D.C.: CQ Press, 1990), 443–470.

12. Kenneth Prewitt and William McAllister, "Changes in the American Executive Elite, 1930–1970," in *Elite Recruitment in Democratic Politics*, ed. Heinz Eulau and Moshe Czudnowski (New York: John Wiley and Sons, 1976), 105–132.

13. James Fallows, "The Presidency and the Press," in *The Presidency and the Political System*, 3d ed., ed. Michael Nelson (Washington, D.C.: CQ Press, 1990), 315–334.

14. Thomas E. Patterson, *Out of Order* (New York: Vintage Books, 1994).

15. Mark Hertsgaard, *On Bended Knee: The Press and the Reagan Presidency* (New York: Schocken Books, 1989).

16. Michael B. Grossman and Martha J. Kumar, *Portraying the President: The White House and the News Media* (Baltimore: Johns Hopkins University Press, 1981), 316.

17. Ibid., 315.

18. Jeffrey M. Berry, *The Interest Group Society*, 2d ed. (New York: HarperCollins, 1989), 121.

19. Hugh Heclo, "Issue Networks and the Executive Establishment," in *The New American Political System*, ed. Anthony King (Washington, D.C.: American Enterprise Institute for Public Policy Research, 1978), 88.

20. David M. Ricci, *The Transformation of American Politics* (New Haven: Yale University Press, 1993).

21. John P. Heinz et al., *The Hollow Core: Private Interests in National Policy Making* (Cambridge: Harvard University Press, 1993).

22. Kay L. Schlozman, review of *The Hollow Core: Private Interests in National Policy Making*, by John P. Heinz et al., *American Political Science Review* 88 (June 1994): 475–476.

23. Quoted in John W. Moore, "Going to Extremes, Losing the Center," *National Jour-*

nal, June 18, 1994, 1395–1398.

24. Moore, "Going to Extremes," 1395.

25. Ibid., 1396.

26. Thomas Mann quoted in Moore, "Going to Extremes," 1396.

27. See Samuel Kernell, *Going Public: New Strategies of Presidential Leadership,* 2d ed. (Washington, D.C.: CQ Press, 1993), esp. chap. 2.

28. See, for example, Lawrence C. Dodd and Bruce I. Oppenheimer, "Consolidating Power in the House: The Rise of a New Oligarchy," in *Congress Reconsidered,* 4th ed., ed. Lawrence C. Dodd and Bruce I. Oppenheimer (Washington, D.C.: Congressional Quarterly Inc., 1989); and Kenneth Shepsle, "The Changing Textbook Congress," in *Can the Government Govern?* ed. John E. Chubb and Paul E. Peterson (Washington, D.C.: Brookings Institution, 1989), 250–262.

29. Kernell, *Going Public.*

30. Quoted in Bert Solomon, "Do We Ask Too Much of Presidents?" *National Journal,* June 18, 1994, 1390–1393.

31. Quoted in Solomon, "Do We Ask Too Much of Presidents?" 1391.

32. Solomon, "Do We Ask Too Much of Presidents?" 1391.

33. For a good overview of this approach, see Ronald Heifetz, *Leadership Without Easy Answers* (Cambridge: Harvard University Press, 1994), chap. 1. In addition, Linda Fowler's *Candidates, Congress and the American Democracy* (Ann Arbor: University of Michigan Press, 1993) recognizes various approaches to leadership within the electoral context. A closer examination of this approach to leadership reveals further distinctions among avenues of inquiry. Some, for example, define leadership styles in terms of their roots in political theories (see David K. Nichols, *The Myth of the Modern Presidency* (University Park, Pa.: Penn State University Press, 1994)). Others view leader-follower relations through the perspective of the president's personality and cognitive style (see Erwin Hargrove, *Researching the Presidency: Vital Questions, New Approaches,* ed. George Edwards III, John Kessel, and Bert A. Rockman (Pittsburgh: University of Pittsburgh Press, 1993); and Alexander L. George, *Presidential Decisionmaking in Foreign Policy* (Boulder, Colo.: Westview Press, 1980)). Scholars such as William Riker have also begun to use a public choice perspective to examine the actions and incentives of leaders and followers. See William Riker, *The Theory of Political Coalitions* (New Haven: Yale University Press, 1962).

34. See, for example, Lester G. Seligman, "Leadership: Political Aspects," in *International Encyclopedia of the Social Sciences,* vol. 9, ed. David L. Sills (New York: The Macmillan Company and The Free Press, 1968); and Lester G. Seligman, "The Study of Leadership," *American Political Science Review* 44 (1950): 904–915.

35. David Held, *Models of Democracy* (Stanford, Calif.: Stanford University Press, 1987), chap. 7.

36. Kernell, *Going Public,* chap. 2.

37. Jeffrey K. Tulis, *The Rhetorical Presidency* (Princeton, N.J.: Princeton University Press, 1987).

38. Barbara Kellerman, *The Political Presidency: Practice of Leadership from Kennedy Through Reagan* (New York: Oxford University Press, 1984).

39. Brace and Hinckley, *Follow the Leader.*

40. Richard E. Neustadt, *Presidential Power and the Modern Presidents* (New York: The Free Press, 1990).

41. Richard E. Neustadt, "Presidency and Legislation: Planning the President's Program," *American Political Science Review* 49 (1955): 980–1021.

42. For a discussion of the impact of crisis situations on decision making, see Ole R. Holsti, "Theories of Crises of Decision Making," in *Diplomacy: New Approaches in History, Theory, and Policy,* ed. Paul G. Lauren (New York: The Free Press, 1976), 99–136.

43. William E. Leuchtenburg, *Franklin D. Roosevelt and the New Deal* (New York: Harper Torchbooks, 1963), 42–43.

44. Kernell, *Going Public,* chap. 5.
45. Unless otherwise indicated, the narrative account of Clinton's attempt to enact health care reform in 1993–1994 and the reactions of the public, Congress, and interest groups described in this section are based upon stories written by Julie Kosterlitz or William Schneider and published by *National Journal* during those two years.
46. William Schneider, "Political Pulse: Coverage for All Isn't Catching On," *National Journal,* July 9, 1994, 1654.
47. Bert Solomon, "Code Blue for Health Care Reform," *National Journal,* July 16, 1994, 1702.
48. Julie Kosterlitz, "Health: Stress Fractures," *National Journal,* February 19, 1994, 412.
49. See Elizabeth Drew, *On the Edge: The Clinton Presidency* (New York: Simon and Schuster, 1994); and Bob Woodward, *The Agenda: Inside the Clinton White House* (New York: Simon and Schuster, 1994).
50. Anthony King, "The American Polity in the Late 1970s: Building Coalitions in the Sand," in *The New American Political System,* ed. Anthony King (Washington, D.C.: American Enterprise Institute for Public Policy Research, 1978), 371–395.
51. Charles O. Jones, *The Presidency in a Separated System* (Washington, D.C.: Brookings Institution, 1994).

5

One Vote at a Time:
Building Presidential Coalitions in Congress

Leroy N. Rieselbach

Pondering the 1992 election returns, pundits predicted an end to "grid-lock," to divided government, and the start of a new effort to resolve the nation's most pressing policy problems. Controlling both the White House and Congress, the Democratic victors could confront crises in health care, crime, education, and a host of other matters. Such an optimistic forecast may well have misread contemporary political realities. The Constitution, lest we forget, empowers Congress, whose members are elected for fixed terms from single-member constituencies, to authorize and fund federal programs and to override the president's veto should he object to its policy choices.[1] President Clinton, like his predecessors, may have underestimated Congress's willingness to exploit its prerogatives; in any case, the new administration encountered a legislature loath to let its legitimate authority lapse.

The astonishing Republican seizure of Congress in the 1994 midterm election, which once again established divided government, underscores the point. The triumphant GOP majority moved forcefully to impose a new policy agenda: the Contract with America in the House and a more modest, but still substantially conservative, set of proposals in the Senate. These dramatic initiatives compelled the president to confront a Congress determined to enact its vision of a smaller, more efficient national government and to devolve large pieces of federal authority to the states. The veto, unused in the 103d Congress (1993–1995), became, of necessity, the administration's weapon of choice in the 104th. These revolutionary developments pose, once again, the issues of interbranch cooperation and conflict. Who is to lead: the executive or the legislature? How can the nation balance the need for action with the need to avoid precipitous change? This chapter takes up the matter of presidential leadership, with particular attention paid to President Clinton's efforts to enact the Democratic administration's program in the 103d Congress.

The Setting: The Constitution and Two Aphorisms

The Constitution and convention shape and constrain the president's capacity to lead Congress. The former, establishing, in Neustadt's classic formulation, "separate institutions sharing power," gives both the executive and legislative branches the authority and opportunity to influence the substance of public policy.[2] The latter, reflecting the evolution of practice over two centuries, defines the starting point for interbranch interaction. Two well-known aphorisms capture these basic truths. The Constitution offers the president and Congress "an invitation to struggle" over the content of government programs.[3] Convention suggests that "the president proposes and Congress disposes" of the executive's initiatives;[4] that is, the president, acting as "chief legislator," sets the nation's policy agenda and Congress reacts to it, sometimes kindly, sometimes with hostility.

The constitutional allocation of authority and the expectation of presidential leadership set the stage for executive-legislative conflict and cooperation. To enact the administration's program, the president must both propose attractive bills and work to convince Congress to enact them. More specifically, his task is to assemble majorities, to construct winning coalitions (most commonly, but not always, 218 votes in the House of Representatives and 51 in the Senate) to pass favored legislation or to block undesirable bills. This is no easy chore; the chief executive cannot command legislative obedience but rather must marshal an impressive but not unlimited array of resources in an effort to persuade Congress to comply with his policy requests.[5] Congress, of course, has ample resources of its own, particularly its authorization and appropriations powers, with which to resist presidential blandishments or to impose its own priorities on a reluctant executive. The president's authority, in short, rests on his "power to persuade," his capacity to elicit congressional support for the administration's program.[6]

The paradigmatic pattern of executive-legislative relations, then, reflecting the two aphorisms, is for the president to propose a policy agenda and seek to persuade Congress to dispose of it favorably. Each side brings substantial resources to the struggle, and the results vary widely from one issue to the next. Each matter is a separate contest where particular interests attempt to win the conflict or forge a consensus around an acceptable compromise. There is no guarantee that the president will attain his objectives in any given legislative battle.

Presidential leadership, moreover, must take account of a number of relatively fixed features. For one thing, the basic organizational structure of Congress changes only very slowly. This means that the chief executive must maneuver his proposals through a decentralized institution in which action may occur only after considerable exertion. Similarly, the president is powerless to alter the nature of the constituencies that send the members of Congress to Washington. The kinds of people who live in the states and districts change slowly. To the extent that legislators feel the need, which elections induce, to react to local sentiments, they may respond to constituency pressures and resist presidential entreaties. Finally, events—both foreign and domestic—lie beyond presidential control. The bombing of a federal installation in Oklahoma City, a Supreme Court decision overturning gun control legislation, strained trade relations with the nations of Europe and Asia, or unrest overseas (for example, in Bosnia) will tax the president's leadership skills as he attempts to take account of such events. Thus, the president will have to contend with forces that congressional structure, constituency considerations, and the flow of events generate— forces that lie outside his power to shape to any great degree. Passing his program will not be easy.

Who Wins the Struggle? Clinton Proposes and Congress Disposes in the 103d Congress

In many ways, the 103d Congress offered an ideal setting to test the possibilities and limits of presidential leadership of Congress. The 1992 election returned the Democrats to the White House, albeit with a modest plurality of the vote (43 percent) in a three-way race. The Clinton campaign offered a platform of change, to which the electorate seemed to respond positively. The Democrats retained a slightly reduced congressional majority, holding 256 House and 56 Senate seats. Moreover, the legislative party, energized by the restoration of one-party, unified government and a putative popular mandate, seemed committed to move ahead vigorously not only on the high-profile items of the Clinton agenda but also on the second-tier matters. Conditions seemed propitious for successful presidential leadership. The inability of the chief executive to forge winning congressional coalitions under these favorable circumstances cast doubt on his capacity to achieve his purposes in the less conducive conditions that obtained in the wake of the 1994 midterm elections.

Some Statistical Evidence

How well did the president do under these promising circumstances? It is instructive to look first at the aggregate evidence. The initial lesson to emerge from the statistics of the 103d Congress is that if he could get a vote on his favored proposals, Clinton stood a strong chance of winning. One gauge of Congress's independent impact is the extent to which it accepts or rejects the chief executive's initiatives. Lower levels of support for the president indicate that the lawmakers are prepared to block the administration's ideas or to modify them substantially. There has been wide variation, both between and within administrations, in legislative compliance, as the percentages of presidential victories in Table 5-1 demonstrate.

These data show that Clinton achieved a higher success rate than any of his immediate predecessors; the 103d Congress approved 86.4 percent of the measures the president supported. The figures also reveal that divided government, when one party occupies the presidency while the other controls at least one chamber of Congress, reduces presidential success.[7] Democratic presidents, including Clinton, with Democratic congressional majorities, fared better than GOP chief executives who faced a Congress in which the opposition controlled at least one chamber. Even the allegedly weak

Table 5-1   Legislative Success Rate by President, Eisenhower through Clinton, 1953–1994

President	Legislative Success Rate (percent)
Eisenhower (1953–1960)	72.2
Kennedy (1961–1963)	84.6
Johnson (1964–1968)	82.6
Nixon (1969–1974)	67.2
Ford (1974–1976)	57.6
Carter (1977–1980)	76.4
Reagan (1981–1988)	61.9
Bush (1989–1992)	51.6
Clinton (1993–1994)	86.4

Note: These percentages are the proportion of roll-call votes on which the president's announced position prevailed. The figures must be taken as approximations. For one thing, the president may ask for something that he knows Congress will not pass. Second, the legislature may alter a proposal to barely recognizable form, but if the president initially suggested it, he will get credit for its passage. Finally, a president's success ratio will reflect the degree of controversy surrounding the administration's program; success may be inflated if requests include numerous less important items.

Source: Norman J. Ornstein, Thomas E. Mann, and Michael J. Malbin, *Vital Statistics on Congress, 1995–1996* (Washington, D.C.: Congressional Quarterly Inc., 1996), 203–204.

leadership of Jimmy Carter secured a higher success rate (76.4 percent) than the most successful Republican president (Eisenhower, 72.2 percent).[8] Overall, then, Clinton won congressional approval of five out of every six of his requests in 1993 and 1994.

Second, the primary basis of the president's support on these roll calls was a strongly unified Democratic party. Clinton won the backing of the average Democrat on three-fourths of the House votes and five-sixths of the Senate ballots on which he expressed a preference (see Table 5-2, panel A). Moreover, he secured the votes of some Republicans, suggesting that on a few issues at least, he was able to assemble a bipartisan coalition. In 1993, the typical Republican voted with the president on 39 percent of the House roll calls; the average GOP senator backed him on 29 percent of these votes. A year later, the figures rose to 47 and 42 percent, respectively. The minority may have been less inclined to oppose the chief executive as the 1994 midterm elections approached. Clinton secured this support from across the aisle from Republicans representing the East and Midwest in particular; members from southern and western constituencies were somewhat less inclined to back him. Among his own partisans, the president received support in equal proportions across the regional spectrum (Table 5-2, panels B and C).[9]

Table 5-2   Presidential Support in the 103d Congress (percent)

A. By Party

	House	Senate
1993		
Democrats	77	87
Republicans	39	29
1994		
Democrats	75	86
Republicans	47	42

B. By Region: House

	East	West	South	Midwest
1993				
Democrats	76	78	78	74
Republicans	49	34	35	38
1994				
Democrats	74	77	75	73
Republicans	56	43	43	46

C. By Region: Senate

	East	West	South	Midwest
1993				
Democrats	92	86	82	87
Republicans	37	27	23	34
1994				
Democrats	87	88	84	85
Republicans	52	40	35	47

Note: Each number is the percentage of the time the average member voted in accord with the announced position of the president.

Source: Congressional Quarterly Weekly Report, "Guide to CQ's Voting Analyses," December 31, 1994, 3651–3678, at 3654.

Third, turning to specific issues, Clinton compiled a mixed but generally positive record on his most significant initiatives. On many major matters, particularly in the House, he was able to get sufficient backing from Democrats alone to pass his preferred bills; on others, he was forced to rely on Republican votes (Tables 5-3, 5-4, and 5-5). Of twenty high-priority bills, Clinton managed to get the House and Senate to vote on fourteen, and eleven became law; six others failed without getting a roll call in one or both chambers.[10]

Looking first to the House, it is obvious that the chamber leaders—Speaker Thomas Foley, D-Wash., and his team—though much maligned "inside the Beltway," managed to provide the president with the votes needed to move the administration's agenda forward. Seventeen of the twenty priority items cleared the House: eleven became law (Table 5-3); three passed the House, but were voted down in the Senate (Table 5-5, panels A

Table 5-3   Coalition Building in the 103d Congress: Clinton Victories (House)

	Votes for "Win" [a]	Dem. Votes	Dem. "Surplus"	Rep. Votes
National service (conf. report) [b]	214	248	+34	26
California desert protection (prev. question) [c]	213	241	+28	4
Balanced budget amendment	142	153	+11	1
Family leave	215	224	+9	40
Goals 2000 (recommittal) [d]	214	223	+9	8
Deficit reduction (conf. report)	218	218	0	0
Abortion clinic access (conf. report)	208	200	−8	17
Anti-crime bill (rule: conf. report) [e]	215	196	−19	42
Brady bill (recommittal)	215	191	−24	37
GATT	218	167	−51	121
NAFTA	218	102	−116	132

[a] "Votes for 'Win'" is the number of votes needed for victory, given the number of members voting.

[b] A conference report is a document prepared by a joint House-Senate conference committee to resolve interchamber differences on a particular bill. Both the House and Senate must accept the report for the bill to pass.

[c] A previous question motion ends debate, precludes additional amendments, and brings a bill to a vote. It is nondebatable.

[d] A recommittal, or motion to recommit, is a procedure that returns a bill to the committee that originally considered it; if adopted, the recommittal usually kills the bill.

[e] A rule is a resolution reported by the House Rules Committee that defines the terms and conditions for floor consideration of legislation. Failure to pass the rule delays or defeats the bill.

Source: Compiled from 1993 and 1994 issues of *Congressional Quarterly Weekly Report.*

and B); three others—telecommunications legislation, safe drinking water act amendments, and mining law reform—won in the House but died without a direct vote in the Senate (Table 5-5, panel C). Sixteen of the bills that the House enacted received roll-call votes and eleven of these would have passed without a single Republican vote. Some votes were exceedingly close. In a widely reported case, Marjorie Margolies-Mezvinsky, D-Pa., cast the decisive 218th vote that ensured the adoption of the conference report on the administration's deficit reduction package (Table 5-3);[11] in two votes on lobby disclosure legislation, Independent Bernard Sanders, of Vermont, cast the critical ballot (Table 5-5, panel A). On the other five roll calls, Republican support put the Clinton proposals over the top. In the extreme case, on the North American Free Trade Agreement, the Democrats came up 116 votes short, but were saved by the backing of 132 Republicans.

On the Senate side, the picture was about the same, although the president's success rate was lower. He secured passage of eleven of the bills that the House had passed (Table 5-4). Of those, six victories required no Republican votes. The remaining five wins depended on GOP support:

Table 5-4   Coalition Building in the 103d Congress: Clinton Victories (Senate)

	Votes for "Win" [a]	Dem. Votes	Dem. "Surplus"	Rep. Votes
Family leave	51	55	+4	16
California desert protection	51	53	+2	16
Abortion clinic access (conf. report)	51	52	+1	17
Deficit reduction (conf. report)	51	51[b]	0	0
National service (conf. report)	51	51	0	6
Balanced budget amendment	34	34	0	3
Brady bill	51	47	−4	16
Anti-crime bill (cloture) [c]	60	54	−6	7
Goals 2000 (cloture)	60	53	−7	9
GATT (budget waiver) [d]	60	37	−23	31
NAFTA	51	27	−24	34

[a] "Votes for 'Win' " is the number of votes needed for victory, given the number of members voting.

[b] Vice President Albert Gore cast the decisive tie-breaking vote.

[c] Cloture limits further consideration of a pending proposal in order to end a filibuster.

[d] A waiver eliminates procedural obstacles to a bill's passage by suspending points of order that might be raised against the measure. A point of order is an objection to an alleged violation of a rule.

Source: Compiled from 1993 and 1994 issues of *Congressional Quarterly Weekly Report.*

Republicans provided 7 votes to invoke cloture and end debate on the anti-crime bill and 34 votes to pass NAFTA. On the negative side, the president lost on nine occasions. On three measures—an economic stimulus package, reform of campaign finance, and regulation of lobbyists—the Democrats were unable to secure the 60 votes necessary to end late-in-the-session fili-busters (Table 5-5, panel B).

Overall, the president won on eleven of the twenty key issues.[12] Five victories needed no Republican help in either chamber; two required GOP votes in one house; and four passed only with bipartisan backing in both House and Senate. The implication of these aggregate figures is that the president can, at least in circumstances of unified government, use the avail-able resources to win a significant number of his public policy struggles with Congress. An assessment of the ways the chief executive, Clinton in the pre-sent case, uses those resources to build successful congressional coalitions in support of his proposals requires a closer look at the details of campaigns to pass specific pieces of legislation.

Some Case Studies

Examination of specific cases demonstrates that each piece of legisla-tion necessitates a carefully tailored coalition-building effort. The president

Table 5-5   Coalition Building in the 103d Congress: Clinton Losses

	Votes for "Win" [a]	Dem. Votes	Dem. "Surplus"	Rep. Votes
A. House				
Economic stimulus package	213	231	+18	3
Campaign finance (rule)	214	216	+2	3
Lobby disclosure (rule: passage)	212	211	−1 [b]	9
Lobby disclosure				
(rule: conf. report)	211	210	−1 [b]	5
B. Senate				
Economic stimulus package				
(cloture)	60	56	−4	0
Campaign finance				
(cloture: passage)	60	55	−5	7
Campaign finance				
(cloture: conf. report)	60	51	−9	6
Lobby disclosure (cloture)	60	46	−14	9
C. No direct votes (Senate)				
Gays in the military				
Health care reform				
Superfund renewal				
Telecommunications reform				
Safe drinking water				
Mining law reform				

[a] "Votes for 'Win' " is the number of votes needed for victory, given the number of members voting.
[b] Independent Bernard Sanders, of Vermont, voted with the Democrats on the lobby disclosure bill.
Source: Compiled from 1993 and 1994 issues of *Congressional Quarterly Weekly Report.*

must employ his resources in appropriate ways to win votes for his proposals. He needs to discover which members of Congress support him and which do not; he must shore up the backing of the former and, if he still lacks the requisite votes, he must induce those on the fence or convert those opposed to take his side. Some campaigns will be relatively easy, requiring only a minimal effort. Others will be fraught with peril and demand an all-out struggle. Still others will be lost regardless of the time and energy committed to them.

The Clinton administration's record in the 103d Congress illustrates the fundamental distinctiveness of individual campaigns for particular bills. The Family and Medical Leave Act, which allowed employees to take unpaid leave from their jobs to attend family members, for example, was enacted without major controversy.[13] With Clinton publicly committed to sign the bill, both the House and Senate passed it easily, and the former accepted the latter's changes, obviating the need for a conference and clearing the bill for the president.

The administration also pursued a party-based coalition-building strategy on its deficit reduction (reconciliation) package, but this time there was far less margin for error.[14] The Republican minority was unanimously opposed; some conservative Democrats dissented on the grounds that the bill did not cut the deficit sufficiently, and the Congressional Black Caucus protested that social programs were scaled back excessively. In the House, the bill passed, 219–213, without a single Republican vote and in the face of defections from thirty-eight Democrats. To secure the narrow victory, Clinton "worked the phones incessantly," Vice President Gore lobbied face-to-face out of his Senate office, and cabinet members made "repeated phone calls" to members. Clinton made substantive concessions; he promised to add entitlement program cuts to the Senate version. The administration was prepared to use the "stick" as well as inducements. It "threatened some senior members with loss of their committee or subcommittee chairmanships" if they voted against the bill. Agriculture Secretary Mike Espy warned three California Democrats that he would cancel scheduled meetings with constituents in their districts (only one of the three voted for the bill). These efforts enabled the president to eke out a six-vote victory.

The Democrats' partisan go-it-alone strategy was equally precarious in the Senate. Disdaining compromise with the Republican minority (and thus getting no GOP votes), the majority was hard put to pass the bill. It held its defections to seven only after the president pledged to renegotiate several hotly contested items in conference, and even then the bill carried 50–49 on a tie-breaking vote by Vice President Gore.

To win approval of the conference report was no simpler. In the House, Democratic leaders "cut a variety of deals to win votes." Their bill preserved social programs and thus mollified the Black Caucus. They agreed to allow two floor amendments to cut additional spending and supported Clinton's promise to propose further expenditure reductions later in the year. Representative Margolies-Mezvinsky provided the critical vote after winning a commitment from the president to hold a conference in her district on cutting entitlement spending. The administration survived 41 Democratic "no" votes to win acceptance of the report, 218–216. In the Senate, the leadership, with no votes to spare, redoubled its efforts when David Boren, D-Okla., who had voted for passage, announced his opposition to the conference report. They "redrafted or removed more than 100 provisions" to consolidate support. They prevailed, 51–50 (without a Republican vote), when Dennis DeConcini, D-Ariz., reversed his earlier position to vote "aye," creating a tie that the vice president broke in the administration's favor. "Both my arms feel twisted," DeConcini said, but he won a provision cutting back a tax increase that his upper-income retiree constituents would have to pay.

On some issues, relying on Democrats alone was infeasible. There were too many fissures within party ranks on an anti-crime package, and a bipartisan coalition-building strategy was the president's only recourse.[15] In general, controversy surrounded both the sums to be spent and the allocation of the funds between prevention (for example, education) and punishment (more police, for instance). More specifically, the administration proposed to ban nineteen types of automatic assault weapons frequently used by criminals. The National Rifle Association (NRA) asserted that the ban infringed on Americans' Second Amendment "right to bear arms," and lobbied extensively against the provision. The Congressional Black Caucus demanded inclusion of a "racial justice" title authorizing the courts to use statistics to demonstrate the unfairness of death penalty sentencing. Republicans pushed for an item reducing the use of habeas corpus provisions to appeal and delay endlessly the imposition of the death penalty. Polls revealed that the public demanded action against crime, giving both branches an incentive to pass some legislation.

The Senate acted first: a "two-week tougher-than-thou" bidding war produced a bill with an acceptable allocation of funds between prevention and punishment and a ban on assault weapons. The limitation of the use of habeas corpus appeals to delay executions was abandoned. Republican votes provided the margins for the weapons ban and the deletion of the habeas corpus provision. The compromise passed easily, 95–4.

The going in the House was much rougher. The 285–141 passage belied considerable controversy. The Black Caucus was split, even after the racial justice provisions were narrowly retained, 217–212. The habeas corpus provisions were dropped, and the bill contained no assault weapons ban. The Republican motion to recommit failed, 192–235, with only 4 GOP votes against it; 65 Republicans eventually supported passage.[16] In a surprising development, the House subsequently enacted the assault weapons ban as separate legislation. The administration played a major role in producing a two-vote, 216–214, margin for the ban. Clinton "called dozens of members, as did Attorney General Janet Reno," relying on "moral persuasion" rather than conventional horse-trading. Ex-presidents Jimmy Carter, Gerald Ford, and Ronald Reagan endorsed the bill. Only 4 Republicans supported the rule governing floor consideration of the measure, but when the roll was called for final passage, 38 Republicans, including Robert Michel, of Illinois, the party leader, supported it, perhaps unwilling to let the president claim full credit for a popular piece of legislation. Thirty members who had opposed a similar ban in 1991 reversed themselves and voted for it in 1994 (only 5 of them received NRA support). Freshman members, perhaps in tune with citizen sentiment, backed the ban, 64–51.

Securing approval of the conference report was even more contentious. The administration suffered an embarrassing and almost fatal defeat when the House rejected the rule for consideration of the report (overall, 58 Democrats opposed the rule).[17] The administration lobbied the Republicans "intensely," but the GOP made crime a party issue—the bill spent too much on social programs aimed at prevention and too little on law enforcement—and only 11 of their number voted for the rule, which lost 210–225. Unable to convince enough Democrats to switch, the administration cut a deal with the Republicans. While insisting on retaining the ban on automatic weapons, the president agreed to reduce spending by $3.2 billion, most of it from the prevention side of the ledger. He accepted several other changes as well; for instance, the compromise called for the states to track sex offenders and notify local communities to which they moved. GOP moderates were reluctant to scuttle a popular measure; 42 of them voted for a revised rule (which passed, 239–189) and 46 joined 188 Democrats (64 Democrats deserted the president) to approve the conference report, 235–195. Republican moderates enabled the president to prevail in the Senate as well. After negotiations between Majority Leader George Mitchell, D-Maine, and Minority Leader Robert Dole, R-Kan., failed to produce an acceptable compromise, the GOP moderates cast their lot with the Democrats. Six voted (with 55 Democrats) to provide the three-fifths' majority needed to waive a budgetary point of order against the bill, and 7 supported both cloture to end the debate and final passage of the conference report.

In extreme cases, such as the North American Free Trade Agreement with Mexico and Canada, the president secured a victory with greater support from the minority in Congress than from his own party.[18] On NAFTA, the administration needed only a single victory; the agreement was considered under "fast-track" procedures that allowed only one up-or-down vote on the text of the compact. On the other hand, there was massive opposition within Democratic ranks, particularly in the House. The labor movement, fearful of a huge loss of jobs to Mexico where wages were low, and environmentalists, worried that the pact would erode conservation efforts along the U.S.-Mexican border, strenuously opposed the agreement. The Republicans were divided as well. The bulk of the minority members, a "free trade" bloc, supported the agreement—originally negotiated during the Republican Bush administration—but a conservative faction was concerned that American commitment to specific dispute resolution procedures might cede the nation's sovereignty to an unfriendly international organization. Initially, the administration's prospects seemed bleak. Only one of the three House committees (Ways and Means, chaired by party loyalist Dan Rostenkowski) with jurisdiction over NAFTA reported it favorably. Worse still, the top House Democratic leaders—Majority Leader Richard Gephardt, of Missouri, and Majority Whip David Bonior, of Michigan—declined to support Clinton. To gain acceptance of the agreement would be "a come from behind victory of impressive proportions." Yet many members seemed willing to listen to the president. "Right now my vote is no," said Rep. Tom Lewis, R-Fla., "but the door's ajar."

Clinton orchestrated a major coalition-building campaign, featuring a "barrage of deal cutting" and considerable "arm twisting." He singled out some groups for special attention. "Many deals were struck to help farmers...": the administration won over nine members of the Florida delegation with arrangements to "help the state's citrus, sugar, and vegetable growers." Ten members from textile states responded to a promise to extend the phase-out of import quotas from ten to fifteen years by backing the agreement. The president also worked on individual members. When the dust from these and other arrangements settled, NAFTA triumphed, 234 (132 Republicans, 102 Democrats) to 200 in the House, and 61 (34 Republicans, 27 Democrats) to 27 in the Senate.

If a president's skillful efforts, sometimes modest, often extensive, can regularly succeed, there remain instances when the legislative terrain is so hostile that the struggle for congressional backing seems fated to fail. The Clinton administration was unable to forge winning coalitions in a number of such circumstances, to which its own shortcomings contributed, in the 103d Congress. In three instances, presidential programs, deftly steered through a House mine field, fell before the withering fire of a Senate filibuster. The president's economic stimulus package (fiscal 1993 supplemental appropriations bill) was one such defeat.[19] The Clinton proposals for "investment in America" did not generate an expected "groundswell of public support." The administration expected its 56–vote majority to prevail and was caught unprepared by a Republican filibuster. Clinton pursued the partisan strategy, typical of 1993, and refused to negotiate; he rejected a compromise offered by three middle-of-the-road Democrats. West Virginia Democrat Robert Byrd's use of obscure parliamentary procedures to preclude Republican amendments hardened the opposition. Three cloture votes fell short of the 60 votes needed to end debate. The bill was then rewritten to cut spending by one-fourth, but the minority would have none of it. A fourth cloture motion won only 56 votes, all from Democrats, and the bill was abandoned.

Campaign finance reform, a major 1992 Clinton campaign pledge, met a similar fate.[20] Both chambers enacted reform legislation in 1993, but no effort to convene a conference ensued until late in the 1994 session. Although a tentative House-Senate agreement on the ticklish issue of political action committee contributions was on the table, the Republican Senate minority chose to filibuster a motion to proceed to conference; the strategy was to deny the Clinton administration a legislative victory to trumpet in the upcoming midterm elections. At the same time, "many Democrats," for obvious electoral reasons, opposed limits on contributions or campaign spending. In the end, 4 Senate GOP moderates and 6 Democrats refused to support a cloture motion, which garnered only 52 of the needed 60 votes, and the reform bill died.[21] Though billed as a "top priority," the administration did not seem to do much to round up support for the measure.[22]

If these measures got more lip service than serious persuasive effort from the president, health care was an entirely different story.[23] The issue was important in the 1992 Clinton-Bush campaign. The challenger promised a comprehensive reform bill within one hundred days of his inauguration. Eventually, well past the self-imposed deadline, the administration sent Congress a massive 1,342–page bill that truly boggled the mind (see James P. Pfiffner, chapter 9, for details of the plan). The public found the bill incomprehensible; a widely broadcast series of TV ads, featuring an ordinary couple, "Harry and Louise," played on public doubts and fear of unpredictable reform. Those affected—health care providers, insurance companies, employers—all found objectionable features in the proposal. The question quickly became mired in controversy.

Five congressional committees—three in the House, two in the Senate—took up the confusing and contentious health care issue. Nothing remotely resembling consensus ever emerged, despite substantial prodding by the Clinton administration. Two years of sustained effort failed to make any headway on the health care question.

Congress also rejected another high priority Clinton campaign pledge, a promise to improve the lot of gays in the military.[24] Candidate Clinton vowed to end discrimination against homosexuals serving in the armed forces, but his proposals to do so ran into heavy seas. Public opinion was clearly hostile, the military resisted changing the policy in place, and social conservatives of both parties in Congress were unsympathetic to the president's initiative. In the end, Clinton not only failed to get a vote on his proposals, but also the existing "longtime ban on homosexual conduct" was written into law "with only slight modifications" in the 1994 defense authorization bill. Observers proclaimed the affair a major setback for the president.

Summary

The foregoing aggregate and case analyses strongly suggest that the conventional wisdom contains considerable truth, at least under the unified government that prevailed in the 103d Congress. Bill Clinton sent the legislature an extensive program, adeptly applied his persuasive resources in some instances, and through his coalition-building efforts won some significant victories. His party provided the needed votes in some cases; in others, Republican votes were essential. Congress, for its part, exercised its independence, negotiating some compromises that modified administration initiatives and rejecting some programs outright. The policy process, in short, worked in the expected fashion: each branch could justifiably claim credit for the programmatic accomplishments of 1993–1995.

Cooperation and Conflict: From the 103d to the 104th Congress

The traditional aphorisms seem appropriate to describe the relationships between the executive and legislative branches in the 103d Congress. Accepting the constitutional invitation to struggle, Bill Clinton proposed an extensive agenda; Congress disposed of its items, sometimes to the president's satisfaction, sometimes to his extreme displeasure. Politics, conducted "as usual," produced the ordinary mix of policy outcomes, reflecting the complex interbranch bargaining, compromise, and coalition building typical of the way Washington ordinarily conducts the nation's business.

The 104th Congress (1995–1997), however, remarkable in many ways, offers the opportunity to assess the continuing applicability of the accepted aphorisms. In the 1994 midterm elections, the Republicans, with their Contract with America, succeeded in overcoming the "all politics is local" orientation of the majority Democrats, making the election a referendum on the performance of the Clinton administration. Their striking seizure of Congress was widely viewed as a mandate for the bold policy changes the contract offered the voters. In sharp contrast to the usual "member individualism," rooted in the electoral safety of incumbents, the 73 House and 11 Senate Republican freshmen, many avid conservatives, displayed unprecedented party loyalty. They voted cohesively for many elements of the contract, which provided them with a clearly articulated alternative agenda to that of the president. The Senate was somewhat less ideological than the House; moderate Republican senators were less inclined to abandon their policy independence. Nonetheless, to an unusual degree, congressional lawmaking in the first year of the 104th Congress revolved around the Republicans' aggressive pursuit of their own rather than presidential proposals. The new majority, especially in the House, seemed singularly determined to reform welfare, balance the budget, and shrink the size and scope of the federal government.

Two broad scenarios seem plausible in the late 1990s. The first envisions permanent change. A forceful majority would continue, like the GOP in the early days of the 104th Congress, to eschew pragmatism and to insist on its own agenda. The legislature would propose and enact its preferred programs, leaving it to the president to dispose of, to react to, congressional initiatives. This sort of outcome would move the policy process in the direction of a "responsible party system," where a disciplined majority in Congress would pass its program subject to voter approval or rejection in the next election.[25] Alternatively, the old order might reappear. Members, concerned about keeping their seats, would assert their autonomy to vote consistently with constituent sentiments even if that meant abandoning ideological purity or throwing over the party traces. The familiar process of coalition building through negotiation and compromise would resurface to produce, most often, incremental rather than boldly innovative policy making.

The responsible parties outcome would radically reduce the capacity of the president (Republican or Democratic) to shape legislation to his liking. A return to the status quo ante would permit the president to struggle to win congressional concurrence with his preferences, a battle with continually uncertain prospects. In either case, the president's road will be an uphill climb; Congress will remain a formidable obstacle in his path to policy leadership.[26]

Notes

1. For stylistic convenience, and because to date all presidents have been men, I use the masculine pronoun throughout without pejorative intent.

2. Richard E. Neustadt, *Presidential Power and the Modern Presidents: The Politics of Leadership from Roosevelt to Reagan* (New York: The Free Press, 1990), 29.
3. Edward S. Corwin, *The President: Office and Powers* (New York: New York University Press, 1957), 208.
4. Robert A. Dahl, *Congress and Foreign Policy* (New York: Harcourt, Brace and World, 1950), 58.
5. Neustadt, *Presidential Power.*
6. For more on the context of interbranch collaboration and conflict, see chapter 1 of this volume. The literature on the president and presidential leadership generally is extensive. Neustadt's *Presidential Power* (first published in 1960) remains the starting point. See also, inter alia, Bert A. Rockman, *The Leadership Question: The Presidency and the American System* (New York: Praeger, 1984); Theodore J. Lowi, *The Personal Presidency: Power Invested, Promise Unfulfilled* (Ithaca, N.Y.: Cornell University Press, 1985); Stephen Skowronek, *The Politics Presidents Make: Leadership from John Adams to George Bush* (Cambridge: Harvard University Press, 1993); and Charles O. Jones, *The Presidency in a Separated System* (Washington, D.C.: Brookings Institution, 1994). On presidential leadership of Congress specifically, consult George C. Edwards III, *At the Margins: Presidential Leadership of Congress* (New Haven: Yale University Press, 1989); Mark A. Peterson, *Legislating Together: The White House and Capitol Hill from Eisenhower to Reagan* (Cambridge: Harvard University Press, 1990); and Jon R. Bond and Richard A. Fleisher, *The President in the Legislative Arena* (Chicago: University of Chicago Press, 1991). For recent scholarship on Congress, see Arthur Maass, *Congress and the Common Good* (New York: Basic Books, 1983); Barbara Sinclair, *The Transformation of the U.S. Senate* (Baltimore: Johns Hopkins University Press, 1989); R. Douglas Arnold, *The Logic of Congressional Action* (New Haven: Yale University Press, 1990); D. Roderick Kiewiet and Mathew D. McCubbins, *The Logic of Delegation: Congressional Parties and the Appropriations Process* (Chicago: University of Chicago Press, 1991); Keith Krehbiel, *Information and Legislative Organization* (Ann Arbor: University of Michigan Press, 1991); David W. Rohde, *Parties and Leaders in the Postreform House* (Chicago: University of Chicago Press, 1991); and Gary W. Cox and Mathew D. McCubbins, *Legislative Leviathan: Party Government in the House* (Berkeley: University of California Press, 1993).
7. There has been an ongoing scholarly controversy about whether divided government inhibits the adoption of important legislation. At the most general level, looking at all votes on which the president expressed a preference, the aggregate evidence suggests that it does. On the debate, see David R. Mayhew, *Divided We Govern: Party Control, Lawmaking, and Investigations* (New Haven: Yale University Press, 1991); Gary W. Cox and Samuel Kernell, eds., *The Politics of Divided Government* (Boulder, Colo.: Westview Press, 1991); Morris P. Fiorina, *Divided Government*, 2d ed. (Boston: Allyn & Bacon, 1996); James A. Thurber, "Representation, Accountability, and Efficiency in Divided Party Control of Government," *PS: Political Science & Politics* 24 (1991): 653–657; and Sean Q Kelly, "Divided We Govern? A Reassessment," *Polity* 25 (1993): 475–488.
8. Interestingly, when Eisenhower had a Republican congressional majority in 1953 and 1954, he won on 89.2 and 82.8 percent, respectively, of his initiatives; once the Democrats reclaimed majority status, his success rate never exceeded 75.0 percent and fell to a low of 52.0 percent in 1959. Similarly, Ronald Reagan began well; in 1981 and 1982, with a Senate majority and working closely with conservative, mostly southern, Democrats in the House, he secured passage of 82.3 and 72.4 percent of his requests. By the end of his term, with the Democrats once again in control of the Senate, his success rate plummeted to 43.5 and 47.4 percent (1987 and 1988).
9. These data support Rohde's contention (in *Parties and Leaders*) that as the South sent more Republicans to Washington, the remaining Democrats resembled their northern colleagues, and the party as a whole became ideologically more homogeneous.

10. *New York Times, Washington Post,* and *Congressional Quarterly Weekly Report* reviews of Congress's performance in the 103d Congress identified the major elements of the Clinton program. The analysis here includes fourteen bills that appeared on all three lists, that the president favored, and that got roll-call votes, one of which the *Weekly Report* identified as a "key vote," on the floors of both the House and Senate. It also considers six additional measures on all three lists that the president backed and that failed to get record votes in one or both chambers. See *New York Times,* "The 103rd Congress: What was Accomplished and What Wasn't," October 9, 1994, 16; *Washington Post,* "The Record of the 103rd Congress," October 9, 1994, A21; and *Congressional Quarterly Weekly Report,* "Assessing the 103rd Congress ... What Passed and What Didn't," November 5, 1994, 3146–3147.

11. Margolies-Mezvinsky lost her seat in the 1994 midterm election, in part because of her challenger's attacking her as a "big spender" on the basis of this vote.

12. The 103d Congress enacted several other significant bills—including "motor voter" registration, Hatch Act reform, student loan legislation, and reinstitution of investigatory independent counsels—on which there were no "key votes," and which, thus, were not included in the tabulations. If these are considered, the Clinton record appears substantially more impressive.

13. Jill Zuckman, "As Family Leave Is Enacted, Some See End to Logjam," *Congressional Quarterly Weekly Report,* February 6, 1993, 267–269.

14. George Hager and David S. Cloud, "Democrats Pull Off Squeaker In Approving Clinton Plan," *Congressional Quarterly Weekly Report,* May 29, 1993, 1340–1345; Hager and Cloud, "Test For Divided Democrats: Forge a Budget Deal," ibid., June 26, 1993, 1631–1635; Hager and Cloud, "Democrats Tie Their Fate To Clinton's Budget Bill," ibid., August 7, 1993, 2123–2129; Cloud, "The Final Hours," ibid., May 29, 1993, 1343.

15. Phil Kuntz, "Tough-Minded Senate Adopts Crime Crackdown Package," *Congressional Quarterly Weekly Report,* November 20, 1993, 3199–3201; Kuntz, "Hard-Fought Crime Bill Battle Spoils Field for Health Care," ibid., August 27, 1994, 2488–2493; Holly Idelson, "More Cops, Jails: House Takes a $28 Billion Aim at Crime," ibid., April 23, 1994, 1001–1005; Idelson, "In Surprising Turnaround, House OKs Weapons Ban," ibid., May 7, 1994, 1119–1123; Idelson, "Clinton, Democrats Scramble To Save Anti-Crime Bill," ibid., August 13, 1994, 2340–2343; Holly Idelson and Richard Sammon, "More Than Talks Produce New Anti-Crime Bill," ibid., August 20, 1994, 2449–2454; David Masci, "$30 Billion Anti-Crime Bill Heads To Clinton's Desk," ibid., August 27, 1994, 2488–2493.

16. A motion to recommit is a procedure that returns a bill to the committee that originally considered it; if adopted, the motion usually kills the bill.

17. A conference report is a document prepared by a joint House-Senate conference committee to resolve interchamber differences on a particular bill; it contains the agreements reached to reconcile the differing versions each chamber enacted. Both the House and Senate must accept the report for the bill to pass. A rule is a resolution reported by the House Rules Committee that defines the terms and conditions for floor consideration of legislation. Failure to pass the rule delays or defeats the bill.

18. David S. Cloud, "As NAFTA Countdown Begins, Wheeling, Dealing Intensifies," *Congressional Quarterly Weekly Report,* November 13, 1994, 3104–3107; Cloud, "Decisive Vote Brings Down Trade Walls with Mexico," ibid., November 20, 1994, 3174–3178; Cloud, "Routine Approval in Senate Wraps Up NAFTA Fight," ibid., November 27, 1994, 3257; Jon Healey and Thomas H. Moore, "Clinton Forms New Coalition To Win NAFTA Fight," ibid., November 20, 1994, 3181–3183.

19. Jon Healey and Chuck Alston, "Stimulus Bill Prevails in House, But Senate Battle Awaits," *Congressional Quarterly Weekly Report,* March 20, 1993, 649–652; Healey, "Democrats Look To Salvage Part of Stimulus Package," ibid., April 24, 1993, 1001–1004; Healey, "Saga of a Supplemental," ibid., April 24, 1993, 1002.

20. Beth Donovan, "Republicans Plan Filibusters, Imperiling Senate Schedule," *Congressional Quarterly Weekly Report*, September 24, 1994, 2655; Donovan, "Democrats' Overhaul Bill Dies on Senate Procedural Votes," ibid., October 1, 1994, 2757–2758.
21. Senate rules allow unlimited floor debate. A minority may use nonstop discussion (the filibuster) to obstruct—delay or defeat—legislation. In this case, the Republicans sought to prevent convening of a conference committee to reconcile differing campaign finance bills. A constitutional three-fifths' majority of senators (sixty) may vote to end debate (invoke cloture) to move the legislation ahead.
22. The story of the administration's lobbying disclosure legislation was nearly identical to the scenario played out over campaign finance reform. (See David S. Cloud, "Leaders Turn To Arm Twisting to Pass Gift Ban in House," *Congressional Quarterly Weekly Report*, October 1, 1994, 2756; and Cloud, "GOP and Interest Groups Dig In To Dump Gift Ban in Senate," ibid., October 8, 1994, 2854–2855.) Despite "private misgivings," both chambers enacted restrictions on lobbyists but waited until adjournment was at hand before producing a conference agreement. In support of Republican obstructionist tactics, intended to deny the administration a victory, eight Democrats voted against cloture, and the filibuster killed the bill. Similarly, a "prolonged effort" to sort out telecommunications policy and to redefine relationships among the long distance and local telephone companies, the cable TV industry, the press, and the Hollywood filmmakers petered out in the crush of business as adjournment neared. The House easily passed two telecommunications bills, but agreement in the Senate proved elusive. Senate Commerce Committee Chairman Ernest Hollings, D-S.C., sought a compromise, but three senators threatened a filibuster, and Minority Leader Dole proposed a "non-negotiable" amendment that bill sponsors refused to consider; Hollings "pulled the plug on a committee-approved bill" without pushing for a floor vote. See Jon Healey, "Stumped by Bells' Objections, Hollings Kills Overhaul," *Congressional Quarterly Weekly Report*, September 24, 1994, 2669–2670.
23. Adam Clymer, Robert Pear, and Robin Toner, "For Health Care, Time Was a Killer," *New York Times*, August 29, 1994, A1, A8; David S. Cloud, "Mitchell Trying to Find A Graceful Exit," *Congressional Quarterly Weekly Report*, September 24, 1994, 2693–2695; and Alissa J. Rubin, "Overhaul Issue Unlikely To Rest in Peace," ibid., October 1, 1994, 2797–2801.
24. Pat Towell, "Months of Hope, Anger, Anguish Produce Policy Few Admire," *Congressional Quarterly Weekly Report*, July 24, 1993, 1966–1970; Towell, "Battle Over Gay Ban Policy Moves Into the Courts," ibid., July 31, 1993, 2075; *Congressional Quarterly Weekly Report*, "The Legislative Word on Gays," July 31, 1993, 2076.
25. Political Science Association, Committee on Political Parties, *Toward a More Responsible Party System* (New York: Rinehart, 1950).
26. Further down the road, the old aphorisms might again apply more fully. The Contract with America proposed three measures—term limits for legislators, a balanced budget amendment to the Constitution, and some form of presidential line-item veto ("enhanced rescission" authority)—with profound implications for executive-legislative relations. While the first two failed, at least temporarily, in the early days of the 104th Congress, if enacted they would have enhanced the president's ability to move his program forward. After 1996, if the Republicans recapture the White House and retain their congressional majority, a more powerful (and conservative) GOP president could propose a party agenda and a weaker (also conservative) GOP Congress could dispose of it, most likely to the chief executive's satisfaction.

6

An Overview of the Empirical Findings on Presidential-Congressional Relations

Jon R. Bond, Richard Fleisher, and Glen S. Krutz

Research on the presidency tends to be less quantitative than research on other political institutions. Because the personality and character of each individual occupying the Oval Office, as well as each president's governing strategy, play such a large part in understanding the politics of the presidency, many presidential scholars view in-depth case studies as the most appropriate method of analysis.[1] The small "sample" of presidents and a lack of quantitative measures of some key variables have also hindered the statistical analysis of the presidency.

The study of presidential-congressional relations, however, is an exception. Since the mid-1970s, quantitative studies of presidential-congressional relations have proliferated. In some instances these studies reinforced generalizations based on case study material. But other quantitative studies of presidential-congressional relations produced results that challenged those produced by other methods. In addition, quantitative analysis demands greater precision about the definition of concepts and their operational indicators. The purpose of this chapter is to give an overview of this literature.

Although case studies are valuable for illuminating the rich details and idiosyncratic elements of political interactions, generalizing from a single case is risky. As a prominent political scientist once said, "The plural of case study is data." But multiple case studies may not cumulate toward generalizations because of the way cases are selected. Cases chosen for in-depth analysis tend to be those involving major presidential initiatives where the president's interest and involvement are high. Such cases are neither typical nor representative of presidential-congressional relations. If the cases analyzed are atypical, the explanations they offer are unlikely to be generalizable.

To make valid generalizations about politics requires analysis of large and representative samples of observations. While quantitative studies sacrifice many of the nuances of politics found in qualitative case studies, quantitative analysis based on representative samples allows research to build toward a broader theoretical understanding of relations between the president and Congress.

We do not intend, however, to belittle the important contributions of case-specific research on presidential-congressional relations. Such works are important because they display detailed information on particular cases of legislative-executive interaction. Case studies also help empirical researchers know where to begin looking for generalizable relationships by suggesting hypotheses that can be tested with larger, more representative samples. Though we concentrate here on the quantitative study of presidential-congressional relations, we hope that qualitative approaches will continue. Because different methodologies illuminate different parts of the puzzle, methodological pluralism is the best way to build a comprehensive understanding of presidential-congressional relations.[2]

We organize our overview of the quantitative literature on presidential-congressional relations along the stages of the policy-making process in Congress: agenda setting, committee action, floor decision making, and vetoes. Public policy making is not predictably chronological, but this framework is useful. It allows us to see where we in political science have made advances in studying the interactions of the president and Congress, and where we have farther to go. As we move through the literature, we will comment on where future quantitative research might be focused in order for political scientists to obtain a broader theoretical understanding of presidential-congressional relations.

Before we discuss the research on relations between the president and Congress along the stages of policy making, however, we need to consider two other issues: (1) What is the basic question these studies attempt to answer? and (2) What are the alternative measures of presidential success?

Influence vs. Success

The extraordinary legislative accomplishments during Franklin Roosevelt's first one hundred days in 1933 set the benchmark against which all modern presidents are judged—they lead " in the shadow of FDR." [3] Since Roosevelt, presidents have been judged more by their legislative success than by their executive ability.

The legislative success of modern presidents varies considerably. The primary question in the study of presidential-congressional relations, therefore, is: Why do some presidents experience greater legislative success than others?

The search for answers to this question must begin with Richard Neustadt's seminal work, *Presidential Power*. Neustadt defined the problem of presidential-congressional relations in terms of personal influence: what a president "can do, as one man among many, to carry his own choices through that maze of personalities and institutions called the government of the United States." [4] Neustadt argued persuasively that to be successful, the president must rely on the powers of persuasion, bargaining, and compromise; he focused on the president's professional reputation as a skilled leader and his popularity with the public as key determinants of presidential influence. Because leadership skills and popularity with the public are based on perceptions of what the president does (or fails to do), these variables may be viewed as president-centered explanations of success.[5]

The president-centered perspective dominated the literature on presidential-congressional relations for over three decades. Following Neustadt, many students of presidential-congressional relations searched for data and research designs to analyze the extent to which the president's leadership skills and popularity with the public *influence* Congress to do something it otherwise would not have done. President-centered researchers are interested in presidential success only if it is associated with influence.

Although presidential influence may increase success in Congress, the president's preferences may prevail for reasons other than influence. A high "success" rate, for example, may result if the president and Congress have similar policy preferences. In such a situation, regardless of whether the president is weak or strong, his preferences prevail because they correspond to what most members of Congress want to do anyway. The 103d Congress passed the Family and Medical Leave Act and the "motor voter" bill with President Bill Clinton's support. A president-centered analyst, however, would be reluctant to count these as Clinton victories because they were not his initiatives, and Congress had passed both bills before, only to see them vetoed by President George Bush.

The study of presidential influence is appropriate, but it provides an incomplete understanding of presidential-congressional relations. The problem of governmental responsiveness in the American system of separate institutions sharing powers makes it important to analyze the conditions that lead to presidential success, regardless of whether success results from the president's influence or from forces beyond his control. Because the public holds the president more accountable than Congress for national conditions, the question of whether outcomes of the legislative process are consistent with presidential preferences is important for understanding the extent to which government is responsive to popular preferences. The question of success is broader and more important than the question of presidential influence.

A concern for governmental responsiveness, therefore, suggests that students of presidential-congressional relations should also look at Congress-centered explanations of presidential success.[6] This perspective argues that the president's legislative success results in large part from the extent to which the president and members of Congress share policy preferences; the degree of their shared preferences is fixed by the results of the last election. Continuing with the example of the family leave and motor voter bills, a Congress-centered analyst would argue that these ought to count as Clinton victories. While it is true that President Clinton did not have to personally persuade a recalcitrant Congress to pass these bills, support for them was a part of his successful campaign for the presidency, and neither would be law if George Bush had been reelected.

Members of Congress are strong-willed politicians who bring with them to Congress partisan and ideological predispositions. With the decline of presidential coattails, the partisan and ideological mix in Congress is largely beyond the president's control.[7] The electoral system forces these representatives and senators to be more responsive to parochial interests than to the national concerns of the president. The Constitution grants Congress institutional autonomy from the executive, and members of Congress have structured the institution to help them achieve their goals. Hence, if the last election brings individuals to Congress who share the president's partisan and ideological preferences, the president will enjoy greater success. If, on the other hand, the last election chooses individuals who have different partisan and ideological preferences, the president will suffer more defeats. No amount of bargaining or popularity with the public can move members of Congress very far from their partisan and ideological predispositions.

And so, legislative success is an appropriate dependent variable. But how should it be measured? Different studies have used different measures based on different units of analysis. Each measure has advantages and limitations.[8]

Measures of Legislative Success

Presidential "success," as Bert Rockman has aptly observed, "is both multidimensional and frequently inextricable from dumb luck." [9] *Legislative* success is only one of four indicators of presidential success that Rockman discusses.[10] Even legislative success, the focus of research on presidential-congressional relations, has been defined in different ways.

What do we mean when we say that one president is more successful in Congress than another? Ultimately, the meaning of any indicator of legislative success involves subjective judgments about the content, complexity, and importance of the issues on which the president prevails. Is a cautious president who endorses a large number of simple, routine issues that Congress is sure to pass more successful than a bold president who pushes a small number of complex, difficult issues through the congressional obstacle course? Because the meaning of legislative success inevitably involves subjective value judgments, no empirical indicator is completely satisfactory. Empirical indicators can be devised, however, that minimize some of the problems and permit valid comparisons across presidents over time.

Several features are necessary for an acceptable empirical measure of presidential legislative success. First, the measure must be reliable. Constructing a quantitative measure of presidential success requires one to decide how to aggregate individual and collective decisions. To have a measure that is comparable across presidents and over time, the decision rules must be clear and precise so that different researchers will come to the same conclusion about whether to score a case as a success or failure. Second, the measure must be valid. The activity observed must bear a close relation to what is ordinarily meant by legislative success, and it should accurately reflect the major components of decision making in Congress. Third, the sample of cases must be representative of presidential-congressional relations in general, and there must be enough cases of presidential success and failure to generalize the findings. Fourth, the measure should differentiate between more important and less important issues, as well as between different types of policies. Finally, the measures should permit the researcher to analyze the behavior of different types of members to determine sources of presidential support and opposition in Congress.

Students of presidential-congressional relations have used several measures of legislative success involving different units of analysis and different types of aggregation. Following is an evaluation of the three major alternatives.

Presidential Box Scores

One measure of success is a box score that indicates the percentage of presidential proposals that are approved by Congress over a period of time. The measure is analogous to a batting average—number of hits as a proportion of times at bat.

Two features of box scores make them appealing. First, since it is based on presidential initiatives, it gives an indication of the proportion of the president's program that is enacted into law. Thus, presidency-oriented analysts are attracted to this measure because it focuses on issues that are important to the president. Second, the measure takes into account the multiple decision points in the legislative process. To count as a victory, a presidential proposal must receive favorable action at each stage of the process. A proposal may fail either because Congress takes some positive action to kill it (in committee or on the floor of one chamber) or because Congress takes no action. Failure to clear both chambers for any reason counts as a defeat.

Despite these appealing features, box scores suffer from serious problems of reliability and validity. Since there are several different ways to count how many times the president went to bat as well as how many hits he got, one can calculate several different presidential box scores for the same president and the same record.

The first problem is to determine what counts as a *presidential* request and whether the Congress approves it. These are subjective decisions that may substantially alter the indication of presidential success. The best known and most used presidential box score is the one reported by Congressional Quarterly every year from 1954 to 1975.[11] But several administrations released their own versions of the president's success rate that differed considerably from what CQ reported. The differences resulted from what was counted as a proposal and what was counted as passed—that is, the measures are not reliable because different researchers used different decision rules that produced different numbers indicating a success rate. CQ considered only proposals requested by the president personally and counted them as victories if they cleared both chambers in the year they were proposed. White House reports prepared by staffers whose job it was to make the president look good sometimes counted proposals from cabinet departments if they passed, divided large proposals into several parts and counted each part as victory, and left off some presidential proposals that did not pass. Not surprisingly, these White House reports were invariably higher than CQ's.[12]

Some scholars argue that if we want to know how much of a *president's* program passes, then the president's subjective judgment of what's important to him is what we should use in the analysis. Although the president's perception is an important element of presidential-congressional relations, we should not rely exclusively on subjective lists compiled by the White House that in effect let the president be the judge of his own success or failure. Some analysts have used assessments of congressional support found in presidential papers to identify lists of bills that were important to the president.[13] Since these lists are compiled only for internal use to identify friends and foes in Congress, they are generally valid indicators—the White House has no incentive to fudge the numbers they use to distribute favors. But these subjective presidential assessments are not available in presidential libraries until several years after a president leaves office. Moreover, serious reliability problems remain because different White House staffers may use different criteria to construct their box scores.

In addition to reliability problems, any attempt to calculate a success ratio (as the box score did) must deal with the problem of deciding what is the appropriate unit of time for aggregating congressional action on presidential proposals. Congressional Quarterly made annual calculations. A proposal that eventually passes two or more years after it is introduced counts as a victory in the year it passes, but it is scored as a defeat in every year in which it failed to complete the process in both houses of Congress. Because many proposals, especially major programs and reforms that are key elements of the president's agenda, require more than a year to work their way through Congress, a yearly box score may underestimate presidential success. But the underestimation does not affect all presidents to the same degree. Presidents who make a few simple proposals that go through quickly each year are likely to have higher box scores than presidents who propose a long list of complex bills that ultimately pass after two or three years.

Recalculating a box score for a longer period such as a Congress (two years) or a presidential term to give the president credit for proposals that take longer to pass lessens the problem of underestimating success. But this procedure creates another problem for the analyst who seeks to explain variation in presidential success: it further reduces an already small number of cases. And because this small sample consists of only presidential initiatives, it is not representative of all the issues on which the president and Congress interact. Many important issues initiated by Congress can be missed in box scores.

The level of aggregation necessary to calculate box scores creates yet another problem. A box score reflects the final result of a series of congressional actions and inactions over a specified period of time. The point at which a proposal passes is clear—when it clears Congress and is sent to the president.[14] With rare exceptions, to succeed a proposal must receive favorable *action* at each point in the process. The point at which a proposal fails, however, is often ambiguous. Some proposals die because of congressional action to kill them (in committee or on the floor); others die because Congress takes no action and makes no decision. Because this measure reflects both decisions and nondecisions that occur at different points for different proposals, one cannot match up possible explanatory variables at the time the definitive action (or inaction) occurs.

The editors at Congressional Quarterly recognized many of these problems and ceased publishing box scores in 1975 because they "decided it was a dubious measure of the president's record." [15] Some recent studies, however, have used box scores in innovative ways that overcome some of these problems.[16]

The other two most common quantitative measures of the president's legislative success are based on roll-call votes. One measures the president's success in attracting roll-call support across individual members of Congress; the other measures the president's success across roll-call votes.

Presidential Support Scores

A presidential support score indicates the percentage of time during a specified period of time (a calendar year in CQ's measure) that each member of Congress votes in agreement with the president's position when he expresses one. Note that presidential support scores measure a different type of success than a box score. Whereas box scores indicate something about the president's programmatic success, presidential support scores indicate the president's relative success in attracting votes from individuals in Congress over a specified period.

Individual presidential support scores have several advantages. First, they are generally reliable and valid. All that is required for the calculation is to accurately identify positions of members of Congress and the president. Members' positions on roll-call votes are available in the public record. Determining the president's position on roll calls is more difficult, but from public statements made by the president CQ has been able to identify presidential positions with a high degree of accuracy since 1953.[17] Once the positions have been identified, one can reliably calculate what percentage of the time each member supported the president's position.

Second, there is an adequate number of cases for a valid analysis. Calculating presidential support scores requires aggregating each member's behavior (votes) over time. CQ uses a calendar year, but shorter or longer periods of aggregation are possible. And adding support scores for more years increases the number of cases.

Third, because CQ's support scores are based on all votes on which the president expressed a position, this measure is more representative of presidential-congressional relations in general than are box scores, which are limited to legislative proposals initiated by the president. As noted earlier, issues that do not require legislation (for example, nominations) and legislation initiated by Congress are often important to the president and should be part of a measure of presidential success.

Finally, because presidential support scores reflect behavior of members, we can identify which members support the president more than others, and how members' party, ideology, and constituency characteristics affect their level of support.

Although individual presidential support scores offer several advantages over box scores, several limitations suggest the need for another measure. First, including all votes on which the president takes a position mixes trivial and routine votes with more important issues. Including routine, noncontroversial issues on which almost all members of Congress vote in agreement with the president's position inflates the level of "support." But this inflation has a partisan bias: support scores of presidents in the minority party are inflated more than are those of majority party presidents. Some of this partisan bias may result because a minority president has an incentive to posture and endorse routine issues to improve his apparent success rate. But much of the difference results from simple arithmetic: support scores of opposition party members are inflated more by nonconflictual votes than are the scores of the president's partisans, and by definition the number of opposition party members is greater for minority presidents. Regardless of the cause of distortion, measures of presidential success ought to exclude nonconflictual victories that introduce systematic error. Excluding these votes will not eliminate all bias, but it will increase validity without threatening the measure's reliability. Some recent studies have adopted the practice of excluding all votes on which more than 80 percent voted in agreement with the president's position.[18]

Individual support for the president's publicly stated positions is certainly one valid measure of success; discovering what causes some members of Congress to support the president more than others is an important part of presidential-congressional relations. But this approach does not tell us much about the most important issue in presidential-congressional relations: the president's policy success. Because policy making in Congress requires collective decisions, a variable may systematically increase support from individuals but fail to improve the president's programmatic success: the variable's effect on each member may be too small to raise the collective support above the threshold necessary to win, or it may increase support on votes the president would have won anyway.

A complete understanding of presidential-congressional relations requires analysis of the president's success and failure across collective policy decisions, as well as analysis of presidential support across members of Congress. Fortunately, another approach—measuring presidential victories and defeats across roll-call votes—focuses on policy success and overcomes many of the limitations of the other two measures.

Success on Winning Roll-Call Votes

A third measure of legislative success is the percentage of the time that the president's publicly stated preference prevails on floor votes—pass or fail. The unit of analysis is the vote, as opposed to the member.

Measures of the president's legislative success based on roll-call votes miss much of presidential-congressional relations. Actions of committees and party leaders determine whether issues of interest to the president ever come to the floor for a vote; the fate of issues that do come to a vote are often determined by the rules, and the way congressional leaders have framed the issue. Occasionally, intense conflict between the president and Congress is not reflected in this measure because the issue never reaches the floor for a vote. Two recent examples illustrate the problem. President Clinton made health care reform his primary legislative priority in 1994. Although Clinton's roll-call success rate was about 86 percent in 1994, the "defeat" of his number one priority is not reflected in that number because health care reform never got to the floor for a vote. In 1995 when Clinton experienced congressional resistance to his proposal to prop up the Mexican peso with loan guarantees, he found a way to achieve his goal on his own executive authority without having to get legislation from Congress; this "success" will not show up in his roll-call success rate for 1995.

Although some important interactions between the president and Congress occur at times and places other than floor votes, several considerations justify using roll-call votes to measure presidential success. First, a roll-call vote may not be the only important decision point in the legislative process, but it is *one* of the important points. Most important issues eventually show up on the floor of the House and Senate for resolution by roll call. Some type of health care reform, for example, is likely to come up for a vote at some point. Analyzing interaction between the president and Congress at the roll-call vote stage, therefore, is likely to produce a representative picture of presidential-congressional relations.

Second, behavior on roll-call votes is the only part in the process where we can observe the preferences of both the president and members of Congress on a large number of cases. The point here is not that we should analyze roll-call votes simply because we can observe them—as in the old joke about the drunk who looked for his keys under the streetlight where he could see instead of in the dark part of the block where he dropped them. Because roll-call votes are a fundamental part of the democratic process, interactions at this stage are *exactly the right place to look* to test important explanations of presidential-congressional relations. If we seek to understand how elected policy makers in the presidency and Congress interact in a democratic process, it is appropriate to analyze their behavior at the only point that is readily observable to the media, interest groups, and voters. Of course, all public behavior is not relevant. As noted above, presidential victories on nonconflictual issues may result from posturing or the routine nature of the issue. But within the universe of votes on which the president expresses a position, there is a subset that can provide the basis for reliable and valid generalizations.

The third and most important justification is that despite their limitations, roll-call votes are a reliable and valid indicator of presidential success. Because the observations are from the public record, the measure will be reliable so long as decision rules used to calculate it are explicit. We believe that the measure is valid because other political actors involved in the process at earlier stages use roll-call votes to evaluate success and support in Congress. Interest groups compute ratings based on roll-call votes and urge their members to reward friends and punish opponents based on those ratings. But more importantly, presidents use the way members of Congress vote on roll calls as a basis for distributing rewards and punishments to them.[19] It seems unlikely that participants involved in the process would rely on roll-call votes to make such critical decisions if they did not indicate something important about support.

Using votes as the units of analysis offers several advantages over presidential support scores. First, this approach focuses on the most important component of presidential success—whether the president wins or loses on policy decisions in Congress. The outcomes of votes can be aggregated over different periods of time to give some indication of programmatic success, but because each vote is a case, presidential success can be disaggregated to analyze the effects of forces occurring at the time the vote is taken. Thus, this approach incorporates a principal advantage of box scores while overcoming some of their major limitations.

Second, on each roll-call vote, we can identify which types of individuals (liberal Democrats, conservative Democrats, liberal Republicans, conservative Republicans, committee leaders, party leaders, and so on) supported or opposed the president. This is not the same as analyzing individual support scores, but it allows us to answer some of the same questions addressed in studies of individual support.

A final advantage of roll-call votes is that we can analyze all votes or particular subsets classified by policy type (for example, foreign vs. domestic) or level of importance.[20]

Conclusion

Students of presidential-congressional relations have used different measures of legislative success and different units of analysis. All have advantages and limitations. Which measure is most appropriate is determined mainly by which aspect of presidential-congressional relations is being analyzed. The focus of box scores on presidential initiatives makes them useful for analyzing questions relating to agenda setting, but they are less useful for identifying specific reasons for presidential success or failure. Presidential support scores are useful for analyzing how individual and constituency characteristics affect members' support for the president, but they do not reveal much about the president's policy success. Roll-call vote success seems to be the best overall approach to analyze most of the important issues of presidential-congressional relations. Table 6-1 shows presidential success rates on conflictual roll-call votes from 1953 to 1994.

We turn now to a review of the quantitative research on presidential-congressional relations at different stages of the policy-making process.

Agenda Setting

Agenda setting consists of those activities that influence which problems are put forward for government attention, how those problems are defined, and which policy proposals intended to solve those problems are acted on in the policy-making process. Students of presidential-congressional relations are concerned with the roles of the president and Congress in this process and with the effects of agenda control on presidential legislative success.

Agenda Setting: Shared Between the President and Congress

Conventional wisdom presents a picture of the president as the major—if not dominant—actor setting the legislative agenda. "Congressmen need an agenda from outside, something with high status to respond to or react against," Richard Neustadt explains.[21] "Congressmen expect the executive to present them with bills," writes Samuel Huntington. "The President now determines the legislative agenda of Congress...."[22]

This view of the president as a dominant actor in setting the agenda has persisted from the 1960s, when Neustadt and Huntington were writing, to the 1990s. In the most comprehensive study of agenda setting to date, Frank Baumgartner and Bryan Jones analyzed nine policy issues being pursued in Congress over several decades to observe the ebb and flow of congressional agenda activity and identify its causes. Their major finding is that over long periods of time, the incremental nature of the agenda can be disrupted by short periods of dramatic change in which issues are redefined and institutional policy-making authority may be altered significantly. Political leaders have the potential to influence such periods of dramatic change, and Baumgartner and Jones suggest that the president is the dominant leader if he wants to be:

> No other actor can focus attention as clearly, or change the motivations of such a great number of other actors, as the president. We saw in several cases ... how the involvement of the president pushed those issues high onto the agenda. We also have noted a number of cases where similar processes worked without any significant personal involvement by the president. So we conclude that the president is not a necessary actor in all cases, but when he decides to become involved, his influence can be decisive indeed.[23]

Table 6-1 Presidential Victories on Roll-Call Votes, 1953–1995

President and Year	All Votes				Conflictual Votes			
	House		Senate		House		Senate	
	%	(N)	%	(N)	%	(N)	%	(N)
Dwight D. Eisenhower								
1953	91.2	(34)	87.8	(49)	88.5	(26)	84.6	(39)
1954	78.9	(38)	77.9	(77)	61.9	(21)	72.1	(61)
1955	63.4	(41)	84.6	(52)	44.4	(27)	68.0	(25)
1956	73.5	(34)	67.7	(65)	55.0	(20)	61.1	(54)
1957	58.3	(60)	78.9	(57)	47.9	(48)	69.2	(39)
1958	74.0	(50)	76.5	(98)	65.8	(38)	69.3	(75)
1959	55.6	(54)	50.4	(121)	45.5	(44)	35.5	(93)
1960	65.1	(43)	65.1	(86)	61.5	(39)	55.9	(68)
Mean	68.4		70.7		57.4		61.0	
John F. Kennedy								
1961	83.1	(65)	80.8	(125)	78.0	(50)	77.4	(106)
1962	85.0	(60)	84.9	(126)	79.1	(43)	79.6	(93)
1963	83.1	(71)	88.8	(116)	77.8	(54)	84.5	(84)
Mean	83.7		84.7		78.2		80.2	
Lyndon B. Johnson								
1964	88.5	(52)	91.2	(203)	84.6	(39)	90.4	(167)
1965	93.8	(112)	91.9	(162)	90.7	(75)	89.4	(123)
1966	89.4	(104)	68.0	(125)	84.5	(71)	55.1	(89)
1967	75.6	(127)	81.4	(167)	62.2	(82)	71.0	(107)
1968	83.5	(103)	69.1	(165)	72.1	(61)	58.5	(123)
Mean	85.5		81.6		78.0		75.2	

Richard M. Nixon								
1969	72.3	(47)	74.6	(71)	61.8	(34)	64.7	(51)
1970	84.6	(65)	71.4	(91)	73.0	(37)	53.6	(56)
1971	82.1	(56)	69.5	(82)	77.8	(45)	60.3	(63)
1972	81.1	(37)	54.3	(46)	76.7	(30)	38.2	(34)
1973	48.0	(125)	52.4	(185)	38.7	(106)	30.7	(127)
1974	67.9	(53)	54.2	(83)	57.5	(40)	47.2	(72)
Mean	68.1		61.3		58.2		46.4	
Gerald R. Ford								
1974	59.3	(54)	57.4	(68)	43.6	(39)	44.2	(52)
1975	50.6	(89)	71.6	(95)	43.6	(78)	57.8	(64)
1976	43.1	(51)	64.2	(53)	37.0	(46)	50.0	(38)
Mean	51.0		65.3		41.7		51.3	
Jimmy Carter								
1977	74.7	(79)	76.4	(89)	66.1	(59)	65.0	(60)
1978	70.2	(114)	84.8	(151)	64.2	(95)	81.6	(125)
1979	71.7	(145)	81.4	(161)	66.4	(122)	75.4	(122)
1980	76.9	(117)	73.3	(116)	69.7	(89)	65.2	(89)
Mean	73.2		79.7		66.6		73.5	
Ronald Reagan								
1981	72.4	(76)	88.3	(128)	66.7	(63)	82.1	(84)
1982	55.8	(77)	82.5	(120)	41.4	(58)	77.7	(94)
1983	47.6	(82)	85.7	(84)	46.3	(80)	82.6	(69)
1984	52.2	(113)	85.7	(77)	44.3	(97)	81.0	(58)
1985	45.0	(80)	71.6	(102)	43.4	(66)	65.5	(84)
1986	33.3	(90)	82.3	(79)	32.4	(71)	77.4	(62)
1987	33.3	(99)	56.4	(78)	28.3	(56)	30.0	(56)
1988	32.7	(104)	54.8	(88)	22.8	(91)	43.6	(55)
Mean	46.5		75.9		40.7		67.5	

(Continued on next page)

Table 6-1 *(Continued)*

President and Year	All Votes				Conflictual Votes			
	House		Senate		House		Senate	
	%	(N)	%	(N)	%	(N)	%	(N)
George Bush								
1989	49.4	(85)	73.3	(101)	43.2	(74)	59.1	(66)
1990	33.3	(105)	66.3	(89)	30.0	(90)	58.9	(73)
1991	43.2	(111)	69.1	(81)	32.3	(93)	59.7	(62)
1992	37.1	(105)	54.2	(59)	33.3	(99)	45.8	(49)
Mean	40.8		65.7		34.7		55.9	
Bill Clinton								
1993	86.3	(102)	85.4	(89)	84.4	(90)	82.7	(76)
1994	87.2	(78)	85.5	(62)	83.3	(50)	80.4	(46)
Mean (103d Congress)	86.7		85.5		83.9		81.0	
1995	26.3	(133)	49.0	(102)	18.4	(114)	41.2	(84)

Source: Presidential victories on "all votes" are from *Congressional Quarterly Almanac*, 1953–1994 (annual editions) (Washington, D.C.: Congressional Quarterly Inc., 1954–1995). Victories on "conflictual votes" were calculated by the authors. Victories on conflictual votes from 1953 to 1984 were published previously in Jon R. Bond and Richard Fleisher, *The President in the Legislative Arena* (Chicago: University of Chicago Press, 1990), 72–73.

Although Baumgartner and Jones contribute much to our understanding of agenda setting in general, a shortcoming for our purposes here is the absence of generalizable quantitative evidence beyond theoretical argument and case evidence to track the president's influence over the congressional agenda.

Some analysts challenged this presidency-dominated view of agenda setting, arguing that Congress plays a significant role.[24] Indeed, the study by Baumgartner and Jones also reveals that Congress can be a significant agenda setter.[25] Most empirical research supports the conclusion that while the president enjoys significant agenda-setting powers, these powers are not unlimited and under certain conditions Congress can play an influential role in setting the nation's policy agenda.

In a study of agenda setting in the areas of federal health and transportation policy over four years (1976–1979), John Kingdon finds that Washington elites perceive that both the president and members of Congress are important in the setting of the agenda.[26] Utilizing 247 in-depth interviews with Washington elites working in the general areas of health or transportation policy, he found that the administration was discussed as being important in 94 percent of the interviews; members of Congress were mentioned (without prompting) as important in 91 percent.

Paul Light conducted a study of presidential agenda setting from the Kennedy through the Reagan administrations based on 126 interviews of presidential staff members and on legislative clearance documents from the Office of Management and Budget, which documented 266 legislative proposals.[27] Light discovered that the contemporary president faces a multitude of crosspressures in setting the agenda. Presidents have the most potential to influence the agenda early in their terms, because that is when they have the most "capital"; if they do not act quickly before their capital runs out, Congress will dominate.

Presidents do not start from scratch in deciding what issues to include on the agenda. The most utilized source of ideas for domestic policy agenda proposals for the president is the Congress, mentioned by 52 percent of the respondents. Only 17 percent of the respondents mentioned the president as a source of ideas for domestic policy agenda proposals. Light concludes, "Congress is a wholesaler of presidential issues, in part because of the availability of tested ideas." [28]

Party control seems to affect the extent to which the president looks to Congress for agenda items. Congress was a more important source of ideas for the Democratic administrations of Kennedy, Johnson, and Carter than for the Republican administrations of Nixon and Ford. Of Democratic staff members interviewed, 62 percent mentioned Congress as an important source of ideas on domestic policy, compared with only 30 percent of Republican staffers.[29]

Charles O. Jones has attempted to determine whether the president or Congress controls the agenda by analyzing twenty-eight major bills enacted during the period 1953 to 1989. His findings suggest that agenda-setting powers are shared between the two branches and heavily affected by the incremental nature of the continuing governmental agenda. He found that of the twenty-eight bills studied, six were presidential preponderant, seven were congressional preponderant, and fifteen exhibited joint action. These findings suggest that neither the president nor Congress dominates agenda setting. Rather, the "national government has an agenda that is continuous because much of it is generated from existing programs." [30]

Perhaps the most important question raised by the study of agenda setting is: What difference does it make? Is the president more successful in those instances when he dominates agenda setting?

The Effects of Agenda Control on Policy Success

More than three decades ago, E. E. Schattschneider elegantly stated the importance of agenda setting: "The definition of the alternatives is the supreme instrument of power." [31] Despite its importance, little quantitative work has been done on the connection between control of the agenda and ultimately prevailing in the legislative process.

A critical issue related to determining the effects of agenda control on success is whether the president is sincere or strategic in deciding what issues to put on the agenda. Finding a correlation between agenda control and success would not mean much if presidents act strategically to manipulate their apparent success rate by publicly supporting popular issues destined to sail through Congress and avoiding taking positions on divisive issues that seem destined to die. Covington found evidence that President Kennedy (1961–1963) and President Johnson (1963–1965) did act strategically in some instances. [32] The number of such instances, however, was small and probably had only a marginal effect on the success rate. Moreover, the finding does not seem to apply in general. Patrick Fett analyzed the public announcements of Presidents Carter and Reagan and found that they did not duck contentious issues nor did they tout easily winnable proposals with an eye toward improving their apparent success. [33] Mark Peterson's study of presidents from Eisenhower to Reagan also found that presidents are generally sincere in public announcements of support or opposition to legislation. [34] Presidential agendas are probably not greatly contaminated by strategic position taking. But what evidence is there that presidential agenda-setting activities affect success?

In the study mentioned earlier, Jones distinguished between bills that moved through the legislative process as a result of bipartisanship (both sides in agreement and participating in the development of the legislation) and crosspartisanship (when a few from one party join with the other party to form a majority). [35] Jones found that bipartisanship happened rarely; crosspartisanship was much more frequent. His evidence suggests that crosspartisanship is the normal path to success, but because the number of cases is small (only twenty-eight), no definitive claims can be made. More importantly, since these twenty-eight major bills all succeeded, this analysis does not tell us much about the effects of agenda control (presidential preponderant, congressional preponderant, or shared control) on success. We need a larger sample of cases that includes both successes and failures.

Mark Peterson's extensive quantitative analysis of 299 presidential initiatives from the Eisenhower to the Reagan administrations (1953–1984) is such a study.[36] Peterson traced these agenda items through the legislative process to passage or failure. He discovered that 11 percent exhibited presidential dominance, 20 percent exhibited opposition party dominance in Congress, 24 percent exhibited some sort of compromise between Congress and the president, and 25 percent received no action. Thus, presidential agenda setting rarely dominates in Congress. Indeed, Congress ignores the president's agenda much more often than he dominates. Furthermore, the large number of bills on which Congress is dominant or where the two branches compromise indicate that successfully setting the policy agenda provides no guarantee that the ultimate policy decision will reflect the president's preferences. Peterson's study is useful mainly for its description of what happened to presidential initiatives and how often the outcome was favorable or unfavorable to the president. His statistical models, however, shed little light on the conditions that lead one branch to dominate the other. Thus, this comprehensive quantitative study does not move us much beyond Kingdon's observation that "setting the agenda and getting one's way ... are two very different things. The president may be able to dominate and even determine the policy agenda, but is unable to dominate the alternatives that are seriously considered, and is unable to determine the final outcome."[37]

A recent quantitative study by Cary Covington, J. Mark Wrighton, and Rhonda Kinney provides evidence of a linkage between agenda strategy and success in Congress.[38] Covington and his associates analyze presidential success and failure on roll-call votes from 1953 to 1973. They find that regardless of majority or minority status, presidents are more likely to win on the floor if the bill is on the president's agenda and he is supporting passage. Minority presidents, however, are less likely than majority presidents to have bills on their agenda that they support on the floor for a vote. Majority presidents apparently are better able to push items on their agenda through the legislative obstacle course.

A president's publicly revealed agenda priorities can influence legislative decisions. Fett found that the number of times Presidents Carter and Reagan mentioned an issue during their first year in office had a statistically noticeable effect. Presidential issue advertisement, however, did not affect all members in the same way. The president's core partisans (liberal Democrats for Carter, conservative Republicans for Reagan) were most responsive to presidential advertisement, but core opponents were not persuaded. The results also varied by president: Carter's efforts at issue advertisement seemed to have a negative effect on members outside his party base, while

Reagan's efforts had a positive effect on support from crosspressured liberal Republicans. Fett suggests that the size of the president's agenda and the nature of the issues might account for this difference. Reagan pushed 107 proposals compared with Carter's 232. Reagan more effectively focused congressional attention, and his top priorities (cutting taxes and increasing defense spending) offered members of Congress considerable political benefits. Signals about priorities may have become muddled in the larger Carter agenda, and his energy proposal imposed significant costs on many members' constituencies. Fett's evidence, based on only the first year in office of two presidents, is not conclusive, and we don't have systematic measures of the nature of the policy proposals on the presidents' agendas.[39]

Although the recent progress in systematic, quantitative analysis of agenda setting is impressive, our knowledge remains limited. The evidence is clear that agenda control is shared between the president and Congress; the evidence about which conditions and circumstances explain why agenda control varies is speculative. Our ability to generalize about the effects of agenda control is even more limited.

Committees

Congress is a decentralized institution that performs a great deal of its work in committee and subcommittee. We are interested in presidential success at the committee stage of the legislative process—that is, the conditions under which congressional committees take actions consistent with the president's preferences.

Presidential Influence in Different Committees

Some studies suggest presidential influence is greater on some committees than others.[40] A classic study by Richard Fenno relied on semistructured interviews with committee members, committee staff, executive branch officials, representatives of clientele groups, and congressional leaders to analyze behavior in twelve congressional committees (six in each chamber) from 1955 to 1966.[41] He found that the executive branch affects the deliberations and decisions of some committees but not others. In particular, the executive was a significant actor affecting the behavior of members on the Ways and Means, Appropriations, Foreign Affairs, and Education and Labor committees. In contrast, Fenno found little evidence that the executive had any impact on either the Interior Committee or Post Office and Civil Service Committee. He found similar results in his analysis of the equivalent Senate committees.

Fenno's classic study suggests that agenda-setting powers are a major source of the president's influence on some committees. Members of the Appropriations, Ways and Means, and Foreign Affairs committees are frequently responding to policy recommendations originated by the executive branch. In the Education and Labor Committee, however, the significance of the president stemmed less from the president's agenda-setting powers than from the observation that the committee often dealt with visible national issues on which the two political parties were divided.

Although Fenno's analysis provides great insights about committee activities and behavior, the evidence of *presidential* influence and success is quite dated and based on the experience of only three presidents. What does it mean that the president is a significant actor on some committees? Does it mean that the policy agendas of these committees are more likely to be defined by the executive? Does executive dominance of the committee agendas mean that members on these committees are more likely to follow presidential preferences and directions than are members of other committees? Or does it mean that the president is more likely to have an interest in these committees because of their policy jurisdiction? Saying that presidents are more likely to lobby some committees than others is different from saying that presidents are able to influence the deliberations and decisions of such committees.

Committee Decision Making

At this point we know very little about the ability of presidents to influence committee decisions concerning whether or not to hold hearings, mark up legislation, or report bills to the floor. Peterson found that on about one-fourth of presidential initiatives, Congress took no significant action.[42] Since he studied only presidential bills, we cannot say whether or not this figure is higher than for major nonpresidential bills. As an absolute statement, Peterson's findings clearly demonstrate that simply because the president desires a congressional committee to act (hold hearings, mark up a bill, report it to the floor) is no guarantee that such actions will be taken.

Some studies have searched for presidential influence on the behavior of individual members of a committee. Richard Hall analyzed members' participation in committee deliberations.[43] Participation, he hypothesized, is a function of a member's goals, his or her place in the committee structure, and contextual variables. One of the goals Hall suggested may influence participation was the member's desire "to carry out the president's agenda." Those who placed greater importance on this goal were more likely to formally participate and to participate in full committee mark-up. This effect was limited only to the first year of the president's term.

Others, such as Glenn and Suzanne Parker, have searched for presidential influence on committee voting.[44] Data on voting in congressional committees first became available with the reforms of the early 1970s. In many ways we might expect voting in committee to reflect the same causal processes as voting on the floor, but the context is different (fewer members and less visibility). This at least raises the possibility that presidential influence in committee and on the floor may differ.

Establishing presidential influence on congressional voting is a difficult task. It requires showing that members behave differently than they would in the absence of such presidential activities. Demonstrating such effects may be analogous to finding the proverbial needle in the haystack. Parker and Parker may be correct when they suggest that the influence of presidents is subtle and indirect and may be masked by the more direct influence of party and ideology. It is also possible that members vote their partisan and ideological predispositions without any significant influence of presidents.

While Parker and Parker's factor analysis of committee voting fails to provide direct evidence that presidential activities alter committee behavior, one aspect of their research suggests some indirect influence of the president.[45] They find that the conservative coalition was more likely to form under Republican presidents than under Democratic ones. (The conservative coalition forms when a majority of Republicans and conservative Democrats vote against a majority of liberal Democrats.) This finding raises the possibility that presidents may be able to affect the probability that a particular voting cue will come into play. Put another way, because the extent to which members are crosspressured by partisan or ideological considerations varies, presidents may be able to alter the likelihood that partisanship or ideology will structure the vote. Herbert Asher and Herbert Weisberg's analysis of the dynamics of floor voting provides some evidence supporting this interpretation.[46] They find that partisanship on votes on two recurring issues important to the president—raising the debt limit and foreign aid authorizations—may be influenced by which party controls the presidency. But at this point, the empirical research is insufficient to allow us to state with confidence the conditions under which party and ideology will influence roll-call voting either in committee or on the floor.

Researchers have also analyzed the support that presidents receive from leaders of congressional committees. Bond and Fleisher report that committee leaders from the president's party are usually supportive of the president when Congress is considering a bill on the floor.[47] Committee leaders, however, are less supportive than are elected party leaders. This finding should not be surprising because committee leaders, chosen mainly on the basis of seniority, are somewhat insulated from party—and presidential—pressure. And choosing committee leaders on the basis of seniority elevates members with policy views outside the party mainstream to important leadership positions. Party leaders, in contrast, are selected by the party caucus; they are more likely to come from their party's mainstream and are expected to support the party—and the president. Since reforms in the mid-1970s forced committee leaders to be more responsive to the party majority, the difference in presidential support provided by the two types of leaders has diminished.[48]

Bond and Fleisher also find that unified support from the president's party and committee leaders is associated with higher levels of party unity.[49]

In addition, they present evidence that support from party and committee leaders increases the probability of winning on the floor. Covington, Wrighton, and Kinney find that committee leaders of both parties are more likely to support items on the president's agenda than items on which the president expresses a position but does not make a priority.[50] This evidence, they argue, suggests that the president has influenced congressional decisions.

This evidence, however, does not necessarily demonstrate that the president influenced the behavior of committee leaders. The measure of support is based on agreement between them and the president. Such agreement may result from processes other than presidential influence, including shared preferences or committee leaders influencing the president to follow them. Another limitation of the Bond and Fleisher study is the reliance on floor votes to analyze presidential support from committee actors. While the floor behavior of committee leaders is probably consistent with the positions they took in committee, it is certainly not the same as observing their behavior inside the committee. For example, floor votes may overestimate the level of agreement because committee leaders prevent some presidential proposals from ever getting out of committee. Peterson's finding that some presidential initiatives are ignored provides evidence that this is the case.[51] These limitations point directly to the need for more studies analyzing the interaction of the president and congressional committees if we are to develop a greater understanding of the effect of separated institutions making policy in a decentralized system.

Floor Decision Making

The vast majority of quantitative research on presidential-congressional relations has been conducted on floor roll-call votes. While analysis of roll-call votes has come under criticism in certain circles of the discipline, we believe the study of presidential-congressional relations at this stage of the process is crucial.

Four linkage agents may serve as sources of support for the president's policy preferences on the floor of Congress: political parties, political ideology, the president's popularity with the public, and the president's leadership skill.[52] Note that party and ideology are properties that members bring with them to the institution of Congress. Because the president has little control over the partisan and ideological mix in Congress, these agents may be viewed as Congress-centered explanations of linkage. Presidential popularity and leadership skill, on the other hand, focus on perceptions and activities of the president. Because perceptions of the president's popularity and leadership are determined by what he does, these agents may be viewed as president-centered explanations of linkage.

Party and Ideology

Political scientists have long noted that political parties are an important explanation of how members of Congress vote. Even with the well-documented decline in party voting in Congress over much of the twentieth century, there is unambiguous evidence that party exerts a crucial influence on presidential-congressional relations: members of the president's party in Congress are more likely to support his policy positions than are members of the opposition, and majority presidents have higher success rates on roll-call votes than do minority presidents.[53] Furthermore, the resurgence of party voting in the 1980s and 1990s has made party an even stronger determinant of presidential success in Congress.[54]

Partisan support is important in explaining the policy success of both majority and minority presidents. Having members of their own party in Congress provides all presidents with a base upon which to build majority coalitions in support of their policy preferences. For example, President Reagan's success on his budget and tax cut proposals in the Democratically controlled House in 1981 resulted from unusually unified Republican members coalescing with conservative Democrats.

Members of the president's party are predisposed to support his policy preferences for several reasons. First, politicians decide which political party to join in part because of policy compatibility. Even in the context of weak parties, members of Congress are likely to have more policy preferences in common with colleagues of their party than with individuals in the other party. Second, because members of the same political party must satisfy similar electoral conditions, they are even more likely to share—or at least support—many of the same goals and policy preferences. Third, because members of the president's party who seek reelection must run on his record as well as their own, they have an incentive to help him succeed. Kingdon found that Republican members of Congress "often referred to their stake in the administration's success" as a reason for supporting President Nixon's policy positions.[55] But Kingdon's evidence is based on interviews in the 1970s. Since then the electoral process has become more candidate-centered and presidential coattails have weakened.[56] Today members of the president's party may feel less need to support the president out of self-interest. Finally, members of the same party share a psychological attachment to a common political symbol; they are members of the same political family. George Edwards notes that "members of the president's party typically have personal loyalties or emotional commitments to their party and their party leader, which the president can often transfer into votes if necessary." [57]

While party affiliation clearly affects a legislator's floor votes, the congressional parties are ideologically diverse. The weakness of American political parties stems in part from this ideological diversity. Traditionally, within each party there has been a faction with ideological predispositions closer to the average member of the other party than to their own. These members are crosspressured: party pulls them in one direction, ideology in the other. Crosspressured members support the president less than do members of the president's base and more than do members of the opposition base. But even members of the party bases, for whom party and ideology are reinforcing, unify less often than in disciplined party systems. Defining a party faction as unified if 75 percent of the members vote together, Bond and Fleisher found that the president's party base unified in support of the president on only 60 percent of conflictual roll calls, while core opponents unified in opposition on approximately half of the votes.[58] The lack of discipline in American political parties seems to result from more than just ideological diversity.

When it comes to winning and losing, majority party presidents are more likely to prevail on the floor than are minority party presidents.[59] Between 1953 and 1984, the least successful majority party president won a larger percentage of conflictual roll calls than did the most successful minority party president (see Table 6-1, pp. 114–116). Since the mid-1980s, the increase in party voting and the greater likelihood of party unity have had a dramatic impact on presidential success. During this more partisan period, minority party presidents (Reagan and Bush) lost much more often than they won. In contrast, Clinton's first two years in office (1993 and 1994) produced many more legislative victories than defeats. With the Republican takeover of Congress in the 1994 elections, Clinton's success in 1995 dropped sharply.

While the evidence strongly indicates that presidents from the majority party are treated differently than those from the minority party, it is uncertain whether the size of the president's majority is what is important. Bond and Fleisher reported that the size of the president's party base and opposition base were significantly related to success, but they did not control for majority status.[60] Covington, Wrighton, and Kinney replicated Bond and Fleisher's analysis for a shorter time period and found no significant effect for the party size variable.[61] Perhaps having members of the president's party in control of the institutional levers of power in Congress—committees and floor scheduling—is a more important benefit of majority status than having a larger number of partisan supporters on the floor.

The partisan and ideological composition of Congress is constant between elections, yet presidential success varies over time within a given Congress. A president's popularity with the public and leadership skills may help explain this variation.

Presidential Popularity

Presidential popularity, in contrast to party and ideology, is relatively fluid. All presidents since Franklin Roosevelt have experienced during their terms wide variation in public support.[62] Because members of Congress are elected representatives who are supposed to be responsive to popular preferences, the president's popularity might influence congressional decisions to support or oppose his policy preferences on floor votes. The belief that the popularity of the president affects support in Congress is widely accepted among Washington insiders. Some quantitative studies also provide evidence that popularity affects support in Congress.[63]

Other researchers have identified methodological and theoretical reasons to question the veracity of the presidential popularity hypothesis. A growing body of research suggests that the influence of presidential popularity on roll-call support may be marginal at best.[64] Bond and Fleisher found that popular presidents were no more likely to win in the legislative arena than were presidents who were less popular.[65] Kenneth Collier and Terry Sullivan replicated this analysis using headcount data (pre-vote polls of members' positions). They found that presidential popularity is not related to shifts in a member's support from the initial count to the final vote.[66]

The expectation that members of Congress will respond to the president's level of popular support is based on two suppositions.[67] The first and most important is electoral—members' fear electoral retribution if they oppose a popular president or support an unpopular one. A second reason for the popularity hypothesis is that some members define their role as representatives of the people and believe they ought to follow the public's lead.

Both suppositions may be challenged. First, with the weakening of presidential coattails, members of Congress have less incentive to pay much attention to the president's popularity. In all likelihood, the public's evaluation of the president plays only a small role in deciding the outcome of congressional elections. Although some voters may use presidential popularity as a voting guide, very few have sufficient knowledge of their representative's presidential support score to make a connection between their evaluation of the president and the voting behavior of their representative. If presidential popularity is a significant cue in congressional elections, it most likely works through political party, helping or hurting members of the president's party without regard to their specific levels of presidential support. Furthermore, because presidential popularity is so fluid, using it as a guide in casting roll-call votes is risky. The president's popularity on election day is much more important than his popularity several months earlier when most roll-call votes occur. But presidential popularity on election day cannot be predicted with any certainty from levels of popularity in the past. Electoral self-interest may not cause members of Congress to alter their support of the president in response to his popularity with the public.

The second supposition focusing on role orientation is equally suspect. Roger Davidson found that only about one-third of House members agreed with the statement, "a representative ought to work for what his constituents want even though this may not always agree with his personal views." [68] Although this study of the role orientation is dated, there is no reason to believe that the number of such members has increased. Since only a minority of members subscribe to the delegate role, there is little reason to expect presidential popularity to strongly affect the decisions of many members.

The preponderance of the systematic quantitative evidence suggests that popularity with the public has only a marginal influence on the president's legislative success. Closer scrutiny of the theoretical underpinnings of the popularity hypothesis reveals little theoretical reason to expect anything more than a marginal effect.

Presidential Leadership Skills

Of all the forces that might lead to success in Congress, the president's reputation as a skilled leader is the one over which he has the most control. According to Neustadt, the president's "professional reputation" is defined by the perceptions of Washington elites, but the president has the capacity to mold perceptions: "Everything he personally says and does (or fails to say, omits to do) becomes significant in everyone's appraisals." [69] The idea that a skilled president can persuade members of Congress to support his policy preferences is the foundation on which the search for evidence of presidential influence rests.

Political pundits and politicians certainly believe in the skills hypothesis: a skilled president is more likely to succeed than a less skilled one. The empirical evidence supporting the skills hypothesis is based almost exclusively on case studies. [70] As noted above, the evidence from case studies is suspect. Some analysts have examined the president's congressional liaison operation and have found, not surprisingly, that the operation worked better for some presidents than for others. [71] Others have described how presidents use the resources at their disposal in an attempt to build political support. [72] The assumption behind these studies is that an effective liaison operation produces a greater probability of presidential success.

Recent quantitative studies attempt to systematically analyze the effects of skills on presidential-congressional relations. Their results provide little support for the skills hypothesis. Edwards found that presidents reputed to be skilled did not receive more support from individual members than did presidents reputed to be unskilled. [73] Fleisher and Bond used a statistical model to estimate a baseline of how often members of the House should be expected to support the president given the effects of party, ideology, and presidential popularity. They compared the forecasts from this baseline model to actual levels of support for Carter (perceived as unskilled) and Reagan (perceived as skilled) during their first year in office. Consistent with perceptions, House members generally supported Carter less often than predicted. But contrary to perceptions that Reagan was unusually influential with members of the House, he received less support than expected. [74] A similar analysis of Bush's first year suggested that support for Bush was also below predicted levels, even for individuals identified as his close friends and political allies. [75]

Bond and Fleisher also analyzed success rates of presidents from Eisenhower through Reagan.[76] This analysis suggests that presidents reputed as highly skilled did not win more roll-call votes than did less skilled presidents. Some may argue that the null results in the Bond and Fleisher analysis are due to the use of crude, global assessments of presidential skill. Bond and Fleisher characterized presidents as high skill (Johnson, Ford, and Reagan), medium skill (Kennedy and Eisenhower), or low skill (Nixon and Carter) based on the descriptive writings about each of these presidents. Clearly, such a "measure" of leadership skill may be criticized as post hoc and impressionistic. In addition, some may criticize this measure based on assessments of an entire presidential administration for being static. Perceptions of presidential skills are probably not as fluid as popularity, but perceptions are likely to vary over time; Light, for example, discusses the cycle of "increasing effectiveness" as a president's knowledge and expertise grow.[77]

Brad Lockerbie and Stephen Borrelli constructed a measure of presidential reputation that varies from month to month.[78] In this study they recorded the number of favorable and unfavorable mentions of presidential skills in a given month by two noted journalists, George Will and Meg Greenfield. They coded each article from 1 (very low skill) to 5 (very high skill) with a code of 3 being considered a neutral article. Their findings produce only limited support for the skills hypothesis. Initially, they found that media reports of the president's skills in a given month were not significantly related to the president's success in that same month. When they reestimated the model separating "high skill" months from all others, they found that presidents were more successful in months when journalists reported most favorably on their legislative skills.

Several problems lead us to question this evidence. One problem with Lockerbie and Borrelli's measure is the assumption that a president's reputation undergoes meaningful month-to-month change. While they did find month-to-month variability in their measure of reputation, it is entirely possible that these monthly changes were the result of measurement error. The potential for measurement error is increased by relying on only two journalistic impressions. Moreover, the study fails to consider the possibility that these journalistic impressions were formed on the basis of legislative success rather than independent of it. It is quite possible that journalists are more likely to see and report about presidential competence when he wins than when he loses. The skills hypothesis never suggested that high skills help, but low skills will not hurt. Given these limitations, this evidence hardly supports the notion that presidential reputation has a direct and independent effect on success.

Others have searched for evidence of presidential influence missed by Edwards and Bond and Fleisher. Using data from administration headcounts, Sullivan reports that some members changed their position between the first poll and the final vote.[79] The vast bulk of switchers were either predisposed to support the president or in a neutral category. A "hard-core opponent" was much less likely to switch to a pro-administration position. Sullivan attributes some of the switching to presidential influence, although this conclusion is inferred rather than the result of some direct measure of presidential activity. In addition, Sullivan's data also show that some opponents and neutral members reverted to an anti-administration position between the initial count and the final vote. In a subsequent analysis Sullivan found that at least some of the conversion to a pro-administration position reflected an insincere, strategically based position taken by the member at the time of the original count.[80]

Both Covington and Sullivan suggest that presidents may influence congressional voting by convincing some partisan opponents to abstain rather than vote against the administration.[81] Fett found that the more often a president mentioned an issue, the more likely core supporters were to vote with the president; Covington found that mobilization of core supporters was greater on issues important to the president than on less important issues.[82] While presidents may induce their core supporters to higher levels of support, it is also possible that presidents give priority to those issues on which they and their core supporters already agree. If this is the case, then these findings do not necessarily imply that presidents are able to influence congressional actors to do something they otherwise would not have done.

Despite the limited systematic support, many politicians and observers close to the process believe that presidential skills play a key role in explaining presidential success. Although those who study presidential-congressional relations from a more detached perspective have an obligation to take the explanation of participants seriously, the consistent negative findings of systematic studies cannot be dismissed. While skills may alter outcomes in some cases, it is appropriate to ask if the evidence from these cases is representative and generalizable.

Presidential Vetoes

The constitutional power to veto legislation passed by Congress furnishes the president with considerable leverage in the legislative process. The leverage, however, is mainly negative, allowing the president to stop or at least resist congressional efforts to pass bills he opposes. There is scant evidence that the veto or a veto threat can be used in a positive way to prod Congress to craft specific legislation desired by the president.

Although the veto power provides mainly negative leverage, it is a powerful weapon when the president wants to kill a bill. Table 6-2 shows the number of vetoes and overrides for all presidents from George Washington to Bill Clinton. Overall, only 7 percent (105 of the 1,459) of regular vetoes have been overridden by Congress.[83] The requirement of a two-thirds majority in both chambers to override the veto explains why vetoes are rarely overridden. Mustering a two-thirds' majority normally requires bipartisan support, which means that some of the president's partisans must publicly oppose him. But party loyalty may be higher on veto override votes than on other issues because some members of the president's party who initially supported the bill vote to sustain the president's veto. Moreover, to override a veto, Congress must muster two-thirds in both chambers; to sustain a veto, the president needs only one-third plus one in one chamber.

The analysis of presidential vetoes seeks to discover why presidents veto bills passed by Congress, as well as the conditions under which Congress will override a veto.

Reasons for Presidential Vetoes

Presidents veto legislation for many reasons, and these reasons have changed over time. Early presidents tended use the veto to kill legislation they felt was unconstitutional. Andrew Jackson was the first president to widely use the veto in policy disagreements. Throughout the remainder of the nineteenth century, vetoes based on constitutional or policy grounds fluctuated from president to president until the administration of William Howard Taft. Taft began the trend of using the veto mainly for policy reasons and on important public legislation. Prior to the twentieth century, many vetoes were on "private" legislation that pertained to a particular individual or entity as opposed to matters affecting broad groups of Americans. Vetoes of private bills have been less prevalent in the twentieth century, while vetoes of public bills with broader consequences have become the most common.[84]

A study by Richard Watson reveals that presidents in the modern era (that is, beginning with the Franklin Roosevelt administration) most often used policy grounds as the reason for their vetoes.[85] From 1933 to 1981, nearly two-thirds of the time (65.7 percent) presidents listed policy differences as the first reason for the veto in their messages explaining the veto to Congress. Other reasons included congressional encroachment on the executive (3.6 percent), constitutionality (5.9 percent), administrative unworkability (5.3 percent), and fiscal problems (19.5 percent).

Since policy grounds have become the primary reason presidents resort to the veto, we might expect that the same resources and conditions associated with lack of success on floor votes will explain when policy differences will be intense enough to lead to vetoes. Studies of roll-call votes on presidential issues discussed above suggest that party control of Congress and popularity with the public might explain vetoes.

Studies of vetoes find that minority presidents are more likely to veto than are majority presidents. Divided government intensifies partisan and ideological differences between the president and Congress. Because minority presidents are unable to dissuade the opposition majority from passing legislation they oppose, minority presidents must resort to the veto more than majority presidents do. Between 1933 and 1981, minority presidents averaged more than eight vetoes per year, while majority presidents averaged

Table 6-2   Presidential Vetoes, 1789–1995

President	Regular Vetoes	Overrides	Pocket Vetoes
George Washington	2	0	0
John Adams	0	0	0
Thomas Jefferson	0	0	0
James Madison	5	0	2
James Monroe	1	0	0
John Quincy Adams	0	0	0
Andrew Jackson	5	0	7
Martin Van Buren	0	0	1
William Henry Harrison	0	0	0
John Tyler	6	1	4
James K. Polk	2	0	1
Zachary Taylor	0	0	0
Millard Fillmore	0	0	0
Franklin Pierce	9	5	0
James Buchanan	4	0	3
Abraham Lincoln	2	0	5
Andrew Johnson	21	15	8
Ulysses S. Grant	45	4	48
Rutherford B. Hayes	12	1	1
James A. Garfield	0	0	0
Chester A. Arthur	4	1	8
Grover Cleveland (1st term)	304	2	110
Benjamin Harrison	19	1	25
Grover Cleveland (2d term)	42	5	128
William McKinley	6	0	36
Theodore Roosevelt	42	1	40
William H. Taft	30	1	9
Woodrow Wilson	33	6	11
Warren G. Harding	5	0	1
Calvin Coolidge	20	4	30
Herbert Hoover	21	3	16
Franklin D. Roosevelt	372	9	263
Harry S. Truman	180	12	70
Dwight D. Eisenhower	73	2	108
John F. Kennedy	12	0	9
Lyndon B. Johnson	16	0	14
Richard M. Nixon	26	7	17
Gerald R. Ford	48	12	18
Jimmy Carter	13	2	18
Ronald Reagan	39	9	39
George Bush	29	1	17
Bill Clinton	11	1	0
Total [a]	1,459	105	1,067

[a] Through December 31, 1995.

Sources: Vetoes from 1789 to 1992: Harold W. Stanley and Richard G. Niemi, *Vital Statistics on American Politics,* 4th ed. (Washington, D.C.: Congressional Quarterly Inc., 1994), 278. Vetoes from 1993 to 1995: *Congressional Quarterly Weekly Report,* January 6, 1996, 10.

fewer than four.[86] Although majority control is probably more important, there is evidence vetoes become less likely as the number of seats held by the president's party in Congress increases.[87]

Another presidential resource is public opinion. Several studies suggest that popular presidents veto less than do unpopular presidents.[88] If the president's popularity is high, presumably he will be able to persuade Congress and rely on vetoes less; as popular support erodes, persuasion is less effective, and the president must turn to the veto. Between 1933 and 1981, presidents with approval ratings below 50 percent vetoed an average of ten times, while those with ratings between 50 percent and 66 percent vetoed only five times.[89]

The findings linking presidential approval and the number of vetoes points to the limits of our theoretical and empirical understanding of presidential-congressional relations. The explanation for the effect of popularity on vetoes rests on the assumption that popular presidents are better able to persuade members of Congress to support their preferences. But as we discussed earlier, the evidence supporting this assumption is not strong. Thus, if it is indeed the case that popular presidents veto fewer bills, then the theoretical explanation of this result is not clear.

Research on vetoes also finds that vetoes increase as inflation and employment increase, and vetoes are more likely on domestic legislation than on foreign policy legislation. Domestic issues, particularly economic ones, are the greatest source of conflict between the president and Congress. Furthermore, the electoral calendar seems to affect vetoes. As elections approach, conflict between the president and Congress tends to escalate. Thus, presidents veto more in election years.[90]

Factors affecting vetoes may be different on vetoes of major and minor bills. John Woolley finds that the lack of political resources, such as minority party status and low popularity, are related to vetoes of major bills.[91] This finding is consistent with those above for all types of vetoes.[92] But because minor bills are less visible to the public, partisanship is reduced, and the popularity of the president becomes less important as a resource to influence Congress. Thus, vetoes of minor bills are affected less by these resources.

Congressional Overrides

The issue of congressional overrides involves two questions: (1) Under what conditions will Congress attempt the unlikely effort to override a presidential veto? (2) What explains whether vetoes are overridden? Congress does not attempt to override all vetoes. Of the 169 regular vetoes between 1933 and 1981, Congress attempted to override 61.5 percent of them. When Congress attempts to override, it succeeds about one-fourth (24.3 percent) of the time.[93]

Research analyzing why Congress does or does not attempt an override is quite limited. David Rohde and Dennis Simon found that the type of policy and the partisan voting alignment prevailing at the time of passage of the legislation were influential. Specifically, overrides were more likely to be attempted on domestic policy (namely social welfare and government management issues) and if the original voting coalition for passage was bipartisan rather than heavily partisan.[94]

Research analyzing whether or not override attempts succeed is also sparse. Richard Watson as well as Rohde and Simon found that presidents sustained vetoes at a higher level on foreign policy legislation than on domestic policy legislation.[95] Specifically, Watson found that Congress in the modern era failed to override 59 percent of foreign policy vetoes (17 of 29) compared with only 28 percent of domestic policy vetoes (47 of 167).

Rohde and Simon found presidents were more successful using the veto early in their administrations when public opinion was high. As the president's popularity eroded, Congress was more likely to override a veto. They also found that if the original vote to pass the legislation was a divisive partisan vote, the president was more likely to have a veto sustained.

An important question for scholars researching veto overrides is the size and composition of the original coalitions passing the vetoed bill. Simple arithmetic may be the primary explanation of why Congress does not attempt an override. If the original coalition supporting the bill in either chamber is smaller than two-thirds, there is virtually no chance of overriding a veto. Members of Congress sometimes do change their votes, but it's unlikely that enough opponents will switch to expand a slim majority passing the bill to the two-thirds necessary to override a veto. In fact, switches from initial support to opposition to overriding a veto are more likely, because some members of the president's party are reluctant to oppose the president even if they like the vetoed bill. Thus, Congress is unlikely to override a veto—or even attempt an override—unless there is strong bipartisan support, and the initial vote in both chambers is large enough to absorb some defections and still exceed two-thirds.[96] Analysis of overrides, therefore, needs to control for the size of the initial coalitions.

Veto Threats

Although a presidential veto is an effective tool to kill a measure after Congress has acted, we found little hard evidence that the threat of a veto can influence the content of legislation as it is developed and passed in Congress. There is, nonetheless, an intuitive appeal to the proposition that the presidential veto has more than a post hoc effect on congressional policy making. Commenting on President Bush's nearly perfect record of sustaining his vetoes, James Thurber noted, "Bush has been trying to govern through the veto, and trying successfully in some cases to change the nature of bills by threatening to veto. That's one of the only strengths a minority president has."[97] Additional research ought to systematically explore this possibility.

Robert Spitzer presents a preliminary analysis of the effects of direct presidential veto threats between 1961 and 1986 as searched in the *New York Times* Index.[98] He finds that these public veto threats are rare—only fifty-six over twenty-five years—but they have increased gradually over time. Neither Kennedy nor Johnson issued a public veto threat. Of the remaining presidents, the greatest number of public veto threats (forty-four of the fifty-six) were made by Republican presidents who faced Congresses controlled partially or entirely by the Democratic party. If the threat of a veto is intended to persuade Congress to change legislation so the president will sign it, the strategy was a failure for Nixon and Ford—80 percent of Nixon's veto threats and 100 percent of Ford's ended up with legislation being vetoed. Reagan's use of the veto threat appears more successful; he had to carry through on only 31 percent of his threats. The one instance of unified government during this period is Carter. Carter issued twelve veto threats, ten of which were resolved without the use of a veto, suggesting that the strategy is more effective for majority presidents.

These findings, however, may not be generalizable because the author looks only at veto threats that are public and on issues important enough to get reported in the *New York Times* Index. This single source may not report all veto threats or even a representative sample of them. Furthermore, the analysis does not identify the conditions that explain why veto threats succeed or fail.

Thus, we have sparse research on the president's strategic use of a veto threat. But members of Congress also have the capacity to act strategically; under certain conditions congressional leaders can signal intentions to pass legislation to elicit a response from the president. We have little understanding of how both branches use signals strategically. Systematic research on this question would be welcome.

Conclusions

The quantitative study of presidential-congressional relations has grown during the past two decades. Different facets of this institutional relationship have been explored, including the influence of both branches of the federal government on agenda setting, the determinants of presidential support and success in Congress, and the forces that influence the propensity of the president to use the veto power. As is often the case in the normal scientific study of social phenomenon, progress measured in terms of new empirical insights and theoretical understandings has been largely incremental.

The systematic study of separation of powers is in its relative infancy. The existing empirical literature has confirmed some of our prior understandings of shared policy-making responsibilities while mounting significant challenges to other conventional wisdom. Much more work needs to be done in all areas of presidential-congressional relations, but further research is especially needed in the areas of agenda setting and committee decision making. We hope future assessments of the literature in this area will show that continued progress has been made.

Notes

1. James David Barber, *Presidential Character: Predicting Performance in the White House,* 3d ed. (Englewood Cliffs, N.J.: Prentice Hall, 1985); Richard E. Neustadt, *Presidential Power: The Politics of Leadership* (New York: John Wiley and Sons, 1960); and Samuel Kernell, *Going Public: New Strategies of Presidential Leadership,* 2d ed. (Washington, D.C.: CQ Press, 1993).
2. Elsewhere, Bond and Fleisher have sharply criticized the use of case studies. The focus of that critique was on the problems of making reliable and valid generalizations about the effects of presidential skills given the problems of potentially biased case selection and ambiguities in interpreting evidence. See Jon R. Bond and Richard Fleisher, *The President in the Legislative Arena* (Chicago: University of Chicago Press, 1990), 36–38.
3. William E. Leuchtenburg, *In the Shadow of FDR: From Harry Truman to Ronald Reagan,* rev. ed. (Ithaca, N.Y.: Cornell University Press, 1983).
4. Neustadt, *Presidential Power,* i.
5. Bond and Fleisher, *The President,* 13.
6. Ibid., 4.
7. On the decline of presidential coattails, see Lyn Ragsdale, "The Fiction of Congressional Elections as Presidential Events," *American Politics Quarterly* 8 (October 1980): 375–398; John A. Ferejohn and Randall L. Calvert, "Presidential Coattails in Historical Perspective," *American Journal of Political Science* 28 (February 1984): 127–146; Gary C. Jacobsen, *The Electoral Origins of Divided Government* (Boulder, Colo.: Westview Press, 1990); and James E. Campbell, *The Electoral Pulse of Congressional Elections* (Lexington: University of Kentucky Press, 1993).
8. The following section relies on Bond and Fleisher, *The President,* chap. 2.
9. Bert A. Rockman, *The Leadership Question: The Presidency and the American System* (New York: Praeger Publishers, 1984), 211.
10. The others are retrospective reputation provided by experts; public approval by the mass public; and the management of decisions that successfully solve crises and problems. Ibid., 190–194.
11. *Congressional Quarterly Almanac* (Washington, D.C.: Congressional Quarterly Inc., 1954–1975).
12. See Bond and Fleisher, *The President,* 56–57.
13. For examples of research based on lists of votes compiled by presidential administrations, see the following articles by Cary R. Covington: "Congressional Support for the President: The View from the Kennedy/Johnson White House," *Journal of Politics* 48 (August 1986): 717–728; "Mobilizing Congressional Support for the President: Insights from the 1960s," *Legislative Studies Quarterly* 12 (February 1987): 77–96; "Staying Private: Gaining Congressional Support for Unpublicized Presidential Preferences on Roll Call Votes," *Journal of Politics* 49 (August 1987): 737–755; "Building Presidential Coalitions Among Cross-Pressured Members of Congress," *Western Political Quarterly* 41 (March 1988): 47–62; and "Guess Who's Coming to Dinner: The Distribution of White House Social Invitations and Their Effects on Congressional Support," *American Politics Quarterly* 16 (July 1988): 243–265. See also these articles by Terry Sullivan: "Headcounts, Expectations, and Presidential Coalitions in Congress," *American Journal of Political Science* 32 (August 1988): 567–589; "Explaining Why Presidents Count: Signaling and Information," *Journal of Politics* 52 (August 1990): 939–962; and "The Bank Account Presidency: A New Measure of Evidence on the Temporal Path of Presidential Influence," *American Jour-*

nal of Political Science 35 (August 1991): 686–723.

14. Assuming, of course, that the amendments and changes in the bill have not altered it so much that it is no longer what the president proposed. In computing the CQ box score, the editors "tried to determine if, on balance, congressional action was more favorable than unfavorable." See Congressional Quarterly Almanac (Washington, D.C.: Congressional Quarterly Inc., 1954), 43. How to handle compromises is a problem with all measures, but it is more severe with box scores, which focus on entire bills that often involve many issues.

15. Congressional Quarterly Almanac (Washington, D.C.: Congressional Quarterly Inc., 1982), 19.

16. Mark A. Peterson, Legislating Together: The White House and Capitol Hill from Eisenhower to Reagan (Cambridge: Harvard University Press, 1990); and Cary R. Covington, J. Mark Wrighton, and Rhonda Kinney, "A Presidency-Augmented Model of Presidential Success on House Roll Call Votes," American Journal of Political Science 39 (November 1995): 1001–1024.

17. Covington's analysis of support scores compiled by the Kennedy and Johnson administrations revealed that CQ missed between one and eight presidential votes per year between 1961 and 1967. See Covington, "Congressional Support for the President," table 1.

18. Jon R. Bond, Richard Fleisher, and Michael Northrup, "Public Opinion and Presidential Support," Annals 499 (September 1986): 47–63; and George C. Edwards III, At the Margins: Presidential Leadership of Congress (New Haven: Yale University Press, 1989).

19. Covington, "Congressional Support for the President"; and Covington, "Guess Who's Coming to Dinner."

20. A recurring issue in the study of presidential-congressional relations is whether the president is more successful on foreign and national security policy than on domestic policy. For an assessment of the literature on this topic, see Steven A. Shull, The "Two Presidencies": A Quarter Century Assessment (Chicago: Nelson-Hall, 1991).

21. Neustadt, Presidential Power, 8.

22. Samuel P. Huntington, "Congressional Responses to the Twentieth Century," in The Congress and America's Future, ed. David B. Truman (Englewood Cliffs, N.J.: Prentice Hall, 1965), 23.

23. Frank R. Baumgartner and Bryan D. Jones, Agendas and Instability in American Politics (Chicago: University of Chicago Press, 1993), 241.

24. Ronald C. Moe and Steven C. Teel, "Congress as Policy-Maker: A Necessary Reappraisal," Political Science Quarterly 85 (September 1970): 443–470.

25. Baumgartner and Jones, Agendas and Instability. Baumgartner and Jones have a more comprehensive agenda-setting project under way that includes exploration of measures in addition to those reported in their 1993 study. For information on that project, see Frank Baumgartner et al., "Committee Jurisdictions in Congress, 1980–1991" (Paper presented at the annual meeting of the American Political Science Association, New York, September 1-4, 1994); and Bryan Jones et al., "Producing Legislation in Congress: Four Controversies and a Research Program to Address Them" (Paper presented at the annual meeting of the American Political Science Association, Chicago, August 31–September 3, 1995).

26. John W. Kingdon, Agendas, Alternative and Public Policies (Boston: Little, Brown & Co., 1984).

27. Paul Charles Light, The President's Agenda: Domestic Policy Choice from Kennedy to Carter (With Notes on Ronald Reagan) (Baltimore: Johns Hopkins University Press, 1982).

28. Ibid., 89.

29. Ibid.

30. Charles O. Jones, The Presidency in a Separated System (Washington, D.C.: Brookings

Institution, 1994), 164.
31. E. E. Schattschneider, *The Semi-Sovereign People* (New York: Holt, Rinehart and Winston, 1960), 68.
32. Covington, "Congressional Support for the President"; Covington, "Staying Private."
33. Patrick J. Fett, "Truth in Advertising: The Revelation of Presidential Legislative Priorities," *Western Political Quarterly* 45 (December 1992): 895–920.
34. Peterson, *Legislating Together.*
35. Jones, *The Presidency.*
36. Peterson, *Legislating Together.*
37. Kingdon, *Agendas, Alternatives and Public Policies.*
38. Covington, Wrighton, and Kinney, "A Presidency-Augmented Model."
39. Patrick J. Fett, "Presidential Legislative Priorities and Legislators' Voting Decisions: An Exploratory Analysis," *Journal of Politics* 56 (May 1994): 502–512.
40. Richard F. Fenno, *Congressmen in Committees* (Boston: Little, Brown & Co., 1973); and Glenn R. Parker and Suzanne L. Parker, *Factions in House Committees* (Knoxville: University of Tennessee Press, 1985).
41. Fenno, *Congressmen in Committees.*
42. Peterson, *Legislating Together.*
43. Richard L. Hall, "Participation and Purpose in Committee Decision-Making," *American Political Science Review* 81 (March 1987): 105–128.
44. Parker and Parker, *Factions in House Committees.*
45. Ibid.
46. Herbert B. Asher and Herbert F. Weisberg, "Voting Change in Congress: Some Dynamic Perspectives on an Evolutionary Process," *American Journal of Political Science* 22 (May 1978): 391–425.
47. Bond and Fleisher, *The President,* 132–133.
48. David Rohde, *Parties and Leaders in the Post Reform House* (Chicago: University of Chicago Press, 1991); and Jon R. Bond and Richard Fleisher, "Clinton and Congress: A First Year Assessment," *American Politics Quarterly* 23 (July 1995): 355–372.
49. Bond and Fleisher, *The President,* 144–145.
50. Covington, Wrighton, and Kinney, "A Presidency-Augmented Model."
51. Peterson, *Legislating Together.*
52. Bond and Fleisher, *The President,* chap. 2.
53. Jon R. Bond and Richard Fleisher, "The Limits of Presidential Popularity as a Source of Influence in the U.S. House," *Legislative Studies Quarterly* 5 (February 1980): 69–78; George C. Edwards III, "Presidential Party Leadership in Congress," in *Presidents and Their Parties: Leadership or Neglect,* ed. Robert Harmel (New York: Praeger Publishers, 1984); Light, *The President's Agenda*; and Bond and Fleisher, *The President.* On the decline of party voting, see David Brady, Joseph Cooper, and Patricia Hurley, "The Decline of Party in the U.S. House of Representatives, 1887–1968," *Legislative Studies Quarterly* 4 (August 1979): 381–406; and Patricia Hurley and Rick Wilson, "Partisan Voting Patterns in the U.S. Senate, 1877–1986," *Legislative Studies Quarterly* 14 (May 1989): 225–250.
54. Rohde, *Parties and Leaders*; Richard Fleisher and Jon R. Bond, "Assessing Presidential Support in the House: Lessons from Reagan and Carter," *Journal of Politics* 45 (May 1983): 745–758; and Richard Fleisher and Jon R. Bond, "The President in a More Partisan Legislative Arena," *Political Research Quarterly* (forthcoming).
55. John W. Kingdon, *Congressmen's Voting Decisions,* 2d ed. (New York: Harper & Row, 1981), 180.
56. Martin P. Wattenberg, *The Rise of Candidate-Centered Politics: Presidential Elections of the 1980s* (Cambridge: Harvard University Press, 1991).
57. Edwards, "Presidential Party Leadership," 184–185.
58. Bond and Fleisher, *The President,* 97–105.
59. Ibid., 74–75.

60. Ibid., 225–227.
61. Covington, Wrighton, and Kinney, "A Presidency-Augmented Model."
62. John Mueller, "Presidential Popularity from Truman to Johnson," *American Political Science Review* 64 (March 1970): 18–34; and George C. Edwards III, *Presidential Approval: A Sourcebook* (Baltimore: Johns Hopkins University Press, 1990).
63. George C. Edwards III, *Presidential Influence in Congress* (San Francisco: Freeman, 1980); Douglas Rivers and Nancy Rose, "Passing the President's Program: Public Opinion and Presidential Influence in Congress," *American Journal of Political Science* 29 (May 1985): 183–196; Charles W. Ostrom and Dennis M. Simon, "Promise and Performance: A Dynamic Model of Presidential Popularity," *American Political Science Review* 79 (June 1985): 334–358; and Paul Brace and Barbara Hinckley, *Follow the Leader: Opinion Polls and the Modern Presidents* (New York: Basic Books, 1992).
64. Bond, Fleisher, and Northrup, "Public Opinion"; Kenneth Collier and Terry Sullivan, "New Evidence Undercutting the Linkage of Approval with Presidential Support and Influence," *Journal of Politics* 57 (February 1995): 197–209; Edwards, *At the Margins*; Calvin Mouw and Michael MacKuen, "The Strategic Configuration, Personal Influence, and Presidential Power in Congress," *Western Political Quarterly* 45 (September 1992): 579–608. For a discussion of methodological problems with previous research analyzing the connection between popularity and success, see Bond and Fleisher, *The President*, 25–26.
65. Jon R. Bond and Richard Fleisher, "Presidential Popularity and Congressional Voting: A Reexamination of Public Opinion as a Source of Influence in Congress," *Western Political Quarterly* 37 (June, 1984): 291–306; Bond and Fleisher, *The President*.
66. Collier and Sullivan, "New Evidence."
67. Edwards, *Presidential Influence.*
68. Roger H. Davidson, *The Role of the Congressman* (Indianapolis: Pegasus, 1969), 118–119.
69. Neustadt, *Presidential Power*, 80.
70. Barbara Kellerman, *The Political Presidency: Practice of Leadership from Kennedy through Reagan* (New York: Oxford University Press, 1984).
71. Eric Davis, "Congressional Liaison: The People and the Institutions," in *Both Ends of the Avenue: The Presidency, the Executive Branch, Congress in the 1980s*, ed. Anthony King (Washington, D.C.: American Enterprise Institute, 1983), 59–95.
72. Covington, "Mobilizing Congressional Support"; Covington, "Building Presidential Coalitions"; Covington, "Guess Who's Coming to Dinner."
73. Edwards, *Presidential Influence*; and Edwards, *At the Margins*, 183–185.
74. Fleisher and Bond, "Assessing Presidential Influence."
75. Richard Fleisher and Jon R. Bond, "Assessing Presidential Support in the House II: Lessons from George Bush," *American Journal of Political Science* 37 (May 1992): 525–541. For a critique of Fleisher and Bond and a different interpretation of Bush's success using a different baseline, see Mark R. Joslyn, "Institutional Change and House Support: Assessing George Bush in the Postreform Era," *American Politics Quarterly* 23 (January 1995): 62–80.
76. Bond and Fleisher, *The President.*
77. Light, *The President's Agenda.*
78. Brad Lockerbie and Stephen A. Borrelli, "Getting Inside the Beltway: Perceptions of Presidential Skill and Success in Congress," *British Journal of Political Science* 19 (January 1989): 97–106.
79. Sullivan, "Headcounts, Expectations, and Presidential Coalitions"; and Sullivan, "The Bank Account Presidency."
80. Sullivan, "Explaining Why Presidents Count."
81. Covington, "Building Presidential Coalitions"; and Sullivan, "Headcounts, Expectations, and Presidential Coalitions."

82. Fett, "Presidential Legislative Priorities"; and Covington, "Mobilizing Congressional Support."
83. Pocket vetoes—which occur if Congress has adjourned and the president fails to sign a bill within thirty days—are not subject to congressional override.
84. Richard A. Watson, *Presidential Vetoes and Public Policy* (Lawrence: University Press of Kansas, 1993), 31–35.
85. Ibid., 139.
86. Ibid., 45.
87. David Rohde and Dennis Simon, "Presidential Vetoes and Congressional Response: A Study of Institutional Conflict," *American Journal of Political Science* 29 (August 1985): 397–427. Watson, *Presidential Vetoes.*
88. Rohde and Simon, "Presidential Vetoes"; Watson, *Presidential Vetoes*; and John T. Woolley, "Institutions, the Election Cycle, and the Presidential Veto," *American Journal of Political Science* 35 (May 1991): 279–304.
89. Watson, *Presidential Vetoes*, 49.
90. Rohde and Simon, "Presidential Vetoes"; Watson, *Presidential Vetoes*; and Woolley, "Institutions."
91. Woolley, "Institutions."
92. Rohde and Simon, "Presidential Vetoes"; Watson, *Presidential Vetoes.*
93. Watson, *Presidential Vetoes.*
94. Rohde and Simon, "Presidential Vetoes."
95. Ibid. See also Watson, *Presidential Vetoes.*
96. Rohde and Simon, "Presidential Vetoes."
97. Quoted in Mike Mills, "Bush Asks for a Sign of Loyalty; Congress Changes the Channel," *Congressional Quarterly Weekly Report*, October 10, 1992, 3147–3149. President Bush had only one of his twenty-nine vetoes overridden. A perfect record of sustaining vetoes would have made Bush unique as the only minority president to achieve the feat. Although eleven presidents who cast vetoes have perfect records sustaining them, all had partisan majorities in Congress.
98. Robert J. Spitzer, *President and Congress: Executive Hegemony at the Crossroads of American Government* (Philadelphia: Temple University Press, 1993).

7

Congressional Support for Presidential Action
Scott R. Furlong

An explanation of the president's ability to influence legislative outcomes or how successful he is in getting his agenda through Congress is essential to an understanding of the rivalry between the president and Congress. There are two ways one can study congressional support for presidential actions. First, one can examine whether Congress as an institution supports presidential actions.[1] Second, by using tools such as Congressional Quarterly's (CQ) presidential support scores, one can explore whether individual members of Congress support the president. This chapter examines the voting behavior of members of the U.S. House of Representatives, but the theory could apply to senators as well. The chapter presents a model of congressional support of the president that builds on the work of Jon R. Bond and Richard Fleisher in *The President in the Legislative Arena*. Bond and Fleisher's hypothesis is that presidential-congressional relations, or in this case congressional support, should focus on congressional and not presidential variables. This chapter explores the effect of party, ideology, position in Congress, public support, and independence of the member on individual support for the president. The chapter also explores whether the presidential honeymoon period affects support. These relationships are important in the understanding of policy formation and may help to explain why government is sometimes deadlocked.

Presidential-Congressional Relations

Ever since publication of Richard Neustadt's classic work, *Presidential Power*, thinking about presidential-congressional relations has centered on presidential variables. According to Neustadt, leadership skill, persuasion, and public support, when used correctly by the president, can exert a strong influence on his relationship with Congress. Others have extended this hypothesis or have tried to provide additional evidence using quantitative analysis.[2]

A major problem with using presidential variables is the difficulty in measuring concepts such as leadership skill or persuasion. For example, scholars have attempted to measure the concept of skill by analyzing editorials to see how the president is faring with political elites who in turn influence the public.[3] But this type of study is often difficult to replicate and may suffer from a number of measurement or theoretical problems. Moreover, many studies suggest that presidential variables have only a minor effect on congressional support. If presidential variables do not explain the difference in congressional support for the president, one must turn to alternate explanations.

Another way of examining presidential-congressional relations is to look at congressional variables (see chapter 6, "An Overview of the Empirical Findings on Presidential-Congressional Relations," for a review of the literature on this topic). Although they focus on institutional support, Bond and Fleisher's works in this area have led to the development of a model to test the impact of congressional variables on support for the president. This analysis expands on their findings.

Congressional Support for Presidential Actions

Congressional support for the president can be approached from two different levels. The first is the aggregate level, which explores whether Congress as a whole supports the president. For example, one could calculate the degree of support by figuring out how many issues supported by the president the House passes and how many it defeats or fails to consider.[4] The second level is that of the individual House member. This chapter focuses on the individual members and looks at the correlates of presidential support within the House. The purpose is to determine the impact of certain independent congressional variables on presidential support. Previous scholarship provides many variables that may affect this relationship. This study adds to Bond and Fleisher's model the party/ideology interactive variable and includes a different measure for public presidential support. Six variables provide the regression model.[5] These variables, and the specific hypotheses associated with them, follow.

Political party. A primary component of congressional voting is party-line voting. One would expect, both intuitively and theoretically, that members from the president's political party are more likely to support his agenda. This hypothesis should hold despite the notion that the party system is on the decline.[6] In fact, the alleged decline is barely evident within Congress. Party unity scores over the past thirty-five years have been stable or have increased slightly in both houses and in both political parties.[7] Members use the party as a voting cue, which represents loyalty between partisans. For those members seeking reelection, party serves as a representation of a certain electoral constituency.[8]

Other studies have argued that the effect of party on presidential success in Congress is overstated. These studies connect the weakening of the president's coattails to a decline in party linkage.[9] Because there may not be any political liability "owed" to the president, individual members' electoral independence can ultimately affect the party link. Melissa Collie and David

Table 7-1 Average Presidential Support Scores by Political Party, 1989, 1992, and 1993 (percent)

Year	President	Republicans	Democrats	All Members
1989	Bush	69.8%	37.2%	49.4%
1992	Bush	70.6	25.3	42.6
1993	Clinton	39.0	77.3	61.8

Notes: For 1989, n = 383; 143 Republicans and 240 Democrats. Data for this year were obtained from the 1992 edition of *Politics in America* and therefore do not include those who did not return to Congress in 1990.

For 1992, n = 434; 166 Republicans and 268 Democrats. As Speaker of the House, Tom Foley voted at his own discretion, and therefore Congressional Quarterly did not compute a presidential score for him.

For 1993, n = 433; 175 Republicans and 258 Democrats.

Source: Politics in America 1992 and *1994* (Washington, D.C.: Congressional Quarterly Inc., 1993 and 1995).

Brady provide evidence that presidential support, as it relates to partisan loyalties, is not as great as it once was.[10] Although these arguments may be persuasive, party still plays an important role in presidential support. Therefore, one expects that a member of Congress of the president's political party will have a higher presidential support score than a member from the opposition party.

Table 7-1 provides the average presidential supports scores by political party for three years—the first and last years of the Bush presidency (1989 and 1992) and the first year of the Clinton presidency (1993). It provides descriptive support of this first, intuitive hypothesis, that political party matters in presidential support.

Ideology. Ideology is another factor that researchers often include in models of presidential-congressional relations. The reasoning is similar to that concerning political party. A member with similar ideological perspectives as the president will be more likely to support presidential programs. There is a correlation between ideology and party, with liberal perspectives typically represented by Democrats and conservative by Republicans. Although the correlation exists, it is not absolute; there are conservative Democrats and liberal Republicans. This variation allows presidents to look for support across party lines by appealing to ideological leanings that may be stronger than party ties. Examples include southern Democratic support for Ronald Reagan's programs in 1981–1982 and Republican support for the North American Free Trade Agreement (NAFTA) during Bill Clinton's first year in office.

The relationship between ideology and presidential support within Congress is strongly related to how ideology affects congressional voting behavior. John Kingdon provided evidence showing ideology as a strong cue for congressional voting.[11] Others have also established the importance of this correlation in support of policy positions and to reflect constituent interests.[12] Obviously, the closer a presidential policy is to a member's ideological tilt, the more likely he/she is to support it. Evidence reporting the crossing of party lines in support of what Kingdon describes as "simple attitudinal agreement" is readily available and demonstrates that ideology affects presidential support.[13] However, Kingdon notes that ideology is a less important cue for moderate members than for those holding extreme positions. Still, one must focus on the norm in congressional behavior rather than the exceptions and accept the importance of ideology in predicting congressional support for the president.

In this study, the member's Americans for Democratic Action (ADA) support score was used to measure ideology. The ADA compares a member's vote to the position taken by the ADA and places the member on the liberal-conservative scale. A score of "0" indicates a very conservative member, and a score of "100" a very liberal member. The score has been shown to be an accurate measure of member ideology.[14] Because "a president's policy positions tend to reflect his party's ideological mainstream," [15] one would expect a member with a similar ideology to support the president. In other words, a member with high ADA scores will be more likely to support a liberal (Democratic) president and less likely to support a conservative (Republican) president.

Party/ideology interaction. In general, the literature that posits the influence of party and ideology on congressional support of the president does not consider the possible and likely interaction between these two variables. For example, one implicitly expects the voting behavior of northern and southern Democrats to be different, and, indeed, Lewis A. Froman Jr. found that southern Democrats supported John F. Kennedy's domestic programs 27 percent less than northern Democrats.[16] It would therefore seem important to measure the effects of the interaction between party and ideology more directly in a study of presidential support in Congress.

Bond and Fleisher refer to this interaction and provide an analysis of the impact of the interactive variable. They reintroduce the theory that there are four parties in Congress—the president's political base, cross-pressured members of the president's party, cross-pressured members of the opposition party, and the opposition political base—and measure each group's presidential support.[17] Their conclusions support their theory of the interactive nature of party and ideology, and their analysis shows the differences in presidential support that occur within the parties when ideology is included.

A problem with the Bond and Fleisher theory is that it limits the party-ideology variable to a categorical phenomenon even though it may be possible to think of the interaction as a continuum. One can use a variable that combines the two-party scheme and ADA score and develop an ideological score that changes depending on the party of the member.[18] Again the relationship of this variable with presidential support will change depending on the president's party and ideological stance. When the president and a congressional member have similar ideologies and are from the same party, presidential support should increase. Different ideologies and parties would lead to the least amount of presidential support.

Congressional leadership. As a congressional leader, especially Speaker of the House, majority leader, or minority leader, a member may support or oppose a president out of duty to party or to the institution. Two examples illustrate how differently leaders see their official duties. Howard Baker, R-Tenn., described his role as majority leader as "the president's spear carrier in the Senate." [19] But, in characterizing Robert Byrd, D-W.Va., an aide to Jimmy Carter said, "God, is he independent. He ain't our man—he's the Senate's man." [20] It is apparent that the effects of participating in the president's party leadership on the Hill are difficult to sort out. In addition, committee leaders, who have many variables affecting their opinions, may be more insulated than party leaders from party pressures. [21]

For this study, members of Congress are divided into three types: party leaders (Speaker, majority or minority leaders, and majority or minority whips); committee chairs or similar positions (full committee chairs, ranking minority members, subcommittee chairs of the Appropriations Committee, and members of the Rules Committee); and the rank and file. A leader from the president's party should have a higher presidential support score than a nonleader, and party leaders should have higher scores than committee chairs. [22] Bond and Fleisher look at support from the party leaders and find that they generally behave as expected; that is, congressional leaders of the president's party are more supportive than committee chairs of the same party. In the opposing party, leaders are less supportive than are committee chairs. Again, an interaction takes place with the party variable. Leaders from the same party as the president are likely to be more supportive than are their opposite numbers across the aisle.

Public presidential support. If a president is popular with the electorate, then individual representatives should be more likely to support him. Both Richard Neustadt and George C. Edwards III posit the importance of public prestige and how members react to it. [23] Edwards finds a strong correlation between presidential popularity and overall support. Many studies have detected a statistically significant relationship between support and success, but the effect is minimal. [24] Others have stated that the relationship between support and success is more complicated than a simple bivariate relationship. This could lead to an underestimation of the effect of public support and presidential success in Congress. [25]

Two problems with the study of public support of the president and its effect on an individual member of Congress are the breadth of the data collected and the inappropriateness of data to the question. [26] Most studies use survey data to determine public support for a presidential position, but a random sample of the entire U.S. population does not provide a true measure of attitudes within a congressional district. Aggregate data may obscure certain district variations of public support that occur across the country. Therefore, as Bond and Fleisher argue, members of Congress are more concerned with the public's support for the president within their district than with a national public support score.[27] Moreover, it is very difficult to determine how popularity may affect the final presidential support score based on one survey result during the year. To partially address these concerns, this study uses the district's electoral support—the percentage that voted for the president. This measure has the advantage of providing district-level data and represents the actual support for a president at least at the time of the election.[28] One would expect that the higher the presidential vote (percentage) in a member's district, the higher that member's presidential support will be.[29]

Independence of member. Today, members of Congress tend to be more independent than in the past. A number of changes in Congress as an institution and in elections have contributed to this independence. The result is that some members have electoral bases that are very independent of party: they do not have to rely on party help or the president to get reelected. And, as seen during the 1994 congressional races, same party candidates explicitly run against a president's record or ask him not to campaign in their behalf. One would expect that as a member becomes more independent, he/she will be less likely to feel a need to support the president, but this will vary according to the member's party. One potential measure of independence is the member's margin of victory as measured by his/her percentage of the district vote. As a member's margin of victory increases, his/her support for the president may decrease.

Data Testing and Analysis

The unit of analysis for this study is the member of the U.S. House of Representatives in 1989, 1992, and 1993, the first and final years of the Bush administration and the first year of the Clinton administration.[30] Congressional Quarterly's presidential support score for each member will be the measure of this dependent variable.[31] CQ calculates this score by first determining what legislation the president does and does not want based on his unambiguous messages. The score is a percentage based on the number of times a member supports the presidential position.

Russell D. Renka raises a concern about examining data over a year-long period. He argues that a year is too long for an accurate measure of presidential support. For example, President Bush's average approval rating in 1991 was 71 percent, but it varied from 80 percent in the first quarter (after Desert Storm) to 58 percent in the fourth quarter. Renka raises an important issue: district-level support can and does change throughout the year, not to mention over a four-year period.[32]

Table 7-2 shows the multiple regression results for the three years using the president's support scores as the dependent variables. More than 80

Table 7-2 Factors Determining Congressional Support of the President

Variable	1989	1992	1993
Intercept [a]	67.78	38.91	72.37
	(4.34)	(4.21)	(2.95)
Political Party	1.90	22.20*	−40.66*
	(1.92)	(2.09)	(2.12)
Ideology	−0.50*	−0.40*	0.06*
	(0.02)	(0.03)	(0.03)
Party/Ideology Interaction	0.15*	−0.14*	0.50*
	(0.04)	(0.05)	(0.06)
Public Presidential Support	0.10*	0.27*	0.06
	(0.04)	(0.04)	(0.05)
Congressional Leadership	1.46*	−0.20	3.14*
	(0.76)	(0.94)	(1.09)
Margin of Victory	0.02	0.05	−0.05
	(0.03)	(0.03)	(0.04)
Adj R^2	0.89*	0.91*	0.84
n	383	431	433

[a] Intercept value represents presidential support if every other variable equals zero.

* Represents significant value.

Note: Regression coefficients are unstandardized. Numbers in parentheses represent standard error.

percent of the variance is explained by the included variable in the three years.[33] One could hypothesize that the presidential variables discussed by Neustadt explain the remainder of the variance in presidential support scores. Because the table explains less variance in Clinton's support score, the variables associated with the power to persuade may have been more important for the first year of his administration. Although party and ideology explain most of the reasons why a member may support the president, the other variables are also noteworthy.

As one would expect, the party of the member of Congress is an important determinant of presidential support. According to the results, a member of the president's party supported the president 22 percent more in 1992 and 41 percent more in 1993.[34] The ideology of the member is also relevant in every year, but less dramatic for Clinton.[35] Liberal members of Congress (those with the highest ADA scores) were less likely to support the Bush administration and more likely to support the Clinton administration. For example, the 1989 results show that for every ten-point increase in ADA score (movement from conservative to liberal), there was a 5 percent decrease in support for Bush.

The results dealing with party and ideology together are not as intuitive.[36] During Bush's first year (1989), the more liberal the member of Congress the less he/she supported the president. But this decrease in support was not as great if the liberal member was also a Republican. In other words, as one would expect, liberal Republicans were more likely to support Bush than were liberal Democrats.[37] These expected results do not occur for the last year of the Bush presidency (1992) or the first year of the Clinton presidency (1993). In 1992 a liberal Republican was less likely than a liberal Democrat to support Bush. In addition, in 1993, a liberal Democrat was less likely than a liberal Republican to support Clinton.[38] One possible explanation is that liberal Democrats expected more favorable positions than Clinton was willing to endorse and therefore voted against him. Clinton's "new Democrat" positions may have hurt his support from liberal members. For example, Clinton supported the legislation creating NAFTA, which many Democrats opposed. The results in all three years, however, support the idea that one must consider party and ideology together when examining presidential support.

Public support for the president was important for the two Bush years examined. In 1989 a ten-point increase in public support led to a one-point increase in congressional support, which increased to almost three points in 1992. The higher support in 1992 is counterintuitive because congressional support should be higher in the first year of an administration, the so-called "honeymoon" period. Public support during the first year of the Clinton administration did not lead to more presidential support by members of Congress. Ross Perot's candidacy may partially explain this result. With Perot in the presidential race and capturing 19 percent of the vote, the potential support for Clinton decreased. Clinton won the election with only 43 percent of the popular vote, hardly a show of public support that would persuade a member of Congress to march behind him. It would appear that Clinton did not enjoy a honeymoon period during the first year of his administration.

The Republican leadership in the House was more supportive of President Bush in 1989 than ordinary Republicans.[39] Party leaders had a support rate 13.5 percent higher than the rank and file, and Republican committee chairs had a rate almost 3 percent higher. Contrary to what one might expect, the 1993 results show that Republican party leaders appeared to support President Clinton more than Democratic party leaders. In terms of specific leadership positions, Democratic committee chairs and Republican party leaders were more supportive than the rank and file.[40] Leadership position does not appear to have had an effect on presidential support in 1992.

Conclusions

This study examines how different congressional variables impact Congress's presidential support at the individual level. Using data from 1989, 1992, and 1993, the study tests some common variables often associated with congressional voting behavior and explores the interaction between party and ideology discussed by Bond and Fleisher. In addition, the study uses a measure of public support for the president that is truly district-based and finds some evidence to support, but also to discount, earlier theories regarding the relationship between public and congressional support for the president.

The reasons a member of Congress supports a president explained a great deal of the variance in presidential support scores. Political party and ideology are the most important determinants of presidential support, but other variables also help determine it. Results from the study support most of the hypotheses presented with some notable exceptions. The results provide evidence to support the interaction between the party of the member and his/her ideology. Further studies in this area, as well as others dealing with determinants of congressional voting, for example, should include this interactive variable.

In terms of public support for the president and its effect on congressional support, the study uses available district-level data to get a more accurate reading of public support as it relates to specific members of Congress. While the results support the theory that public support for the president affects congressional support, further research is needed. The results suggest that the honeymoon presidents are thought to have may be overstated. For President Bush, district support in the 1988 elections increased congressional support more in his last year in office than in his first, and for President Clinton, public support had no significant effect at all. The support going to a viable third party candidate may have eliminated any congressional perception of public support for Clinton and his honeymoon period.

This measurement of public support has its problems, not the least of which is its validity throughout the president's term in office. The electoral vote for the president as a measure of public support, while better in terms of getting district-level data, is problematic because public opinion changes. But, until pollsters conduct surveys and report data on the district level, the actual impact of public opinion on congressional support will be difficult to explain. Nationwide polls measuring support for the president also have problems, as discussed earlier.

Leadership provided an interesting contrast in this study. As one would expect, Republican leaders were more likely than Democratic leaders to support Bush. But, according to the results, there was some evidence to suggest that Republican leaders were also more likely to support President Clinton. One can think of situations during the first year of the Clinton presidency, such as the NAFTA vote, that demonstrate this result. Many of the Democratic party leaders did not support the NAFTA position, while Republicans did. The result is still surprising on an aggregate level. If Clinton cannot rely on the Democratic party leaders to support his agenda and programs, on whom can he rely?[41]

Such a situation again raises the question of whether one-party control of government matters in terms of governance.[42] Divided government is not only a phenomenon of party control of the legislative and executive branches, but also of many other situations. Ideological, policy, regional, and constituency differences also divide support for certain programs. One of President Clinton's most vocal opponents in the health care debate was Jim Cooper, a Democrat from Tennessee, who replaced Vice President Gore in the Senate. If one wanted to choose a potential supporter of a Clinton program, Cooper would be the logical but, in this case, incorrect choice.

The results of the interactive variable support the idea that divided government is a larger issue than which party controls the institutions of government. As some of the results suggest, in certain situations the opposition party is more supportive of the president than his own party. If David Mayhew is correct in his assessment that divided government does not make a difference in passing legislation, then perhaps there are other kinds of divergence that lead to a nontraditional form of divided government. This study has mentioned a few possibilities in this area, all of which require additional study.

What other areas should be explored? One possibility is a reexamination of the use of the ideology measures. Scholars typically look at this variable in terms of liberal and conservative scores, but perhaps a more relevant measure would compare a member's ideology to the president's. As the difference increases, presidential support should decrease. In addition, as mentioned, further research in the area of other divisions between the executive and legislative branches seems warranted. For example, regional disparities and electoral concerns—impacts on the district—may need to be included in congressional support research.

This study has provided support for existing theories, but it also developed some new insights into current thinking on the interaction between party and ideology. One must consider party and ideology when examining support for the president, but the results may not be as intuitive as one would think. Research will continue in this area because of the ever-changing nature of the two branches and the subsequent changes in the relationship between them. Republican control of the 104th Congress provides an interesting scenario for studies on divided government that has not occurred in forty years. Congressional support for the president is an important topic, but the bottom line in this relationship is its impact on public policy. The nature of the presidential-congressional partnership will determine the policies and direction of the nation. It could also result in an impasse that cripples policy development.

Notes

1. See Richard E. Neustadt, *Presidential Power: The Politics of Leadership* (New York: Wiley, 1980); George C. Edwards III, *Presidential Influence in Congress* (San Francisco: Freeman, 1980); and Jon R. Bond and Richard Fleisher, *The President in the Legislative Arena* (Chicago: University of Chicago Press, 1990).
2. See Theodore Lowi, *The Personal Presidency* (Ithaca, N.Y.: Cornell University Press, 1985); and Edwards, *Presidential Influence in Congress.*
3. For example, see Brad Lockerbie and Stephen A. Borrelli, "Getting Inside the Beltway: Perceptions of Presidential Skill and Success in Congress," *British Journal of Political Science* 19 (January 1989): 96–106.
4. Congressional Quarterly's presidential box scores used between 1954–1975 would be such a measure.
5. The model to test this hypothesis is: SUPPORT = a + b1POLITICAL PARTY + b2IDEOLOGY + b3PARTY/IDEOLOGY INTERACTION + b4LEADERSHIP + b5PUBLIC PRESIDENTIAL SUPPORT + b6MARGIN OF VICTORY + e where: SUPPORT is the member's presidential support score, POLITICAL PARTY is whether the member is of the same political party as the president, IDEOLOGY is the member's ideology measured by his/her ADA score, PARTY/IDEOLOGY INTERACTION is the interactive variable for ideology and party for each member, LEADERSHIP is whether the member is a congressional leader, PUBLIC PRESIDENTIAL SUPPORT is the public support for the president measured by district-level voting support for the president in the last election, MARGIN OF VICTORY is the member's margin of victory in his/her last election. In addition, variables are added to represent the slope dummy variables associated with certain theories.
6. For example, see David S. Broder, *The Party's Over: The Failure of Politics in America* (New York: Harper and Row, 1972); and William J. Crotty and Gary Jacobson, *American Parties in Decline* (Boston: Little, Brown, 1980).
7. This is documented in Norman J. Ornstein, Thomas Mann, and Michael J. Malbin, *Vital Statistics on Congress, 1993–1994* (Washington, D.C.: American Enterprise Institute, 1994).
8. For a discussion of reelection and representation, see Morris P. Fiorina, *Representatives, Roll Calls, and Constituencies* (Lexington, Mass.: Heath, 1974); Heinz Eulau and Paul K. Karps, "The Puzzle of Representation: Specifying Components of Responsiveness," *Legislative Studies Quarterly* 2 (1977): 233–254; and Richard Fenno, *Home Style: House Members in Their Districts* (Boston: Little, Brown, 1978).
9. For example, see John A. Ferejohn and Randall L. Calvert, "Presidential Coattails in Historical Perspective," *American Journal of Political Science* 28 (February 1984): 127–146; and Morris A. Fiorina, "The Presidency and the Contemporary Electoral System," in *The Presidency and the Political System,* ed. Michael Nelson, (Washington, D.C.: CQ Press, 1984).
10. Melissa P. Collie and David W. Brady, "The Decline of Partisan Voting Coalitions in the House of Representatives," in *Congress Reconsidered,* 3d. ed., ed. Lawrence C. Dodd and Bruce I. Oppenheimer (Washington, D.C.: CQ Press, 1985).
11. John W. Kingdon, *Congressmen's Voting Decisions,* 2d ed. (New York: Harper and Row, 1981).
12. For discussion on the impact on ideology and voting behavior, see also Jerrold E. Schneider, *Ideological Coalitions in Congress* (Westport, Conn.: Greenwood, 1979); Fenno, *Home Style;* and Barbara Sinclair, "Coping with Uncertainty: Building Coalitions in the House and the Senate," in *The New Congress,* ed. Thomas E. Mann and Norman J. Ornstein (Washington, D.C.: American Enterprise Institute, 1981).
13. Discussion on the crossing of party lines due to ideology can be found in *Congressman and their Constituencies,* by Lewis A. Froman Jr. (Chicago: Rand McNally, 1963);

Jon R. Bond and Richard Fleisher, "The Limits of Presidential Popularity as a Source of Influence in the U.S. House," *Legislative Studies Quarterly* 5 (February 1980): 69–78; David W. Brady and Charles S. Bullock III, "Is There a Conservative Coalition in the House?" *Journal of Politics* 42 (May 1980): 549–559.

14. See Eric R. A. N. Smith, Richard Herrera, and Cheryl L. Herrera, "The Measurement Characteristics of Congressional Roll-Call Indexes," *Legislative Studies Quarterly* 15 (May 1990): 283–295. This article provides support for the use of certain indexes (specifically ADA and Conservative Coalition) in the measurement of ideology within Congress.

15. Bond and Fleisher, *The President in the Legislative Arena*, 21.

16. See Froman, *Congressman and their Constituencies*.

17. See also James MacGregor Burns, *The Deadlock of Democracy: Four-Party Politics in America* (Englewood Cliffs, N.J.: Prentice-Hall, 1963).

18. This is done by creating a slope dummy variable. For a discussion on slope dummy or dummy interaction effects, refer to Larry D. Schroeder, David L. Sjoquist, and Paula E. Stephan, *Understanding Regression Analysis: An Introductory Guide* (Thousand Oaks, Calif.: Sage), 58.

19. Cited by Walter J. Oleszek in *Congressional Procedures and the Policy Process*, 2d ed. (Washington, D.C.: CQ Press, 1984), 225.

20. Cited by George C. Edwards III in "Presidential Leadership in Congress," *Presidents and Their Parties: Leadership or Neglect?* ed. Robert Harmel (New York: Praeger 1984), 187.

21. See Bond and Fleisher, *The President in the Legislative Arena*.

22. Coding for this variable is as follows: −2 for a party leader of the opposition party, −1 for a committee chair of the opposition party, 0 for any nonleader, 1 for a committee chair of the same party, and 2 for a party leader of the same party. One would expect that support for the president increases as one moves from −2 to 2. One could also code this variable with a series of dummy variables representing each type of congressional member and determine the amount of support for each type. I will also do this when presenting the results.

23. See George C. Edwards III, "Presidential Influence in the House: Presidential Prestige as a Source of Presidential Power," *American Political Science Review* 70 (1976): 101–113; Edwards, *Presidential Influence in Congress;* and Neustadt, *Presidential Power*.

24. For a discussion of the limited impact of popular presidential support, see Bond and Fleisher, "The Limits of Presidential Popularity"; and Jon R. Bond, Richard Fleisher, and Michael Northrup, "Public Opinion and Presidential Support," *Annals of the American Academy of Political and Social Science* 499 (September 1988): 47–63.

25. For example, see Douglass Rivers and Nancy Rose, "Passing the President's Program: Public Opinion and Presidential Influence in Congress," *American Journal of Political Science* 29 (May 1985): 183–196; and Charles W. Ostrom and Dennis M. Simon, "Promise and Performance: A Dynamic Model of Presidential Popularity," *American Political Science Review* 79 (June 1985): 334–358.

26. See Bond and Fleisher, *The President in the Legislative Arena*, for a discussion of the difficulties of this measurement.

27. Ibid., 25–30.

28. Anita Pritchard, "An Evaluation of CQ Presidential Support Scores: The Relationship Between Presidential Election Results and Congressional Voting Decisions," *American Journal of Political Science* 30 (May 1986). Pritchard argues that it may not be appropriate to attribute influence to district presidential vote, but given the alternative, it is a useful measure of the constituency. The measure of this variable may also be a measure for the party identification of the district. One expects a Democratic district to support a Democratic presidential candidate. A Republican member from this district, therefore, may support the Democratic president because the district identifies more with the Democratic party and he/she wants to remain in office. This

could also be considered another form of public support.

29. One would expect that the impact of the presidential vote in the district will decline during the president's term. Therefore, this measure may not be as useful for the model using 1992 data.

30. All data were gathered from *The Almanac of American Politics 1990* (Washington, D.C.: National Journal, 1991); and *Politics in America 1992 and 1994* (Washington, D.C.: Congressional Quarterly, 1993 and 1995).

31. For a discussion on other measures of presidential support and the relative advantages and disadvantages, the reader should refer to George C. Edwards III, *At the Margins* (New Haven, Conn.: Yale University Press, 1989). Edwards develops and compares four indexes of presidential support; overall support (CQ support score), nonunanimous support (support for president when the winning side numbered less than 80 percent of those who voted, single-vote support, and key votes (uses only votes that are considered very important).

32. See Russell D. Renka, "The Locus of Presidential Success and Failure with Congress," paper presented at the Annual Meeting of the American Political Science Association, New York (September 1-4, 1994).

33. Eighty-nine percent of the variance is explained for the year 1989, the first year of the Bush presidency, while 91 percent is explained in the last year (1992) and 81 percent in the first year of the Clinton administration (1993). These adjusted R2 values are significant at better than the 0.0001 level.

34. The negative coefficient in 1993 signifies the change in party administration, so that Republicans, coded as 1, supported President Clinton 41 percent less than Democrats. Although the party variable in the 1989 model was not significant, this is likely due to multicollinearity problems with the interactive variable. When the interactive variable is not included in the model, party affiliation is highly significant with a parameter estimate of 8.34. The effect of party in the 1989 model is much less than the other two.

35. A ten-point increase in ADA led to only a 1.4 percent increase in support.

36. This parameter estimate is interpreted by adding the ADA score parameter with the interactive variable for a Republican (because Republicans are coded as 1).

37. Adding the estimates together shows support decreasing by 0.35 rather than 0.50.

38. During 1992, the last year of the Bush administration, the decrease in presidential support by liberal Democrats was less (-0.40) than a liberal Republican (-0.54). During 1993, the first year of the Clinton administration, the increase in presidential support was greater for liberal Republicans (0.58) than liberal Democrats (0.14).

39. When this variable is separated into a series of four dummy variables, one can see the impacts of the leadership position more clearly. Of the four variables, Democratic party leader, Democratic committee chair, Republican committee chair, and Republican party leader, neither of the Democratic leadership categories is significant, but both Republican positions are.

40. One must keep in mind concerning this result that a presidential support score was not furnished for the Speaker of the House, and therefore a potential major party leader supporter is eliminated from the analysis.

41. One could argue against the measurement of the party leader variable used in this study. For example, this study did not include subcommittee chairs as leaders, yet one could argue that they are leaders. In addition, certain "party positions," such as deputy majority whip, are not included as "leaders." All these omissions could be included. The problem, however, is that soon almost everybody is some type of leader. And while many scholars would make such an argument concerning the legislative process, from a practical research standpoint, it does not make sense.

42. See David Mayhew, *Divided We Govern: Lawmaking and Investigation, 1946–1990* (New Haven, Conn.: Yale University Press, 1991), for evidence to support the idea that divided government is unimportant in terms of passing legislation.

8

Congress, the President, and Automatic Government: The Case of Military Base Closures

Christopher J. Deering

In 1801, during the waning days of the Federalist administration of President John Adams, the United States purchased land in Philadelphia and five other cities and commenced the construction of six naval shipyards.[1] That same year the new president, Thomas Jefferson, attempted to halt spending on the shipyards. A year later, Samuel L. Mitchill, chairman of the House Committee on Naval Affairs, charged that $200,000 had been spent on the yards without legislative authority. But the Jefferson administration found the yards difficult to abandon, and they were retained, partially complete, as public property. By 1825 the six yards had been supplemented by a seventh, in Pensacola, Florida. That same year John Quincy Adams's navy secretary, Samuel L. Southard, argued that "the greater part, if not the whole, of our Navy Yards, are badly located; and ... a very large proportion of the public money, which has been, and continues to be, expended upon them, might have been saved, by a wiser location at the commencement." Philadelphia, for example, was far from the open sea and tended to freeze up during long, cold winters. Thus, ironically, the backbone of America's modern system of navy yards was established during "anti–navy yard" administrations early in the nation's history. All but one of the original seven naval shipyards are still in operation. After a protracted battle, the Philadelphia navy yard was closed in September 1995.

The yard was closed—along with numerous other shipyards, forts, bases, reservations, labs, and installations—by a complicated law first passed by Congress in 1988. Under that law a base closure and realignment commission was given the task of producing a list of military bases that could be closed (or realigned) without harm to the national security. As we will see, the commission is a legislative by-product of Congress's pork barrel nature and its endemic distrust of the executive branch. It also is emblematic of an age of policy making frequently called "dedistributive." The purpose of this chapter is to examine the military base closure process as an example of how the legislative and executive branches have sought to solve collective decision-making problems in an age of dedistributive politics.[2]

In order to understand the pattern of policy making displayed here, we must first understand several important concepts about collective decision making and congressional-presidential relations. These are the subjects of the chapter's first section. In the following three sections, the case study

shows how the base closure controversy came about and why the base closure commission was created—to solve a collective decision-making problem faced by Congress. The chapter concludes with a discussion of lessons
to be learned from the base closure process.

Collective Decision-Making Problems, Delegation, and Blame Avoidance

Congress is well known for its distributive policy making, the result of
which is laws with focused benefits and widely dispersed costs. Distributive
policy making thrives during periods of national economic growth. As long
as the federal budget was expanding, a process facilitated by inflation-based
revenue increases (sometimes called "bracket creep"), more money was available to expand government programs. This was the situation in the United
States throughout most of the nation's history. By the late 1970s, however,
America found itself in a fiscal crisis. Chronic deficits, acute inflation,
unemployment, and the disappearance of the Vietnam peace dividend
brought an end to a long period of government expansion and distributive
politics.[3] This painful reversal of distributive politics has been aptly characterized as the advent of the age of dedistributive politics.[4]

Rather than continuing to distribute targeted benefits, Congress was
forced by economic circumstances to impose targeted reductions. These
reductions would be visible, costly, painful, and politically risky. Congress,
collectively, could not cope very well with making such decisions. Politicians, writes R. Kent Weaver, need to "concern themselves with avoiding
blame for perceived or real losses that they either imposed or acquiesced in,
as well as with claiming credit for benefits they have granted."[5] Accepting
blame for targeted reductions is not the only cost associated with collective
decision making. As public choice scholars have shown, decisions require
time and information. For legislators both may be in short supply. Typically
the legislator's solution in these situations is to delegate authority for decision making to the president or to executive agencies. At first glance, these
delegations may appear to be the perfect solution: cede to experts the
authority and responsibility for making policy decisions. Unfortunately,
there are costs to delegation as well, since the agent to whom responsibility
is ceded may not always do what members of Congress might wish. Formally, Congress will delegate whenever it expects the benefits of delegation
to exceed the likely costs—which may be measured in terms of bureaucratic error, noncompliance, or even willful disobedience.[6] To limit the costs of
delegation and help ensure executive compliance, Congress frequently
amends legislation by adding conditions, provisions, procedures, and reporting requirements.[7]

Mistrust of the executive branch—the president, cabinet departments,
and other federal agencies—is likely to exacerbate these interbranch problems. Whether the mistrust reflects partisan politics or simply interinstitu-

tional competition makes little difference. When such mistrust is combined with Congress's collective decision-making difficulties, a complex yet common set of barriers to making important policy decisions comes to the fore. This combination of structural, procedural, and political impediments frequently goes by the generic title of "gridlock." Congress must face up to difficult decisions that have real costs for constituents. Institutional rules frequently allow a minority of members disproportionate power to block those costly decisions. Mistrust of the executive makes legislators hesitant to delegate in an open-ended way. Increasingly, therefore, as R. Kent Weaver tells us, Congress has adopted discretion-limiting devices as a means of overcoming these barriers.[8] The military base closure process is but one example of how the government makes collective decisions in a time of limits. Current debates about the line-item veto, balanced budget amendments, nuclear waste disposal, and many other policy issues feature the same interbranch political dynamics.

Military Bases and the Triumph of Distributive Politics

The roots of the base closure controversy run deep in American history. They are the product of Congress's jealous control over base openings. For two centuries military bases (forts, arsenals, reservations, shipyards, and other facilities) have been the most visible manifestations of the defense establishment in congressional districts. The pork barrel character of their construction, location, and relocation has animated legislative decision making for just as long. For example, the establishment of a string of military trading posts—the U.S. Indian factory system—along the northwestern frontier was among Congress's first acts. In addition to serving military and foreign policy interests, the posts had important economic impacts—albeit in areas not yet admitted as states—and were precursors of the U.S. Army's system of frontier forts that formed the backbone of the land army's structure into the twentieth century.[9]

Under the Constitution, Congress is granted explicit and exclusive legislative authority for the acquisition and construction (Article I, Section 8) of military bases (forts, magazines, arsenals, dockyards, and other buildings) and for their disposal (Article IV, Section 3). Congress has used this power to broaden the authority of the executive and, in the case of some perceived or real abuse of that power, to restrict the executive's power within the narrowest of confines. As a general rule, congressional action has been more exacting during peacetime and much more expansive during wartime. Broad grants of authority during the Civil War, for example, gave way to explicit postwar restrictions. An act of 1877, for instance, required specific congressional authorization for any construction project costing more than $20,000.[10] As Elias Huzar points out, however, the primary land problem during postwar periods was disposal rather than acquisition. And in this, as with construction and land purchase legislation, members could be no less exacting. A 1931 act, for example, forbade the sale or disposal of any real estate by the War Department without the express authority of Congress.[11]

In the modern era, bases, in a variety of shapes and sizes, continue to be important community assets. Indeed, many adults are familiar with communities that are identified and dominated by a nearby installation. San Diego, Charleston, and Norfolk are all "navy towns." Major military installations require large tracts of land, employ and house thousands of people, have a strong impact on schools, and influence local culture. Of the many facilities operated by the Defense Department, these installations have frequently been the most visible. But the military has long owned thousands of smaller tracts of lands—for radar sites, recruiting centers, laboratories, or coat manufacturing plants. It is not surprising, therefore, to hear a House Armed Services Committee aide of the 1960s say: "Our committee is a real estate committee. Don't forget that. If you study our committee, you are studying real estate transactions." [12]

During World War II, Congress suspended its practice of annually authorizing military public works projects, which included real estate purchases. Rather quickly thereafter, as Cold War politics led to large-scale and widespread construction projects, executive-legislative relations deteriorated.[13] Congress's role in the authorization process reemerged in 1947 and was cemented in 1951 with an amendment to the military construction bill that required the Defense Department to "come into agreement" with the House and Senate Armed Services Committees prior to any real estate transaction of more than $25,000.[14] Raymond Dawson argues that congressional intervention was more pronounced in missile defense systems than in any other strategic program precisely because the purchase and construction of missile sites involved real estate and public works projects. In 1961, according to Barry Blechman, only 2 percent of the defense budget required annual authorization; but 90 percent of all military construction had to be authorized each year.[15]

On November 18, 1964, Secretary of Defense Robert S. McNamara announced that the administration intended to close or phase out ninety-five military installations during the following eighteen months. Of the ninety-five "bases," perhaps one-third were the same radar and missile sites that the Armed Services Committees had fought to gain control of during the late 1940s and the 1950s. But McNamara's list also included the historic Portsmouth Naval Shipyard, which had been established in 1801 along with the other five original naval shipyards.[16]

In response, the House Armed Services Committee added an amendment to a bill authorizing nearly $2 billion in military construction at 427 bases during fiscal year 1966. The amendment required the Department of Defense to notify the House and Senate Armed Services Committees anytime it planned to close a military installation and permitted either chamber of Congress to prevent closure by passing a simple resolution (sometimes called a legislative veto). A revised form of this amendment—without the legislative veto—was contained in the bill that emerged from the House-Senate conference committee. The bill was sent to President Lyndon Johnson, who promptly vetoed it because he found the base closure restriction "repugnant to the Constitution." [17] Although a watered-down version of the base closure provision was included in a revised bill signed by President Johnson, the terms of debate for the following two decades were set. Presidents would continually defend their powers as commanders in chief to manage the military establishment. Congress, ever worried about the local impact of base construction and even more worried about the perceived adverse impacts of closures or realignments, would continually defend its constitutional authority to "raise and support" the armed forces. Passage of this amendment, it turns out, coincided with expansion of the war in Vietnam and of military spending in general. As a result, the debate about base closure became largely moot until the end of U.S. military involvement in Southeast Asia.

During the early 1970s nearly 500 military bases were closed in the United States.[18] This reduction was caused by U.S. withdrawal from the war in Vietnam and made possible by open-ended authority provided to the Pentagon by the Armed Services Committees. Distressed at the potential for adverse economic impacts and convinced that base closings were being used by the administration to punish uncooperative members, a large number of members rallied in support of a floor amendment offered by House Majority Leader Thomas P. "Tip" O'Neill, D-Mass., and Rep. William S. Cohen, R-Maine. The amendment was drafted in response to a Ford administration announcement that 160 more bases would be closed or reduced in size. Among the bases to be closed was Loring Air Force Base in northern Maine. The base was something of a throwback to an era of more-limited-range manned bombers. But Loring was expensive to run and difficult to keep open during the region's extraordinarily cold and snowy winters. Newer bombers, submarines, and intercontinental ballistic missiles had weakened the national security rationale for keeping the base open. But with the support of Majority Leader O'Neill—and like-minded but less vocal potential losers in the battle over the Ford administration's list—a solution was at hand.

O'Neill's first attempt at thwarting the base closure plan, an amendment to the defense procurement authorization, failed on a floor vote of 152-202, on April 9, 1976. But his second, slightly revised, attempt—an amendment to the fiscal year 1977 military construction authorization—succeeded. To O'Neill's regret, however, the bill was vetoed by President Ford. Ford's July 2, 1976, veto message challenged the amendment on budgetary and efficiency grounds and suggested that it placed an impermissible limitation on the power of the presidency. Unable to override the veto, Congress revised the provision once again, and the military construction bill was signed into law. From the members' viewpoint, the military construction bill now had two compelling advantages. First, it featured $3.3 billion in construction funds for over 400 projects at bases and installations in the United States and abroad.[19] Thus, it had the distributive impact favored by legislators. Second, it provided a bureaucratic roadblock to base closures or realignments, thus protecting from dedistributive harm not only the representatives of districts in which the 160 targeted bases were located, but also those of districts in which future base closures might occur. Moreover, the new procedures provided political cover to members who might claim that voting for the bill made economic good sense (due to potential future cost savings) and resulted in environmental benefits (due to a provision that required adherence to the National Environmental Policy Act (NEPA)).

As finally passed, the law said that no base with more than 500 employees could be closed and that no base could have its civilian work force cut by more than 1,000 people or 50 percent unless

- Congress was notified of the intended closure or realignment;
- all provisions of the NEPA had been complied with, including the requirement that an environmental impact statement (EIS) be filed;
- the House and Senate Armed Services Committees had been notified of a final decision to close or realign a base and had been given a report of its financial, military, and environmental impacts; and
- a sixty-day period had elapsed.

Although these requirements applied only to Pentagon activities during fiscal year 1977, the procedures were altered slightly and made permanent on August 1, 1977. The provisions were revised somewhat in 1978, 1982, and 1985. Supported by a massive military buildup during the Reagan administration, they had their intended effect. From 1977 to 1987 not a single military base in the United States was closed. Indeed, under a controversial plan to expand the navy, a homeport project was implemented that significantly increased the number of bases and made subsequent base closures even more difficult politically.

Without actually prohibiting base closures, the O'Neill amendment erected a very high wall for the Pentagon to scale. Procedural barriers ensured that any base closure would require early congressional notification and time-consuming effort. During that time, members would be given ample opportunity to marshal local or national opposition to specific closures. Nothing would prohibit powerful members from simply blocking the use of appropriated funds for the closure of particular bases. At bottom, therefore, dedistributive policy making in this context was simply distributive policy making in the negative. Rather than making specific incremental distributions, Congress made specific incremental prohibitions.

The Base Closure and Realignment Act: A(nother) Bad Idea Whose Time Had Come[20]

Although subsequent reenactments allowed the base closure issue to resurface briefly during the late 1970s and early 1980s, the 1977 law ended debate about base closures as effectively as it ended the closures themselves. All this changed in 1987. During floor debate on the fiscal year 1988 defense authorization bill, Rep. Dick Armey, R-Texas, offered an amendment that would have empowered a congressionally appointed commission on base closures to generate a list of bases to close or realign. Armey's amendment also would have severely limited Congress's ability to alter the list, removed the regulatory roadblocks to closures (including NEPA regulations), and resulted in $5 billion in budget savings. Offered on the open floor, the proposal came within seven votes of passage.

Even in defeat, the vote on the Armey amendment proved instructive in four ways. First, $5 billion in defense budget savings from base closures was a powerfully attractive idea. Second, in order to succeed, base closure legislation would require support from legislators with little to lose in order to overcome opposition from legislators with bases in their districts. (Armey's Texas district had no military bases.) Third, the vote would have to be on a procedure for accomplishing the base closure process rather than on specific closures or realignments. And fourth, the new process could not simply delegate open-ended base closure authority to the president or the secretary of defense.

Armey explained why Congress would not allow the executive branch to control the base closure process:

> At issue is who will have control of the pork. Any congressional veteran will tell you that pork is power—both the ability to distribute it and the ability to deny it. If the executive branch has unrestricted freedom to close bases, the argument runs, it would have a potent political weapon in its hands to retaliate against anyone who defies the president on key legislation. Congress has an institutional interest in insuring that the executive branch does not have it. And while parochial interests can be defeated ... institutional interests cannot.[21]

To be successful, therefore, base closure legislation had to accomplish two objectives: eliminate Congress's impulse to legislate in a distributive fashion and avoid empowering the executive in a manner that allowed political blackmail.

During the year following Armey's original amendment, legislative and executive politics followed a familiar path. On the Hill, Armey's near miss spawned the sincerest form of political flattery—imitation. On the Senate side, several Armed Services Committee members, including Chairman Sam Nunn, D-Ga., began to shape base closure provisions, which became part of the defense authorization bill reported by that committee. On the House side, Armey sought to reintroduce his own legislation in somewhat altered form as a new amendment to the authorization. In addition, other members, including Rep. Les Aspin, D-Wis., chairman of the House Armed Services Committee, and Rep. William L. Dickinson, R-Ala., the ranking Republican member of the committee, jointly offered their own version of the original Armey proposal.

Meanwhile, opponents sought to stall or defeat Armey's new legislation on jurisdictional grounds. Reps. Jack Brooks, D-Texas, and Walter B. Jones, D-N.C.—chairmen of the Government Operations Committee and the Merchant Marine and Fisheries Committee, respectively, and members with major military installations in their districts—asked the Rules Committee to block consideration of Armey's new amendment on the House floor, arguing that consideration would bypass their own stake in the process. The Rules Committee agreed, and Speaker Jim Wright, D-Texas, subsequently referred the legislation to all three committees (as HR 4481). This multiple referral procedure assuaged the jurisdictional jealousies that existed in the House but also made passage less likely. Armey was diplomatic but pointed in the face of this setback: "I understand the problem is a committee jurisdictional dispute. However, I cannot overlook the possibility that the jurisdictional dispute could be a ruse to kill the bill." [22]

Despite legislative momentum in both chambers, the bill had trouble reaching the floor. In the spring, both Armed Services Committees reported defense authorization bills that contained base closure provisions. A House-Senate conference committee was convened to reconcile the differences between the two provisions, but House conferees later dropped their provision in deference to the other panels examining the issue. House Majority Leader Thomas S. Foley, D-Wash., began to backtrack from his own assurances that the legislation would come to a floor vote. Meanwhile, each of the three House committees assigned to review the Armey amendment—Government Operations, Merchant Marine and Fisheries, and Rules—began to alter the legislation in numerous small ways. These alterations were a testament to the power of the base closure idea but also a typical means of congressional opposition. Indeed, one Pentagon wag characterized the numerous revisions as "death by pinpricks." [23] Finally, a much-altered version of the original Armey proposal reached the House floor in early July 1988—having been reported by Armed Services, Government Operations, and Merchant Marine and Fisheries and merged by Rules. Before the floor vote, however, Armey was able to gain permission for an up-or-down vote on his own bill as a substitute for the much-altered, multiple-committee bill. Armey's substitute passed, by a 223-186 vote, on July 12, 1988. The conference report was approved by both chambers on October 12 and became law (PL 100-526) on October 24, 1988. In its final form, the Base Closure and Realignment Act of 1988:

- created a twelve-member base closure commission;
- provided for its appointment by the secretary of defense;

- required the commission to report recommendations for closure and realignment by December 31, 1988;
- required the secretary to approve or reject the list in total;
- permitted Congress forty-five days to reject the entire package by joint resolution; and
- severely limited the use of environmental impact statements as a dilatory tactic.

Would the law work? In November, as the newly appointed Commission on Base Closure and Realignment went about its work, House Armed Services Committee Chairman Les Aspin offered this calculus for why it would:

> Right now, a hundred or more congressmen are worried that bases in their districts might be closed. Once the base list appears, most will breathe a sigh of relief. For, at that point, the overwhelming majority of the members of Congress will have a vested interest in seeing that the closure program goes through—because approval will mean the issue is dead for a decade or better, and bases in their districts will be safe from the ax for a long time.[24]

Aspin's prognostication was almost perfect. On December 29, 1988, the commission recommended the closure of eighty-six bases and partial closure of five others. Secretary of Defense Frank C. Carlucci III endorsed the list on January 5, 1989. On March 1, after a layover period required by the new law, the forty-five-day congressional clock began. In April all but four members of the House Armed Services Committee voted to oppose a resolution to keep the bases open. That resolution was then defeated on the House floor, on April 18, by a vote of 43-381.[25] As expected, votes in favor of the resolution came from members slated to lose bases in or near their districts.

Representative Aspin might have erred in one respect. The 1988 law provided for only a single round of base closures and operated, in effect, as a one-time exception to the legal barriers Congress had constructed during the previous decade. Once the 1988 round was complete, the existing legal barriers once again became operative. Therefore, when Secretary of Defense Dick Cheney proposed closing an additional thirty-five domestic bases in early 1990, Congress simply reverted to previous political form. As before, however, base closure had sufficient political appeal to generate support for the formation of a commission. The commission process was resuscitated in revised form in the fiscal year 1991 defense authorization bill, and three more rounds of cuts were mandated—in 1991, 1993, and 1995.

Under the Base Closure and Realignment Act of 1990, the roles of the defense secretary and the (now) eight-member commission reversed, and Congress added a role for the General Accounting Office (GAO). Now it was up to the Pentagon to produce a base closure list and a justification for each action. It then became the commission's job to hold public hearings and to review those recommendations. GAO would simultaneously audit the secretary's recommendations, determine whether they had been based on "proper criteria," and make a report to Congress. During its review, the commission could add to or subtract from the Pentagon's list of bases. The list would be referred directly to the president, who was empowered to accept or reject the list in whole or in part. But if the list changed, it would be sent back to the commission. The commission's final list had to be approved by the president by September 1 or the process would come to a halt. As before, congressional referral was governed by so-called fast track procedures that precluded delay or amendment. Congress could vote to disapprove the package—via a joint resolution subject to presidential veto—but no action was required for the package to go forward. Also as before, procedures were designed to defeat opponents of base closure.

While it is beyond the scope of this chapter to review in detail the three subsequent rounds of cuts, it is useful, nevertheless, to briefly summarize their outcomes. The first set of cuts under the revised law—proposed by the secretary of defense, reviewed by the commission, and approved by President George Bush—was sustained by the House on July 30, 1991, when a resolution to defeat the package was itself defeated, 60-364.[26] That package included twenty-five major military installations. During a more contentious second round of cuts under the revised law, the commission ordered the closing of thirty-five more major bases and numerous minor installations. That list, although somewhat different than the one Defense Secretary Les Aspin had proposed, was quickly approved by President Bill Clinton. A resolution to disapprove the list was defeated on the Senate floor by a vote of 12-83, on September 20, 1993.[27] The third and final round of cuts was cleared by the House on September 8, 1995, when a joint resolution to reject the commission's list failed on the House floor by a vote of 75-343. This final package—the fourth since passage of the Base Closure and Realignment Act of 1988—closed an additional seventy-nine bases, realigned twenty-six others, and was expected to save almost $20 billion over twenty years.[28]

Why Base Closure Works

In July 1991, two days before President Bush approved the first round of base closures under the revised law, Sen. Arlen Specter, R-Pa., filed a suit in federal court in an attempt to block the closure of the Philadelphia Naval Shipyard. In the suit Specter alleged that the commission's decision to recommend closure of the Philadelphia yard was based upon improper criteria and, further, that the commission had violated the law's disclosure requirement by failing to place information regarding its decision in the record in a timely fashion. The district court dismissed the complaint on the grounds that the law itself precluded judicial review of the president's approval order. But a divided appeals court reversed that ruling, determining that the president's order was reviewable. This ruling also was appealed, this time to the Supreme Court. After considering the petition of Navy Secretary John H. Dalton, the Court agreed to hear the case.

On May 23, 1994, the Supreme Court reversed the appeals court decision favorable to Specter and held that the president's order was not reviewable.[29] In so deciding, the Court made clear that while the joint decision-making process established by the law and the discretion granted to the president at the final stage of that process might raise questions of error and merit, "how the president chooses to exercise the discretion Congress has granted him is not a matter for our review." [30] With this decision, the last remaining obstacle to the base closure process was eliminated.

The Court explicitly recognized the political character of the law and the problem it was designed to solve. In his concurring opinion, Justice David H. Souter referred to the base closure law as an "unusual statutory scheme." The law represented, he argued,

> a considered allocation of authority between the Executive and Legislative Branches to enable each to reach important, but politically difficult, objectives.... If judicial review could eliminate one base from a package, the political resolution embodied in that package would be destroyed; if such review could eliminate an entire package, or leave its validity in doubt when a succeeding one had to be devised, the political resolution necessary to agree on the succeeding package would be rendered the more difficult, if not impossible.[31]

As Justice Souter's opinion and the events recounted above make clear, the base closure law represents a delicate balance of ingredients. So while the justice's characterization is certainly on the mark, to some degree it begs the inevitable question: Why does this process succeed?[32]

As we have seen, the base closure process succeeds because it solves the collective decision-making problems of dedistributive politics. Three characteristics of the process have made success possible: *delegation* of authority, symbolic *opposition*, and the *automation* of the decision-making process. There is no way of knowing whether the absence of any one of these characteristics would have doomed the base closure process. But it is clear that each contributed to the success that the process has enjoyed. It is also clear that these same characteristics are crucial to other areas of policy making in a dedistributive age with frequent divided government.

Delegation of Authority

A key component of both the 1988 and 1990 base closure laws was the creation of a bipartisan, independent commission. Commissions are products of the progressive era in American politics, and they are evidence of the divided nature of the American democracy.[33] The most important defining element of the base closure commissions is that they are neither wholly legislative nor wholly executive in character. If Congress can affect the commissions' work, then the base closure process becomes part of the collective decision-making problem the law is designed to solve. If the executive branch can influence the commissions' work excessively, then the process fails to address legislators' concern that delegating to the executive is too costly.

Under the law, the costs of delegating to the executive are reduced in four ways. First, the commission's eight members are drawn from both parties—indeed, six of the eight are congressionally recommended—and must be confirmed by the Senate. Second, the law places several restrictions on the sources for and longevity of the commission staff. Third, under the 1988 law the commission was charged with establishing its own list of base closures or realignments, thus ensuring its independence. Under the 1990 law the responsibility for generating the list was ceded to the Pentagon, but the commission could subtract or add to the secretary of defense's list. And fourth, the Pentagon must make explicit its rationale for closing or realigning bases. In concert, these requirements help to ensure a relatively narrow delegation of authority to the secretary of defense, with independent authority vested in the commission as a check on executive power. To prevent legislators from influencing the commission's work, Congress has created an arm's-length relationship between the commission and itself. Most important, Congress may reject the commission's list, but only in total.

Symbolic Opposition

Political scientists have long recognized the importance of symbolic opposition as a means of legitimizing political decisions.[34] For the base closure process to succeed, members in affected districts had to be accorded the opportunity to oppose the commission's decisions. The utility of symbolic opposition is captured nicely in the words of Sen. Phil Gramm, R-Texas:

> The beauty of this proposal is that: If you have a military base in your district—God forbid one should be closed in Texas, but it could happen—under this proposal, I have sixty days. So I come up here and I say, "God have mercy. Don't close this base in Texas. We can get attacked from the south. The Russians are going to go after our leadership and you know they are going to attack Texas. We need this base." Then I can go out and lie down in the street and the bulldozers are coming and I have a trusty aide there just as it gets there to drag me out of the way. All the people of Muleshoe, or wherever this base is, will say, "You know, Phil Gramm got whipped, but it was like the Alamo. He was with us until the last second." [35]

Writing symbolic opposition into the law requires careful legislative drafting since legislators are practiced in the art of using procedure to their advantage. Under the 1988 law, for example, members were allowed to introduce a resolution of disapproval and to have a recorded vote opposing the commission's recommendations. But the law did not provide funding for carrying out the decisions of the commission, and the process was nearly upset when opponents threatened to amend, delay, or filibuster the appropriations bill that provided those funds. The 1990 law fixed this defect by giving the commission budget, as well as program authority.

Like the appropriations challenge, Senator Specter's lawsuit was a real threat to the viability of the process—a threat that Justice Souter explicitly recognized in his opinion. Thus, the long legal process that resulted in defeat for Specter and the Philadelphia Naval Shipyard served a purpose in terms of symbolic politics. This is not to suggest that Senator Specter's lawsuit was calculated to fail. Without question, Specter opposed the decision of the commission and hoped for the success of his lawsuit. But just as certainly, Justice Souter saw the danger in allowing the pieces of the closure package to be separated from the whole.

Under the 1990 law, members have two opportunities to oppose commission actions. First, the law provides for open hearings after the initial list of proposed closures is promulgated. These hearings, which may persuade the commission to alter the list, allow members and other interested parties to make a case for their particular base or installation. In this way, due process is assured and at least symbolic opposition is allowed. Second, as noted, a resolution disapproving the closures is virtually assured a roll-call vote in at least one chamber prior to the conclusion of the process. In this way, members can go on record as opposing the closure of a base in their state or district.

Automation of the Decision-Making Process

It is a well-known fact that Congress is slow and deliberative and that its structure allows numerous veto points. In both chambers, though more pronouncedly in the Senate, minorities have influence disproportionate to their numbers. Time is one of an opposition minority's most important resources.[36] Forces opposed to change are never in a hurry. Delay is an ally, and strict adherence to House and Senate rules inevitably causes delay. A Senate filibuster, after all, does not actually preclude decisions; it simply makes them too painful and too costly in terms of legislative time. For base closure to work, therefore, the capacity for delay must be overcome. Base closure legislation overcomes the capacity for delay through automation of the decision-making process.

Both the 1988 and 1990 laws featured fixed deadlines for each step in the base closure process. Under the 1990 law, every base closure action— from commission appointment to final closure—must take place according to a legislatively mandated schedule. Two of these are most important. First, the president's discretion is limited because he must submit an approved list to Congress by September 1 or the process simply stops for that round. The law presumes, of course, that the executive wants to close or realign bases.

And second, Congress must act within forty-five days or the closures are deemed approved. In order to guarantee that this deadline is met, the law establishes "fast-track" procedures that ensure rapid Armed Services Committee consideration of joint resolutions to disapprove the list. These resolutions must be reported to the floor even if (as has been the case) they are opposed by the Armed Services Committees. As a result, each of the base closure lists submitted to date has been subject to a floor vote to disapprove. Not surprisingly, each resolution opposing closures has been defeated by a comfortable margin.

The Lessons of Base Closure: Dedistributive Politics in a Divided Age

The authors of the Constitution established divided government more than two hundred years ago.[37] Since then, one political party has controlled either or both of the two popular branches of government. But inasmuch as the Founders never anticipated organized political parties of the kind we have today, they were unconcerned with divided party control of government as we know it today. For most of the post–World War II period, the legislative and executive branches have been controlled by opposing parties. This has not been the advent of divided party government in the United States; rather, it simply is a new manifestation of it.

The politics of base closures highlights two key elements of divided (or separation of powers) government. First, in a system of blended rather than absolutely divided powers, political accommodation among the branches is difficult but necessary. In the presence of partisan division, real disagreements about policy are inevitable. Within the separation of powers system, interbranch competition and a certain level of mistrust are inevitable. Thus, each branch and each party must explore institutional and policy solutions that allow collective decisions to be reached without irrevocably compromising the independence of the parties or branches. The base closure process succeeds, perhaps better than other, similar policy solutions, because of its delicate balance of accommodation.

Second, the legislature frequently makes difficult political decisions by fashioning complicated, blame-avoiding procedural solutions. Delegation of authority, symbolic opposition and automation of the decision-making process are oft-utilized ingredients in these solutions. Likewise, Congress now frequently separates the adoption of a procedure aimed to achieve a widely supported collective good from the actual decision to reach the desired goal. Base closure legislation was widely supported because it promised to save billions of dollars at a time when budget deficits were widely regarded as a top political problem. The base closure process allowed members to boast that they had established a procedure that short-circuited their own tendencies toward political self-interest.

In sum, the base closure process works. It recognizes the difficulty of making collective decisions in a system that protects minority rights. It solves the problem of interbranch mistrust by careful and considered delegation and a sharing of decision-making authority. And it solves the problems of dedistributive policy making by permitting the allocation of targeted costs while at the same time ensuring due process to the losers.

Notes

1. The other cities were Washington, D.C.; Portsmouth, N.H.; Charlestown, Mass.; New York, N.Y.; and Norfolk, Va. Events reported in this paragraph are from Leonard D. White, *The Jeffersonians* (New York: Macmillan, 1951), 285–287.
2. Although structurally different, this chapter is similar to, but was undertaken quite independently of, Kenneth R. Mayer's "Closing Military Bases (Finally): Solving Collective Dilemmas Through Delegation," *Legislative Studies Quarterly* 20 (August 1995): 393–414.
3. See James A. Thurber, "The Consequences of Budget Reform for Congressional-Presidential Relations," *The Annals* 499 (September 1988): 101–113.
4. The term is used by Paul Light in *Artful Work: The Politics of Social Security Reform* (New York: Random House, 1985), 15.
5. R. Kent Weaver, *Automatic Government: The Politics of Indexation* (Washington, D.C.: Brookings Institution, 1988), 19.
6. See, among others, Mathew D. McCubbins and Talbot Page, "A Theory of Congressional Delegation," in *Congress: Structure and Policy*, ed. Mathew D. McCubbins and Terry Sullivan (New York: Cambridge University Press, 1987), 409–425; D. Roderick Kiewiet and Mathew D. McCubbins, *The Logic of Delegation: Congressional Parties and the Appropriations Process* (Chicago: University of Chicago Press, 1991), esp. chap. 2; Morris P. Fiorina, "Legislator Uncertainty, Legislative Control, and the Delegation of Legislative Power," *Journal of Law, Economics, and Organization* 2 (Spring 1986): 33–51; and Terry M. Moe, "The New Economics of Organization," *American Journal of Political Science* 28 (November 1984): 739–777.
7. McCubbins and Sullivan, 410–414. See also Mathew D. McCubbins, Roger G. Noll, and Barry R. Weingast, "Administrative Procedures as Instruments of Political Control," *Journal of Law, Economics, and Organization* 3 (Fall 1987): 243–276.
8. Weaver, 18–19.
9. See Carl P. Russell, *Guns on the Early Frontier* (Berkeley: University of California Press, 1957), esp. chap. 1. On the latter point regarding the role of frontier forts, see Stephen Skowronek, *Building a New American State: The Expansion of National Administrative Capacities, 1877–1920* (Cambridge: Cambridge University Press, 1982), 212–247.
10. Elias Huzar, *The Purse and the Sword: Control of the Army by Congress Through Appropriations, 1933–1950* (Ithaca, N.Y.: Cornell University Press, 1950), 224.
11. Ibid., 233.
12. This frequently repeated and reprinted quote is found in Lewis Anthony Dexter's "Congressmen and the Making of Military Policy," in *New Perspectives on the House of Representatives*, ed. Robert L. Peabody and Nelson W. Polsby (Chicago: Rand McNally, 1969), 182. It should be pointed out that Dexter's study predated the full expansion of the annual authorization process. Hence, the committee's control over real estate and construction was much more pronounced at the time.
13. See Raymond H. Dawson, "Congressional Innovation and Intervention in Defense Policy: Legislative Authorization of Weapons Systems," *American Political Science Review* 56 (1962): 42–57.

14. Ibid., 47.
15. Barry M. Blechman, *The Politics of National Security: Congress and U.S. Defense Policy* (New York: Oxford University Press, 1990), 29–31.
16. The list is contained in a story in *Congressional Quarterly Weekly Report*, November 20, 1964, 2724.
17. *Congressional Quarterly Weekly Report*, August 27, 1965, 1722.
18. The figure is reported in the *CQ Almanac* but not substantiated in any way. See "Bases: A History of Protection by the System," in *The 44th Annual CQ Almanac, 1988* (Washington, D.C.: Congressional Quarterly Inc., 1988), 441. Nonetheless, the figure is corroborated by President Ford's July 2, 1976, veto message to Congress, in which he stated that from 1969 to 1976 the Defense Department took 2,700 "actions to reduce, realign, or close military installations and activities," which resulted in the reduction of defense costs by more than $4 billion. Also, during the earlier controversy, Secretary McNamara claimed that 574 bases had closed since 1961.
19. The floor vote on the O'Neill amendment can be found in *Congressional Quarterly Weekly Report*, April 17, 1976, 924–925. For broad figures on the military construction bill, see *Congressional Quarterly Weekly Report*, September 25, 1976, 2630.
20. The reference is to Sen. Warren Rudman's characterization of the Gramm-Rudman-Hollings mandatory deficit reduction act as a "bad idea whose time had come." Like deficit reduction, base closures forced members to distribute painful costs to their constituents, and only a discretion-limiting, automatic procedure offered a way out of the political cul-de-sac members found themselves in.
21. Dick Armey, "Base Maneuvers: The Games Congress Plays With the Military Pork Barrel," *Policy Review* 43 (Winter 1988): 70–75.
22. "Base Closing Issue: Back to Drawing Board," *Congressional Quarterly Weekly Report*, April 30, 1988, 1145. The Rules Committee establishes the conditions for debating major legislation on the floor. In this case the Armey amendment could be debated only if it was among those specifically allowed by Rules. It was not.
23. "Members Go on the Offensive to Defend Bases," *Congressional Quarterly Weekly Report*, July 2, 1988, 1815.
24. David C. Morrison, "Caught off Base," *National Journal*, April 1, 1989, 801.
25. Having failed in the House, the resolution was never voted on in the Senate.
26. The vote can be found in *Congressional Quarterly Weekly Report*, August 3, 1991, 2196
27. The vote can be found in *Congressional Quarterly Weekly Report*, September 25, 1993, 2596.
28. Some lawmakers suggested that this final round of closures and realignments, expected to hit electorally important states like California, Florida, and Texas particularly hard, be put off until after the 1996 presidential election or that it be broken into two smaller pieces. But there was insufficient support for the delay, and President Clinton named former Illinois senator Alan Dixon (a critic of the base closure process) to chair the 1995 commission. The commission's list commanded greater attention than previous lists because it deviated sharply from the recommendations of the secretary of defense. Most important, it ordered closure of large bases in California and Texas. The announcement of these additional closures was perceived to be a blow to President Clinton's reelection chances because of the importance of those two states' large blocks of electoral votes. An angry Clinton criticized the commission for deviating so widely from the Defense Department's recommendations and seriously considered rejecting the list. In the end, however, Clinton approved the list and forwarded it to Congress to complete the process. For background see Elizabeth A. Palmer, "Former Sen. Dixon To Oversee Painful New Round of Cuts," *Congressional Quarterly Weekly Report*, October 8, 1994, 2898; Donna Cassata, "Californians Pressure Clinton To Reject Panel's List," *Congressional Quarterly Weekly Report*, July 1, 1995, 1939–1941; and Donna Cassata, "Angry Clinton Accepts List, Seeks to Privatize Jobs," *Congressional Quarterly Weekly Report*, July 15, 1995. For commentary see Tyrus W. Cobb,

"Close the Bases—Now," *Washington Post*, June 1, 1995, A19.

29. *Dalton* v. *Specter*, 114 Sup. Ct. 1719 (1994). Specter was joined in the suit by Philadelphia Naval Shipyard employees and by trade unions.

30. More formally, the Court determined that the commission's actions were not reviewable under the Administrative Procedures Act because its recommendations did not represent "final agency actions." Specter's claim that the president had exceeded his authority was not, the Court said, a constitutional claim and, therefore, was not reviewable.

31. *Dalton* v. *Specter*, 114 Sup. Ct. 1719 (1994).

32. The use of the term *succeed* here is advised and narrow. Critics of the base closure law assert that it has been bad policy and that it has been poorly implemented. They also point out that many bases slated for closure do not actually close or simply get transferred to a different service or to the private sector for rental back to the government. The presence of toxic wastes on former bases also raises questions about whether abandoned properties are of use to anyone. This chapter is in no way intended to address those issues. For present purposes, success is defined as the ability to reach collective decisions about which bases to close. In that respect, certainly, the law must be considered a success.

33. Relatively little work is available on commissions. But see Thomas R. Wolanin, *Presidential Advisory Commissions: Truman to Nixon* (Madison: University of Wisconsin Press, 1975); Wilson K. Doyle, *Independent Commissions in the Federal Government* (Chapel Hill: University of North Carolina Press, 1939); David Flitner, Jr., *The Politics of Presidential Commissions: A Policy Perspective* (Dobbs Ferry, N.Y.: Transnational Publishers, 1986); and Patricia W. Ingraham, "Commissions, Cycles, and Changes: The Role of Blue-Ribbon Commissions in Executive Branch Change," in *Agenda for Excellence: Public Service in America*, ed. Patricia W. Ingraham and Donald F. Kettl (Chatham, N.J.: Chatham House, 1992), 187–207.

34. Murray Edelman, *The Symbolic Uses of Politics* (Urbana: University of Illinois Press, 1964).

35. Gramm's statement was made in support of his own version of the base closure law—hence, the sixty-day deadline is not consistent with deadlines in versions later passed by Congress and signed into law. Nonetheless, the utility and futility of symbolic opposition are well stated. Gramm's comments are reproduced in Armey, "Base Maneuvers," 74.

36. For a discussion of time, deliberation, and decision making, see George E. Connor and Bruce I. Oppenheimer, "Deliberation: An Untimed Value in a Timed Game," in *Congress Reconsidered*, 5th ed., ed. Lawrence C. Dodd and Bruce I. Oppenheimer (Washington, D.C.: CQ Press, 1993), 315–330.

37. Charles O. Jones, *Separate But Equal Branches: Congress and the Presidency* (Chatham, N.J.: Chatham House, 1995).

9

President Clinton and the 103d Congress: Winning Battles and Losing Wars

James P. Pfiffner

B ill Clinton began his administration with elaborate promises and high expectations. His ambitious agenda was based on two premises: that the 1992 presidential election signaled the voters' demand for change and that, with the Democrats in control of the presidency and both houses of Congress; the era of gridlock was over. His policy agenda included reducing the deficit; stimulating the economy; and cutting the taxes of the middle class; establishing a national service program; overhauling the health care and welfare systems; instituting administrative reforms; rewriting campaign finance and lobbying laws; ensuring equitable treatment for gays in the military; and implementing various other policies that he had spoken about over the course of the campaign.

In winning a number of significant legislative battles, Clinton nevertheless lost the broader war for his ambitious policy agenda. And he also lost the partisan war in the sweeping Republican victory in the 1994 elections. Clinton's legislative performance was marked by two paradoxes:

(1) he enjoyed a high success rate on the roll-call votes on which he took a stand, but his first two years were marked by only partial success with his major priorities; and

(2) his high success rate was accompanied by high party unity scores, yet he did not receive the level of support from Democrats that he needed or had expected.

In both 1993 and 1994 Clinton won 86.4 percent of the time on the congressional votes on which he took a stand. This unusual success rate has been exceeded only by Presidents Dwight Eisenhower (89.0 percent) and Lyndon Johnson (88.0 percent) in their first years in office, and by Johnson (93.0 percent) in his second year as president.[1] President Clinton also enjoyed unusually high party unity scores from the Democrats in Congress. The percentage of party unity votes, in which a majority of one party votes against a majority of the other party, was historically high in 1993, with 67.1 percent of Senate votes and 65.5 percent of House votes being partisan. In 1994 the percentages dropped off to 51.7 percent in the Senate and 61.8 percent in the House, still very high scores relative to others reported since the 1950s.[2] The higher partisanship was a mixed blessing; while it meant that the Democrats most often voted together, it also meant that they picked up little support on the Republican side of the aisle.

Despite the impressive presidential support and party unity scores, the Clinton record was mixed, with some major accomplishments, particularly deficit reduction and the North American Free Trade Agreement (NAFTA), but with some major lost opportunities, such as health care reform, welfare reform, and political reform. The opportunity cost of the failed health care reform initiative was high. Much of 1994 was dominated by legislative maneuvering on health care, to the exclusion of other pressing issues (for example, welfare reform). As many as a dozen policy initiatives with good chances of becoming law were lost in the legislative pileup at the end of the 103d Congress.[3]

Clinton suffered from a number of problems in his relations with Congress. Despite clear Democratic majorities, Clinton had no natural coalition of votes for his agenda. For each important issue he had to cobble together a different combination of members to forge a winning coalition. For instance, in the two major votes on the 1993 budget reconciliation bill and on NAFTA, only 78 of 435 members of the House and 27 of 100 senators voted with the president in both cases.[4] Democrats in Congress, despite the high party unity scores, did not support Clinton consistently or wholeheartedly. Often members of his own party did not support him in key legislative battles or demanded policy concessions or personal favors for their votes.

Clinton knew the policy issues in detail (unlike Ronald Reagan) and enjoyed the personal politicking necessary to win votes in Congress (unlike Jimmy Carter). He did all the right things in courting Congress and was generous in the time he devoted to courting individual members. Although he had denounced insiders and special interests in his campaign and inaugural address, Clinton (like Reagan, but unlike Carter) embraced the Washington establishment and took advice from its "old hands." He was also flexible in his policy priorities, often willing to compromise to win votes. But these assets were also cited as his weaknesses. At what point is willingness to compromise seen as "caving in" to the opposition? After how many calls and personal appeals is the president "overexposed" and in danger of devaluing the currency of personal presidential appeals? The administration also suffered from problems with momentum and timing in pushing its legislative agenda, hurting its overall record and perceptions of its effectiveness.

This chapter will first take up the initial agenda of the Clinton administration, which was marked by a number of minor legislative victories, but marred by unfavorable media coverage of several administration embarrassments while budget priorities were debated internally. The following section will take up the major budget battles in which the president achieved a significant deficit reduction package without a single vote from the congressional Republicans. Finally, after a brief look at Clinton's NAFTA victory, the ill-fated health care campaign will be analyzed and the many factors that led to its defeat will be laid out. The conclusion will try to determine why the president's record in the 103d Congress was so decidedly mixed. The assessment will try to separate those factors for which the president himself was responsible from those over which he had no control.

The Initial Agenda

Realizing that there would be a narrow window of opportunity for policy change early in his presidency, Clinton promised to "focus like a laser beam" on the economy and to have an economic plan ready to go "on day one" of his administration. But because of disagreements within the administration about whether to stimulate a lagging economy or to pursue deficit reduction to improve long-term economic performance, the Clinton White House was not ready to move on budget issues until late in its first month in office.

Even before the inauguration trouble was brewing over Clinton's nominee to be attorney general, Zoë Baird. The press was running stories that Baird and her husband had hired illegal immigrants for domestic work and that they had not, until recently, paid Social Security taxes on the workers' wages. Baird's status as a wealthy lawyer who had not paid taxes and, perhaps more important, as a prospective attorney general who had broken the law made her an easy political target, and Clinton decided to withdraw the nomination on January 21, 1993. The administration stumbled a second time in its first week when it settled on Kimba Wood as its replacement for Baird, only to withdraw her nomination when it was discovered that she too had hired an illegal alien to care for her child. Even though Wood had broken no law and had paid Social Security taxes, the administration decided that her situation was too similar to Baird's. The White House finally nominated Janet Reno to be attorney general, and she was easily confirmed.

In his first two days in office Clinton signed several executive orders, the first of which imposed additional ethics guidelines that prohibited members of his administration from lobbying their former agencies for five years after they left government. Several other executive orders reversed those of the Bush and Reagan administrations that concerned abortion counseling, use of fetal tissue in scientific research, and U.S. aid to U.N. population control programs.[5]

The administration had three early legislative victories when Congress passed, and Clinton signed, three bills that had been vetoed by President Bush or stopped by Republicans in Congress. The Family and Medical Leave Act required employers to permit workers to take unpaid leave for the birth of a child or to care for a sick parent. The "motor voter" law allowed citizens to register to vote while applying for or renewing a driver's license. The Hatch Act was liberalized to enable federal career civil servants to participate in more aspects of political campaigns, though safeguards against political coercion were left in place.

In his first year in office President Clinton also signed bills that were part of his agenda. His national service proposal, allowing students to earn money for college by performing several years of community service, was passed, though on a smaller scale than he had hoped. Responsibility for administering higher education loans was shifted from banks to the Department of Education, reducing the interest rates charged. The Brady bill, which imposed a waiting period for those wishing to purchase hand guns, was passed late in 1993.

Despite these legislative victories, the headlines of the first month of the administration were dominated by the problems in the search for the attorney general and by Clinton's efforts to ensure equitable treatment for homosexuals in the armed services. In the presidential campaign Clinton had not made the gay issue a major part of his program, but he had consistently said that he was against discrimination against homosexuals and had received considerable financial support from organized gay political action committees. He had said during the campaign that, if elected, he would issue an executive order to end the ban on gays in the military.

Though Clinton saw the gay issue as a civil rights issue, the military establishment was dead set against any change in the status of homosexuals, arguing that such a change would undermine unit cohesion and personal privacy. The chairman of the joint chiefs of staff, Colin Powell, spoke out publicly against lifting the ban, and the rest of the joint chiefs also spoke against it in a meeting with Clinton on January 25, 1993.[6] Just as important politically, Sen. Sam Nunn, D-Ga., publicly criticized Clinton's proposed change, thus legitimizing other Democratic opposition, since Nunn was the Democrats' foremost military spokesman in Congress. Congress warned that if Clinton pursued his plan by executive order, it would pass a bill and lock the present policy in law. (Despite the president's status as commander-in-chief, Congress clearly has the constitutional right to "make Rules for the Government and Regulation of the land and naval Forces" (Art. I, Sec. 8).) Given the array of political forces against the policy and the likelihood of its defeat in Congress, Clinton accepted a compromise: Secretary of Defense Les Aspin would prepare a policy on gays in the military by July 15. In the meantime, applicants to the military would not be asked their sexual orientation.

This compromise took the contentious issue off the front burner and out of the newspaper headlines, but it also signaled an important defeat for the new administration. Most importantly, the issue dominated the headlines during Clinton's first weeks in office. As a result, it was perceived, mistakenly, as one of the president's foremost priorities. If the budget policy had been ready to go earlier, the political controversy would have been over economic priorities for the country, and the gay issue would have been put in perspective as one of several items on the Clinton agenda. Second, the fight got Clinton off to a shaky start with the military, already wary of a commander-in-chief who had avoided the draft during the Vietnam War. Finally, the public and vocal opposition of Senator Nunn indicated that the Democrats in Congress would be willing to challenge the new president on his policy agenda.

In July the issue was settled with the compromise policy of "don't ask, don't tell," according to which new recruits would not be asked their sexual orientation, but members of the military could not openly declare their homosexuality. Admitted homosexuals could still be expelled from the service. The compromise amounted to a political defeat for Clinton at the hands of some members of Congress and the military. Clinton was also criticized by parts of the gay community for refusing to stand up to the military and Congress. Barney Frank, D-Mass., an openly gay member of Congress, praised the president for having the courage to take on the issue and for making at least some progress. But the issue was a net loss for the president because it confused the public about his primary agenda and delayed progress on his economic priorities.

Budget Battles

The major theme of the 1992 presidential campaign had been the nation's fiscal health, and Clinton had promised to stimulate the economy, cut the deficit, invest in worker training and infrastructure, cut taxes for the middle class, and reform health care financing. During the transition period the president-elect held an economic conference in Little Rock, Arkansas, in which the major economic issues facing the nation were discussed from a variety of perspectives by economic experts and members of the future administration. Everyone was impressed with Clinton's grasp of the issues and with his ability to conduct the discussion of all of the experts. By taking valuable transition time for the conference, Clinton sent a message that the economy was his highest priority and demonstrated his mastery of economic issues.

Preparation

With all of the preparation in December and with his economic team carefully chosen, many expected that Clinton would have a budget plan ready early in his administration, even if not on "day one" of his presidency. Had he dealt with economic policy in the first two weeks of his term, the policy debate would have overshadowed the press flare up over selecting the attorney general and gays in the military. But an economic policy was not ready to go because Clinton had not yet made up his mind about whether the economy should be stimulated to pull it out of the recession or whether the deficit should be attacked to ensure the long-term health of the economy. The first several months of the administration were consumed by a fight for the mind of the president over this issue.

In one corner were the "consultants," who had run the campaign and who continued to be actively involved in policy deliberations and advising the president. Even though they did not hold official positions in the government, James Carville, Paul Begala, Mandy Grunwald, and Stanley

Greenberg were trusted advisers to the president and first lady. They argued that Clinton should stick to his campaign promise for a middle-class tax cut and investments to help people deal with economic dislocations caused by a globalizing economy and layoffs.[7] In the other corner were the "deficit hawks," who believed that the long-term health of the U.S. economy was dependent on reducing the deficit. The national debt had climbed from $1 trillion in 1981 to $4 trillion in 1993, the annual deficit was expected to reach nearly $300 billion by fiscal year 1994 if no changes were made, and interest on the debt approached $200 billion per year and 14 percent of budget outlays.

The deficit hawks argued that in the short term an economic recovery depended upon keeping interest rates down and inflation in check. If the bond markets (money lenders) thought that the Clinton economic plan would encourage inflation by continuing to increase the deficit, they would demand higher interest rates to loan money, and the recovery would be cut short by these higher rates. On the other hand, steep deficit reduction would not guarantee a robust recovery in the short term.

The deficit hawks included Treasury Secretary Lloyd Bentsen, OMB Director Leon Panetta, National Economic Council staff director Robert Rubin, and Deputy OMB Director Alice Rivlin. The chairman of the Federal Reserve, Alan Greenspan, was perhaps the most important deficit hawk, though his role was indirect since he was head of an independent agency. His advice to Clinton implied that if there was sufficient deficit reduction, the Fed would not raise interest rates in order to head off potential inflation. He made this clear in meetings with the president-elect and White House staffers.[8] Greenspan was reinforcing the same message that the deficit hawks were arguing. Clinton understood both economic arguments well and was clearly ambivalent. He realized the necessity of deficit reduction but was not eager to sacrifice his other policy initiatives and devote much of his initial political capital to fighting the deficit reduction battle. For a while he thought he could both reduce the deficit and pursue his own policy initiatives.

A key turning point came during the transition, in a January 7, 1993, meeting of the president and his main economic advisers (including Bentsen, Rubin, Vice President Al Gore, Council of Economic Advisers Chair Laura D'Andrea Tyson, and CEA member Alan Blinder). They warned that the deficit would soar to $360 billion in 1997 and to $500 billion in 2000 if nothing were done to curb it. They admitted that in the short term, cuts in federal programs and higher taxes might slow the economy, but in the long term the economy would benefit. The importance of the bond market to the success of his economic program was made clear to the president. If lenders thought that Clinton was not serious about deficit reduction, they would demand higher interest rates, which in turn would slow the economy, and the Fed might also raise interest rates in order to head off anticipated inflation. The problem was that it was not clear at the time that the economy was undergoing a strong recovery; it might still need stimulus.

Clinton found himself in a difficult position. He was being forced to inflict economic pain during his presidency so that economic benefits would accrue in the future under his successors. "You mean to tell me that the success of the program and my reelection hinges on the Federal Reserve and a bunch of f_____ bond traders?" he asked. The answer was yes.[9] The consultants argued that the deficit hawks were taking over and that Clinton was betraying the coalition that had elected him. They said that his core supporters would want him to spur the economy, invest in infrastructure and retraining, and cut the taxes of the middle class, not pursue a policy of deficit reduction. Stanley Greenberg, one of the consultants, declared that "the presidency has been hijacked."[10]

Unveiling the Plan

In a series of all-day sessions in early February 1993 the outlines of the Clinton economic plan were hammered out. Clinton decided to drop his promise of a middle-class tax cut, raise the taxes of the affluent, propose a broad-based energy tax, and cut spending on some federal programs. The Clinton plan, combining tax increases and spending cuts, would reduce the deficit by $500 billion over five years. The plan also included an investment package that would stimulate the economy in the short run. The budget package was introduced February 17, during a nationally televised address to a joint session of Congress. Despite (or perhaps because of) the fact that aides were unable to load the last-minute version of the speech into the TelePrompTer by the time Clinton was scheduled to deliver it, the president gave an inspired delivery, presenting much of the material from his own intimate knowledge of the details of the policies.

The day after the speech the president hit the road to sell his plan to the public in town meetings, speeches, and interviews with radio and television stations. A carefully orchestrated media and information blitz involved the whole administration in the selling of the plan. Most cabinet secretaries traveled to their home states and then to other targeted locations. Leon Panetta explained the details of the budget plan to 250 business leaders, and other groups were invited to the White House for briefings.[11] Public opinion polls indicated strong support for Clinton's proposal.[12]

The momentum generated by the president's speech and by the media and information campaign lasted a month, until it was time for Congress to vote on the concurrent resolution, which would determine budget totals. On March 18 the House passed the resolution on a party-line vote of 243–183, with 11 Democrats defecting. The vote in the Senate was tougher, but after six days of lobbying and forty-five roll-call votes to defeat Republican amendments, the Senate passed the resolution, 54–45, with Alabama senator Richard C. Shelby the only Democrat voting no. (Shelby became a Republican two years later.)

The Stimulus Package

In order to give the economy an immediate boost, which it seemed to
need at the time, the administration put together a "stimulus package" that
would get spending out immediately, before the next fiscal year. In 1981
President Reagan had authorized a similar package that included a $30 bil-
lion increase in military spending for fiscal year 1981, then in progress. The
Clinton package totaled about $20 billion and included $4 billion in extended unemployment benefits as well as funding for training, infrastructure, and
social programs that would be included in community development block
grants.

After the package was announced it became clear to moderate Democrats that the Republicans would object to much of the plan and argue that
it contained irresponsible spending.[13] To stave this off, Sens. David L.
Boren, D-Okla., and John B. Breaux, D-La., approached the White House
with a scaled-down version of the plan as a proposed compromise. But the
House had already passed the package after voting on the concurrent resolution on March 18, and Sen. Robert C. Byrd, D-W.Va., chairman of the
Appropriations Committee, assured the president that he could pass the bill
over Republican opposition.

The White House had miscalculated. Byrd's parliamentary maneuvering in support of the package irritated many Democrats and alienated most
Republicans, who felt they did not have a fair chance to offer any amendments to the bill. But more important, the Republicans, who at first felt they
could gain political points by decrying Democratic spending, soon realized
that they might be able to defeat the bill entirely with a filibuster (an option
not available to them under the expedited rules governing budget resolutions).[14]

With help from Byrd's heavy-handed parliamentary tactics and the
White House's refusal of several offers to compromise, the Republicans were
able to hold all of their moderate members and to block any Democratic
moves for cloture. Finally, on April 20, the administration gave up and with-
drew the stimulus bill, with only the $4 billion in extended unemployment
compensation passing the Senate.

The defeat of the administration on this relatively small spending bill
affected the president's policy agenda hardly at all, but in symbolic terms the
defeat was devastating for three reasons. First, it stopped the momentum
that the administration had achieved in its total budget package. A whole
month had passed since the media and information blitz, and future budget
votes would be harder to wring out of Congress. Second, the administration
had picked its first big fight with Congress without much planning or
awareness of what was at stake, and it had lost. The administration and
Democrats now appeared weaker, and the Republicans were more unified
and emboldened to fight on other issues. Third, the Republicans were able
to paint a picture of the Clinton administration as "tax and spend" Demo-

crats, and to give the impression that the Clinton budget plan was filled with "pork," when in reality the whole budget and deficit reduction package was rather stringent.

Key Votes

Public perception, which is crucial to presidential power and standing in Congress, was noticeably changed by the stimulus fight. The percentage of voters favoring the Clinton economic plan fell from 62 percent on February 18, 1993, to 45 percent on May 13, according to a *Time* poll.[15] In addition, the public approval rating of the president at the end of April was about 55 percent, among the lowest ratings received by recent presidents after one hundred days in office.. The damage done to the administration was evident in the close votes on the reconciliation bills in the summer of 1993.

In late May the Clinton budget was considered in the House. Although both houses had passed the concurrent resolution, which set out the totals and general outlines of the plan, they had not yet voted on the reconciliation bill, the enforcing document that laid out the details of the spending cuts and tax increases that would be used to reach the totals. The campaign for votes in the House was prodigious, with Clinton buying votes retail by personally calling scores of members and lobbying incessantly. Finally, after a grueling fight and many favors, the president won the battle on May 27 by a vote of 219–213, with 38 Democrats defecting and no Republicans supporting the plan. On June 24, after another exhausting fight, during which the BTU tax was dropped and replaced with a 4.3 cents-per-gallon gas tax, the Senate passed its version of the bill, with Vice President Gore breaking a 49–49 tie.

But the fight was not over. Both houses had passed different versions of the reconciliation bill, and the differences had to be ironed out in a conference committee. Once the conference committee had finished its work, the bill would return to the House and Senate for floor votes before going to the president for his signature. In July, in preparation for the final reconciliation votes, Clinton again became intensely involved in lobbying members for their votes. At one point Clinton had five members of the House on separate phone lines at the same time.[16] The president's personal involvement may have been excessive, but it seemed necessary at the time. The problem was that when members saw how desperate the administration was for votes, they tried to make deals for themselves.

When the House began the roll call on the reconciliation bill, it was still uncertain that Clinton had the votes to win. All the Republicans were voting no, so the president needed 218 Democratic votes. In a last-minute switch at 10:15 P.M. Rep. Marjorie Margolies-Mezvinsky, D-Pa., voted for the bill, putting the vote over the top for a 218–216 win, with no votes to spare. The Senate voted on August 6, and the president had to make a last-minute deal to get Sen. Bob Kerrey, D-Neb., to vote yes. Kerrey switched at 7 P.M., after Clinton promised to let him chair a commission on entitlement spending. In casting his vote Kerrey gave a bitter speech charging that the budget was not stringent enough, saying publicly to the president: "... I could not and should not cast a vote that brings down your presidency." [17] The final Senate tally was 51–50, with the vice president again casting the tie-breaking vote.

The budget votes were important in that they made a significant contribution to deficit reduction, but they also demonstrated how fragile support for the president was in Congress. The reconciliation packages were the only major pieces of legislation since World War II that were adopted without one vote from the opposition party.[18]

The Health Care Campaign

By the beginning of the Clinton administration the president had decided that health care reform would be an essential part of his policy agenda. Opinion polls had indicated that the public was firmly behind major change. Thirty-seven million Americans were without health insurance coverage, costs were escalating, and workers were afraid of losing coverage if they changed jobs or were laid off. Clinton also concluded that serious deficit reduction was impossible without health care cost containment.

In late January 1993 Clinton announced the creation of a major health care task force that would be headed by Hillary Rodham Clinton. He gave the task force one hundred days to produce the administration's proposal. The director of the policy development process was Ira Magaziner, who pulled together a task force of five hundred experts recruited from throughout the government and the private sector.

Tactics and Timing

Although the group was not ready with a plan within one hundred days, by the end of May it had talked with more than five hundred organizations and had had several hundred meetings with members of Congress.[19] Despite the feeling within the administration that it should move quickly on one of its most important priorities, the proposal was not ready for several reasons. For one thing, the task force could not come to terms with the concerns of Clinton's economic team, which thought that sweeping changes might cost too much and therefore favored a more incremental approach. In addition, crucial votes on the administration's economic plan were coming up soon, and the economic team did not want to jeopardize the budget votes by overloading the political and policy agendas. (An earlier proposal to package health care with the concurrent resolution was rejected.)

The health care task force was disbanded in May 1993, and the White House team began work on the administration's package, but without final presidential decisions on many key elements. It was late summer before the budget fights were over and the fall policy agenda had been set. It was decided that when Congress reconvened in September, Vice President Gore would unveil his "reinventing government" program.[20] Soon thereafter, health care reform and passage of the North American Free Trade Agreement (NAFTA) would become the top policy priorities.

Clinton kicked off his health care reform campaign with a speech to Congress on September 22, 1993. The speech, spelling out the principles of universal coverage and managed competition, was a great success with Democrats in Congress and with the public. A majority of the public approved of the president's plan in October 1993.[21] Hillary Rodham Clinton received respectful (Republican) and enthusiastic (Democratic) receptions when she went to Capitol Hill to testify for the administration's health care package. But the actual text of the bill was not yet ready and did not make it to the Hill until October 27. Meanwhile, some momentum was lost when the president had to deal with the killing of twelve U.S. soldiers in Somalia. At the same time, the administration was also fighting the battle over NAFTA.

The administration ended 1993 with the health care proposal before Congress, but its work was far from over. The bill still had to be passed, and it was essential that this happen early enough in the second session of the 103d Congress in order to avoid two potential obstacles: the politics associated with the upcoming 1994 midterm elections and the legislative traffic jam that was bound to occur at the end of the session. The administration was unable to avoid these obstacles for political, partisan, and policy reasons, which will be examined next.

Political and Partisan Dynamics

In December of 1993 allegations about the Clintons' investment in the failed Whitewater real estate venture and questions about the relationship of the Arkansas-based venture to the defunct Madison Guaranty Savings and Loan were raised in the press. When the administration was unable to defuse charges that the Clintons had engaged in shady or illegal activities, a major scandal erupted in the spring.

The unproven allegations undercut the confidence of the general public in the president, and his approval ratings began to fall from the almost 60 percent level they had reached at the end of 1993. At the same time, Republicans were able to label the health care plan as too large, too complex, too costly, and too much government. Public opinion about the health care plan shifted in spring 1994; by summer, the majority in favor of the plan had become a majority opposed.

The shift in public opinion seemed to energize the Republicans, who proceeded to frame the health care issue in terms of trust. Because the administration's plan was too complex to be easily understood by most citizens, the American public would have to place its trust in the president's ability to make wise policy and in the federal government's ability to implement that policy. Perhaps understandably, the public was wary of making this leap of faith. Interest groups were mobilized in opposition to the Clinton plan, spending more than $300 million to defeat it.[22] Included in this figure was $46 million spent by lobbyists between January 1993 and May 1994, according to Federal Election Commission records.[23]

As support for the administration's plan began to erode, Republicans who had previously favored parts of it, such as universal coverage, began to change their minds. It now seemed possible that the health care plan could be defeated completely and that the Democrats could be denied a legislative victory to run on in the 1994 midterm elections. The Republicans might be accused of fostering gridlock, but the Democrats would have been shown unable to govern or to achieve their major policy goal. As the Republicans' confidence in their 1994 election prospects grew, the chances of health care reform faded, and the bill was never brought up for a vote in the 103d Congress.

As with the budget bill, the Clinton administration was criticized for adopting a partisan approach to the health care bill. The criticism was legitimate, but it was not clear whether a bipartisan coalition could have been forged to pass a bill even remotely resembling the one introduced in Clinton's popular speech of September 22, 1993. The administration, in conjunction with the Democratic leadership, had decided on a partisan strategy on the budget bill, and it had worked, but just barely. After Clinton gave his well-received health care speech, the Republicans seemed to accept the fact that some version of health care reform would pass. The administration had met with Republican moderates early on, but each side had decided to work on its own version and leave compromises until later in the process.[24] In a meeting in the Cabinet Room in early February 1994, Democratic House leaders warned Clinton that health care would receive no Republican support but assured him that they could get a health care bill through the House before the end of the year. Sen. Daniel Patrick Moynihan, D-N.Y., demurred, arguing that the Senate was, of necessity, more bipartisan than the House and that the Democrats had no guaranteed votes to end a possible filibuster.[25]

In any case, the political dynamics of the issue led to partisan battling, with no compromise in sight. This made it critical to the passage of some version of health care reform that the administration win the support of all Democrats. But there were early defections, with Moynihan not supporting the Clinton bill almost from the beginning, and Rep. Jim Cooper, D-Tenn., proposing an alternative plan throughout the debate. But the more important reason for the lack of Democratic unity was the divisiveness of the policy issue itself. There may have been a public consensus that health care needed fixing, but there was no consensus on how to do it.

Policy Dynamics

Many Democrats favored a single-payer system (as in the Medicare program), which had the virtue of relative simplicity. Health care would be provided by the private sector, and the government would pay the bills. While a single-payer system was less complex than many other proposed health care plans, , it had the disadvantage of threatening the business of private health insurance and seeming to be "socialized medicine," with high costs and too much government control.

So Clinton rejected that option in favor of private insurance. But the disadvantage of private insurance was that it allowed "creaming," or the practice of insuring only the young and healthy, to the exclusion of those with expensive medical problems. This led to the proposal for health insurance cooperatives, which all Americans would have to belong to and which would bargain with different insurance companies for the best insurance packages for their members. But these cooperatives would be big, their dynamics would be complex, and they would have to be created from scratch.

Clinton decided that a broad new tax to finance his health care plan would be politically unacceptable, so he chose to rely on employer mandates. Although these mandates would have the effect of a tax, the vast majority of health insurance (aside from Medicare) was already provided by employers. In addition, a number of Republicans had, at one time or another, embraced the idea of employer mandates. But the mandates proposal was vulnerable to the claims of smaller businesses that they could not afford to pay for health insurance for their workers and that they would go out of business if they were forced to buy it.

Clinton argued that the bottom line of his health care plan was universal coverage. All other industrialized nations had it, and he threatened to veto any bill that did not provide for it. But achieving the goal of universal coverage, while at the same time containing costs, would not be possible unless the major players in the health care system, including insurance companies, employers, and patients, were coerced into making certain concessions. Insurance companies would have to accept premium caps, employers would be required to purchase coverage for their employees, and patients would have no choice but to participate in cooperatives. The plan did not, however, deny people the option of buying health care services from their own doctors.

These factors added up to a bill of sweeping scope and intricate complexity. The United States has a mixed system of health care, with most doctors and insurance companies in the private sector and with the federal government financing Medicare and Medicaid. Combine these realities accepted by Clinton, with his goals of universal coverage and cost containment, and you have inherent complexity and some government coercion in any plan to deal with all of these factors at once.

Adopting a simpler approach would have meant abandoning some major element of the administration's plan. So the complaint of complexity, while valid, was not so much the issue as were the major elements in the plan. No one else came up with a simpler plan that would accomplish all of the goals of the Clinton proposal. Nevertheless, the complexity issue did play a major role in the defeat of the plan. Members had a hard time explaining it to constituents and defending it. Even though the bill itself was 1,342 pages long, rival plans also were well over 1,000 pages, and the NAFTA and crime bills were not significantly shorter.[26] But the complexity was real in that the proposed changes would have affected up to one-seventh of the U.S. economy and would have entailed many unintended consequences. While most of the elements of the package already existed in various forms, the combination of all of the elements into a sweeping overhaul of such a large portion of the U.S. economy was unacceptable to many.[27]

The failure of the health care campaign pointed out several things. Clinton did not completely understand his vulnerability on the Hill with such a huge piece of legislation. With a 43 percent plurality in the 1992 election, a divided Democratic party, and a contentious and intractable policy issue, how could he have expected to win? The consequences of the failure were not only the loss of the administration's top policy initiative but also the loss of a number of other bills that were pending in Congress when health care went down.

In sum, health care reform failed because of: divided Democrats, emboldened Republicans, high interest group spending against reform, an overly ambitious proposal, Clinton's 43 percent plurality, declining public approval, the Whitewater scandal, the complexity of the proposals, and the resistance of Americans to large governmental programs in the 1990s.

The NAFTA Fight

One of President Clinton's most important victories was getting Congress to approve the legislation implementing the North American Free Trade Agreement (NAFTA). The agreement, which had been negotiated by the Bush administration, eliminated tariffs among the United States, Canada, and Mexico. Major opposition to the agreement came from those who feared that the United States would lose jobs to Mexico. These opponents included traditional Democratic constituencies, such as labor unions, as well as Ross Perot, who launched a highly publicized campaign against the agreement. Clinton took a significant political risk of alienating his own Democratic constituency if he won and looking ineffectual if he lost.

Clinton had been in favor of NAFTA, while maintaining some reservations about side agreements, since spring 1993, but had not wholeheartedly endorsed it. Some attributed the lack of congressional support for NAFTA to the president's failure to come out sooner in favor of it. But after a rousing September 22, 1994, speech in support of the agreement at the

White House, with three former presidents (Ford, Carter, and Bush) in attendance, the administration went into high gear to lobby for it in Congress. Clinton personally spoke with 135 members of Congress, made more than seventy phone calls in the ten days before the vote, and held eighteen public events to improve its chances for passage.[28] As Clinton campaigned, he had to fight the leadership of his own party, since Majority Leader Richard A. Gephardt, D-Mo., and Majority Whip David E. Bonior, D-Mich., were leading the fight against the bill.

On the eve of the vote it was not clear whether Clinton's all-out effort would be successful, and the 34-vote margin belied the closeness of the final tally. The administration won, 234–200, with 156 Democrats against it and only 102 in favor. Most Republicans voted for the bill, 132–43 (with one independent voting no). The vote was important for Clinton because it demonstrated that he was willing to take an issue that was unpopular in his own party and fight for it. It also showed that he could fight a bipartisan battle and win a tough fight in the House. In addition, Clinton's successes with NAFTA, creating the largest free-trade zone in the world, and with the General Agreement on Tariffs and Trade (GATT), the largest multilateral free-trade agreement in history, built a credible record for him as a proponent of open trade in a new global economy.

Conclusion

Clinton's record with the 103d Congress was decidedly mixed. On the positive side, he enjoyed a high success rate on the roll-call votes on which he took a stand, and several major public policy initiatives were passed, notably deficit reduction, NAFTA, and GATT, among other laws. On the negative side, he did not do as well as he had hoped or many had expected. The failure of his health care reform initiative was a major disappointment, and because of the emphasis on health care in 1994, a number of other administration priorities never came to a vote, such as welfare reform, campaign finance reform, lobbying disclosure, hazardous waste cleanup, and congressional reform.

One explanation of the paradox of high support and party unity scores along with a relatively disappointing record with much of the broader Clinton agenda, has been suggested by David Mayhew. He argues that the Democrats had become strong enough organizationally in Congress to prevent votes on issues they were not likely to win. But he points out that this control of internal rules and processes did not signify enough strength to ensure victories on most agenda items. Thus health care, the dominant Democratic agenda item in 1994, did not lead to any roll-call votes in the House and only four minor votes in the Senate. He also lists legislative drives for about fifteen other Democratic agenda items that were not successful.[29]

The question remains, however, as to how much of the legislative record was due to Clinton's personal decisions, strategy, or skills and how much of the outcome was determined by factors beyond his control. Observers of presidential-congressional relations have concluded that several dimensions of presidential behavior seem to enhance chances for success with Congress. At the personal level, presidents are urged to court Congress, to be willing to compromise, and to use carrots and sticks in lobbying for votes on the Hill. At the agenda level, presidents are urged to move quickly in their first year to bring legislation to congressional votes, to pace their legislative demands on the Hill, and to focus their agendas by clearly setting priorities.[30] How well did Clinton perform on these levels?

At the personal level Bill Clinton was an impressive lobbyer of Congress. He took pains to court members of both parties with invitations to the White House and personal phone calls. He was quite effective at the interpersonal level, combining the affability of Ronald Reagan with the detailed policy expertise of Jimmy Carter. In addition, he was empathetic and could communicate that he understood and sympathized with his listener. And he was certainly willing to compromise on substance and pass out favors in seeking votes.

But some critics argued that Clinton was too rigid in his approach to Congress; others argued that he was too willing to compromise on the essence of his programs. Was he courageous or craven? Clinton was clearly courageous in taking on deficit reduction, NAFTA, gun control, and military intervention in Haiti. Despite significant congressional opposition to each of these, he stuck with them and won. Others accused Clinton of "caving" too early (for example, on grazing fees in the West and on the nomination of Lani Guinier to be assistant attorney general). At times Clinton was forced by political reality to compromise, settling for winning a partial victory on his crime bill and his national service program, and compromising and losing on the issues of health care reform and gays in the military.[31] One might argue that these decisions by Clinton were either wise or unwise, but in any case they demonstrate that Clinton was not either too rigid or too accommodating in his approach to Congress.

At the agenda level Clinton conformed less closely to scholarly prescriptions to move quickly and focus his agenda. At the beginning of his term his primary message of budget discipline was interrupted by the search for an acceptable attorney general and by the gays in the military issue. Besides provoking these media flare-ups, the administration was talking about and planning many diverse policy initiatives, from congressional campaign and lobbying reform to national service, environmental improvement, and gun control. It was difficult for citizens to discern in these initiatives one central theme or set of priorities. As Leon Panetta admitted in 1995, "There were so many initiatives and so many efforts that were made that we lost the message...."[32]

When the economic package was finally ready to go in mid-February, Clinton launched it with an effective speech and a carefully planned media blitz. But immediately after the passage of the concurrent resolution, the battle over and eventual defeat of the stimulus package slowed the momentum of the economic plan and embarrassed the administration. The negotiations over reconciliation in Congress were then dragged out over the summer of 1993, delaying introduction of the health care reform proposal. The idea of political momentum is amorphous, but in politics it is more than an abstract concept, as demonstrated by Ronald Reagan's string of budget victories in 1981.[33]

Timing and momentum also affected the prospects of Clinton's health care proposal. When the administration failed to keep its promise to deliver a plan after one hundred days, much of the early enthusiasm for the plan was quelled. It was rekindled with Clinton's speech in September 1993, only to be snuffed out again when the bill's introduction to Congress was delayed for another month. The administration's decision to put off other legislative initiatives until health care had been settled effectively prevented several bills from reaching the floor for votes and kept a welfare reform bill from being introduced. Furthermore, Republicans, anticipating gains in the midterm elections, refused to allow many bills to come to a vote. As one administration official said: "What we've come to realize is the incredible opportunity cost of health care. We really put a lot of things on the back burner in order to focus on health care." [34]

The inability of the Clinton administration to move early and quickly on a focused set of priorities illustrates Lyndon Johnson's advice: "I keep hitting hard because this honeymoon won't last. Every day I lose a little more political capital." [35] As an administration moves closer to midterm elections, Johnson said, members of Congress begin "thinking about their reelections. I'll have made mistakes, my polls will be down, and they'll be trying to put some distance between themselves and me. They won't want to go into the fall with their opponents calling 'em Lyndon Johnson's rubber stamp." [36] Prior to the 1994 elections, many Democrats did not want President Clinton to campaign for them.

The shortcomings of Clinton's own approach to legislation were exacerbated by the problems of the Democrats in Congress. Although some Democrats felt that they would share Clinton's political fate and that their own political success was tied inextricably to their president's, many did not. Despite the high party unity scores, too many Democratic members of Congress abandoned the president on key votes or extracted high concessions for their own special preferences. There was little party discipline for the president or their own congressional leadership. After the budget votes in 1993 R. W. Apple, Jr., of the *New York Times* commented that "members of Congress in the modern era, even members of the President's party, tend to see themselves as soloists. Like prima donnas everywhere, they demand pampering. A senior White House official commented with disgust on Friday [August 6, 1993] that many freshman House members demanded to talk to the President personally." [37] The budget fight provided many examples of Democrats demanding concessions from the vulnerable president in exchange for their votes, and the NAFTA fight witnessed the Democrats' own leadership (Bonior and Gephardt) leading the opposition to the president's program.[38]

While the personal, tactical, and strategic decisions of presidents make a difference in their relationship with Congress, a consensus among scholars has developed that presidential success with Congress is largely determined by factors outside the control of presidents.[39] These scholars stress the importance of partisan balance in Congress. Bill Clinton had 57 Democrats in the Senate, the fewest since Harry Truman, and 258 in the House, the fewest since the large Democratic losses in 1966.[40] In addition, Clinton had no coattails; few Democrats in Congress felt they owed their victory to him, and all of them garnered more votes than he did in their own districts (due to Ross Perot's candidacy). Combine the absence of gratitude with a lack of fear of a president with relatively low public approval ratings, and you have a formula for weak presidential influence on the Hill.

These scholars also argue that presidential actions are not the primary determinants of members' votes. Rather, members of Congress make up their minds on the basis of constituency pressure, ideology, and personal policy preference. Party discipline is very weak in the U.S. system, and despite the high party unity scores on roll-call votes, Democrats in Congress deserted their president in important instances in the 103d Congress. This perspective on the relative weakness of presidential influence with Congress is summarized by George Edwards, who argues that the president is a "facilitator" rather than a "director" of legislative action. "There is no systematic relationship between presidential legislative skills and congressional support for the White House," writes Edwards. "Moreover, [presidents] are *not* more likely to win close votes, on which skills might play the crucial role in obtaining the last few votes needed to pass a program." [41]

In spite of the strength of these arguments about the lack of presidential control over the votes of members of Congress, it still must be admitted that in several crucial budget votes President Clinton was able to eke out victories only by last-minute politicking. If he had lost even one vote for his reconciliation budget package in either the House or Senate, his record would have been significantly diminished, and the consequences might have been disastrous for the rest of the session. There is no doubt that his personal pressure and promises made the difference. Even though the NAFTA vote was won by a greater margin, Clinton's personal efforts were crucial to the final outcome, which was uncertain until the very end. These examples, however, do not significantly undermine the general point that presidential skills are not the determining factor in presidential success on the Hill.

In summary, the factors working against President Clinton as he entered office were considerable. He was elected with only a 43 percent plurality; he ran behind most members of Congress; he had fewer Democrats in Congress than other recent Democratic presidents; and his party lost seats in the 1992 election. Combine these negatives with a very ambitious policy agenda, and you have a prescription for high conflict and low success. From this perspective we should be surprised that he did as well as he did in terms of policy success and congressional support.[42]

Of course public expectations were formed not by these realities, so clear in hindsight, but by the hopes of Democrats and the high expectations created by campaign promises. We might have more realistic expectations of presidential performance if we took the perspective of Charles O. Jones, who emphasizes that the United States is not a *presidential* system but rather a separated system, and that presidential agendas are heavily dependent upon contextual variables. From his perspective: "The American Presidency carries a burden of lofty expectations that are simply not warranted by the political or constitutional basis of the office.... The natural inclination is to make the president responsible for policies and political events that no one can claim a legitimate right to control." [43] Viewing our political system as presidency-dominated leads us to expect too much from the chief executive. Citizens and scholars alike could benefit from a broader perspective.

Notes

For comments on an earlier version of this chapter, the author would like to thank Jim Carter, Tim Conlan, Cynthia Harrison, Chris Hill, Bob Maranto, Tom Stanton, Katie Dunn Tenpas, and Margaret Wrightson.

1. Steven Langdon, "Clinton's High Victory Rate Conceals Disappointment," *Congressional Quarterly Weekly Report*, December 31, 1994, 3619–3623. CQ has been keeping presidential support scores since 1953.

2. See *Congressional Quarterly Weekly Report*, December 18, 1993, 3432; and December 31, 1994, 3624. See also Richard E. Cohen and William Schneider, "Epitaph for an Era," *National Journal*, January 14, 1995, 83. The higher partisanship is due to a number of factors, including an increase in the number of divisive issues confronting Congress and a widening of the ideological divide between the parties since the 1980s. The heightened partisanship is also due to the breakup of the "solid South." In decades past, representatives of this conservative region had no choice but to run as Democrats. As a result, the Democratic party in Congress became bipolar. But as Republicans made inroads into elective offices in the South (beginning with Goldwater in 1964 and increased significantly by Reagan in the 1980s), the Democratic party became more ideologically coherent on the liberal side of the party spectrum. This has helped polarize the two parties in Congress. In addition, the forty-year domination of the House by the Democrats led to the perception on the part of Republicans (partially accurate) that they had been ignored and deprived of resources by the Democratic majority, and made them willing to take extreme and obstructive actions to slow the Democratic majority. This led to a mutually reinforcing dynamic. The consequences for President Clinton were that he had to make a more liberal appeal to the Democrats in Congress in order to hold their votes. But this, of course, tended to alienate potential Republican moderates and prevent bipartisan coalitions. See Nelson Polsby, "Clinton and Congress Navigate the Dog Days," *Public Affairs Report* (University of California, Berkeley: Institute of Governmental Studies, September 1994), 3.

3. *Congressional Quarterly Weekly Report*, October 8, 1994, 2851. Clinton signed all but 2 of the 465 bills that reached his desk (President Bush signed 2 that got to him

before Clinton took office). Clinton was the first president since Millard Fillmore to not veto a single bill during an entire Congress (32d Congress, 1851–1853). See *Congressional Quarterly Weekly Report*, December 31, 1994, 3623.

4. David Broder, "Round-the-Clock Operative," *Washington Post*, December 1, 1993, A25.

5. See Elizabeth Drew, *On the Edge* (New York: Simon and Schuster, 1994), chap. 3.

6. Ibid., 46.

7. The economic agenda of the Clinton administration is the main subject of Bob Woodward's *The Agenda* (New York: Simon and Schuster, 1994). Much of my analysis is based on Woodward's account. See also the insightful review of *The Agenda* by Robert M. Solow, "Advise and Dissent," in *The New Republic*, August 1, 1994, 41–43. On the credibility of Woodward's book, see Bert Solomon, "Seems Like a Messy Way to Decide ... But It Could Be a Whole Lot Worse," *National Journal*, June 25, 1994, 1532–1533. Solomon's interviews with White House staffers found no major disputes with Woodward's account of the early administration.

8. See Woodward, *The Agenda*, passim.

9. Woodward, *The Agenda*, 84.

10. Ibid., 94.

11. Dan Balz and Ruth Marcus, "The Windup For the Pitch," *Washington Post*, March 7, 1993, A1, A16.

12. Woodward, *The Agenda*, 140.

13. See the accounts in Drew, *On the Edge*, 114–122; and in Woodward, *The Agenda*, 151–174.

14. For tactical details see *Congressional Quarterly Weekly Report*, April 3, 1993, 818.

15. *Time*, May 31, 1993, 28.

16. Woodward, *The Agenda*, 298.

17. Ibid., 308.

18. R. W. Apple, Jr., "Clinton Is Pulled From the Brink. He'll Be Back," *New York Times*, August 8, 1993, E1.

19. James Fallows, "A Triumph of Misinformation," *Atlantic Monthly*, January 25, 1995, 26.

20. For an analysis of the politics and policy of the "reinventing government" initiative, see James P. Pfiffner, "The National Performance Review in Perspective," *International Journal of Public Administration* (forthcoming).

21. *Washington Post*, October 11, 1994, A6.

22. Steven Wald and Bob Cohn, "The Lost Chance," *Newsweek*, September 19, 1994, 29.

23. *Washington Post*, October 11, 1994, A6; and *New York Times*, August 29, 1994, A13.

24. Comments of Ira Magaziner at a luncheon at the Brookings Institution, October 12, 1994.

25. David S. Cloud, "Health Care's Painful Demise Cast Pall on Clinton Agenda," *Congressional Quarterly Weekly Report*, November 5, 1994, 3142–3145.

26. Fallows, "A Triumph of Misinformation," 34.

27. See Martha Derthick, "Endless Ramifications," *Washington Post*, August 31, 1994, A25.

28. Ann Devroy, "Clinton's Commitment Evident in His Effort," *Washington Post*, November 16, 1993, A23; and Gwen Ifill, "56 Long Days of Coordinated Persuasion," *New York Times*, November 19, 1993, A27.

29. David Mayhew, "Clinton, the 103rd Congress, and Unified Party Control: What Are the Lessons?" (Paper prepared for presentation at a conference honoring Stanley Kelley, Jr., Princeton University, October 27–28, 1995).

30. For a summary of this advice, see James P. Pfiffner, "The President's Legislative Agenda," *The Annals* 499 (September 1988): 22–35; and Pfiffner, *The Strategic Presidency: Hitting the Ground Running*, 2d ed. (Lawrence: University Press of Kansas, 1996), chap. 7. On the need to focus, see Paul C. Light, *The President's Agenda* (Bal-

timore: Johns Hopkins University Press, 1991); and Light, "The Focusing Skill and Presidential Influence in Congress," in *Congressional Politics*, ed. Christopher J. Deering (Chicago: Dorsey, 1989), 239–261.

31. See Leroy N. Rieselbach, "It's the Constitution, Stupid: Clinton and Congress," *Extension of Remarks* (November 1993): 10–11.

32. Quoted in Ruth Marcus, "Administration Now Sees Its Record at Risk," *Washington Post*, January 24, 1995, A1, A6.

33. See James P. Pfiffner, "The Reagan Budget Juggernaut," in *The President and Economic Policy*, ed. James P. Pfiffner (Philadelphia: ISHI Press, 1986), 108–134. Lyndon Johnson said about momentum: "A measure must be sent to the Hill at exactly the right moment and that moment depends on three things: first, on momentum; second, on the availability of sponsors in the right place at the right time; and third, on the opportunities for neutralizing the opposition. Timing is essential. Momentum is *not* a mysterious mistress. It is a controllable fact of political life that depends on nothing more exotic than preparation." Quoted in Doris Kearns, *Lyndon Johnson and the American Dream* (New York: New American Library, 1976), 237 (emphasis in the original).

34. Quoted in Marcus, "Administration Now Sees Its Record at Risk," A1, A6.

35. Quoted in Jack Valenti, *A Very Human President* (New York: W. W. Norton, 1975), 44.

36. Quoted in Harry McPherson, *A Political Education* (Boston: Little, Brown & Co., 1972), 268.

37. R. W. Apple, Jr., "Small Change," E1.

38. For examples of Democratic disloyalty in the budget fight, see Graeme Browning, "Freelancers," *National Journal*, September 24, 1994, 2203–2206.

39. George C. Edwards, *At the Margins* (New Haven: Yale University Press, 1989); Jon Bond and Richard Fleisher, *The President in the Legislative Arena* (Chicago: University of Chicago Press, 1990); and Mark A. Peterson, *Legislating Together: The White House and Capitol Hill* (Cambridge: Harvard University Press, 1990).

40. Mark A. Peterson, "Clinton and Congress: What Would You Expect?" *Extension of Remarks* (November 1993): 3.

41. George C. Edwards, "Reforming the 'President': The Individual as Leader," *PS: Political Science & Politics* 20, no. 3 (Summer 1987): 623 (emphasis in the original). See also Edwards, *At the Margins*.

42. For a good statement of this argument, see Peterson, "Clinton and Congress: What Would You Expect?" 2–3.

43. Charles O. Jones, *The Presidency in a Separated System* (Washington, D.C.: Brookings Institution, 1994), 281.

10

Congressional-Presidential Battles to Balance the Budget

James A. Thurber

The election of Republican majorities in the House and Senate in 1994 had a direct impact on the battle between Congress and the president over the federal budget of the United States.[1] This first Republican congressional budget agreement, completed in June 1995, was historic in that it ignored President Clinton's budget preferences and directly confronted hundreds of special interests with its proposals: to balance the budget by 2002, cut Medicare, devolve power over Medicaid to the states, reform welfare, cut education funding, reduce environmental regulations, eliminate the Department of Commerce (and hundreds of other federal programs), and provide for a $245 billion tax cut. Upon agreement between the House and Senate over the budget, House Speaker Newt Gingrich, R-Ga., announced, "Throughout the [House Republican Conference], Republicans have been unified in fashioning a budget which keeps our promise to the American people." Senate Majority Leader Bob Dole, R-Kan., stated that the budget agreement would "put more money in the pockets of American families and provide incentives for savings, economic growth, and job creation."[2] Congressional Republicans dismissed President Clinton's budget plan and Clinton the Republican plan; this led to a historic deadlock over passage of the budget and shut down the federal government for almost thirty days (a week in November 1995, two weeks in December 1995, and the first six days of January 1996).

As we will see, the confrontation over the fiscal year 1996 budget revealed a major change in the budgetary strategy of both the president and Congress, but the deadlocked negotiations were a reminder that budget policy in the United States is made by bargaining and compromise. On January 6, 1996, President Clinton compromised with congressional Republican demands for a seven-year balanced budget. Clinton announced, "This plan will show that you can balance the budget in seven years and protect Medicare, Medicaid, education and the environment, and provide tax relief to working families. This is a time of great national compromise. We need to find unity and common ground."[3] Congressional Republicans were also forced to compromise with the president after the extended negotiating sessions by allowing fewer cuts to Medicare and Medicaid, taxes, welfare, and other social programs.

On January 26, 1996, the president and Congress agreed to pass temporary continuing resolutions (with significant cuts in some departments) to keep the federal government open in 1996, thus breaking the budget deadlock until after the 1996 presidential election. Both the president and the congressional Republicans decided to let the American electorate decide what the spending and revenue policy should be, thus setting the stage for a historic election campaign focused on the role of the federal government and whether further cuts should be made in taxes, social programs, education, and government regulations.

At the center of the budget battle was the natural rivalry built on the constitutional separation of powers between the president and the Congress and the tenacious political ambitions of the president, the Speaker of the House, and the majority leader of the Senate. Journalists Michael Weisskopf and David Maraniss summarized how the personalities of Clinton, Dole, and Gingrich influenced events: "There were large political and historical forces at work in the great balanced budget fight of this fall and winter, but in the middle of it all, shaping events and being shaped by them, were three formidable politicians: One who is president, one who wants to be president and one who sometimes acted as though he were president." [4]

Decisions about the federal budget involve major confrontations over where federal money for public programs will be spent, who will pay for them, and whether money will be borrowed to pay for the spending. Since 1969, the last fiscal year with a budget surplus, the president and Congress have focused on the unpleasant task of raising taxes, cutting back on popular federal programs, or running a deficit and adding to the national debt. These battles between the president, Congress, and organized interests in society are at the heart of American politics and reveal the essence of congressional-presidential relations. [5]

The struggles over the federal budget in the 1990s, whether with unified or divided government, with Republicans or Democrats, have continued toward a zero-sum game, trading visible reductions in one program for visible increases in another or tax cuts for some in exchange for tax increases for others. [6] Until the revolutionary 1994 election, battles over the budget tended to be decentralized, favoring existing programs and strong interests over new programs and weak interests. Congressional budgeting became more centralized and independent of the president under the Republican leadership of the 104th Congress, thus causing budgeteers to focus their attentions on major tax and policy changes rather than protecting specific programs. Republican budgeting in the 104th Congress was in direct conflict with President Clinton and the desires of many specialized interests. It was centralized, disciplined, and top-down, designed to limit deliberations and the power of agencies and their supportive interest groups and to discourage individualism by members of Congress. It limited the power of the president in the process. The promise to balance the budget and cut back the scope of the federal government, first made by President Clinton in his 1992 election campaign and continued with greater vigor by the new Republican Congress in 1995, guaranteed an institutional battle between the president and Congress.

To combat rising deficits and improve accountability over the budget process, the congressional budget process has undergone six major reforms in the last two decades: the Congressional Budget and Impoundment Control Act of 1974, the Balanced Budget and Emergency Deficit Control Acts of 1985 and 1987 (Gramm-Rudman-Hollings or GRH I and II), the Budget Enforcement Act (BEA) of 1990, the 1993 Omnibus Budget Reconciliation Act, and the agenda of the Contract with America to cut taxes and balance the budget within seven years.[7] Supporters of these reforms suggested that they would promote more discipline in congressional budgeting, reduce deficits, control runaway spending, and make the process more timely and effective. However, in the years since the adoption of the first five reforms, complaints about spending, taxing, deficits, debt, and the budget process itself have not abated. The GOP takeover in 1995 brought a new round of budget reforms and a major shift in spending and taxing priorities, thus causing major changes in presidential-congressional budgeting strategies. Each reform has layered the budgetary relationship between the president and Congress with new procedures, rules, and powers.

Congressional-Presidential Budgeting and the 1974 Congressional Budget Process

The most important change in the last five decades in the way Congress makes decisions about collecting and spending money was implemented by the 1974 Congressional Budget and Impoundment Control Act (also referred to as the Congressional Budget Act).[8] The Congressional Budget Act forced the president to focus on a more centralized decision-making system in Congress. It created standing budget committees in the House and Senate, which were responsible for setting overall tax and spending levels. It also required Congress to adopt an annual budget resolution, which established total expenditures and revenues, with prescribed procedures for arriving at those spending and income totals. The budget resolution was the only time Congress was required to vote on the size of the deficit, total spending, and budget priorities in one legislative action. The 1974 reforms included three important elements. First, a timetable was established that set deadlines for action on budget-related legislation. This timetable was intended to ensure completion of the budget plan prior to the start of each fiscal year. Second, the Congressional Budget Act required the annual adoption of concurrent budget resolutions (which do not require presidential approval). Initial concurrent budget resolutions establish targets for total budget authority, budget outlays, and revenues for the upcoming fiscal year. Then, a final "binding" resolution, with ceilings on budget authority and outlays and a floor on revenues, is adopted. Finally, the act instituted a reconciliation process to conform revenue, spending, and debt legislation to the levels specified in the final budget resolution.[9] Each of these elements required the president and interest groups to follow the process at a higher level of budgetary aggregation than the traditional decentralized authorization and appropriations processes. It was now more difficult to build cozy relationships between the budget committees and special interests than between those interests and the authorization committees and appropriations subcommittees. The level of conflict was shifted to the budget committees and the leadership that were required to make major changes in popular programs in order to conform revenues and spending to the functional levels set in the budget resolution, rather than allowing a more program friendly, highly decentralized decision-making system to make the final cuts. The president was often left out of these relationships, but was the central player in the more visible reconciliation process.

Reconciliation, established in section 310 of the Congressional Budget Act of 1974, centralized the budget process. It is a procedure in which the House and Senate Budget Committees direct other committees to determine and recommend revenue and/or spending actions deemed necessary to conform authorizations and appropriations to the determinations made in the budget resolutions.[10] The budget committees have the option of mandating that House and Senate committees "report" legislation that will meet budget authority, outlay, and revenue targets.[11] Reconciliation has been used since 1980 exclusively for the purpose of deficit reduction. It has been used to implement broad and highly visible deficit reduction agreements between the president and Congress, as was the case in the historic fiscal year 1996 budget negotiations.

Reconciliation permits actions to be taken in tandem that would never survive alone, thus making it more difficult for presidents to influence the budget process. Combining spending reductions and revenue increases in the same legislation communicates "shared sacrifice" to the American public and allows members of Congress to build a coalition to reduce the deficit, as was the case in 1995. The use of reconciliation in 1995 made spending changes much easier and the task of presidential lobbying over the budget much more difficult. The fiscal year 1996 budget reconciliation was the ultimate compromise between the president and Congress, containing tax cuts, welfare reform, Medicare and Medicaid overhaul, and reductions in hundreds of federal programs. It was used by Speaker Gingrich to battle the president and advance a "conservative agenda" that some argued he could not win without the "cover" of a large omnibus budget bill.

The 1974 Congressional Budget Act did not require that the budget be balanced or keep Congress and the president from increasing the debt and deficits. During the first decade (fiscal years 1976–1985) the deficit averaged more than $110 billion (or 3.8 percent of Gross Domestic Product (GDP)). In the previous decade it averaged $15 billion (or 1.4 percent of GDP). As budget deficits increased (the average grew to more than $200 billion during fiscal years 1983–1986), Congress established annual targets to reduce the deficit.[12]

Congressional-Presidential Budgeting Under Gramm-Rudman-Hollings

The Balanced Budget and Emergency Deficit Control Act of 1985, commonly referred to as the Gramm-Rudman-Hollings (GRH) Act, was passed to force a progressive reduction in the deficit in each fiscal year from 1986 through 1990 for a balanced budget in 1991. The GRH legislation revised established budgetary deadlines for each of the major aspects of the congressional budget process in order to bring more discipline to spending decisions, to make the process more efficient, and to focus attention on reducing the deficit.[13]

The central enforcement mechanism of GRH was a series of automatic spending cuts that occurred if the federal budget did not meet, or fall within ten billion dollars of, the deficit targets (these automatic spending cuts were referred to as sequestration).[14] Sequestration required that federal spending be cut automatically if Congress and the president did not enact laws to reduce the deficit to the maximum deficit amount allowed for that year. If the proposed federal budget did not meet the annual deficit targets established by GRH, then the president had to make across-the-board spending cuts evenly divided between domestic and defense programs until those targets were met. However, most entitlement programs (then approximately 43 percent of the budget) and interest payments (then approximately 14 percent of the budget) were "off-budget," partially or totally exempt from the potential cuts.

The 1985 GRH legislation gave the General Accounting Office (GAO) the responsibility for triggering the across-the-board cuts. In 1986 the Supreme Court declared that part of the legislation was unconstitutional because it gave the GAO, a legislative support agency, executive functions.[15] The Supreme Court's decision would have prevented the implementation of GRH, but Congress responded by passing a revised version of the act in 1987 (GRH II). GRH II altered the original GRH deficit reduction plan by directing the Office of Management and Budget (OMB), an executive agency, to issue the report that would trigger sequestration if deficit reduction targets were not met. GRH II also revised the original deficit reduction targets in accordance with more realistic economic assumptions.

The GRH reform did not change the inclination of members of Congress to spend more than the revenues coming into the federal government. The threat of sequestration did not keep Congress and the president from exceeding the GRH targets.

The Failure of GRH and the Success of Specialized Interests

The Gramm-Rudman-Hollings deficit reduction plan failed to balance the budget and never reached the mandated deficit levels for a number of reasons. The enforcement of the deficit targets was not effective after the final budget "snapshot." That is, prior to the passage of the 1990 Budget Enforcement Act, Congress evaluated the budget only once a year to ascertain whether it was meeting the GRH deficit reduction targets. The result was a snapshot of the budgetary situation. After that evaluation, Congress was free to add new expenditures to the budget, which often increased the budget deficit. After the snapshot was taken, indicating that the deficit target had been met, legislation could be adopted that raised the deficit in the current year and following years as well.[16] The law did not require the actual deficit to be within the target, only the projected deficit at the start of the fiscal year. An increase in the actual deficit during the year did not require an offsetting spending reduction in order to meet the projected deficit in the resolution. Sequestration could be avoided by using overly optimistic economic and technical assumptions as substitutes for actual policy changes. In the end, it was futile to attempt to set fixed dollar limits on annual deficits unless the Congress truly desired to do so.

The failure of GRH reflected the power and success of strong specialized interests pressuring the president and Congress for full funding and tax expenditures for the programs they monitored. Some of the largest parts of the budget that had well-organized interests in society, such as Social Security, Medicare (the American Association of Retired Persons (AARP)), and veterans' programs (seven national veterans groups), were not touched by sequestration.

GRH sequestration was supposed to threaten the interests of all participants— the president, Congress, and organized interests outside of government—enough to make them want to avoid it. However, the threat of sequestration did not have the intended effect.

In spite of their goals, the Congressional Budget and Impoundment Control Act and GRH did not: curb growth of federal spending; bring an end to the growth in uncontrollable spending; reduce the deficit; force Congress to complete budgeting on time; reorder national spending priorities; allow Congress to control fiscal policy; eliminate the need for continuing resolutions; or reduce the power of specialized interests. Clearly something needed to be done to counteract these problems, and that was the 1990 Budget Enforcement Act.

Congressional-Presidential Budgeting in a Zero-Sum Game

By early 1990, it was obvious to congressional budgeteers and President Bush that the balanced budget target was not going to be reached. The deficit in 1993 (the year in which the revised GRH targets were to require a balanced budget) turned out to be $255 billion; thus, the budgetary rules were changed again with passage of the Budget Enforcement Act (BEA) of 1990, set forth in Title XII of the Omnibus Budget Reconciliation Act of 1990 (OBRA 1990). The 1990 BEA established a new deficit control process that distinguished between discretionary spending, controlled by annual appropriations, and direct spending, controlled by legislation outside the jurisdiction of the appropriations committees. The BEA procedures and rules were to be effective only for fiscal years 1991–1995, but were subsequently extended to fiscal year 1998. The significant programmatic and procedural restrictions that were made in spending and taxing reduced the deficit by almost $500 billion over a five-year period (1991 through 1995). The bipartisan agreement was intended to bring more control over spending while easing potential conflicts over the budget, thus allowing more efficient negotiated compromises to difficult economic and political questions, solving the problems of increasing deficits, and providing political cover over unpopular election-year decisions.[17]

The 1990 BEA reforms further centralized power within Congress by forcing Congress and coalitions of interest groups to make "zero-sum" choices: that is, trading visible reductions in one program for visible increases in another, or tax cuts for some in exchange for tax increases for others, and limiting the degrees of freedom for the president in the process. The BEA included changes in substantive law and budgetary procedures designed to bring more top-down party leadership control over the budget process, with the goal of reducing the deficit. The BEA thus had the effect of further increasing the centralization of congressional budgetary decision making. In December 1990 the Congressional Budget Office (CBO) estimated that the tax hikes, spending cuts, and procedural changes of the BEA summit agreement promised to reduce the cumulative deficit by about $496 billion for the 1991–1995 period.[18]

The BEA included three major changes in the congressional budget rules: adjustable deficit targets, caps on discretionary spending, and pay-as-you-go (PAYGO) rules for revenues and direct spending. The BEA also gave the president the option of adjusting the maximum deficit amount when he submitted his budget to Congress. President Clinton did this for both fiscal year 1994 and 1995, thus eliminating the possibility that money would be sequestered because the maximum deficit limit had been exceeded. In fact, under the BEA rules any level of deficit was permitted.

Perhaps the most significant aspect of the BEA reforms was the spending ceilings it established for annual appropriations, about one-third of the budget.[19] The budget agreement set a spending limit on total discretionary budget authority and outlays. The ceiling of each discretionary spending category (defense, domestic, and international) was enforced by an end-of-session sequestration applied across-the-board to all of the programs within the category. It also applied to categories that exceeded their spending limits (for example, if the ceiling for discretionary spending in the international category was exceeded, the end-of-session sequester applied to all programs within the international category). This process was referred to as "categorical sequestration." If congressional appropriations breached the limit of budget authority or outlays, the president had to sequester sufficient funds to compensate for the excess spending. The sequester was triggered only if the spending limits of any or all of the categories were exceeded due to changes in legislation (for instance, an extension of the benefits of a program or of the number of people eligible to receive benefits or tax cuts). If the spending limits were exceeded because of changes in economic conditions (or, as was the case with many domestic programs, because of increases in the number of eligible recipients), sequestration would not be triggered. If more money was appropriated for discretionary spending than was allowed under the discretionary limits, automatic sequestrations would be imposed, but only on the accounts in the category in which the breach occurred. Two small sequesters were applied to discretionary spending during the first four fiscal years (1991–1994) that the caps were in place.

The PAYGO rules in the BEA created a zero-sum game in the budget process.[20] They stated that legislation increasing direct spending or decreasing revenues had to be fully offset so that the deficit was not increased. Direct spending consisted mainly of entitlement programs, such as Social Security, Medicare, and Medicaid. PAYGO did not prevent Congress from passing revenue or spending bills that would add to the deficit. Rather, it required that the deficit increase caused by such laws be fully paid for by legislation raising revenues or cutting direct spending.

In fiscal years 1994–1995, the congressional budget system was supposed to return to fixed deficit targets enforced by the same sequestration rules used prior to the 1990 act, but it did not. President Clinton wanted to reduce the deficit further so he proposed another five-year deficit reduction package with discretionary spending limits, pay-as-you-go requirements, and maximum deficit amounts extended through fiscal year 1998. This Omnibus Budget Reconciliation Act of 1993 (OBRA 1993) embodied President Clinton's five-year deficit reduction plan. The goal of this plan was to reduce cumulative budget deficits by a total of $500 billion between fiscal years 1994 and 1998. With few changes, the Congress passed the 1993 OBRA, which embraced tax increases, discretionary spending cuts, and more stringent limitations on discretionary spending. The BEA's enforcement procedures, including the discretionary caps and PAYGO process, continued the spending ceilings for defense, international, and domestic discretionary programs in fiscal years 1994–1995. The consequence of all of these changes was to create a highly centralized zero-sum game, the most important consequence of the budget reforms of the 1990s for the battle between the president and Congress. These reforms forced organized interests to fight each other or join broad coalitions to lobby for tax expenditures or increases in spending.[21]

According to former CBO Director Robert D. Reischauer, "To date, this pay-as-you-go requirement has proved to be an effective poison pill that has killed a number of legislative efforts to cut taxes and expand entitlement." [22] The primary impact of PAYGO has been to dampen both presidential and congressional demands for new spending. The difficulty of either raising taxes or cutting popular existing mandatory programs (like Social Security) has resulted in PAYGO effectively closing out new mandatory programs (like Clinton's 1993 health care reforms) and allowing for major cuts in existing federal programs, as in the fiscal year 1996 budget. In the deadlock over the fiscal year 1996 budget, the PAYGO provision made it much more difficult to negotiate an agreement to balance the budget in seven years. The major cuts in revenues had to be offset by major cuts in federal spending programs or increases in revenues, creating a major confrontation between the president and Congress and among hundreds of specialized interests outside of government.

The Foundations of Centralized Budgeting

Before the series of budget reforms starting in 1974 were passed, the stable roles, relationships, and routines of the president, executive branch agencies (including the Bureau of the Budget, renamed the Office of Management and Budget in 1970), congressional party leaders, congressional committees, and interest groups led to few surprises in the federal budget process. Predictable "preferential" pluralistic incrementalism, with a narrow scope and low level of political conflict, predominated over distributive budgetary processes. [23] Preferential pluralistic incrementalism is a theory of budgetary strategy and process with three basic characteristics. [24] First, congressional budget actors make simple decisions, usually linked with organized interests with strong preferences, when confronted with complexity. Second, congressional and executive branch budgetary roles are determined by formal institutional positions. Third, congressional budgetary bargaining is stable, consensual, and often linked to special interests. Since passage of the 1974 Congressional Budget Act, however, two oil crises, stagflation, high interest rates, Reaganomics, large deficits, and debt have changed the economy and destabilized the budget process. Reagan-era tax cuts forced Congress to make redistributive budget decisions that widened the number of organized interests in the conflict over the budget and increased the conflict's visibility. A latent consequence of the budget reforms of the last two decades has been increased budgetary conflict, confusion, visibility of decisions, and stalemate between Congress and the president.

The budget reforms centralized budget decisions and caused some jockeying for jurisdictional turf between the budget committees and the other standing committees, especially the appropriations and taxing committees, thus shifting the focus of lobbying the process. Just about every committee is part of the congressional budget process; however, the authorization committees have lost power because of the appropriations committees' right to cap new backdoor spending.[25] The 1974 budget reforms restricted the authorization committees' use of contract authority and borrowing authority. But pre-1974 entitlement programs and net interest payments continue to reduce the ability of both Congress and the president to control the budget.

The 1974 budget act required all standing committees to estimate the cost of programs within their jurisdiction early in the budget cycle. These estimates of authorization tended to limit the committees' freedom and that of executive agencies and interest groups, which had a natural tendency to push for new programs and higher authorizations. The committees were forced to state priorities and to make difficult choices among programs very early in the process; they were much less vulnerable to twelfth-hour lobbying by agencies and strong, well-organized interest groups.

The Impact of Budget Reforms in the 1990s

The budget reforms of the 1990s have affected the budget process, the internal workings of Congress, congressional-presidential budgetary powers, and lobbying by external organized interests.[26] Collectively, the budget reforms of the 1990s established more budget control, expanded the power of the appropriations committees, and narrowed the scope of influence other committees had enjoyed because the changes created a zero-sum budget game. However, duplication of effort and fragmentation of responsibility are pervasive in the congressional budget process. The congressional budget process is now more accessible and accountable to the public, interest groups, and the president by publicly revealing the trade-offs that must be made in discretionary and entitlement program spending. Although an open and more accountable zero-sum budget game may have the potential for more conflict over the budget, the 1990 reforms were intended to create a more congenial budget process. The Budget Enforcement Act of 1990 and the OBRA of 1993 ensured that the president and the Congress would not fight over balancing the budget, but they would battle over domestic discretionary spending in a controlled zero-sum budget game. However, the battle to balance the budget within a specific time period was center stage again in the 104th Congress.

Notably, the 1990 and 1993 reforms have had mixed consequences for the distribution of power within Congress and for the power of the president and lobbyists outside Congress. The pay-as-you-go, zero-sum reforms had a centralizing impact: the reforms discouraged individual members from initiating their own "budget proposals" (with the help of outside interests) because cuts and revenue enhancements had to be instituted in other programs in order save their proposals. Stricter enforcement of categorical sequestration, PAYGO provisions, and taking the Social Security Trust Fund "off-budget" also increased the public's understanding and the visibility of the trade-off between spending and revenue policies. The exchange between tax cuts vs. Medicare and Medicaid cuts while trying to balance the budget was clear.

The BEA rules also centralized budget decision making with the party leadership and the budget committees, institutions with the power to negotiate trade-offs in the zero-sum game, as shown clearly with the Republican leadership in the 104th Congress. Reconciliation constrained the power of special interests and their favorite committees, and the 1990 BEA categorical sequestration centralized power by calling for more top-down budgeting.

Although the more rigid constraints set by the 1990 BEA have further reduced the autonomy of the appropriations committees, most budget participants argue that these committees were the big winners in the 1990 pact. The 1990 budget process rules diminished the role of the House and Senate Budget Committees by giving more freedom to the appropriations panels. One budget expert summarized this shift: "Since the pot of money the appropriations committees will have to work with has already been decided, they needn't wait for a spending outline from the budget committees before divvying it up." [27]

Appropriators are more able to determine the legislative details within the BEA constraints than through the old reconciliation process and sequestration under GRH. The appropriators have more control over backdoor spending, which has been determined regularly by the authorizers in reconciliation bills. The budget process reforms of the 1990s have also encouraged appropriators to favor "pain-deferral budgeting," or slow spending programs, over fast spending programs in order to reduce the projected spending for the next year. An example of pain deferral budgeting in the early 1990s was the failure of Congress (and the president) to terminate major programs whose budgetary requirements were likely to escalate sharply in future years, such as the space station, although they did cut the Superconducting Supercollider (SSC). "The camel's nose is being allowed under the tent; next year the camel's shoulders will want in, and then his hump," according to Robert Reischauer.[28] The power of the appropriators changed dramatically in the House with the drive by the Republican 104th Congress to balance the budget in seven years.

According to budget process scholar Irene Rubin, "closing the budget process is often considered one way to help control increases in expenditures; opening it is usually a way of increasing expenditures." [29] The BEA attempted to do the opposite: it opened up the process and placed more controls on expenditures. It also revealed the trade-offs within mandatory spending and the three discretionary spending categories, thus putting tough spending and taxing decisions in full public view. The decision-making process over the fiscal year 1996 budget was often closed and controlled by the Republican party leadership in their drive to control spending and reduce the deficit.

The 1990 and 1993 budget agreements simplified the process only if members abided by the agreements. The 1990 budget reforms have tended to work at cross-purposes when it comes to timeliness. A five-year budget agreement theoretically should make it easier to pass budget resolutions on time. It did not, as shown by the delay and deadlock in the fiscal year 1996 budget. When there are major differences in policy, no matter what the procedure, there will be conflict and gridlock. The budget resolutions will not be passed on time just because the reforms seem to make it easier.

Although the reforms of the 1990s simplified major aspects of the budget process, other changes increased its complexity and thus the potential conflict between the president and Congress. President Clinton and his agents found it necessary to work Congress continually in order to win spending battles. The process was relatively open and thus more difficult for the president, forcing him to bargain more openly with members of Congress and to monitor the budget process carefully. The president's budgeteers still attended budget hearings and markups, but they also tried to sit at the bargaining table with budget committee leaders to negotiate the final budget resolutions. Steps in the process have multiplied, as have the decision-making rules. Budget resolutions, reconciliation bills, PAYGO rules, discretionary spending caps, impoundment procedures, and sequestration have all created more complexity for the president and Congress. Typically, the more complex the process, the more time it consumes, as has been shown in the mid-1990s. Confrontations increase complexity and delay in the process as more cuts (or tax increases) are required to meet the caps on discretionary spending and the deficit. The complexity of the budget process simply reflects the diverse demands from organized interests in society and the policy differences between the president and Congress. Budget conflict and complexity cannot be eliminated simply by reforming the decision-making process. The only way to simplify the budget process is to have more consensus in society, which is not likely to happen soon in the United States.

Congressional-Presidential Budgeting Under the Contract with America

Republican members of Congress argued that voters sent a clear, undeniable message from the 1994 congressional elections: balance the budget, cut taxes, reform welfare programs, and cut the scope of the federal government. Not a single incumbent Republican congressman, senator, or governor was defeated, with most Republican candidates supporting the "Fiscal Responsibility Act," which required a balanced budget/tax limitation amendment and a line-item veto to "restore fiscal responsibility to an out-of-control Congress." [30] The 1994 election transformed the budget reform agenda dramatically. The major impact of the 1994 election and the Republican Contract with America was to bring the Balanced Budget Amend-

Table 10-1 Major Budget Process Reform Proposals of the 104th Congress

---

H.J.Res. 1: Balanced Budget Amendment
H.R. 2: Line-Item Veto Act
H.R. 5: Unfunded Mandate Reform Act
H.Res. 6: Abolish baseline budgeting; require a super majority (three-fifths' vote) for passing tax increases
Biennial budgeting (Senate)
Prohibit authorizations of less than two years
Restore "firewalls" between defense and nondefense spending
Balance the budget by 2002

Sources: H.J.Res. 1; H.R. 2; H.R. 5; H.Res. 6, adopted by the U.S. House of Representatives on January 4, 1995; and the Contract with America.

ment, the line-item veto, and the unfunded mandate reform to the top of the congressional budget reform agenda. Another consequence of the election was conflict, delay, and eventually deadlock between the president, Republican party congressional leaders, and Democratic party congressional leaders over the shape and size of the budget. The election brought divided party control of government and little consensus between the president and Congress.

The foundation of the budget reforms in the contract was a series of proposals developed in the 1990s. A CBO listing of budget process reform legislation supported by most Republican members of the 103d Congress included 186 major budget process reform proposals (most being the Balanced Budget Amendment and the line-item veto).[31] The Joint Committee on the Organization of Congress considered dozens of budget proposals, but none was adopted in the 103d Congress.

The first promise in the Contract with America was the Balanced Budget Amendment (H.J.Res. 1), a constitutional amendment requiring the president to propose, and Congress to adopt, a balanced budget each fiscal year starting in fiscal year 2002 (see Table 10-1). Under this proposal, Congress could not adopt a budget resolution in which total outlays exceeded total receipts unless three-fifths of the membership of each house approved. This was a popular proposal with the public. A Gallup poll conducted November 28, 1994, revealed that 77 percent of those questioned ranked the Balanced Budget Amendment either a top or a high priority for the 104th Congress. Congress had previously rejected several balanced budget amendments since the first one was introduced in 1936. Congress came close to passing such an amendment in 1986, when the Senate defeated the proposal by a single vote. This occurred again in 1995, when moderate Republican senator Mark Hatfield of Oregon voted against the balance budget amendment, thus defeating the proposal by one vote.

The second major budget reform of the 104th Congress from the Contract with America was the Line-Item Veto Act (H.R. 2), which would have given the president a permanent line-item veto. Under this procedure, the president could strike or reduce any discretionary budget authority or eliminate any targeted tax provision in any bill. The president had to prepare a separate rescissions package for each piece of legislation and was required to submit his proposal to Congress within twenty working calendar days after the original legislation arrived on his desk. The president's proposed rescissions would take effect unless Congress passed a disapproval bill within twenty days after receiving them. The disapproval bill had to pass by a two-thirds' vote in both houses. This conferred substantial new budgetary powers on the president. Proponents of the line-item veto maintained that, given large deficits, the president should have the authority to single out "unnecessary and wasteful" spending provisions in bills passed by Congress. Critics of the line-item veto argued that it ceded too much power to the executive branch to control federal spending, a responsibility clearly given to the legislative branch in the U.S. Constitution. This reform passed the House and Senate early in 1995, but the Republican leadership did not appoint conferees to reconcile the differences between the House and Senate versions of the bill until late September 1995, being reluctant to give President Clinton such substantial power under the line-item veto.

The Unfunded Mandate Reform Act (H.R. 5), restricting the imposition of unfunded requirements (mandates) by the federal government on state and local government entities, was the first bill to pass the House and Senate and be signed by President Clinton in the 104th Congress. Unfunded mandates are provisions in federal legislation that impose enforceable duties on state and local governments without appropriating funds to pay for them. Examples of unfunded mandates include provisions in most environmental legislation (for example, the Clear Air Act Amendments of 1990, the Clean Water Act, and the Safe Drinking Water Act), the "motor voter" law, and the Americans for Disabilities Act. The Unfunded Mandate Reform Act established a Commission on Unfunded Federal Mandates to investigate and review the impact of current unfunded state, local, and private entities. According to the reform, the Commission had to report to Congress and the president (within nine months after enactment) recommendations for suspending, consolidating, simplifying, or terminating mandates, as well as for instituting flexible means and common standards for complying with mandates. The law required federal agencies to assess the effects of federal regulations on state, local, tribal, and private sector entities. CBO was required to prepare an impact statement assessing the cost of the proposed mandates for any legislation. The CBO statement would detail estimates of the total direct costs of compliance exceeding $100 million in the first five years. The law repealed mandates at the beginning of any fiscal year in which no funds were provided to cover their costs, and assigned responsibility to determine the appropriate mandate funding levels to the budget committees. There was widespread consensus among Democratic and Republican state governors that an unfunded mandate act was needed to reduce the burden of federal regulations. A former governor, President Clinton strongly supported the reform, and there was no conflict between the president and Congress over its provisions.

These three budget reforms had several potential and actual consequences for presidential-congressional budgeting. The Balanced Budget Amendment, line-item veto, and unfunded mandate reform all: (1) favored a more conservative agenda for federal spending, (2) increased the complexity of the budget process, and (3) shifted power between the president and Congress.

Further cutbacks in federal spending and federal legislation would occur as a result of these three Contract with America reforms. The Republican drive to balance the budget in seven years (if not to pass a balanced budget amendment) and a cut in taxes meant major cuts in federal spending. The Republican leadership's desire in the 104th Congress to balance the budget helped to centralize budget decisions around the leadership and the budget committees. It increased the level of conflict and forced President Clinton to change his policy agenda (he produced three different budgets in 1995 and one in 1996). He appealed directly to the American people through a clear strategy, theme, and message in late 1995 in an attempt to build support for his limits on cuts in education, social programs, and taxes. Clinton argued in the crucial final days of budgetary negotiations that the time had come to "put aside partisanship and work to craft a balanced-budget agreement that upholds our values. It is time now to do what our parents have done before us: to put the national interests above narrow interests." [32]

Congressional-Presidential Budget Politics
After the 1994 Election

The major impact of the 1994 election and the Contract with America was on the House of Representatives in the budget process. Speaker Newt Gingrich centralized power in the House and may have become the strongest speaker since Thomas Brackett Reed and Joseph G. Cannon around the turn of the twentieth century. Because of a strong unified party that ran on a common ideology, the contract, Gingrich effectively consolidated power in the speakership and dominated the budget process to the detriment of the president (and the Senate). This centralization forced the president to threaten vetoes, build moderate coalitions in the Senate, and work on the most visible changes in the budget. A direct impact of the Republican cuts in Medicare, Medicaid, welfare, food stamps, the earned-income tax credit, education, and environmental programs was that President Clinton went "public" over the heads of Congress and used grass-roots strategies in lobbying the budget process. He made dozens of direct appeals to the American public through the media to save programs that were scheduled to be cut or eliminated by the congressional Republicans.

Speaker Gingrich enjoyed high levels of loyalty from the House GOP in the first session of the 104th Congress, as shown in Table 10-2. The strong loyalty of Republicans (especially Republican freshmen) to their party and against President Clinton is clearly shown in the table (see column labeled "party unity").[33] The loyalty of the Republican budget committee members, an essential factor in the Republicans' budget strategy, was especially impressive when compared with Democrats' party unity scores in the 102d Congress. The House and Senate GOP members of the budget committees in the 104th Congress had party unity scores of 93 and 91, respectively, compared with the House and Senate Democrats in the 102d Congress, with party unity scores of 82 and 78. Also, the party unity scores of House GOP Budget Committee members increased dramatically from the 102d Congress (when they had a score of 79), which showed the impact of centralization and discipline by the Republicans on the budget process. The highest party unity score (96) of budget committee members was achieved by the House freshmen GOP in the 104th Congress. The House GOP freshmen were a major force behind Speaker Gingrich's drive to balance the budget in seven years. The Republicans were more loyal and disciplined in both the 102d and 104th Congresses. Congressional Democrats generally, and Democratic budget committee members particularly, had low party unity and presidential support scores, making it difficult for President Clinton to build a coalition around his budget. The close vote in the House for Clinton's fiscal year 1993 budget (with a majority of one vote) and the absence of a natural coalition among House Democrats were clearly explained by the low support scores among the veteran Democrats.

The symbiotic relationship between the House GOP freshmen and Speaker Gingrich paid off in their strong support for his prolonged negotiations over the fiscal year 1996 budget. The exceptionally high party unity scores among House GOP freshmen revealed their loyalty to his leadership and to the drive to balance the budget, a key element of the contract.

Gingrich built this unity through several dramatic reforms that helped him to centralize power in the House.[34] He effectively appointed all of the chairs of House committees (including the Appropriations Committee), ignoring seniority by passing over the most senior members in several cases. Chairmen felt they owed their positions to him (and the House Republican Conference) rather than to seniority. He restricted the power of the chairs by placing term limits of six years on their positions. He also pushed through a ban on proxy voting by the chairs, which undermined their ability to act independently of the Speaker in the budget process. He made all freshman committee assignments, putting freshmen on the Rules, Ways and Means, Appropriations (nine out of eleven open Republican appointments), and Commerce Committees. Putting freshmen on the four most important committees in the House was unprecedented, and that helped to build

Table 10-2 Party Unity in the 102d and 104th Congresses: Comparing Parties, Budget Committees, Freshmen, and Veterans

	Party Unity	Presidential Support
Budget Committee Members		
102d Congress		
House Budget Republicans	79	70
House Budget Democrats	82	31
Senate Budget Republicans	87	83
Senate Budget Democrats	78	37
104th Congress		
House Budget Republicans	93	24
House Budget Democrats	80	73
Senate Budget Republicans	91	34
Senate Budget Democrats	85	83
Freshmen and Veterans in the 104th Congress		
House		
Overall	88	48
Freshmen	93	31
Veterans	87	52
Freshman Republicans	94	23
Freshman Democrats	87	78
Veteran Republicans	92	25
Veteran Democrats	82	75
Budget Freshman Republicans	96	21
Budget Freshman Democrats	92	26
Budget Veteran Republicans	92	26
Budget Veteran Democrats	78	72
Senate		
Overall	88	58
Freshmen	93	33
Veterans	87	61
Freshman Republicans	93	33
Freshman Democrats	NA	NA
Veteran Republicans	90	38
Veteran Democrats	84	82
Budget Freshman Republicans	87	36
Budget Freshman Democrats	NA	NA
Budget Veteran Republicans	94	34
Budget Veteran Democrats	85	83

Notes: All party unity and presidential support scores are preliminary calculations for the 104th Congress for all relevant roll-call votes as of October 1, 1995. All 102d Congress voting scores are final. "NA" means not applicable.

Source: This analysis is compiled from unpublished data gathered by Rhodes Cook, senior writer, *Congressional Quarterly Weekly Report,* October 20, 1995. Used with permission of Stephen Gettinger, senior editor.

exceedingly high party unity scores from House GOP freshmen both on and off the Budget Committee. Three-fifths of the House Republicans had been elected in the last two elections; many felt they owed their seats to Gingrich and were his backers generally and in the budget process specifically. The consequences of the 1994 election and of the subsequent reforms in the House have been to centralize budget power in the House leadership. There are fewer roadblocks within the House in putting together a balanced budget.

The centralization also has reduced the power of most specialized interests in the budget process. Take, for example, the cuts made in agriculture appropriations in the fiscal year 1996 budget. When the House Agriculture Committee failed to approve the Republican leadership's cuts in farm spending, the leadership pulled the farm bill from the Agriculture Committee and sent it to the Budget Committee (which did not have the same specialized farm interests pressuring it) for insertion into the budget reconciliation package. This led one observer to conclude: "Cross the Republican House leaders and be prepared to reap the whirlwind. They will threaten your livelihood, take your bill away and then do what they want anyway, all in the name of progress." [35] The zero-sum budgetary game has gotten tighter with the requirement to make major cuts in social programs, cut taxes, and balance the budget in seven years. [36]

Conclusions

Specific policy outcomes did not change dramatically as a result of the budget process reforms during the last twenty years. Change came as a result of the transformational 1994 election and the dramatic shift in the will of Congress and the president to balance the budget within a specific number of years. Over the last fifty years, the real growth in government spending happened almost automatically through pluralistic incrementalism—that is, through the collective strength of specialized interests influencing Congress and the president to make gradual changes in policy. Interest groups, agencies, and committees were as successful under the 1974 budget process and GRH in protecting their base funding and securing their "fair share" of increases as they were before Congress centralized budgetary decision making. No major groups were significantly disadvantaged by budget reform until the new budgetary priorities of the Republican 104th Congress were established. No major programs were cut by presidents or Congress (except taxes by Reagan) until the partisan change came in both the House and Senate after the 1994 election. No congressional committees tried to abolish major programs under their jurisdictions until the 104th Congress. Presidential and congressional spending priorities were not greatly changed as a direct result of the 1974 budget process reforms, GRH I and II, and the 1990 and 1993 BEA. Spending changes came with a new desire by the House Republicans to balance the budget in seven years.

The BEA further diffused the target of responsibility for spending and the deficit (although the latter is dropping rapidly). In a complex budget process, who will be blamed (or get credit) for the deficit? Not the budget committees, the tax committees, the appropriations committees, the party leadership, or the president. President Clinton understood this, as shown in his fiscal year 1996 budget proposal that abandoned serious deficit reduction. Clinton's 1996 budget invited the Republicans to show how they could balance the budget while cutting taxes and increasing defense spending. Realizing that he was not getting credit for deficit reduction, Clinton "punted the ball" to the Republicans to pursue this politically thankless task. They did so with proposed major cuts in Medicare, Medicaid, education, the earned-income tax credit, and other social welfare programs. This led to a major confrontation over the scope and role of the federal government and pushed the president to the sideline of the budget battle temporarily. Ultimately, the president has the power of the veto and the power of persuasion (which President Clinton used to overcome the budget deadlock with the congressional Republicans).

The president and the Republican Congress ended the historic budgetary deadlock on January 26, 1996, when Congress passed legislation that President Clinton signed to fund the federal government until March 15 with $100 billion in spending cuts as a "down payment" on deficit reduction. The budget cease-fire between the president and Congress was not a victory for either side. Compromise and a political rapprochement between Speaker Gingrich and his more conservative freshmen, Majority Leader Dole and the House Republicans, and President Clinton and the more liberal Democratic House members were ultimately necessary for the struggle to end. The issues of tax cuts, reduction in social spending, devolution of the federal government, and deregulation would be fought over in the next election and the next Congress.

Budgets are political documents, and budgetary battles will continue to hold center stage for presidents and Congress. Budget and party leaders will continue to build coalitions in the formulation of the budget and to negotiate with the president about spending priorities, as was the case with divided party control of government under President Bush, and with unified party government under President Clinton, and again with divided party government after the 1994 election. The major impact of the 1990 pact and the 1994 Republican win on the president was a tighter zero-sum budget game, with more controlled, top-down, centralized budgeting by the congressional party leadership. The trade-offs between program reductions and increases were more visible, as were tax reductions and increases. The emphasis of the 1990 BEA reforms was on spending, not deficits, whereas the budget battles of the 104th Congress focused on deficits and program cuts. Presidential budget strategies concerned spending priorities and cuts in programs within the zero-sum limits defined by the reforms of the 1990s and the realities of a more conservative and centralized leadership in the

House. These reforms made spending trade-offs more visible and imposed more control over the process. Reforms added more complexity to budget making (for example, categorical caps on discretionary spending and PAYGO) and enlarged the roles of budget and party leaders, thus reducing individualism and the power of the president in the process. Ultimately, conflict over further centralization of budget power is inevitable; however, the consequence of the centralized budget process in the 104th Congress was to reduce the power of the president and specialized interests.

The Budget Enforcement Act, Gramm-Rudman-Hollings Act, and other reforms in the late 1980s and 1990s insulated Congress from accountability and made it difficult to assign responsibility for the growth of the federal budget or the size of the deficit. The reality of the congressional budget process in the 104th Congress was the opposite. The process was open and transparent. The policy differences between the president and Congress were clear. The centralized drive in Congress to balance the budget hurt many specific organized interests. Accountability was clear in the era of the Contract with America.

Budgeting by the president and Congress has become more democratic, yet more conflicted. Frequently, the result is policy-making gridlock, as was the case in the battle over the fiscal year 1996 budget. Congress is fundamentally a representative institution. Because it responds to political pressures from organized groups and public preferences generally, any effort to make the budget process more efficient is in direct conflict with its constitutional design and natural state. The struggle inside Congress vacillates between centralization and decentralization of authority, and it will continue to cause delay, deadlock, and even a breakdown in congressional-presidential budgeting until the American people wish something different.

The centralization of power over the budget process in the House in the 104th Congress and the increased discipline of the congressional Republican party reduced the power of the president and many organized interests outside of Congress, which in turn led to increased campaign contributions, grass-roots activity, coalition building among specialized interests, and direct lobbying tactics. Further change in the relationship between the president and Congress in the budget process will come as a result of elections, as it did in 1994. The 1994 voters seemed to want a balanced budget, cutbacks in the size of the federal government, lower taxes, and welfare reform; the Republican Congress clearly responded. Ultimately, the desires of the American electorate have the most important impact on the battle between the president and Congress over the budget. Congressional budget reform that is disconnected from the will of the American public will have little impact on presidential-congressional relations.

Notes

I would like to thank the School of Public Affairs and the Center for Congressional and Presidential Studies at the American University for supporting the research for this analysis. This chapter is partially based upon interviews with White House staff, House and Senate members and staff, and informed observers. I am grateful for the time they gave and for their observations about the congressional budget process. I would especially like to thank Dr. Patrick J. Griffin, assistant to the president for legislative affairs, for sharing his insights about the relationship between President Clinton's White House and Congress in the budget process in 1994 and 1995. I would also like to thank the following individuals, who were most helpful in sharing their knowledge about the congressional budget process: Roy T. Myers, Department of Political Science at the University of Maryland, Baltimore County; Dr. Phillip G. Joyce of the Congressional Budget Office; James V. Saturno and Edward Davis of the Government Division, Congressional Research Service, Library of Congress; Dr. Joe White at the Brookings Institution; and Dr. Nicholas Masters, former senior staff, House Budget Committee, and adjunct professor at American University.

1. For an analysis of the impact of the 1994 election on Congress, see James A. Thurber, "Remaking Congress After the Electoral Earthquake of 1994," in *Remaking Congress: Change and Stability in the 1990s*, ed. James A. Thurber and Roger H. Davidson (Washington, D.C.: Congressional Quarterly Inc., 1995), 1-8.

2. Eric Pianin, "Hill Leaders Agree on 7-Year Budget," *Washington Post*, June 23, 1995, A1. For an analysis of Speaker Gingrich's leadership over the budget negotiations, see Jason DeParle, "Rant/Listen, Exploit/Learn, Scare/Help, Manipulate/Lead," *New York Times Magazine,* January 28, 1996, 34-41, 48, 56, 60-61, 66.

3. Ann Devroy, "Bill Signed to Fully Reopen Government," *Washington Post,* January 7, 1996, A1.

4. Michael Weisskopf and David Maraniss, "Personalities Shaped Events as Much as Ideology," *Washington Post,* January 20, 1996, A1.

5. See James A. Thurber, "The Impact of Budget Reform on Presidential and Congressional Governance," in *Divided Democracy: Cooperation and Conflict Between the President and Congress*, ed. James A. Thurber (Washington, D.C.: CQ Press, 1991), 145-170.

6. For a discussion of the impact of divided government on presidential-congressional relations, see Thurber, *Divided Democracy*; and James A. Thurber, "Representation, Accountability, and Efficiency in Divided Party Control of Government," *PS: Political Science and Politics* (December 1991): 653-657.

7. For a discussion of these reforms, see James A. Thurber, "If the Game is Too Hard, Change the Rules: Congressional Budget Reform in the 1990s," in *Remaking Congress*, 130-144; Thurber, "The Impact of Budget Reform"; James A. Thurber, "Budget Continuity and Change: An Assessment of the Congressional Budget Process," in *Studies of Modern American Politics*, ed. D. K. Adams (Manchester, England: Manchester University Press, 1989), 78-118; Louis Fisher, "Ten Years of the Budget Act: Still Searching for Controls," *Public Budgeting and Finance* 5 (Autumn 1985); Harry Havens, "Gramm-Rudman-Hollings: Origins and Implementation," *Public Budgeting and Finance* 6 (Autumn 1986): 4-24; Lance T. LeLoup, Barbara Luck Graham, and Stacy Barwick, "Deficit Politics and Constitutional Government: The Impact of Gramm-Rudman-Hollings," *Public Budgeting and Finance* 7 (Spring 1987): 83-103; and Raphael Thelwell, "Gramm-Rudman-Hollings Four Years Later: A Dangerous Illusion," *Public Administration Review* 50 (March/April 1990): 190-197.

8. One of the important reforms instituted by the 1974 Congressional Budget Act was the creation of the Congressional Budget Office (CBO). This agency serves as Congress's principal source of information and analysis on the budget and on spending

and revenue legislation. The CBO has a specific mandate to assist the House and Senate Budget Committees and the spending and revenue committees. Secondarily, it responds to requests for information from other committees and individual members of Congress. Prior to the creation of CBO, Congress was forced to rely on the president's budget estimates and economic forecasts and on the annual analysis of the economy and fiscal policy done by the Joint Economic Committee.

9. James A. Thurber, "Budget Continuity and Change: An Assessment of the Congressional Budget Process," 80.

10. Authorizations are laws that establish federal programs or agencies and specify how appropriated funds are to be used. An appropriation is a provision of law providing budget authority that enables an agency to make payments or incur obligations.

11. See Allen Schick, *Reconciliation and the Congressional Budget Process* (Washington, D.C.: American Enterprise Institute, 1981); D. Tate, "Reconciliation Breeds Tumult as Committees Tackle Cuts: Revolutionary Budget Tool," *Congressional Quarterly Weekly Report*, May 23, 1981, 887–891.

12. Another measure of the budget deficit is the imbalance of outlays and receipts as a percentage of the Gross National Product (GNP). The deficit is decreasing as a percentage of GNP. For example, outlays were 24.3 percent of GNP and receipts were 18.1 percent of GNP in 1983; 23.7 percent outlays to 18.4 percent revenues in 1986; and 22.2 percent outlays to 19.2 percent revenues in 1989. See U.S. Congress, Congressional Budget Office, *The Economic and Budget Outlook: Fiscal Years 1991–1995*, January 1990, Appendix E, Table E-2, at 123.

13. These deadlines significantly altered prior budget process deadlines. Notably, the new deadlines have been delayed or modified informally each year since GRH I and GRH II were passed, especially in 1990 and 1995.

14. See Rudolph G. Penner and Alan J. Abramson, *Broken Purse Strings: Congressional Budgeting 1974–1988* (Washington, D.C.: Urban Institute Press, 1988), 97.

15. *Bowsher v. Sinar*, 106 Sup. Ct. 3181 (July 7, 1986).

16. See Senate Committee on Governmental Affairs, "Proposed Budget Reforms: A Critical Analysis," in *Proposed Budget Reform: A Critical Analysis*, prepared by Allen Schick, 100th Cong., 2d sess. (Washington, D.C.: Congressional Research Service and the Library of Congress, April 1988), 52.

17. John E. Yang and Steven Mufson, "Package Termed Best Circumstances Permit," *Washington Post*, October 29, 1990, A4.

18. U.S. Congress, Congressional Budget Office, *The 1990 Budget Agreement: An Interim Assessment*, December 1990.

19. Budget Enforcement Act of 1990, Public Law 101–508, sec. 13101, 1990 U.S.C.C.A.N. (104 Stat.), 1388–1574.

20. Budget Enforcement Act of 1990, Public Law 101–508, sec. 13204, 1990 U.S.C.C.A.N. (104 Stat.), 1388–1616.

21. U.S. Congress, Congressional Budget Office, *Pay-as-You-Go Budgeting*, a staff memorandum, March 1990.

22. Robert D. Reischauer, speech to the National Tax Association, 84th Annual Conference on Taxation, Williamsburg, Virginia, November 11, 1991.

23. For a discussion of preferential pluralism, see Charles O. Jones, *The Presidency in a Separated System* (Washington, D.C.: Brookings Institution, 1994).

24. M. A. H. Dempster and Aaron Wildavsky, "On Change: Or, There is No Magic Size for an Increment," *Political Studies*, September 1979, 371–389.

25. There are three kinds of backdoor spending techniques: *Contract authority* permits agencies to enter into contracts that subsequently must be liquidated by appropriations. *Borrowing authority* allows agencies to spend money they have borrowed from the public or the Treasury. *Mandatory entitlement authority* grants eligible individuals and governments the right to receive payments from the national government. Entitlements for Medicare, for example, establish judicially enforceable rights without

reference to dollar amounts.

26. See Thurber, "The Impact of Budget Reform"; and James A. Thurber and Samantha Durst, "Delay, Deadlock, and Deficits: Evaluating Congressional Budget Reform," in *Federal Budget and Financial Management Reform*, ed. Thomas D. Lynch (Westport, Conn.: Greenwood, 1991).

27. John E. Yang, "Budget Battle Set to Begin on New Terrain," *Washington Post*, February 3, 1991, A12.

28. U.S. Congress, Congressional Budget Office, *The 1990 Budget Agreement*.

29. Irene Rubin, *The Politics of Public Budgeting* (Chatham, N.J.: Chatham House, 1993), 66.

30. Ed Gillespie and Bob Schellhas, eds., *Contract with America* (New York: Times Books, 1994), 9.

31. See memos by Phil Joyce to Bob Reischauer (and others) on "Budget Process Legislation" from January 22, 1993, to September 1, 1994.

32. Adam Clymer, "Clinton Approves a Bill Returning Workers to Jobs," *New York Times*, January 7, 1996, 1. For a discussion of the internal conflict in the House Republican Conference that eventually led to the compromise with President Clinton, see David Maraniss and Michael Weisskopf, "GOP Lost Control of Members and Public Perception," *Washington Post*, January 19, 1996, A1.

33. *Party unity scores* are a measure of party-line voting commonly measured as the percentage of all recorded votes on which a majority of voting Democrats opposed a majority of voting Republicans. Party unity scores give a picture of how loyal a member of Congress is in their voting behavior. A high score means more loyalty and partisanship.

    Presidential support scores show the annual percentages of presidential victories on votes on which the president took clear-cut positions. Congressional Quarterly determines what the president wants in the way of legislative action by analyzing his messages to Congress, public comments in press conferences, documents, and other public remarks. Presidential support scores also reflect the position of the president at the time of a vote even though he may have made a major concession from an earlier stand. The measure gives a rough indication of the state of relations between the president and Congress and reveals the loyalty of members to the president's positions. A high presidential support score indicates greater loyalty to the president's legislative agenda than a low score.

    The characteristics and limitations of both voting scores are discussed in chapter 6 of this volume, "An Overview of the Empirical Findings on Presidential-Congressional Relations," by Jon R. Bond, Richard Fleisher, and Glen S. Krutz (pp. 103–139).

34. For further discussion of these reforms, see Thurber and Davidson, eds., *Remaking Congress*.

35. Guy Gugliotta, "Democratic Tactics Prove Useful to GOP Leaders," *Washington Post*, September 17, 1995, A4.

36. See Thurber, "Remaking Congress After the Electoral Earthquake of 1994," in *Remaking Congress*, 1-8; and James A. Thurber, "Thunder from the Right: Observations About the Elections," *The Public Manager* (Winter 1994–1995): 13–16.

11

President Clinton as Commander in Chief

Louis Fisher

President Bill Clinton embraced a broad definition of the power of commander in chief, claiming that it enables him to send troops anywhere in the world—even into combat—without first seeking prior authority from Congress. During October 1993, when Congress debated restrictions on his use of American troops in Somalia and Haiti, Clinton vigorously objected to any congressional interference: "I would strenuously oppose such attempts to encroach on the President's foreign policy powers." [1] While promising to *consult* with members of Congress, he claimed that "the Constitution leaves the President, for good and sufficient reasons, the ultimate decisionmaking authority." [2] Acknowledging that the president has an obligation to define and justify the use of U.S. force, Clinton insisted that "the President must make the ultimate decision." [3]

Over the next two years, Clinton continued to press an expansive view of presidential power over military initiatives. In February 1994, while contemplating air strikes in Bosnia, he looked for authority not to Congress but to the U.N. Security Council and to the North Atlantic Treaty Organization (NATO). [4] At a press conference on August 3, 1994, Clinton said that he was not "constitutionally mandated" to receive approval from Congress before invading Haiti. [5] Regarding his authority to commit ground troops to Bosnia, he wrote to Sen. Robert C. Byrd, D-W. Va., on October 19, 1995, claiming that he could act without seeking the authority of Congress. Clinton agreed only to request an expression of "support" from legislators while maintaining the "constitutional authorities of the Presidency." [6] A month later he took the same position in a letter to Speaker Newt Gingrich, asking only for "support" and insisting that he must "reserve my constitutional prerogatives in this area." [7]

Clinton's interpretation of presidential war power would have astonished the framers of the Constitution. They deliberately rejected the British models of John Locke and William Blackstone that gave the executive exclusive control over foreign affairs and the war power. Instead, the framers vested in Congress the decision to initiate and authorize war. It gave to Congress also the power over foreign commerce, approval of treaties, confirmation of ambassadors, power of the purse, and other authorities over external affairs. [8] In recent decades, however, Congress has failed to protect its prerogatives. Nor have the courts chosen to place any restrictions on the president's ability to take the country to war. The result is a presidency that acts unilaterally in war making without effective checks from the other two branches.

Clinton's Constitutional Framework

The 1992 presidential campaign contains a few clues about Bill Clinton's readiness to use military force. Unlike recent Democrats who ran for the White House, he appeared to endorse an activist, interventionist philosophy. Although much of Clinton's campaign centered on economic recovery, health care, and other domestic issues, he projected himself as a strong leader in foreign affairs and indicated a willingness to resort to military action.

In an interview in June 1992, Clinton said that he had been more detailed and forthright about his foreign policy "even than President Bush and certainly than Mr. Perot." For those reasons, "I can be trusted to be Commander in Chief." Criticizing Bush's foreign policy, Clinton said he would be willing to use military force—in concert with other nations—to bring humanitarian aid to the citizens of Bosnia and Herzegovina.[9] In August, he said that he would not relish the prospect of sending citizens into combat, "but neither do I flinch from it." Clinton pointed out that World War I and World War II were led by presidents who came to the White House after serving as governor.[10] U.S. foreign policy, he said,

> cannot be divorced from the moral principles most Americans share. We cannot disregard how other governments treat their own people—whether their domestic institutions are democratic or repressive, whether they help encourage or check illegal conduct beyond their borders. It should matter to us how others govern themselves.[11]

Implicit in these statements is the message that if other nations govern badly, the United States may have an obligation to intervene in some form: through economic means, political influence, or military action. In a number of specific regions of the world, Clinton criticized Bush for failing to address foreign policy more assertively: (1) "[Bush's] failure to articulate clear goals or a rationale for an engaged foreign policy has fueled a dangerous new isolationism," (2) "The Administration sat on the sidelines for too long while the former Yugoslavia slipped into chaos and civil war," and (3) "The Administration turned its back on those struggling for democracy in China and on those fleeing Haiti." [12]

Clinton's image as a credible commander in chief was damaged by conflicting stories about his draft record during the Vietnam War. Various accounts surfaced on the techniques he used to avoid military service. Repeatedly he tried to put the issue behind him, but the controversy remained alive and kept him on the defensive. Given Clinton's background and history, it may have been tempting for him to see political benefits in military action.

Clinton's reputation as commander in chief suffered a serious setback early in his term when he proposed that gays be allowed to serve in the military. The initial strategy would have deferred the issue for up to six months by asking Secretary of Defense Les Aspin to draft an executive order and prepare Defense Department instructions for standards regarding sexual conduct in the military. The administration hoped to push the issue to the sidelines so that Clinton could concentrate on economic and domestic issues. However, when the Joint Chiefs of Staff complained that they had not been properly consulted, the dispute began to look like a rebellion within military ranks against Clinton. His hand was also forced when the Senate threatened to write the existing administration ban into law.[13] The controversy became more explosive and emotional on March 23 when Clinton was asked at a news conference:

> Mr. President, you seem to be having some difficulty with the Pentagon. When you went to the U.S.S. *Theodore Roosevelt*, the sailors there were mocking you before your arrival, even though you are the Commander in Chief. The services have been undercutting your proposal for permitting gays to be in the military.... Do you have a problem, perhaps because of your lack of military service or perhaps because of issues such as gays in the military, in being effective in your role as Commander in Chief, and what do you propose to do about it?[14]

Clinton denied that he had a problem being commander in chief. Within a few months he would have what White House officials saw as an opportunity to show his "toughness."[15]

Launching Missiles Against Baghdad

On June 26, 1993, President Clinton ordered air strikes against Iraq. In an address to the nation, he explained that the Kuwaiti government in April had uncovered what they suspected was a car bombing plot to assassinate former president Bush during a visit to Kuwait. Sixteen suspects, including two Iraqi nationals, had been arrested. Although the trial of those suspects was still under way in Kuwait, the CIA concluded that there was "compelling evidence" of a plot to assassinate Bush and that this plot, including the use of a powerful bomb made in Iraq, was directed and pursued by the Iraqi intelligence service.[16] Clinton called the action against Bush "an attack against our country and against all Americans."[17] In a message to Congress on June 28, he said that the attack was ordered "in the exercise of our inherent right of self-defense as recognized in Article 51 of the United Nations Charter and pursuant to my constitutional authority with respect to the conduct of foreign relations and as Commander in Chief."[18]

Clinton did not consult with members of Congress before ordering the launching of twenty-three Tomahawk cruise missiles against the Iraqi intelligence service's principal command-and-control facility in Baghdad. The facility was badly damaged, but three of the missiles destroyed homes in the surrounding neighborhood, killing eight people and wounding at least twelve others.

News analyses suggested that the White House appreciated that the use of force would help rebuild Clinton's image into that of a strong and decisive leader. After Clinton's difficult start as president, members of Congress and the public had questioned his ability to lead the nation. The cruise missile attack, a White House aide commented, would "serve notice to one and all that Americans are prepared first of all to exercise leadership and to remain engaged and to act with military forces as appropriate." A senior administration official said, "We were showing that Bill Clinton can take the challenge." Aides disclosed that Clinton, shortly after making an address from the Oval Office, returned to the White House residence to watch a movie with his wife and slept "a solid eight hours." [19]

President Clinton said that the attack on Baghdad "was essential to protect our sovereignty, to send a message to those who engage in state-sponsored terrorism, to deter further violence against our people, and to affirm the expectation of civilized behavior among nations." He further noted that there should be no mistake about the message being sent to Iraq and to other nations: "We will combat terrorism. We will deter aggression. We will protect our people." [20] That argument was not credible. As two attorneys of constitutional law noted, "calling the U.S. bombing of Iraq an act of self-defense for an assassination plot that had been averted two months previously is quite a stretch." [21] If the United States had evidence of terrorist activity by Syria, it would not have launched cruise missiles against its intelligence facilities located in cities. Other responses, less confrontational, would have been used. Iraq was attacked because, like Cambodia, Grenada, and Libya, it fell into the category of a weak and isolated nation vulnerable to the use of American military force.

Combat Operations in Somalia

Congress urged the Bush administration to intervene in Somalia to feed the starving people. After the 1992 election, Bush announced that U.S. troops would be sent to Somalia as part of a multinational effort. A quarter of a million people had died in the famine. Without prompt humanitarian assistance, another million could have starved to death. Over time, this humanitarian initiative acquired a military face. American forces, operating under the umbrella of the U.N. Security Council but without congressional authority, used military force and air attacks against a so-called warlord, Mohamed Farad Aideed. In these efforts, troops from the United States and other nations suffered substantial casualties.

On December 3, 1992, the U.N. Security Council enacted a resolution authorizing the use of "all necessary means to establish as soon as possible a secure environment for humanitarian relief operations in Somalia." A day later Bush authorized the sending of U.S. troops to Somalia as part of a multinational relief effort. Bush explained to the nation that the mission had a limited objective: "To open the supply routes, to get the food moving, and to prepare the way for a U.N. peacekeeping force to keep it moving. This operation is not open-ended. We will not stay one day longer than is absolutely necessary." [22] There were no plans "to dictate political outcomes." [23] In a letter to congressional leaders a few days later, Bush said that there was no intention for U.S. armed forces in Somalia to become "involved in hostilities." [24] President-elect Clinton commended Bush for taking the lead in the humanitarian effort. [25]

The Senate passed legislation on February 4, 1993, authorizing the use of U.S. armed forces in Somalia. Senate majority leader George Mitchell noted in debate that U.N. Security Council resolutions "are no substitute for congressional authorization." [26] The House also acted, on May 20, to authorize the use of U.S. armed forces in Somalia, but Congress could not reconcile the different House and Senate versions of the bill. [27] In the end the authorizing legislation was never enacted.

The humanitarian effort turned bloody in June 1993 with the killing of twenty-three Pakistani peacekeepers. U.N. officials blamed the deaths on Aideed. U.S. warplanes launched a retaliatory attack, hitting a radio station and four weapons storage sites. What began as a nonpolitical effort to help starving Somalis turned into a personal operation against Aideed. President Clinton explained that armed force was needed

> to undermine the capacity of Aideed to wreak military havoc in Mogadishu. He murdered 23 U.N. peacekeepers. And I would remind you that before the United States and the United Nations showed up, he was responsible for the deaths of countless Somalis from starvation, from disease, and from killing.
> The military back of Aideed has been broken. A warrant has been issued for his arrest.... [28]

In August 1993, four U.S. soldiers were killed when a land mine blasted apart their Humvee vehicle in Mogadishu. The killings were again attributed to Aideed, who remained at large. Earlier conflicts had killed four other American soldiers. Because of the transformed nature of the effort in Somalia, the Pentagon began awarding American soldiers "hostile fire pay" for service in Somalia and authorized U.S. Army troops to wear a combat patch on their uniforms. Moreover, officials in the Clinton administration began to talk of "nation building": rebuilding political structures in Somalia to form a stable order.

By September 1993, members of Congress were drafting legislation that would require Clinton to remove American troops within a fixed period of time unless Congress enacted legislation authorizing that they remain. Indiana Democrat Lee Hamilton, then chairman of the House Foreign Affairs Committee, objected to the new mission of U.S. troops in Somalia:

"I do not believe that the United States should be engaged in nation building in Somalia. That is the task of the United Nations." [29] Early in October, Clinton hoped to defuse the confrontation with Congress by seeking a compromise and greater recourse to executive-legislative cooperation. [30]

Within a few days that strategy floundered when two U.S. helicopters were shot down trying to capture, or kill, Aideed. Twelve American soldiers lost their lives in the assault; another seventy-four were wounded. TV footage showed the body of one of the American soldiers dragged through the streets of Mogadishu. Under pressure from Congress, Clinton announced on October 7 that all American troops would be out of Somalia no later than March 31, 1994, except for a few hundred support personnel in noncombat roles. [31] He repeated the March 31 pledge a week later in a message to Congress, at which time he said the U.S. military mission "is not now, nor was it ever one of 'nation building.'" [32]

In the defense appropriations bill, Congress provided that no funds for the operations of U.S. armed forces in Somalia could be obligated for expenses after March 31, 1994, although that date could be extended "if so requested by the President and authorized by the Congress." Congress asserted the power of the purse to regain control. The legislation further provided that funds could be obligated after the March 31 date to protect American diplomatic facilities and American citizens. Moreover, to ensure that American forces would not be under U.N. control, the measure provided that U.S. combat forces in Somalia "shall be under the command and control of United States commanders under the ultimate direction of the President of the United States." [33] Clinton removed U.S. military forces prior to the March 31 deadline.

Deciding to Invade Haiti

Clinton's position on what to do about the military regime in Haiti fluctuated from month to month depending on shifting political pressures, many of them of his own making. Jean-Bertrand Aristide, the island's first democratically elected president, was overthrown in a military coup on September 30, 1991. Political repression by the military rulers produced a flood of refugees trying to reach the United States. The Bush administration, maintaining that the Haitians were fleeing because of economic conditions, not political persecution, refused to qualify them for asylum and returned the refugees to Haiti. Bush also cut off aid to Haiti and complied with a trade embargo adopted by the Organization of American States (OAS). Officials in the Bush administration believed that economic sanctions would force the military leaders out of office and restore democratic rule. However, the embargo proved to be ineffective because European nations and other countries continued to ship goods to Haiti.

During the 1992 campaign, Clinton criticized President Bush's policy of turning back boats carrying refugees from Haiti to the United States. In his campaign book, *Putting People First*, he accused the Bush administration of turning its back "on those fleeing Haiti." [34] Even before taking office, however, Clinton reversed course and accepted the policy of the Bush administration. Reports predicted that thousands of Haitians were prepared to leave their country on homemade boats as soon as Clinton took office. His aides appealed to Aristide to advise Haitians to stay home. [35] Aristide issued that statement, and a few days later Clinton announced that he would continue the Bush administration policy of returning any fleeing Haitians. [36] Allowing (or encouraging) Haitians to reach the United States would have created, for the Clinton administration, unacceptable political conditions in Florida. [37] Democrat Lawton Chiles, running for reelection as governor, needed the refugee issue resolved.

Once in office, President Clinton tried to formulate a strategy on Haiti. Pressure mounted for him to act. The Congressional Black Caucus, which in the past had opposed the use of American military force to intervene in other countries, now strongly advocated U.S. troops to topple the military government in Haiti and reinstate Aristide. On June 4, 1993, Clinton issued a number of sanctions against Haiti "to increase the pressure on the military." He prohibited the entry into the United States of Haitian nationals who "are impeding a solution to the Haitian crisis." He also froze the U.S. assets of Haitians acting for or on behalf of the military junta. [38] On June 16 the U.N. Security Council imposed a worldwide embargo against Haiti.

In July, the Haitian military leaders promised to step down for the orderly transition to constitutional rule under Aristide. The plan was to restore Aristide to power by October 30. After much internal debate, the Clinton administration concluded that the Accord would be advanced by sending military engineers to Haiti to work on roads, bridges, and water supplies. A contingent of 600 U.S. soldiers reached Haiti on October 11, only to be prevented from docking by a group of armed civilians. Lightly armed, the U.S. troops were instructed by their commanders not to use force but to leave the area. The retreat in the face of tiny Haiti was widely interpreted as a humiliation to the United States. A policy shift followed. President Clinton implied that he might have to use military force, and on October 15 ticked off the telltale signs of an impending U.S. intervention: a thousand American citizens lived in Haiti, Americans helped to operate the embassy, and the United States had "an interest in promoting democracy in this hemisphere." [39]

To enforce economic sanctions imposed by the U.N. Security Council, Clinton ordered six destroyers to patrol the waters off Haiti and reported this to Congress pursuant to the War Powers Resolution. He also ordered an infantry company to be on standby at the Guantanamo Naval Base in Cuba. Madeleine K. Albright, U.S. ambassador to the United Nations, said that the administration had "not ruled out" a unilateral use of force in Haiti. Lt. Gen. Raoul Cedras, Haitian army commander, countered that there was "no threat against any American on Haitian soil." [40] Congress threatened to limit Clinton's power to send troops to Haiti, unless specifically authorized by statute, but in the end settled for nonbinding language making it the "sense of Congress" that funds appropriated should not be obligated or expended for U.S. military operations in Haiti unless authorized in advance by Congress. There were two exceptions for advance authorization: when it became necessary to protect or evacuate U.S. citizens from a situation of "imminent danger," and when "vital to the national security interests of the United States" and there was "not sufficient time" to seek and receive congressional authorization. [41]

The drumbeat for military action continued in 1994. In May, Clinton said with regard to Haiti "we cannot afford to discount the prospect of a military option." [42] In expressing a desire to work peacefully with nations in the Caribbean and in Latin America, he announced that the United States "never will interfere in the affairs of another country to try to seek to thwart the popular will there. This is a different case." [43] Later that month the House of Representatives debated several amendments designed to limit Clinton's military options in Haiti. The amendment that passed, 223 to 201, declared it to be the sense of Congress "that the United States should not undertake any military action directed against the mainland of Haiti unless the President first certifies to Congress that clear and present danger to citizens of the United States or United States interests requires such action." [44] Even that amendment, weak as it is, was voted down two weeks later on a separate vote. [45]

On June 10, Clinton increased the sanctions against the military regime by cutting off commercial air travel between the United States and Haiti and barring most private financial transactions between the two countries. [46] Congress continued to express uncertainty about its authority to constrain Clinton. On June 29, the Senate rejected an amendment stating that funds could not be used for any U.S. military operation in Haiti unless authorized in advance by Congress. However, that limitation would not apply if the president reported to Congress that deployment of armed forces to Haiti "is justified by United States national security interests." [47] What appeared to be a prohibition on the use of funds could be lifted simply by a presidential statement that U.S. force was necessary for national security interests, whatever that meant. In effect, the amendment contemplated delegating legislative prerogatives and duties to the president. That procedure was later adopted by the Senate, on a vote of 93 to 4, after making the amendment a nonbinding "sense of Congress." [48]

One hundred and four members of the House wrote a letter to President Clinton on July 21, stating that they had a "range of views" about whether military intervention in Haiti would serve important national interests. However, they had "a single view" about the responsibility of Congress to address the issue and about the "obligation of the President to obtain authorization from Congress prior to military intervention." Absent a "genuine emergency" that required presidential action to protect the safety of U.S. citizens, they said that the Constitution vests in Congress the power not only to declare war but to authorize the use of force. The letter featured names from prominent Democrats and Republicans.[49]

By late July, there were strong rumors that the U.N. Security Council was about to pass a resolution authorizing an invasion of Haiti. Dante Caputo, the United Nations' special envoy to Haiti, wrote a "confidential" memo to U.N. secretary general Boutros Boutros-Ghali describing political calculations within the Clinton White House. This memo, which found its way into the *Congressional Record*, states that Clinton's advisers believed that an invasion of Haiti would be politically desirable because it would highlight for the American public "the President's decision making capability and the firmness of leadership in international political matters." [50]

On July 31, the U.N. Security Council adopted a resolution "inviting" all states, particularly those in the region of Haiti, to use "all necessary means" to remove the military leadership in that island. On this occasion the Senate spoke promptly and with a clear voice, unanimously passing a "sense of the Senate" amendment that the Security Council resolution "does not constitute authorization for the deployment of United States Armed Forces in Haiti under the Constitution of the United States or pursuant to the War Powers Resolution (Public Law 93-148)." [51] At a news conference on August 3, President Clinton once again denied that he needed authority from Congress to invade Haiti: "Like my predecessors of both parties, I have not agreed that I was constitutionally mandated to obtain the support of Congress." [52]

In early August, Clinton was blindsided by another foreign policy crisis. Boatloads of Cubans headed toward Florida, jeopardizing the reelection effort of Florida governor Lawton Chiles. The migration to the United States was the largest since 1980. In the past, U.S. policy allowed Cubans to flee their homeland and settle in the United States. However, the Clinton administration now intercepted at sea refugees from both Haiti and Cuba and took them to the U.S. naval base at Guantanamo in Cuba. When the population of refugees overwhelmed the naval base, the administration had to seek space in Panama and other countries.

In a nationwide television address on September 15, President Clinton told the American public that he was prepared to use military force to invade Haiti, referring to the U.N. resolution of July 31 and his willingness to lead a multilateral force "to carry out the will of the United Nations." [53] The message to the military leaders, he said, was clear: "Your time is up. Leave now, or we will force you from power." [54] The administration argued that a democracy in Haiti not only would keep the peace and create economic opportunity but also would encourage Haitians to stay on the island and rebuild their future. Political conditions in Haiti had provoked some of the refugee flows, but Clinton's own support for an economic embargo had a greater effect in driving Haitians to the sea.

The public and a substantial majority of legislators assailed the planned invasion. Criticized in the past for currying public favor and failing to lead, Clinton now seemed to glory in the idea of doing something against the grain. Expressing his determination to proceed with the invasion, he said: "But regardless [of this opposition], this is what I believe is the right thing to do. I realize it is unpopular. I know it is unpopular. I know the timing is unpopular. I know the whole thing is unpopular. But I believe it is the right thing." [55]

Clinton never had to invade Haiti. An invasion became unnecessary when former president Jimmy Carter negotiated an agreement in which the military leaders in Haiti agreed to step down to permit the return of Aristide. Initially, nearly 20,000 U.S. troops were sent in to occupy Haiti and provide stability.

Why did Clinton feel compelled to act militarily in Haiti? In part, he had backed himself into a corner by threatening to use force if other options, including economic sanctions, failed to dislodge the military rulers. In the end, only one option remained: invasion. Not to invade would have signaled weakness on Clinton's part. For his own image, if for no other reason, the military card had to be played. One article, written after the deployment of U.S. forces in Haiti, summarizes these political considerations. The administration "surely came to realize" its need

> to demonstrate that it can act forcibly in foreign affairs. Clinton did not need an engagement on the scale of Bush in the Arabian peninsula, but a "splendid little war," like the American action in Cuba in 1898, in which Theodore Roosevelt showed himself to be an effective commander in chief, would do his presidency no harm. Something had to be done to reverse the image of a president whose backing down over Bosnia surely contributed to a successful resistance to American power in Somalia, which in turn presumably emboldened the Chinese, then the Haitians, next the North Koreans, the Cubans, and finally the Iraqis to test American intentions. [56]

House and Senate debates were strongly critical of Clinton's insistence that he could act militarily against Haiti without legislative authority. A resolution was introduced to provide retroactive authorization for the use of U.S. armed forces in Haiti, but that proposal failed. [57] A remark by Sen. Max Baucus, Democrat from Montana, reflected the attitude of many legislators: "The President did not seek my approval for occupying Haiti. And he will not get my approval now." [58] Both Houses passed legislation stating that "the President should have sought and welcomed Congressional approval before deploying United States Forces to Haiti." [59] Even legislators who voted against this legislation agreed that Clinton should have gotten approval from Congress. [60]

Defending Clinton's authority to deploy troops to Haiti, the Justice Department offered three arguments. First, the deployment was not a "war" within the meaning of the Declaration of War Clause in the Constitution because troops were sent "with the full consent of the legitimate government of the country involved" (Aristide). Second, the War Powers Resolution recognizes the existence of unilateral presidential authority to deploy armed forces into hostilities or into situations where imminent involvement in hostilities is likely, at least for sixty to ninety days. Third, legislation passed by Congress in 1993 implied that Clinton need not seek prior authorization for the deployment of troops to Haiti provided that he made certain specific findings and reported them to Congress in advance of the deployment.[61]

This legal analysis has a number of interesting qualities. First, it did not assert broad constitutional claims, such as the president's authority to act as commander in chief. Instead, it relies either on definitions (what is "war"?) or statutory sources. Executive officials usually view the War Powers Resolution as an unconstitutional restriction on the president. It is unusual and ironic to see the War Powers Resolution cited as a source of executive authority. With regard to the legislation passed by Congress in 1993, the language adopted was a "sense of Congress" resolution not meant to be legally binding. If Congress had passed nonbinding language in 1993, telling Clinton that he should not invade Haiti, the Justice Department could easily have argued that the language was merely hortatory and had no legal effect.

Intervention in Bosnia

During the campaign of 1992, Clinton rebuked Bush for failing to act in Bosnia. Age-old rivalries between Serbs, Croats, and Muslims had led to massive deaths from fighting and famine in the former Yugoslavia. Clinton insisted on a stronger U.S. role: "It is time for real leadership to stop the continuing tragedy in the former Yugoslav republics. I urge the Administration to work with the nations of Europe to bring new urgency to ending the bloodshed and ensuring the delivery of humanitarian assistance."[62] He urged President Bush to seek U.N. Security Council authorization for air strikes against the forces opposing and attacking the relief effort. The United States, he said, should be prepared to lend military support for that effort. Air and naval forces adequate to carry out those missions "should be visibly in position."[63]

As a candidate, Clinton continued to press the attack, arguing that the United States should consider the use of military force to open Serbian detention camps and should consider lifting the arms embargo imposed on Bosnia and Croatia.[64] The Bush administration limited itself to supporting economic sanctions against Serbia, participating in humanitarian airlifts, and creating a "no-fly" zone (a ban on unauthorized flights) over Bosnia-Herzegovina.[65]

Once in office, Clinton acted in concert with the United Nations and NATO to authorize humanitarian airdrops of food, helped enforce the no-fly zone, and supported an arms embargo for that region. The U.S. forces initially assigned included thirteen F-15 and twelve F-18A fighter aircraft, equipped for combat and ready to fire in self-defense. Clinton reported to Congress on these flights.[66] The administration considered lifting the arms embargo to enable the Muslims to defend themselves against the Serbs, but no final decision was reached. Large-scale bombing raids on Serb positions were considered and rejected. The administration wanted to take "action" but could not decide what steps to take without making matters worse. The American public, hearing Clinton promise strong measures and military action, discovered that a clear policy had yet to emerge. European allies, such as the French, resisted bombing because their troops were on the ground.

Clinton sketched out some general policies: the United States would act not alone but only as part of a multilateral force; he would not consider the introduction of American ground forces; and the United States would not become involved as a partisan for one side.[67] The use of ground troops was debated within the administration but discarded because of likely congressional opposition.[68] Although Clinton's statements indicated that he would consult closely with Congress and seek its "support," he did not state that prior authorization from Congress would be required before ordering air strikes. He did say, at one point, that for air strikes "Congress would have to agree."[69] Later he stated that he would "welcome and encourage congressional authorization of any military involvement in Bosnia."[70]

Congress considered various restrictions on military initiatives by Clinton in Bosnia. One amendment, never enacted, would have prevented the deployment of additional U.S. forces to Bosnia and Herzegovina unless Congress gave advance approval.[71] In response to pending amendments to restrict presidential actions in Bosnia and Haiti, Clinton objected that they would infringe on his constitutional authority to make foreign policy and deploy troops. He promised to "strenuously oppose such attempts to encroach on the President's foreign policy powers."[72] When asked on October 18, 1993, whether he would veto legislation requiring him to obtain congressional consent before using troops in Haiti and Bosnia, he replied:

> All I can tell you is that I think I have a big responsibility to try to appropriately consult with Members of Congress in both parties whenever we are in the process of making a decision which might lead to the use of force. I believe that. But I think that, clearly, the Constitution leaves the President, for good and sufficient reasons, the ultimate decisionmaking authority....
>
> ... the President should be very circumspect and very careful in committing the welfare and the lives of even our All-Volunteer Army. We need to have a clear American interest there, and there needs to be clearly-defined conditions of involvement, and the burden is on the President to provide those. But still the President must make the ultimate decision, and I think it's a mistake to cut those decisions off in advance.[73]

In a message to Congress the same day, Clinton expressed his "grave concern" about a number of amendments designed to restrict the use of American troops in Haiti, Bosnia, and in U.N. peacekeeping operations. He was "fundamentally opposed" to amendments that "improperly limit my ability to perform my constitutional duties as Commander-in-Chief, which may well have unconstitutional provisions." Adversaries and allies, he said, must know with certainty that the United States can respond decisively "to protect the lives of Americans and to address crises that challenge American interests." Amendments regarding "command and control" of U.S. forces "would insert Congress into the detailed execution of military contingency planning in an unprecedented manner." [74]

Clinton's objections were misplaced. Congress has full constitutional authority to place limits on the deployment of American soldiers, even when such restrictions affect "command and control." Such statutory restrictions are not unprecedented. Indeed, they are consistent with constitutional principles. [75]

After substantial debate on various amendments, Congress and the administration compromised on sense-of-Congress (nonbinding) observations about the placement of U.S. troops under foreign commanders and the conditions for such engagements. [76] Congress also stated its sense that funds appropriated for defense should not be available for deploying U.S. forces to participate in the implementation of a peace settlement in Bosnia-Herzegovina "unless previously authorized by the Congress." [77]

In February 1994, Clinton continued to threaten air strikes to bomb Serbian militias in Bosnia. Such actions would be taken in response to U.N. Security Council resolutions, operating through NATO's military command. As Clinton explained: "the authority under which air strikes can proceed, NATO acting out of area pursuant to U.N. authority, requires the common agreement of our NATO allies." [78] In late February, U.S. jets shot down four Serbian bombers over Bosnia. Clinton reported to Congress: "U.S. Armed Forces participate in these operations pursuant to my constitutional authority to conduct U.S. foreign relations and as Commander in Chief." [79] This was the first time in the history of NATO that its forces had been engaged in combat. In April, U.S. planes bombed Bosnian Serb forces involved in laying a siege around the Muslim-held city of Gorazde. U.N. officials requested the airstrikes ostensibly to protect twelve international peacekeepers deployed in the city. [80] In August, U.S. jets again hit Serbian positions, and in November, thirty NATO jets (American, British, French, and Dutch) bombed Serbian antiaircraft weapons and a Serbian airfield. [81]

NATO continued to conduct limited air strikes during the first half of 1995. In July, the war took a more serious turn when Bosnian Serb forces overran a UN-designated "safe area" of Srebrenica, forcing nearly 30,000 civilians to flee and trapping 430 Dutch peacekeepers. Congress voted to lift the arms embargo on Bosnia to permit the Muslim-led government to better defend itself. Clinton vetoed the bill on the ground that a unilateral lifting of the arms embargo would result in the withdrawal of allied forces in Bosnia, and he called the congressional effort an "attempt to regulate by statute matters for which the President is responsible under the Constitution." [82] At the end of August, several weeks after that veto, NATO aircraft carried out the war's biggest air raid.

The next stage of America's involvement in Bosnia was the introduction of U.S. ground forces by Clinton. In a letter to Senate majority leader Bob Dole, R-Kan., on October 20, 1995, Clinton said "it would be helpful to have a strong expression of support from the United States Congress prior to the participation of U.S. forces in implementation of a Bosnian peace accord. For that reason, I would welcome and encourage congressional authorization of any military involvement in Bosnia." [83] This pledge to seek congressional *authorization* competed with a different proposal: merely a request for congressional *approval.* Under the latter concept, Clinton could act unilaterally in introducing U.S. troops to Bosnia in the event the legislative support was withheld. At a news conference on October 19, Clinton engaged in this give-and-take with reporters:

> Q.... Would you go ahead, then, and send the troops, even if Congress does not approve?
>
> The President. I am not going to lay down any of my constitutional prerogatives here today. I have said before and I will say again, I would welcome and I hope I get an expression of congressional support. I think it's important for the United States to be united in doing this.... I believe in the end, the Congress will support this operation.[84]

The letter Clinton sent Senator Byrd on October 19, 1995, also invited "an expression of support by Congress." [85] White House press secretary Michael McCurry said that President Clinton would not be legally bound by anything Congress did, and "if the President ever felt he had to act as commander in chief to protect American interests he would do it." [86] In a letter to Speaker Newt Gingrich, R-Ga., on November 13, Clinton continued to avoid any suggestion that he needed authorization from Congress before sending U.S. ground forces to Bosnia. He told Gingrich:

> I will submit a request for a Congressional expression of support for U.S. participation in a NATO-led Implementation Force [IFOR] in Bosnia promptly if and when the parties have initialed an agreement that I consider to be a genuine agreement and after I have reviewed the final NATO operational plan.
>
> While expeditious IFOR deployment is desirable, after initialing of an agreement, there will be a timely opportunity for Congress to consider and act upon my request for support before American forces are deployed in Bosnia. However, there is a requirement for some early prepositioning of a small amount of communications and other support personnel.
>
> As I have said previously, I believe Congressional support for U.S. participation is important and desirable, although as has been the case with prior Presidents, I must reserve my constitutional prerogatives in this area.[87]

President Clinton, acting on the basis of what he considered sufficient authority under NATO, ordered the deployment of 20,000 American ground troops to Bosnia without first seeking or obtaining authority from Congress. Using military force through the NATO treaty raises the perennial issue of the meaning of the treaty. The treaty does not authorize offensive actions or general peacekeeping operations. It is a defensive pact, intended to contain the Soviet Union. The treaty's parties were "resolved to unite their efforts for collective defense" and "resist armed attack." The provisions of the treaty were to be carried out "in accordance with [the parties'] constitutional processes." To claim that the president, acting in concert with NATO allies, has the power to order military strikes without advance congressional authority would mean that the president and the Senate, through the treaty process, can obliterate the constitutional power of the House of Representatives to decide whether to take the nation to war. That position, no matter how often asserted, is untenable. The legislative histories of NATO and other military security treaties do not give the president unilateral authority to use military force.[88]

Multilateral Operations

In May 1994, the Clinton administration released an unclassified summary of its policy for reforming multilateral peace operations. Conditions are established to decide on U.S. participation in peace operations, "with the most stringent applying to U.S. participation in missions that may involve combat." [89] The policy directive states that the president "will never relinquish command of U.S. forces," although the president may place American forces under the operational control of a foreign commander when it serves American security interests.[90] Seven proposals are put forth to increase the flow of information and consultation between the executive and legislative branches; one of them calls for "periodic consultations with bipartisan Congressional leaders on foreign policy engagements that might involve U.S. forces, including possible deployments of U.S. military units in U.N. peace operations." [91]

The War Powers Resolution of 1973 attempted to place limits on the president's ability to act unilaterally in sending U.S. troops into hostilities. Under the statute's procedures, which are often conflicting and ambiguous, it was intended that the president would have to withdraw troops after a sixty-day period (which could be extended to ninety days to facilitate the removal of U.S. troops) unless Congress had specifically authorized continued use of American forces in combat. The summary report from the Clinton administration recommends the elimination of the sixty-day withdrawal provision and would introduce a consultative mechanism with a small core of congressional leaders.[92] No longer would the president need the support and authority from Congress as a whole through the regular legislative process.

As a means of diminishing, or extinguishing, the constitutional role of Congress in matters of going to war, it would be difficult to top this position paper. The president, in concert with the U.N. Security Council and such regional alliances as NATO, claims sufficient constitutional authority to use military force without ever seeking, or obtaining, approval from Congress. A regular series of meetings and briefings with key congressional leaders are sufficient gestures to meet the constitutional test, according to the Clinton administration. Will Congress accept this subordinate, second-class role? Will the American people be satisfied with this reallocation of power? Whatever happened to the expectation of the framers that Congress, as the people's representative, would have to approve in advance any use of U.S. forces against foreign governments?

Notes

1. *Weekly Compilation of Presidential Documents*, vol. 29, 2097.
2. Ibid., 2101.
3. Ibid., 2102.
4. *Weekly Compilation of Presidential Documents*, vol. 30, 219–220.
5. Ibid., 1616.
6. U.S. Congress, Senate, *Congressional Record*, daily ed., October 20, 1995, S15393, vol. 141.
7. U.S. Congress, House, *Congressional Record*, daily ed., November 17, 1995, H13228, vol. 141.
8. Louis Fisher, *Presidential War Power* (Lawrence: University Press of Kansas, 1995).
9. *New York Times*, June 28, 1992, 16.
10. *New York Times*, August 14, 1992, A15.
11. Governor Bill Clinton and Senator Al Gore, *Putting People First: How We Can All Change America* (New York: Times Books, 1992), 136.
12. Ibid., 137-138.
13. "Clinton Sets Two-Phase Plan to Allow Gays in Military," *Washington Post*, January 22, 1993, A1; and "Clinton Compromise Delays Showdown over Ban on Gays," *Washington Post*, January 30, 1993, A1.
14. *Weekly Compilation of Presidential Documents*, vol. 29, 469.
15. Elizabeth Drew, *On the Edge: The Clinton Presidency* (New York: Simon & Schuster, 1994), 230.
16. *Weekly Compilation of Presidential Documents*, vol. 29, 1181.
17. Ibid.
18. Ibid., 1183.
19. Ruth Marcus and Daniel Williams, "Show of Strength Offers Benefits for Clinton," *Washington Post*, June 28, 1993, A1, A14.
20. *Weekly Compilation of Presidential Documents*, vol. 29, 1181.
21. Michael Ratner and Jules Lobel, "Bombing Baghdad: Illegal Reprisal or Self-Defense?" *Legal Times*, July 5, 1993, 24.
22. *Public Papers of the President, 1992–93*, II, 2175.
23. Ibid., 2176.
24. Ibid., 2180.
25. *Congressional Quarterly Almanac 1992* (Washington, D.C.: Congressional Quarterly, 1993), 44-E.
26. U.S. Congress, Senate, *Congressional Record*, daily ed., February 4, 1993, S1365, vol. 139.

27. On the House action, see U.S. Congress, House, *Congressional Record*, daily ed., May 25, 1993, H2764, vol. 139.
28. *Weekly Compilation of Presidential Documents*, vol. 29, 1101.
29. U.S. Congress, House, *Congressional Record*, daily ed., September 28, 1993, H7090, vol. 139.
30. "Clinton Seen Calming Hill on Peace Keeping," *Washington Post*, October 2, 1993, A16.
31. *Weekly Compilation of Presidential Documents*, vol. 29, 2024.
32. Ibid., 2066.
33. 107 Stat. 1475–77, § 8151 (1993).
34. Clinton and Gore, *Putting People First*, 137.
35. "Clinton Aides Try to Halt Haitian Flight," *Washington Post*, January 12, 1993, A13.
36. "Aristide Asks Haitians to Stay Home, Await His Return," *Washington Post*, January 13, 1993, A15; and "Clinton to Continue Forcible Repatriation of Fleeing Haitians," *Washington Post*, January 15, 1993, A16.
37. Drew, *On the Edge*, 139.
38. *Weekly Compilation of Presidential Documents*, vol. 29, 1029–1030.
39. Ibid., 2082.
40. *Washington Post*, October 18, 1993, A16.
41. 107 Stat. 1474, § 8147 (1993).
42. *Weekly Compilation of Presidential Documents*, vol. 30, 967.
43. Ibid.
44. U.S. Congress, House, *Congressional Record*, daily ed., May 24, 1994, H3938, H3945, vol. 140.
45. Ibid., June 9, 1994, H4253.
46. "Clinton Ratchets up Sanctions against Haiti Military Regime," *Washington Post*, June 11, 1994, A1.
47. U.S. Congress, Senate, *Congressional Record*, daily ed., June 29, 1994, S7902–32, vol. 140.
48. Ibid., June 29, 1994, S7932–37.
49. Letter of July 21, 1994, to President Clinton signed by Representatives David E. Skaggs, D-Colo.; Richard J. Durbin, D-Ill.; Sherwood Boehlert, R-N.Y.; Larry Combest, R-Texas; Ron Wyden, D-Ore., who is now a senator; and Dan Glickman, a Kansas Democrat who is no longer a member of the House. Attached to the letter were the names of 106 members of Congress.
50. U.S. Congress, House, *Congressional Record*, daily ed., July 28, 1994, H6433, vol. 140.
51. U.S. Congress, Senate, *Congressional Record*, daily ed., August 3, 1994, S10415–33, vol. 140.
52. *Weekly Compilation of Presidential Documents*, vol. 30, 1616.
53. Ibid., 1780.
54. Ibid., 1779.
55. *Weekly Compilation of Presidential Documents*, vol. 30, 1771.
56. Tony Smith, "In Defense of Intervention," *Foreign Affairs* 73 (November/December 1994): 41.
57. U.S. Congress, House, *Congressional Record*, daily ed., October 5, 1994, H10973, vol. 140; and daily ed., October 6, 1994, H11121, vol. 140.
58. U.S. Congress, Senate, *Congressional Record*, daily ed., October 6, 1994, S14343, vol. 140.
59. Ibid., October 6, 1994, S14346, passing S. J. Res. 229; U.S. Congress, House, *Congressional Record*, daily ed., October 6, 1994, H1111–12, H11122, vol. 140, passing H. J. Res. 416. A day later the House, by unanimous consent, agreed to S. J. Res. 229; *Congressional Record*, daily ed. October 7, 1994, H11297, vol. 140; P.L. 103–423, 108 Stat. 4358 (1994).
60. For example, of the eight senators who voted against S. J. Res. 229, at least four agreed

that Clinton should have first obtained approval from Congress: Sen. Max Baucus, D-Mont. (140 *Congressional Record* S14343), Sen. Bill Bradley, D-N.J. (140 *Congressional Record* S14340), Sen. Robert C. Byrd, D-W.Va. (140 *Congressional Record* S14321), and Sen. Russell D. Feingold, D-Wis. (140 *Congressional Record* S14313–14, S14316).

61. U.S. Congress, Senate, *Congressional Record*, daily ed., October 6, 1994, S14314–15, vol. 140; legal memorandum by Assistant Attorney General Walter Dellinger, Office of Legal Counsel, Department of Justice.
62. "Statement by Governor Bill Clinton on the Crisis in Bosnia," National Campaign Headquarters, July 26, 1992, 1.
63. Ibid., 2.
64. *New York Times*, August 10, 1992, A8.
65. *Public Papers of the Presidents, 1992–93*, II, 1738–1739.
66. *Weekly Compilation of Presidential Documents*, vol. 29, 586.
67. Ibid., 652, 654, 659–660, 828, 1237–1238.
68. Drew, *On the Edge*, 274–275.
69. Ibid., 1711.
70. Ibid., 2123.
71. U.S. Congress, Senate, *Congressional Record*, daily ed., September 23, 1993, S12334, vol. 139.
72. *Weekly Compilation of Presidential Documents*, vol. 29, 2097.
73. Ibid., 2101–2102.
74. Ibid., 2104.
75. Fisher, *Presidential War Power*, 199–201.
76. 107 Stat. 1478–80, § 9001 (1993). See also 107 Stat. 1839–40, § 1511 (1993).
77. 107 Stat. 1474, § 8146 (1993).
78. *Weekly Compilation of Presidential Documents*, vol. 30, 219–220.
79. Ibid., 406.
80. "U.S. Jets Strike Serb Forces Near Bosnian Town," *Washington Post*, April 11, 1994, A1; and "U.S. Planes Blast Serb Forces Again," *Washington Post*, April 12, 1994, A1.
81. "U.S Jets Hit Serbs After Raid on Arms," *Washington Post*, August 6, 1994, A1; and "NATO Jets Bomb Serb Airfield," *Washington Post*, November 11, 1994, A1.
82. *Weekly Compilation of Presidential Documents*, vol. 31, 1439.
83. U.S. Congress, Senate, *Congressional Record*, daily ed., September 29, 1995, S14637, vol. 141.
84. *Weekly Compilation of Presidential Documents*, vol. 31, 1878.
85. U.S. Congress, Senate, *Congressional Record*, daily ed., October 20, 1995, S15393, vol. 141.
86. "President to Ask for Bosnia Vote," *Washington Post*, October 21, 1995, A22.
87. U.S. Congress, House, *Congressional Record*, daily ed., November 17, 1995, H13228, vol. 141.
88. Fisher, *Presidential War Power*, 92–97.
89. "The Clinton Administration's Policy on Reforming Multilateral Peace Operations," May 1994, Department of State Publication 10161, Bureau of International Organization Affairs, 1.
90. Ibid., 2.
91. Ibid., 14
92. Ibid., 15

12

Congress Within the U.S. Presidential System

Michael L. Mezey

One of the more distinctive qualities of the U.S. political system is its remarkable continuity. Although the system has altered in several respects during the two centuries that it has functioned, it has done so gradually and for the most part without formal constitutional changes. Its fundamental governing design remains essentially as it was when the Constitution was created: a federal system of divided power between the states and the national government, and within that national government a system of shared powers among a president, a bicameral Congress, and a Supreme Court, with each institution independent of the other and each possessing its own policy-making prerogatives.

The long-term stability of American political institutions is particularly noteworthy in light of the argument advanced by some that presidential systems are prone to instability. Giovanni Sartori has noted that "with the sole exception of the United States, all presidential systems have been intermittent." [1] Why, then, have the institutional arrangements in the United States been so stable? At the national level especially, how does one explain the continued coexistence of a Congress that by comparative standards is the strongest legislative institution in the world and a presidency that for two hundred years has, by most estimates, steadily expanded its policy-making prerogatives? And what lessons, if any, does the experience of the U.S. presidential system have for those nations in central and eastern Europe and in Asia, Africa, and Latin America that are today experimenting with new democratic forms?

My discussion of these questions proceeds in five parts. First, the theoretical link between political stability and political institutions will be reviewed, drawing on analyses of less-developed political systems and on the recent literature suggesting that some modes of legislative-executive relations are more likely to lead to stability than others. Second, the view reflected in this literature will be compared with the one held by the Founders of the American political system. The design of the Founders squared admirably with their understanding of the issue, but the system that they produced, from a modern perspective, should not have been capable of establishing and maintaining political order. That it has done so for more than two hundred years is attributable in part to several noninstitutional factors that will be identified in the third and fourth sections of this chapter.

Finally, the role that the modern Congress plays in maintaining political stability in the United States will be assessed.

Political Institutions and Political Stability

Stability Defined

The word *stability*, when applied to political systems, indicates "the absence of revolutions, the lack of internal violence factors, the lack of continual constitutional revision, the lack of anti-system protest, and the lack of institutional and governmental instability." [2] From the perspective of systems theory, a stable political system exhibits high levels of "support" for the larger national community, for the community's system of government (the regime), and for those who happen to be in power at the time (the authorities). [3] Thus, a stable polity will be characterized by a shared sense of nationhood, by the persistence of governmental forms, and by a gradual and orderly turnover in governing elites. Although these three levels of political stability are analytically separable, they are related in the sense that instability in regard to one may lead to instability in regard to the others. Secessionist activities by a politically disaffected regional minority, for example, can lead to, or be caused by, a drop in support for the constitutional system or incumbent political leaders.

Stability Explained

Most explanations of political stability begin from the premise that stability is more likely if the political institutions of the regime are able to respond to the demands of its citizens. Such demand responsiveness yields "specific support" for the regime and its incumbents and, in the long term, "diffuse support"—support that is not dependent on demand-satisfying outputs—for both the regime and the community. High levels of diffuse support help maintain stability when the regime is unable to respond to the most immediate demands of its citizens. [4]

Among the most salient demands of citizens are those concerning their economic welfare. As Ted Gurr suggests, "men rebel" because of relative deprivation; that is, unrest is caused when people believe that their economic condition is worse than it should be. [5] In developing countries and in the new democracies of central and eastern Europe, widespread economic privations, rapidly rising popular expectations, and high levels of political participation can result in instability when the regime fails to deliver policies that respond to needs. As Joan Nelson has observed, widespread participation often has provoked instability "by heightening group conflict and by escalating demands, prompting frustration when those demands were not met." [6]

Instability may be further exacerbated by the absence of a political culture that supports obedience as well as participation. Gabriel Almond and Sidney Verba suggest that a "civic culture" is characterized by relatively high levels of stability because the citizen's role as a participant "has been added to the subject and parochial roles. This means that the active citizen has maintained his traditional non-political ties as well as his more passive political role as a subject." [7] When, because of rapid movement from a parochial to a participant culture or from a traditional to a modern society, these non-participatory roles or other moral codes of behavior erode or break down entirely, rootlessness, or anomie, can set in. Citizens then can become vulnerable to the appeals of charismatic leaders to join mass movements, which can destabilize the political system. [8]

Social and cultural variables that adversely affect political stability can be mediated by political institutions. If institutions operate effectively to meet the most salient demands of citizens, particularly those demands that arise from severe economic needs, political instability can be averted. The question, however, is whether political institutions have the capacity to respond in such a manner. Samuel Huntington suggests that the threats to political stability engendered by high levels of political participation can be handled by strong political institutions. But when political institutions are weak, high levels of participation can be destabilizing. Huntington argues that "social frustration leads to demands on the government and the expansion of political participation to enforce those demands." He goes on to note that low levels of political institutionalization can make it "difficult if not impossible for the demands upon the government to be expressed through legitimate channels and to be moderated and aggregated within the political system. Hence the sharp increase in political participation gives rise to political instability." [9] If stability is to be maintained, political participation may have to be restricted until political institutions are strong enough to support higher levels of participation.

Stability and Institutional Forms

Another implication of Huntington's argument is that in democratic societies political instability is primarily attributable to the weakness of the state, to its inability to act. [10] This link between the strength of a nation's political institutions and political stability depends upon the following reasoning: political stability is enhanced when the government has the capacity to act in the face of pressing problems. If government is too weak to act, or cannot act effectively, problems will get worse, public discontent will rise, and instability will result. Juan Linz has argued that presidential systems characterized by a legislature and an executive structurally independent of each other are particularly prone to such policy-making inefficiency and, ultimately, political instability. [11]

In Linz's view, presidential systems lead to such results for three reasons. First, because both the president and the legislature are elected by the people, both enjoy "democratic legitimacy," so it is not possible to resolve disputes between the two institutions by appeals to democratic criteria. Second, because the terms of both the legislature and the president are fixed and independent of each other, presidential systems are "rigid." If the political lines shift or new challenges confront the system, it is not possible to adjust the personnel of government until the next scheduled election.

Finally, presidential systems are prone to zero-sum politics, especially when the group controlling the presidency is different from the majority controlling the legislature. In such an event, policy outcomes are viewed either as victories or defeats for one or the other of the separate branches of government. Because of that, such systems may have a tendency toward stalemate, with difficult decisions avoided either because the executive and the legislature cannot reach agreement or because one side sees political advantage in thwarting the plans of the other. In the end, as pressing issues go unaddressed, stalemate leads to public discontent and political instability.[12]

Yet presidential systems are not the only forms of government to demonstrate a tendency toward political instability. This tendency has also been observed in some parliamentary systems. In parliamentary systems with no majority party and a fragile governing coalition, policy making may be as slow and inefficient—and the likelihood of stalemate and therefore instability as great—as in a presidential system. Matthew Shugart and John Carey have suggested that the capacity of the government to act may have more to do with the relative strength of the parties in the parliament, and specifically with the presence of a majority party, than with the parliamentary system itself.[13] In such systems, the introduction of a mixed premier-presidential system—or semipresidential government, to use Maurice Duverger's term[14]—following the model of the French Fifth Republic, may enhance policy-making efficiency. And in a deeply divided nation, an elected presidency, the argument goes, may actually enhance stability, especially if the presidential election system is designed to encourage the election of a centrist.[15] Mixed systems of this sort have become increasingly popular in the nations of central and eastern Europe, which have sought to overcome the tendency of their legislatures toward inaction.[16]

In spite of their growing popularity, mixed systems have been criticized by some scholars. Arend Lijphart, for instance, argues that the term *mixed system* is a misnomer because none of the so-called mixed systems are truly that. Shugart and Carey's findings notwithstanding, Lijphart asserts that there are no actual examples of intermediate systems between parliamentarism and presidentialism.[17] In the case of the Fifth Republic, he says that the two forms have alternated, with the typical system of presidentialism occasionally interrupted by parliamentarism. Exactly which form of government is in operation depends upon whether the president's party enjoys a majority in the parliament. As long as the president has such a majority, the system operates presidentially. But during periods of cohabitation between a president of one party and a premier of another, as occurred between 1986 and 1988 and reappeared with the election results of February 1993, the role of the president is limited. In these situations, what appears to be semipresidential government in fact operates along parliamentary lines.

Furthermore, there is some question as to whether semipresidential systems are actually associated with greater levels of stability. Linz reminds us that the Weimar Republic was a semipresidential system in which the president could dissolve the Reichstag. Although the consent of the chancellor was required for such a step, this was not a problem because the president appointed the chancellor. It was exactly this sequence of events that led to the end of the republic with the election of a Nazi majority in March 1933. And those who point to the stability of the French Fifth Republic over its predecessors as testimony to the stabilizing influence of mixed systems sometimes slight the importance of the consolidation of the party system, which resulted from the abandonment of the proportional representation system of parliamentary elections in favor of the single-member system.[18]

One other possibility is also open: that the manner in which a nation's political institutions are structured may have little independent effect on political stability. Political systems, it can be argued, become unstable because of deep societal cleavages—economic, ethnic, regional, and ideological cleavages that are beyond the capacity of mere political institutions to bridge. From that perspective, institutional arrangements of political power may reflect rather than affect these societal cleavages. While certain institutional forms may ameliorate, and others exacerbate, the forces that create instability, in the end institutions cannot themselves bring stability to an inherently unstable society.

Legislatures and Stability

The role of the legislature in maintaining stability is complex.[19] Because legislatures are typically selected through elections in which virtually the entire adult population is eligible to participate, their creation, especially after a period of authoritarianism, is likely to be accompanied by relatively high levels of political participation and by increased expectations that government will be able to respond to the demands of the electorate. To advance their own careers, political leaders may use their positions in legislatures, or their candidacies for legislative positions, to foment popular discontent with the regime. And because legislatures by their very nature are slow to act, they may impede the state's response to the demands that their members have been partially responsible for inciting. If governments are unable to respond to these demands, the result could well be public frustration, heightened unrest, and greater levels of political instability.

But legislatures can be stabilizing as well. As legislators link the nation's periphery with its center, they act as conduits for popular demands and grievances, thereby contributing to the responsiveness of the regime. Discontent can be reduced by legislators' efforts to resolve problems that individuals and groups in their constituencies have with the central government. And representation in the legislature will provide regional, ethnic, and partisan minorities with an arena within which to express their concerns. Even if policy is not immediately responsive to their demands, such representation can encourage political minorities to view the regime as legitimate, and it may build diffuse support for the regime, even in the absence of policies that will raise levels of specific support. Finally, legislatures can be instruments for making elites accountable to the populace, which in turn should reduce the likelihood that elites will resort to repressive tactics to deal with mass discontent. The absence of elite accountability and the presence of repression are closely associated with political instability.[20]

Summary

The model connecting political stability and political institutions that emerges from this discussion is fairly straightforward. Political stability is threatened when popular discontent is directed against the nation's political institutions and incumbents. Strong, effective political institutions that are able to govern can deal with discontent before it leads to political instability. Weak political institutions are less capable of dealing with discontent, and the result is instability. Legislatures can intensify demands and therefore intensify conflict, and in the case of legislatures operating in presidential systems, legislative obstructionism can lead to stalemate and reduce the likelihood of effective government action. However, these independent legislatures also can contribute to stability by restraining executive elites from pursuing unwise goals or from using repressive means. In parliamentary systems, legislatures may not be as successful in restraining elites, but the proponents of such systems as well as so-called mixed systems argue that they reduce the likelihood of stalemate. In all systems, the representational activities of individual legislators can increase the legitimacy of the regime, either by encouraging responsiveness to demands or by giving citizens the impression that their demands are being heard.

The Founders and Political Stability

Political instability was very much on the minds of those who wrote the U.S. Constitution. One of the reasons that the new Constitution was necessary, they said in the document's preamble, was "to ensure domestic tranquility." James Madison, in the course of justifying the proposed Constitution to the citizens of New York in the *Federalist Papers*, noted that "complaints are heard from our most considerate and virtuous citizens ... that our governments are too unstable." [21] "Stability in government," he would later write, "is essential to national character." [22]

The Founders worried about political instability because of their experiences with the postrevolutionary constitutions of the several states. Most of these documents provided for legislative supremacy and a subservient executive, an understandable reaction to the prerevolutionary abuses that the colonies had experienced at the hands of the king and his royal governors. In the years before independence, it was the colonial assemblies that represented the colonists and articulated their demands; the assemblies, said James Wilson of Pennsylvania, "were the guardians of our rights, the objects of our confidence, and the anchors of our political hopes." [23] It was not surprising, therefore, that the power to govern was consigned to those assemblies after the revolution had been won. In contrast, the upper chambers of the state legislatures had little independent power and, with the exception of New York, most states had weak governors who were almost entirely dependent on the legislature. [24]

These dominant legislatures soon became targets of intense public pressures. Many of the Founders thought that the legislators were too easily intimidated by these pressures and by the threats to public order that sometimes accompanied them. They were appalled by the tendency of the state legislators to knuckle under to popular demands for "the confiscation of property, the paper money schemes, and the various devices suspending the ordinary means for the recovery of debts." [25] The writer Noah Webster lamented the state of affairs: "so many legal infractions of sacred rights, so many public invasions of private property, so many wanton abuses of legislative power." [26]

These experiences led Madison to conclude that in legislatures, "passion never fails to wrest the scepter from reason." [27] At the Constitutional Convention, Edmund Randolph decried "the turbulence and follies of democracy," [28] and Benjamin Franklin suggested that while in prerevolutionary times the problem faced by the American people was an excess of power in the hands of the rulers, "our present danger seems to be a defect in the obedience of the subjects." [29] And with popularly elected legislatures virtually in complete control of the governments of most of the states, there was no way to check the imprudent actions of these legislatures. As historian Gordon Wood notes, by the time the Founders arrived in Philadelphia in 1787, the legislature in their view had replaced the executive as "the institution to be most feared." [30]

In the terminology of the development literature, the Founders saw themselves confronted first by excess political participation and second by political institutions at the state and national levels that they believed were too weak to cope with the resulting popular pressures. Just as development theorists would have advised, the Founders set about strengthening their political institutions and restricting popular participation. Their plan had two components: first, create a strong national government that would control those powers being abused by the state legislatures; second, insulate that government as much as possible from popular pressures, thereby ensuring political stability.

What for many contemporary leaders would be the most obvious strategy for achieving these goals—creating a weak legislature and vesting most governmental power in executive-centered elites—the Founders rejected because of their republican principles and commitment, despite their postrevolutionary experiences, to a strong legislature. In the *Federalist Papers*, Madison tersely acknowledges that in a republic "the legislative authority necessarily predominates,"[31] and he states the republican case for a strong legislature:

> The genius of republican liberty seems to demand on one side not only that all powers should be derived from the people but that those entrusted with it should be kept in dependence on the people by a short duration of their appointments; and that even during this short period, the trust should be placed not in a few but a number of hands.[32]

But, he went on, political stability required institutional characteristics not associated with legislatures:

> Stability required that the hands in which power is lodged should continue for a length of time the same. A frequent change of men will result from a frequent return of elections; and a frequent change of measures from a frequent change of men; whilst energy in government requires not only a certain duration of power, but the execution by a single hand.[33]

For the Founders to have resolved the problem of instability by establishing a weak national legislature and a strong presidency would have been to deny their republican principles and, more practically, to have rendered the task of ratifying the new Constitution all but impossible. Instead, they chose to balance the power of the legislature with a strong executive. The new presidency would be electorally independent of the legislature (unlike in the states, where the governors were often chosen by the legislature) and therefore would supply the desired stability in government. An independent executive, said Alexander Hamilton, would be characterized by energy, and an energetic executive would be able to "protect the community against foreign attacks," provide "steady administration," and secure "liberty against the enterprises and assaults of ambition, of factions, and of anarchy."[34]

When the Founders spoke about "the legislature," they were almost always referring to the popularly elected House of Representatives. A further remedy for the political instability that they associated with the House was bicameralism. The Founders provided for an indirectly elected Senate that would share equal legislative power with the directly and more frequently elected House (senators' terms were six years). Such an arrangement, said Madison, would guard against "the mutability of public councils arising from a rapid succession of new members."[35] Gouverneur Morris suggested at the Constitutional Convention that the Senate would "check the precipitation, changeableness, and excesses of the first branch." [36]

In sum, the Founders strengthened their political institutions by creating a strong national government with broad policy-making powers, especially in important areas such as taxation, commerce, military defense, and foreign affairs. To ensure stability and prevent the abuse of these powers, they prohibited the House of Representatives from taking any action without the agreement of the Senate and the president. Finally, they reduced popular pressures on these institutions by arranging a process for selecting senators that removed them by at least one step from the voting public (indirect election by state legislatures), and a process of presidential selection (the electoral college) with which the people would have as little to do as possible.[37]

But the careful design of the Founders had at least one serious flaw. So acute was their fear of legislative abuses of power that they created institutional arrangements that would make power extraordinarily difficult to exercise. The system of shared powers that they established for the new national government would not simply check legislative abuses but would operate reciprocally, to restrict the power of both the president and the Congress. In truth, this system of power sharing among a popularly elected House, an indirectly elected Senate, and an independently elected president amounted to a constitution against government, a set of institutional arrangements more likely to produce inaction than action.[38]

Whereas modern development theorists argue that a strong state is needed to control political participation and avert political instability, the Founders, convinced that the primary threat to political stability was precipitous government action provoked by popular demands, created a weak state with a questionable capacity to govern. While some of the Founders recognized that such a state might have difficulty governing, its saving grace was that it would not be in a position to govern unwisely or tyrannically. But a weak state of this sort, our contemporary views suggest, should not be particularly effective in maintaining political stability. Why then would political institutions seemingly designed to prevent government action be associated with a political system with a historically high level of stability? The answer, in part, stems from the context in which these institutions developed.

The Context of Political Development

The theory that political instability arises when the government is unable to respond effectively to popular demands presupposes a politically active citizenry making excessive demands upon its political leaders. But this was not the situation when American national political institutions were in their embryonic stage. The volume of demands was relatively low for several reasons.

First, in the United States of the late eighteenth century, the political-ly active and involved public constituted a small percentage of the total pop-ulation. In most states the franchise was available only to white male prop-erty holders, a relatively homogeneous and elite electorate. While certainly there were political differences among these voters, their demands were fair-ly moderate. This situation stands in marked contrast to the universal suf-frage that characterizes most contemporary new democracies. Moreover, the modern institutions of mobilization (such as mass political parties, orga-nized interest groups, and mass communication systems, all of which serve in new democracies today to focus and intensify popular demands) would not emerge in the United States for many years.

Second, demands were moderated by the federal structure of the new government. That is, while the national government had significant powers and responsibilities its scope was still relatively narrow compared with what it is today and, more to the point, what it is today in new nations with rela-tively new political institutions. According to historian James Sterling Young,

> almost all of the things that republican governments do which affect the everyday lives and fortunes of their citizens, and therefore engage their interest, were, in Jeffersonian times, not done by the national government. The administration of justice, the maintenance of law and order, the arbi-tration of disputes, the chartering and supervision of business enterprises, road building and the maintenance of transportation systems, the school-ing of the young, the care of the indigent, even residual control over the bulk of the military forces—these functions fell principally within the province of state and local governments to the extent that any govern-mental bodies performed them.[39]

The federal government's role in those early days was restricted to the important but nonetheless narrow areas of public finance, national defense, and delivery of the mail. Thus, if people had problems, their first instincts were to deal with them on their own or to turn to local authorities for help; their last recourse was the national government, except in matters where it had specific responsibilities, such as dealings with Native American or for-eign nations.

Public demands today are often provoked by economic privations. While eighteenth- and nineteenth-century America had serious economic problems, these problems did not always create political difficulties for the new government. The expectation that government at any level should be responsible for the economic welfare of its citizens had not yet emerged, whereas today it is a given in every nation. Also, the seemingly unlimited availability of land and resources in the West provided the American nation with a safety valve. Those who were suffering economically could pick up and go, and the history of westward expansion in the United States indicates that many took that option. Today, in nations with large populations, clear-ly defined borders, and equally meager opportunities from region to region, there is no such safety valve; there is simply no place for the discontented to go, except perhaps to the cities which, not surprisingly, are usually the primary locus of popular unrest. But the economic wealth of the United States, particularly in terms of land, made its citizens a "people of plenty." [40] American cities did not become magnets for the economically deprived and the politically discontented until a century after the founding of the nation.

Thus in the early years the volume and intensity of the economic and social demands generated in the new nation were quite moderate by contemporary standards. And relatively few of the demands that were generated reached the new political institutions of the nation. As designed, these institutions may have been too weak to resolve the problems that confront new democracies in today's world. When they were created, however, these institutions were not subject to the same popular pressures as they would have been had they been created today. As Young explains, the "modern image of Washington as a vital center and government as a target for citizen demands of every sort ill prepares us for the image of a sequestered and secluded governmental community that emerges from the record of 1800–1828." [41]

Once again, to use the terminology of development theory, political institutionalization in the United States in its early years was aided by relatively weak political participation and by relatively few demands directed at the government. In time, the franchise expanded (and with it the scope of government) and the frontier closed, but not until the political institutions of the new nation had become entrenched. As Seymour Lipset concludes, the "United States gradually acquired legitimacy as a result of being effective," and low participation and manageable demands allowed it to be effective. [42]

The Context of Modern American Politics

There is today significant debate on exactly how effective the American political system really is. The propensity toward stalemate, sewn in the very fabric of the Constitution, continues. Some attribute stalemate to divided government, or the situation in which one party occupies the presidency while the other controls at least one chamber of Congress. [43] Others, most notably David R. Mayhew, argue that the frequency of major lawmaking has little or nothing to do with divided government. As the administration of Jimmy Carter and the first two years of Bill Clinton demonstrated, even unified governments are not immune to stalemate. [44]

Indicators of legislative-executive policy stalemate in both divided and unified contexts are abundant. The 1980s, a period of divided government, witnessed spiraling budget deficits and deadlock between the president and Congress about what should be done (beyond easy accounting gimmicks) to deal with this problem. In 1992 Bill Clinton was swept into the presidency in part on his promise to change a health care system that all agreed was badly in need of reform. Two years later, no health care bill had emerged, despite a unified government with Congress controlled by his copartisans.

Similar stories could be told about agriculture policy, welfare, and a legion of other domestic policy areas, to the point where two prominent scholars ask: "Can the government govern?" Their answer, at least with regard to energy, trade, and fiscal policy, is no; they suggest that "established structures no longer can contain political tensions between Congress, the president, and the bureaucracy, and, riven by conflicts, they often do not permit successful management of the nation's problems." [45]

This marked tendency toward policy stalemate has not led to the political instability that has plagued other nations with presidential systems. The balance of power between president and Congress has shifted over the years, and the power of the presidency has increased dramatically. However, despite repeated predictions to the contrary, Congress has not been eclipsed as a policy-making force by the president. In fact, some would argue that in 1995 we saw a return to a model of congressional dominance, something that many political scientists had thought was an anachronism in the era of the modern presidency. Stability has characterized not only America's political institutions but also the larger society. In the two-hundred-year history of the U.S. Constitution, the Civil War era represents the single period in which the survival of the regime was seriously in question.

During the 1960s an epidemic of urban riots by the poor and civil disobedience by the young in response to racial discrimination and the Vietnam War caused some to fear an era of political instability in the United States. But in the 1970s and 1980s this political activism was replaced by either satisfaction or apathy, depending upon one's point of view. In the 1990s political discontent once again seemed to be on the rise. Americans, we were told, were angry about everything from crime to taxes to welfare and thought that the government in Washington was responsible for all that was wrong. But this discontent took the comparatively benign forms of a centrist third-party presidential candidacy, switches in party control of the presidency (1992) and the Congress (1994), and declining voter turnout.

There are several contextual reasons for this consistent record of stability. Although many of the conditions that gave rise to minimal demands early in the political history of the United States have changed, others continue to reduce the burden on national political institutions. Most important, the federal system remains. Even though the scope of activities of the national government has expanded, especially during the twentieth century, most public services—schools, police, sanitation, and transportation—remain the primary responsibility of state and local governments. While national political institutions have been characterized by stalemate, many state governments have dealt successfully with a variety of difficult policy issues. What some perceive as the poor performance of the national government would be less tolerable to the American people if it resulted in closed public schools, mass transit strikes, and breakdowns in sanitation services, as it sometimes does in other nations and as it well might in the United States if the national government were responsible for these services.

The United States continues to be a nation of plenty. Economic differences persist and economic misery is far from unknown, but resources are sufficient and sufficiently distributed to have produced a large middle class. Whatever economic discontent this class exhibits is seldom translated into truly destabilizing political activity. On the contrary, in recent years this discontent seems to have resulted in higher levels of political apathy. Nor have the economic privations of the lower classes resulted in political instability, partly because, as Lipset suggests, "adaptive mechanisms" within American political culture "reconcile low status individuals to their position and thus contribute to the stability and legitimacy of the larger system." Among these mechanisms are religious beliefs that poor people will enjoy a higher status in heaven and secular beliefs that social mobility is possible (if not for oneself, then for one's children). Another stabilizing factor is the opportunity for citizens to participate in political movements whose ostensible goals are to raise the status of the needy.[46]

The continued strength of capitalism, both culturally and politically, also reduces economic discontent. Capitalism as a culture serves to convince those with less that those with more somehow deserve what they have and that their own lower status is attributable to personal failings rather than to any failings of the regime. Politically, many economic issues that other countries view as primarily national responsibilities—issues such as economic planning, prices and wages, and the allocation of goods and services—are largely viewed in the United States as matters for individuals and corporations to decide and therefore inappropriate concerns of political institutions. People's expectation that government will deal with the economic issues closest to their lives is lower in the United States than in many other countries. The volume of demands that reach U.S. political institutions is lower as well.

Citizens' participation in the U.S. political system continues to be low. Even beyond the well-known statistics showing declining percentages of eligible voters going to the polls, Americans seem not to involve themselves very much in, or even to think very much about, politics. Political involvement is a "sometimes thing," restricted for the most part to elections, primarily presidential elections. Other sorts of political activity—joining interest groups, attending political meetings, participating in demonstrations, signing petitions, writing to legislators, performing acts of civil disobedience—are engaged in by minuscule percentages of the population. Politics, in short, is not high on the personal agendas of most Americans.[47]

There are several possible reasons for this apolitical society, both structural and attitudinal. Lack of participation may indicate that people are pleased with the way the political system operates, although public opinion data suggesting high rates of cynicism and the results of the 1994 congressional elections would tend to discredit such an explanation.[48] Voter turnout may be significantly diminished by institutional barriers to participation (primarily registration laws), and by a lack of political competitiveness.[49] The absence of mass party organizations capable of mounting class-based appeals also may be a contributing factor to citizens' weak political participation.[50] Finally, because capitalism removes from the public agenda the issue that is of most concern to most Americans—their economic well-being—Americans may be apathetic and see no reason to participate. Rather, they are distracted by social and cultural issues such as abortion, ethics, patriotism, and religion, or they distract themselves with the consumer culture, sports, television, and the other diversions that our society provides.

In sum, the continued stability of the U.S. presidential system, despite persistent stalemates on major policy issues, is a product of a political environment characterized, as it was in the period after the Constitution's ratification, by low participation and moderate levels of political demands. After two hundred years, the nation's political institutions are stronger, more firmly entrenched, and more legitimate—a status that indicates, and also contributes to, political stability. But it also may be that the stability of the U.S. presidential system is attributable in part to the unique legislature at the heart of the system. Certain specific characteristics of Congress may allow the American political system to avoid the instability that has characterized other presidential systems. In addition, Congress may contribute to political stability by moderating the forces of change, by encouraging political responsiveness, by enforcing executive accountability, and by acting in a symbolically responsive manner.

The Congress and Political Stability

The U.S. Congress is different in certain crucial aspects from all other legislative institutions.[51] Unlike other legislatures that for the most part react to, and usually approve, proposals from the executive, the Congress is often the source—some scholars claim the dominant source—of major public policy initiatives.[52] Unlike other legislatures that are constitutionally barred from legislating in certain areas of executive prerogative, or whose decisions may be nullified by an executive veto or a popular vote, Congress has a jurisdiction that is virtually coterminous with that of the national government. Congress, rather than the president or the voters, has the final say on public policy questions.[53]

Although policy proposals from the president and executive agencies are accorded serious and often priority consideration by Congress, Congress says no to the president almost as often as it says yes, and even when it supports an executive initiative, such proposals rarely get through the legislative process without significant amendment. Presidents seem able to affect congressional deliberations "at the margins," with their success determined primarily by the number and ideology of their copartisans in the Congress rather than by the specific strategies they adopt or their standing in the public opinion polls.[54]

Of the world's legislative bodies, Congress has a support staff that is unmatched in size and professionalism and a committee system that is highly specialized and autonomous.[55] Members of Congress are well educated and most have had previous political experience at other levels of government. Once elected to Congress, they tend to stay. Salaries are relatively high, fringe benefits generous, and the retirement plan excellent. The institutional power of the Congress is matched by the power individual legislators can exercise in making policy. Through their committee assignments, members acquire policy expertise and with it the ability to shape public policy in the area of their committee jurisdictions But the policy-making influence of individual legislators is not restricted to those policy areas relevant to their committee assignments. For some time the formal and informal rules of the Senate have supported a great deal of individual autonomy so that senators can exercise influence on a wide range of policy issues.[56] And the House, in the view of one observer, is moving toward more collegial decision-making practices, characterized by "egalitarian norms that encourage and tolerate the full participation of any member seeking to influence policy outcomes." [57]

Much of the policy-making autonomy exhibited by the Congress and its members can be traced to the independent political bases of the legislators. National political party organizations in the United States tend to be weaker than they are in many other political systems, which means that representatives and senators must be elected from their local constituencies largely on their own efforts. This arrangement has two important consequences. First, legislators develop strong, personal ties to their constituents and to the interest groups that finance their elections. Second, once in office, members have a great deal of autonomy from their party leaders. To remain in office, members see to the most salient needs of their constituencies and of the groups that back their reelection efforts, and they do so even when this may be contrary to the wishes of the president or their party leaders.

The policy-making strength of the U.S. Congress, its decentralized policy-making processes, and the resistance of its individual members to party and executive leadership undoubtedly have contributed to policy conflict and stalemate between the president and Congress.[58] But these same characteristics may also permit the system of presidential-congressional relations to "work" better than one would expect in a presidential system of government. While the lack of party discipline and the strong constituency ties of members of Congress often foster legislative-executive stalemates, these factors also make legislators susceptible to influence by the president.[59]

In presidential systems with stronger political parties and more nationally oriented legislators than in the United States, control of the Congress by a party different from the president's would always lead to deadlock because the president would have a great deal of difficulty rounding up a majority of votes in support of executive initiatives. But in the American political system, opposition legislators can be induced to support the president by ideological considerations or through favors from the executive that can benefit their constituents. Although President Ronald Reagan never had a partisan majority in the House of Representatives, he was nonetheless able to persuade numerous congressional Democrats to vote his way, especially in the first two years of his administration. A stronger, more disciplined party system might have prevented such bipartisan coalitions from developing. In this context the budgetary stalemate during the 104th Congress is attributable not just to the return of divided government, but also to the surprisingly high levels of discipline and intraparty unity exhibited by the Republican majority.[60]

The congressional committee system, which has more than occasionally frustrated presidents' efforts to implement a broad policy agenda, also has contributed to the stability of the presidential system. First, division of labor has enabled committees to deal with the greatly expanded workload produced by the explosion of federal government activity during the twentieth century. Although the committee system does make the legislative process slow and tedious, without it policy making certainly would come to a halt. In unstable presidential systems, committees typically have little support from staff, little autonomy, and quite broad and amorphously defined jurisdictions.

A second stabilizing feature of the congressional committee system is the close relationship that has traditionally existed between committees and the bureaucracies over which they have jurisdiction. These "subgovernments," while major obstacles to presidents seeking to lead the bureaucracy, make the ties between bureaucrats and legislators stronger than in most other political systems. Whereas in other nations the civilian bureaucracy typically allies itself with the president and the military to threaten parliamentary institutions, in the United States the permanent bureaucracy is often closer to the legislators who serve on the committees that authorize and fund its programs than to the president and his cabinet members—people who could be hostile to the mission of any one of its agencies.[61]

For this and other reasons, presidents bent on potentially destabilizing policy changes may well be defeated by a coalition of congressional and bureaucratic forces allied in defense of current public policy; such a coalition, of course, would be unlikely to appear in most other political systems. The events of 1995 suggested that such coalitions also may be endangered in the American political system. The first Republican-controlled House in forty years seemed intent on reducing the size and power of the federal bureaucracy, and the relationship between the Republican-dominated committees and the bureaucracy was not nearly as "cozy" as it was when the House was under Democratic control.

Mediating the Forces of Change

Instability may result from demands for political participation by previously excluded groups, especially when such demands are resisted by incumbent elites. On the other hand, sudden and dramatic changes in the turnover of political elites also can be destabilizing. This, as noted earlier, was what worried the Founders with regard to the House of Representatives. They feared that a rapid turnover in the membership of the House would lead to destabilizing shifts in public policy from one session of Congress to the next. If such political instability is to be avoided, the trick is to allow for change but to arrange matters so that change will be gradual.

Although the Founders did not anticipate it, Congress became an institution that allowed for exactly this sort of nondestabilizing change in political elites. A careful analysis of biographical data on members of the House finds evidence during the late nineteenth century of "democratization of the congressional elite" and "increasing similarity between characteristics of representatives, on the one hand, and the general population, on the other." But the same analysis uses the adjective "glacial" to describe the pace of this movement toward "increasing openness of the House." [62] Congress thus can be seen as both facilitating and moderating demands for political inclusion. It allows the political system to adapt at a pace rapid enough to avoid rebellion among the excluded, but deliberate enough to prevent destabilizing change.

The pace of change was further slowed, and stability further enhanced, by the emergence of congressional careerism. For most of the nineteenth century, membership turnover in the House of Representatives was quite high; Nelson Polsby counted fifteen elections, the last in 1882, that produced turnover rates above 50 percent.[63] But after that time, turnover declined; for most of the twentieth century, gradual rather than rapid change in the membership of the House and Senate has been the rule. Even in the electoral upheaval of 1994, only 10 percent of the members seeking reelection were defeated.

The average tenure of House members rose from just over six years at the turn of the century to just over eleven years in the 1980s. During most of that decade, no more than 15 percent of House members were serving their first term, while a similar number had served for at least twenty years. This pattern changed somewhat in the early 1990s. At the beginning of the 104th Congress, 20 percent of House members were in their first term of service, an additional 22 percent were in their second, and just over 10 percent of the membership had twenty years or more of service.[64]

Change is also moderated by the kind of people elected to Congress. Contrary to the concerns of the Founders that legislators, particularly members of the House, would be people of relatively little education and status and therefore overly sympathetic to the potentially destabilizing demands of mass publics, most members are well educated, middle- and upper-class citizens. During the twentieth century the electoral role of political parties has declined, and the expense of election campaigns has increased. Consequently, legislators are more likely than in the past to be people who are either wealthy themselves or have close connections to groups or individuals with financial resources. The possibility that legislators would undertake radical actions on behalf of mass publics or would attack the fundamental values of the American political economy is, to the say the least, extraordinarily unlikely. As Philip Brenner concludes, Congress continues to foster the "capitalist mode of production in the United States, and the social relations that attend this mode of production." [65]

One reason Congress has been able to attract and retain the services of people of quality is the congressional committee system. Its highly refined division of labor enables talented politicians committed to careers in Congress to increase their influence and to make their mark on public policy. [66] The committee system's decentralization of power is another source of congressional resistance to radical changes in policy. Committees and subcommittees tend to be dominated by members and staff who continue in place from one legislative session to the next and who have political and personal stakes in current public policy. This has ensured that policy changes will be largely incremental and therefore nondestabilizing. In addition, the decentralized nature of congressional decision making means that passage of most policy initiatives takes a long time and requires the support of a broad coalition of legislators and, ultimately, the support of the president as well.

On the other hand, the 1994 election reminds us that the membership of the House of Representatives can, as the Founders feared, change quickly in response to public unrest, and such change can bring a new political agenda to Washington. Although elements in the Republican Contract with America challenged a great deal of how business was done in Washington, to call these proposals "revolutionary" was to stretch substantially the usual meaning of that term. However, no matter how these proposals were characterized, the stabilizing nature of the policy-making process remained apparent in the moderating impact that the Senate had on House actions as well as in the veto power in the hands of a Democratic president. All of this, just as the Founders planned it, served to blunt the most extreme or radical actions proposed by the newly empowered Republican House majority. On the other hand, what seemed to be emerging from the 104th Congress still constituted a significant break with the past.

The slow and deliberate pace of the congressional process also works to moderate the changes presidents can make. The plebiscitary nature of the modern American presidency has caused presidential candidates to promise during their campaigns more than they can fulfill once elected and to inflate the public's expectations of the victorious candidates. [67] As a result, newly elected presidents may come to office promising a "sea change" in public policy; however, as Bill Clinton discovered in battles over his health care and economic recovery plans, they soon confront the rather conservative congressional policy-making process that will always slow the rate of changes they can initiate and will usually modify, if not reject, their bolder proposals.

Policy Responsiveness

If political systems are to remain stable, their policy-making institutions must be responsive to public pressures. "Responsive" in this sense does not mean doing whatever the constituents wish. Rather, it means "acting in the interests of the represented" and calculating those interests with some degree of public consultation but also with some degree of discretion and judgment.[68] Members of Congress stay responsive by staying in touch with their constituents. The two-year term for members of the House requires continuous contact with constituents if members wish to be reelected. And although senators have a longer term in office, one-third of the Senate's membership is always no more than two years away from the next election day. This electoral connection has sharpened the sensitivity and responsiveness of representatives and senators to constituency concerns. The result is strong personal ties between legislators and their constituencies. In fact, citizens think highly of their legislators even while maintaining a relatively low opinion of Congress as an institution. It seems that citizens evaluate the performance of their legislators primarily in terms of their record of constituency service and their personal characteristics, and they usually conclude that their legislators are doing well on these criteria.[69]

This phenomenon has insulated Congress from the effects of episodic periods of national political discontent. If voters are unhappy, they take their displeasure out on presidential candidates while reelecting members of Congress whom they tend to evaluate on how well they have served the constituency rather than on how they have stood on the salient issues of the day.[70] Although the 1994 elections suggest that this is not always the case, the 1968 elections would appear to be more typical. In that year, in a context of great political unrest, only 13 of the 409 members of the House who sought reelection were defeated. Although the composition of the Congress was virtually unaltered by the events of 1968, an incumbent president was driven from office by members of his own party, one candidate to replace him was assassinated, an extremist third-party candidate garnered more than 13 percent of the popular vote, and the opposition party candidate ultimately captured the presidency.

Today the continuity of congressional membership largely depends on members' ability to serve and benefit their constituents. As the modern administrative state expanded its activities and touched the lives of increasing numbers of citizens, more people came to think of themselves as adversely affected by government or as deserving of government services or funds. Soon they began to expect legislators to resolve their problems and complaints with the administrative apparatus of the modern state. As legislators responded to these expectations, they encouraged a degree of bureaucratic responsiveness that might otherwise have been absent, and to some extent they reduced the incidence and severity of public discontent with government.

Congress also has proven to be responsive to the policy demands of constituents on those occasions when citizens or well-organized interests have made their views clear. One example of the process at work is Congress's decision in 1989 virtually to repeal the catastrophic health care legislation that it had passed with much fanfare the year before. When the members of senior citizens' groups became aware of the law's provisions (particularly the new taxes that many of them would need to pay), they voiced their discontent to their legislators in no uncertain terms. After several failed attempts to "educate" their constituents about the catastrophic health care issue, the legislators finally threw in the towel and repealed most of the benefits and most of the taxes associated with the new program. Whether or not this was wise is not the point here; what repeal of these measures demonstrates is the very real sense in which Congress responds to public pressures, especially pressures generated by an intense minority.

Enforcing Executive Accountability

"To watch and control the Government," John Stuart Mill suggested, is the "proper office" of representative assemblies.[71] Legislatures as open public arenas are admirably suited to perform this oversight function. To the extent that such activities discourage the executive from acting corruptly, arbitrarily, repressively, or unconstitutionally, they enhance the stability of the political system.

Congress, through its committee system, exercises continuous oversight of executive agencies. Although it has been suggested that members' reelection concerns distract them from their oversight responsibilities, these same electoral concerns may well make members more zealous in investigating corrupt or arbitrary bureaucratic action.[72] Hearings during the 104th Congress on the manner in which the Federal Bureau of Investigation and the Bureau of Alcohol, Tobacco, and Firearms conducted themselves in a 1992 shootout at Ruby Ridge, Idaho, are a case in point. Legislators who might have seen no reelection payoff in improving the operation of two federal law enforcement agencies saw a major payoff in the news coverage that they received from ferreting out what appeared to be a serious incident of bureaucratic malfeasance. And to the extent that such instances of intense legislative oversight inhibit the bureaucracy from acting in this manner in the future, the legitimacy and therefore the stability of the political system are enhanced.

Similarly, when presidents have acted corruptly or beyond their prerogatives, Congress has often provided a highly visible institutional check. Some of the most vivid and positive images of Congress in action arise from those episodes when an imperial-minded president has been confronted and ultimately censured or deterred by Congress. The congressional hearings on the Vietnam War during the Johnson administration, the Watergate and impeachment hearings during the Nixon administration, and the Iran-Contra hearings during the Reagan administration all illustrate the capacity of Congress to sanction presidents who have engaged in repressive, illegal, or corrupt activities.

In presidential systems less stable than that of the United States, the legislature has no real capacity to check the actions of presidents or military and civilian bureaucrats. When it tries to do so, it may jeopardize its institutional survival as well as the political and personal security of its members. As a result, power is frequently abused, citizens lose respect for their political institutions, and the likelihood of instability increases.

Symbolic Responsiveness

Finally, Congress and its members play an important symbolic role that both dampens and diverts political discontent. In all political systems, the act of voting for legislators as well as for other officeholders gives citizens the impression that they are involved in political decision making even when their ballots may have little real effect on policy decisions. This sense of involvement contributes to the legitimacy of a political system, even in situations where concrete responses to public discontent may not be forthcoming.

In the same manner, regional, demographic, economic, and ideological groups with minority status in the nation as a whole can achieve representation in Congress by virtue of their strength in particular legislative districts. Representation may then lead to policy actions that speak to certain of the substantive demands of such groups. But even if responsive public policy is not forthcoming, representation, simply by providing these groups with spokespeople for their point of view, will make them more inclined to accept their political lot.

The public articulation of dissenting views also can function as a safety valve for the political system, releasing potentially explosive political pressures before they can have a destabilizing effect. In authoritarian regimes, apparently powerless legislatures seem to perform exactly that function, but legislatures in more open political systems do the same thing, and Congress is no exception.[73] During the summer of 1989, the public furor over a Supreme Court decision that seemed to condone flag burning was in part defused by congressional debate that gave vent to the anger and frustration felt by many Americans about this issue. The action that Congress decided to take was relatively moderate, but it had the effect, at the time, of sidetracking the much more destabilizing response, endorsed by the president, of a constitutional amendment.

Finally, the activities of members of Congress when they are at home in their constituencies have a similar symbolic effect. As members listen to and empathize with the concerns of discontented constituents, they supply them with a safe and relatively inconsequential outlet for their grievances. The appearance of the legislator in the district symbolizes for citizens in a very concrete manner that they are being represented in Washington and that their voices are being heard.

These various symbolic activities make a crucial contribution to political stability. As John Wahlke has observed, such "symbolic satisfaction with the process of government is probably more important than specific, instrumental satisfaction with the policy output of the process." [74] A process of government that is viewed as legitimate has the effect of domesticating conflict by channeling political discontent in relatively benign directions. While certainly such activities by themselves cannot eliminate destabilizing pressures or render legitimate an essentially illegitimate political system, they can, in an essentially stable political system such as that of the United States, help maintain stability or at least head off incipient discontent.

Conclusion

Robert Packenham has suggested that "legislatures tend to represent, all over the world, more conservative and parochial interests than executives, even in democratic polities." [75] While this "conservative legislature" hypothesis might well be exaggerated, it does offer an important corrective to the instinctive view of many democrats that legislatures in general and the U.S. Congress in particular are likely to be progressive, change-oriented institutions. Even if legislatures do function as conservative institutions, however, they will not necessarily contribute to political stability. If legislatures are overly rigid and consistently block necessary changes, then instability certainly will result; however, if legislatures provide an institutional setting for moderating or diverting the forces of change, they are likely to contribute to, more than they will detract from, political stability.

The latter possibility is much more descriptive of the role of Congress in the American political system than the former. Members of Congress, some of whom represent those who are politically disaffected, are drawn disproportionately from those strata of society with the fewest grievances against the political system. The representational activities of these legislators often enhance the responsiveness of the political system to those who do have grievances, and they consistently operate at a symbolic level to reduce the potential impact of popular discontent. The operation of the congressional policy-making process ensures that potentially destabilizing policy proposals seldom make it onto the agenda, let alone the statute books. Congress restrains the president from pursuing radical policy proposals while at the same time providing the votes for the president's more moderate policy initiatives. It also checks any propensity that the president or the bureaucracy might have to act arbitrarily or corruptly. In all of these senses, then, Congress enhances political stability.

Whether legislatures in other nations, particularly those nations experiencing rapid political change, will perform the same stabilizing function as the U.S. Congress is open to debate. As the nations of central and eastern Europe began their transitions toward more open political systems at the end of the 1980s, the previously weak legislatures in those countries came to have an increasingly conspicuous role. In Poland and Czechoslovakia the legislature provided the only institutional setting within which change could take place because it was the only institution that retained some degree of legitimacy among the forces advocating change. Often the first voices of dissent within the Communist parties of these nations came from members of the national legislature. Later, as these parties gave up their monopoly of power, those calling for change from outside the party gained increased representation in the legislature. The legislature became the place for planning and implementing major political change.

On the other hand, these institutions have not always been receptive to change. In Russia the parliament has acted as an impediment to many of the economic reform proposals that have come from President Boris Yeltsin and his advisers. Adam Przeworski has argued that legislatures expose economic reform initiatives to political pressures that may ultimately weaken those initiatives and render them ineffectual. This will result in a certain oscillation between executive dominance and executive solicitation of parliamentary support, leading in turn to a "stop-go" approach to economic reform.[76]

Although many legislative bodies have helped to manage the transition from authoritarian to more open political systems, they will not necessarily develop into powerful legislatures similar to the U.S. Congress. That is because these institutions are not likely, in the long run, to produce much more than symbolic policy responses to the economic and ethnic problems at the root of instability in these political systems. In fact, the confrontation and stalemate that characterize decision making in presidential systems may reduce the likelihood of substantive policy responses, as events in Poland and Russia suggest.[77] And without substantive solutions, higher rather than lower levels of political instability will result.

The modern Congress is able to contribute to political stability because the United States has an essentially stable political system. The political system is stable because of the unique circumstances under which it was permitted to develop and because of the cultural and political norms that have come to characterize the nation. Nations that today seek to foster political stability by emulating the American institutional model are unlikely to succeed because the context in which they try to build new political institutions little resembles the context in which American political institutions developed.

Notes

1. Giovanni Sartori, "Neither Presidentialism nor Parliamentarism," in *The Failure of Presidential Democracy*, ed. Juan J. Linz and Arturo Valenzuela (Baltimore: Johns

Hopkins University Press, 1994), 107. See also Fred W. Riggs, "Bureaucratic Links Between Administration and Politics" (Paper presented at the annual meeting of the American Political Science Association, Atlanta, Ga., September 1989). Charles O. Jones argues that the United States is not a presidential system. He believes that such a designation overemphasizes the importance of the presidency in the American policy-making system. See Charles O. Jones, *The Presidency in a Separated System* (Washington, D.C.: Brookings Institution, 1994). But Matthew Soberg Shugart and John M. Carey define "presidential government" as the popular election of the chief executive, fixed terms for the chief executive and assembly that are not contingent on mutual confidence, and an elected executive who names and directs the composition of the government. Certainly, the United States meets all three criteria of this definition. See Matthew Soberg Shugart and John M. Carey, *Presidents and Assemblies: Constitutional Design and Electoral Dynamics* (Cambridge: Cambridge University Press, 1992), 19.

2. Robert J. Jackson and Michael B. Stein, *Issues in Comparative Politics* (New York: St. Martin's Press, 1971), 196.

3. See David Easton, *A Systems Analysis of Political Life* (New York: John Wiley and Sons, 1965), esp. part 3.

4. Ibid., 269–277. On the distinction between specific and diffuse support, see John Wahlke, "Policy Demands and System Support: The Role of the Represented," *British Journal of Political Science* 1 (July 1971): 271–290; and Gerhard Loewenberg, "The Influence of Parliamentary Behavior on Regime Stability: Some Conceptual Clarifications," *Comparative Politics* 3 (January 1971): 177–200.

5. Ted Robert Gurr, *Why Men Rebel* (Princeton, N.J.: Princeton University Press, 1970).

6. Joan M. Nelson, "Political Participation," in *Understanding Political Development: An Analytic Study*, ed. Myron Weiner and Samuel P. Huntington (Boston: Little, Brown, 1987), 114.

7. Gabriel Almond and Sidney Verba, *The Civic Culture* (Boston: Little, Brown, 1963), 339.

8. William Kornhauser, *The Politics of Mass Society* (New York: Free Press, 1959). See also Nelson, "Political Participation," 110.

9. Samuel P. Huntington, *Political Order in Changing Societies* (New Haven: Yale University Press, 1968), 55.

10. See Joel S. Migdal, "Strong States, Weak States: Power and Accommodation," in *Understanding Political Development*.

11. Juan J. Linz, "Presidential or Parliamentary Democracy: Does It Make a Difference?" in *Failure of Presidential Democracy*.

12. See also Scott Mainwaring, "Presidentialism in Latin America: A Review Essay," *Latin American Research Review* 25 (1989): 157–179; Giuseppe Di Palma, *To Craft Democracies* (Berkeley: University of California Press, 1990); and Arend Lijphart, "Presidentialism and Majoritarian Democracy," in *Failure of Presidential Democracy*.

13. Shugart and Carey, *Presidents and Assemblies*. For another defense of presidential systems, see Thomas O. Sargentich, "The Limits of the Parliamentary Critique of the Separation of Powers," *William and Mary Law Review* 34 (Spring 1993): 679–639.

14. Maurice Duverger, "A New Political System Model: Semi-Presidential Government," *European Journal of Political Research* 8 (June 1980): 165–187.

15. See also David L. Horowitz, "Comparing Democratic Systems," *Journal of Democracy* 1 (Fall 1990): 73–79; Sartori, "Neither Presidentialism nor Parliamentarism."

16. See Alfred Stepan and Cindy Skach, "Presidentialism and Parliamentarism in Comparative Perspective," in *Failure of Presidential Democracy*; and Michael L. Mezey, "Parliaments in the New Europe," in *Governing the New Europe*, ed. Jack Hayward and Ed Page (Oxford, England: Polity Press, 1995).

17. Lijphart, "Presidentialism and Majoritarian Democracy," 94–95.

18. See Linz, "Presidential or Parliamentary Democracy," 48–51; see also Ezra N.

256   Michael L. Mezey

Suleiman, "Presidentialism and Political Stability in France," in *Failure of Presidential Democracy.*

19. See Michael L. Mezey, *Comparative Legislatures* (Durham, N.C.: Duke University Press, 1979), chap. 12; William Mishler and Anne Hildreth, "Legislative Correlates of Political Stability: An Exploratory Analysis" (Paper presented at the Conference on Parliaments, Policy, and Regime Support, Durham, N.C., December 1982); and Robert Packenham, "Legislatures and Political Development," in *Legislatures in Developmental Perspective,* ed. Allan Kornberg and Lloyd Musolf (Durham, N.C.: Duke University Press, 1970).

20. See Douglas A. Hibbs, Jr., *Mass Political Violence: A Cross-National Causal Analysis* (New York: John Wiley and Sons, 1973); and Edward N. Muller, "Income Equality, Regime Repressiveness, and Political Violence," *American Sociological Review* 50 (February 1985): 47–61.

21. James Madison, *Federalist* no. 10, in *The Federalist Papers,* ed. Clinton Rossiter (New York: New American Library, 1961), 77.

22. Ibid., *Federalist* no. 37, 226.

23. Quoted in Charles C. Thach, Jr., *The Creation of the Presidency, 1775–1789* (Baltimore: Johns Hopkins University Press, 1923), 27.

24. See Merrill Jensen, *The Making of the American Constitution* (New York: Van Nostrand Reinhold, 1964), 20. On the New York governorship, see Thach, *Creation of the Presidency,* chap. 2.

25. Gordon Wood, *The Creation of the American Republic, 1776–1787* (Chapel Hill: University of North Carolina Press, 1969), 404.

26. Quoted in Wood, *Creation of the American Republic,* 411.

27. Madison, *Federalist* no. 55, in *Federalist Papers,* 342.

28. Max Farrand, ed., *The Records of the Federal Convention of 1787* (New Haven: Yale University Press, 1966), vol. 1, 51.

29. Quoted in Wood, *Creation of the American Republic,* 432.

30. Ibid., 409.

31. Madison, *Federalist* no. 51, in *Federalist Papers,* 323. The parliamentary system as it is understood today had not yet emerged in Great Britain, so this model could not be emulated by the Founders. They believed a system in which the executive was selected by the legislature would result in one of two undesirable situations: either the executive would be manipulated by the legislature, or the executive would attempt to stay in office by corrupting legislators with bribes and other favors. See Michael L. Mezey, *Congress, the President, and Public Policy* (Boulder, Colo.: Westview Press, 1989), 30–34.

32. Madison, *Federalist* no. 37, in *Federalist Papers,* 227.

33. Ibid.

34. Alexander Hamilton, *Federalist* no. 70, in *Federalist Papers,* 423. See also David F. Epstein, *The Political Theory of the Federalist* (Chicago: University of Chicago Press, 1984), 171–172.

35. Madison, *Federalist* no. 62, in *Federalist Papers,* 380.

36. Farrand, *Records of the Federal Convention,* vol. 1, 511–512.

37. On the Founders' fear of popular election of the president, see James W. Ceaser, *Presidential Selection: Theory and Development* (Princeton, N.J.: Princeton University Press, 1979), chap. 1.

38. Mezey, *Congress, the President, and Public Policy,* chap. 2.

39. James Sterling Young, *The Washington Community, 1800–1828* (New York: Columbia University Press, 1966), 31.

40. See David Potter, *People of Plenty* (Chicago: University of Chicago Press, 1954).

41. Young, *Washington Community,* 34.

42. Seymour Martin Lipset, *The First New Nation: The United States in Historical and Comparative Perspective* (New York: Basic Books, 1963), 59.

43. See, for example, James L. Sundquist, "The Crisis of Competence in Our National Government," *Political Science Quarterly* 95 (1980): 183–208.

44. David R. Mayhew, *Divided We Govern: Party Control, Lawmaking, and Investigations, 1946–1990* (New Haven: Yale University Press, 1991). On the stalemate issue, see Mezey, *Congress, the President, and Public Policy*, chaps. 5 and 6; James Sundquist, *Constitutional Reform and Effective Government* (Washington, D.C.: Brookings Institution, 1986); and John Chubb and Paul E. Peterson, eds., *Can the Government Govern?* (Washington, D.C.: Brookings Institution, 1989).

45. Chubb and Peterson, *Can the Government Govern?* 5.

46. Lipset, *First New Nation*, 271–272.

47. See Sidney Verba and Norman Nie, *Participation in America: Political Democracy and Social Equality* (New York: Harper and Row, 1972).

48. On political cynicism, see Seymour Martin Lipset and William Schneider, *The Confidence Gap: Business, Labor, and Government in the Public Mind* (New York: Free Press, 1983).

49. See Raymond E. Wolfinger and Steven J. Rosenstone, *Who Votes?* (New Haven: Yale University Press, 1980); and G. Bingham Powell, "American Voter Turnout in Comparative Perspective," *American Political Science Review* 80 (March 1986): 17–44.

50. Walter Dean Burnham, "The Appearance and Disappearance of the American Voter," in *Electoral Participation: A Comparative Analysis*, ed. Richard Rose (Beverly Hills, Calif.: Sage, 1980).

51. Among the volumes treating the U.S. Congress comparatively are Mezey, *Comparative Legislatures*; Gerhard Loewenberg and Samuel C. Patterson, *Comparing Legislatures* (Boston: Little, Brown, 1979); David Olson, *The Legislative Process: A Comparative Approach* (New York: Harper and Row, 1980); and John E. Schwarz and L. Earl Shaw, *The United States Congress in Comparative Perspective* (Hinsdale, Ill.: Dryden Press, 1976).

52. See Jones, *Presidency in a Separated System*; Gary Orfield, *Congressional Power: Congress and Social Change* (New York: Harcourt Brace Jovanovich, 1975); Lawrence Chamberlain, *The President, Congress, and Legislation* (New York: Columbia University Press, 1946); Ronald C. Moe and Steven C. Teel, "Congress as Policy-Maker: A Necessary Reappraisal," in *Congress and the President*, ed. Ronald C. Moe (Pacific Palisades, Calif.: Goodyear, 1971); and Mark A. Peterson, *Legislating Together: The White House and Capitol Hill from Eisenhower to Reagan* (Cambridge: Harvard University Press, 1990).

53. See Jean Blondel, *Comparative Legislatures* (Englewood Cliffs, N.J.: Prentice-Hall, 1973), 35–38. On a few issues, of course, the Supreme Court does have the final say, but the Court does not often declare acts of Congress unconstitutional. See Steven Wasby, *The Supreme Court in the Federal Judicial System*, 3d ed. (Chicago: Nelson-Hall, 1988), 79.

54. See George C. Edwards III, *Presidential Influence in Congress* (San Francisco: Freeman, 1980); Mezey, *Congress, the President, and Public Policy*, chap. 5; George C. Edwards III, *At the Margins: Presidential Leadership of Congress* (New Haven: Yale University Press, 1989; Jon R. Bond and Richard Fleisher, *The President in the Legislative Arena* (Chicago: University of Chicago Press, 1990); and Peterson, *Legislating Together*.

55. See Susan Webb Hammond, "Legislative Staffs," in *Handbook of Legislative Research*, ed. Gerhard Loewenberg, Samuel C. Patterson, and Malcolm E. Jewell (Cambridge: Harvard University Press, 1985); and Malcolm Shaw, "Conclusions," in *Committees in Legislatures: A Comparative Analysis*, ed. John D. Lees and Malcolm Shaw (Durham, N.C.: Duke University Press, 1979).

56. See Richard F. Fenno, Jr., *The United States Senate: A Bicameral Perspective* (Washington, D.C.: American Enterprise Institute, 1982).

57. Steven S. Smith, *Call to Order: Floor Politics in the House and Senate* (Washington, D.C.: Brookings Institution, 1989), 4.

58. See Norman J. Ornstein, "The Open Congress Meets the President," in *Both Ends of*

the Avenue: The Presidency, the Executive Branch, and Congress in the 1980s, ed. Anthony King (Washington, D.C.: American Enterprise Institute, 1983); James Sundquist, *The Decline and Resurgence of Congress* (Washington, D.C.: Brookings Institution, 1981), esp. chaps. 7, 14, 15, and 16; and Mezey, *Congress, the President, and Public Policy*, chap. 5.

59. This point is made by Fred W. Riggs, "The Survival of Presidentialism in America: Para-Constitutional Practices," *International Political Science Review* 9 (1988): 247–278.

60. This increasingly rigid partisanship and its consequences for presidential-congressional relations were anticipated by James L. Sundquist, "Needed: A New Theory for the New Era of Coalition Government in the United States," *Political Science Quarterly* 103 (Winter 1988–1989): 613–635.

61. See Riggs, "Survival of Presidentialism in America," for a similar discussion.

62. Allan Bogue et al., "Members of the House of Representatives and the Processes of Modernization: 1789–1960," *Journal of American History* 63 (1976): 287–288.

63. Nelson W. Polsby, "The Institutionalization of the U.S. House of Representatives," *American Political Science Review* 62 (March 1968): 146; also see H. Douglas Price, "Congress and the Evolution of Legislative Professionalism," in *Congress in Change: Evolution and Reform*, ed. Norman J. Ornstein (New York: Praeger, 1975).

64. See Mezey, *Congress, the President, and Public Policy*, 72. The data on the 104th Congress are from "104th Congress by Year of First Election" (chart), *Congressional Quarterly Weekly Report*, November 12, 1994, 3214.

65. Philip Brenner, *The Limits and Possibilities of Congress* (New York: St. Martin's Press, 1983), 188.

66. Kenneth A. Shepsle, "Representation and Governance: The Great Legislative Trade-off," *Political Science Quarterly* 103 (Fall 1988): 461–484.

67. See Theodore Lowi, *The Personal President* (Ithaca, N.Y.: Cornell University Press, 1985).

68. The concept of responsiveness is discussed more thoroughly in Hanna Fenichel Pitkin, *The Concept of Representation* (Berkeley: University of California Press, 1967), chap. 10; and Heinz Eulau and Paul Karps, "The Puzzle of Representation: Specifying Components of Responsiveness," *Legislative Studies Quarterly* 2 (August 1977): 233–254.

69. Glen Parker and Roger Davidson, "Why Do Americans Love Their Congressmen So Much More Than Their Congress?" *Legislative Studies Quarterly* 4 (February 1979): 53–61.

70. There is a vast literature on congressional elections. The best summary continues to be Gary C. Jacobson, *The Politics of Congressional Elections*, 3d ed. (New York: Harper Collins, 1992).

71. John Stuart Mill, *Considerations on Representative Government* (1861; reprint, New York: Liberal Arts Press, 1958), 81.

72. See Lawrence Dodd and Richard Schott, *Congress and the Administrative State* (New York: John Wiley and Sons , 1979), chaps. 5 and 6; Sundquist, *Decline and Resurgence of Congress*, 332–340; and Mayhew, *Divided We Govern*, chap. 2.

73. See Mezey, *Comparative Legislatures*, 266–267; and Packenham, "Legislatures and Political Development."

74. Wahlke, "Policy Demands and System Support."

75. See Packenham, "Legislatures and Political Development," 578. Also see Huntington, *Political Order*, 388ff. For a review of the research relevant to the conservative legislature hypothesis, see Michael L. Mezey, "The Functions of Legislatures in the Third World," in *Handbook of Legislative Research*, 750–754.

76. See Adam Przeworski, *Democracy and the Market: Political and Economic Reforms in Eastern Europe and Latin America* (Cambridge: Cambridge University Press, 1991).

77. See Mezey, "Parliaments in the New Europe," for a fuller discussion.

Index